ONE
STEP
AHEAD

ONE
STEP
AHEAD

A Jewish Fugitive in Hitler's Europe

Alfred Feldman

With a Foreword by
Susan Zuccotti

Southern Illinois University Press
Carbondale

Southern Illinois University Press
www.siupress.com

Copyright © 2001, 2024 by Alfred Philip Feldman
All rights reserved. Cloth edition 2001.
Paperback edition 2024.
Printed in the United States of America

The publication of the cloth edition was partially funded by a subvention grant from the Lucius N. Littauer Foundation.

The epigraph to chapter 13 is reprinted with permission from *The Memoirs of Field-Marshal Kesselring*, Presidio Press, Novato, CA, USA. The translation of the Kiddish in chapter 15 is reprinted with permission from Leon Wieseltier.

First printed November 2001.
First paperback edition 2024.

Cover illustration: by Erin Longwell. *Back cover illustration:* Alfred Feldman and his father, Joachim, toward the end of 1945. Author's collection.

ISBN 978-0-8093-3937-2 (paper)
ISBN 978-0-8093-2411-8 (cloth)
ISBN 978-0-8093-9021-2 (ebook)

Library of Congress Cataloging-in-Publication Data
Names: Feldman, Alfred, 1923– author.
Title: One step ahead : a Jewish fugitive in Hitler's Europe / Alfred Feldman.
Other titles: Jewish fugitive in Hitler's Europe
Identifiers: LCCN 2023052899 | ISBN 9780809339372 (paperback)
Subjects: LCSH: Feldman, Alfred, 1923– | Feldman, Alfred, 1923—Family. | Jews—Germany—Cologne—Biography. | Holocaust, Jewish (1939–1945)—Germany—Cologne—Personal narratives. | Holocaust, Jewish (1939–1945)—Italy—Personal narratives. | Jewish refugees—France—Biography. | Jewish refugees—Italy—Biography. | Feldman family. | Cologne (Germany)—Biography. | BISAC: HISTORY / Modern / 20th Century / Holocaust | HISTORY / Europe / General
Classification: LCC DS135.G5 F33 2024 | DDC 943/.5514086092 [B]—dc23/eng/20231109
LC record available at https://lccn.loc.gov/2023052899

Printed on recycled paper ♻

SIU
Southern Illinois University System

For my wife

Contents

Illustrations

Plates
Following page 120

Alfred's father, Joachim Feldman; Alfred's mother, Paula; her mother, Scheindel Chaja Bauminger; and her husband, Isaac Bauminger. Hamburg, Germany, 1920s.

Passport photo of Alfred's grandmother, Chinka Feldman. Cologne, Germany, 1934.

Aunt Betty Knoll and her son Simon. Cologne, Germany, 1935.

Alfred's sisters Jenny and Hella, Alfred's cousin Ines Rosenbaum, and Alfred's sister Edith at the beach. Knokke, Belgium, summer 1938.

Foreword

Susan Zuccotti

ALTHOUGH WORLD WAR II BEGAN with the German invasion of Poland on September 1, 1939, it had little impact in the west until the following spring. What Americans call the "phony war" ended abruptly on May 10, 1940, when German armored divisions invaded and quickly overran Holland, Belgium, and Luxembourg. General Heinz Guderian's XIX Panzer Corps smashed into France two days later, and Holland surrendered two days after that. The Belgians asked for an armistice on May 27, the day after the British ordered the evacuation of their troops from Dunkirk. France did not hold out much longer. The French government fled first to Tours and then to Bordeaux. The Germans entered Paris on June 14, the government of Paul Reynaud fell on the sixteenth, and the newly appointed premier, Marshal Henri Philippe Pétain, informed his countrymen the following day that France must cease hostilities. The armistice was signed on the twenty-second and put into effect on the twenty-fifth. The Germans celebrated their most astounding success of the war.

Sixteen-year-old Alfred Feldman was living with his parents and three younger sisters in Antwerp, Belgium, at the time of the German invasion. His parents, Paula and Joachim, were Polish Jews, the children of immigrants who had settled in Germany in search of a better life. His father represented a German firm in Belgium. On May 12, the Feldmans abandoned their comfortable house and possessions in Antwerp and joined well over a million refugees fleeing westward into France to escape the German onslaught. Among the refugees were an estimated forty thousand Jews. Most of them entered France without proper identification papers, passports, visas, or residence permits. Once in France, they joined some four million French men, women, and children, including hundreds of thousands of Parisians, all trying to move south out of reach of the invaders. Some two to three hundred thousand of these refugees were Jewish, both French and foreign. Frightened people overran the trains, jammed the highways, ran out of gas, abandoned their cars, slept in barns or fields, and struggled to obtain food, sometimes donated by sympathetic Frenchmen and sometimes purchased at outrageous prices.

Although the tribulations of the Belgium-based branch of the Feldman family did not begin until the German invasion, their relatives back home in the Third Reich had suffered under the Nazi regime since Hitler's rise to power in January 1933. Alfred vividly describes in these pages the growing anti-Jewish hatred and violence in Germany during the 1930s, the impact of the anti-Jewish Nuremberg laws in 1935, and the terrifying pogrom called *Kristallnacht* on November 9, 1938. In the face of increasing persecution, his grandparents, aunts, uncles, and many cousins in Germany scattered over the globe in a desperate attempt to survive. His warm and loving extended family was shattered even before the deportations began. Some family members managed to reach the United States. Others were refused entry by increasingly restrictive American immigration policies. Elsewhere, two aunts, an uncle, and several cousins were among the fifteen thousand Polish Jewish immigrants in Germany stranded on the German-Polish border during the autumn and winter of 1938. In response to a new Polish policy of reevaluating and possibly revoking their passports, the German government had expelled them. The Poles refused to admit them, and the hapless victims spent months in a no-man's-land between the two countries. This was the incident that provoked the unhappy Jewish immigrant Herschel Grynszpan in Paris to murder a German diplomat, Ernst vom Rath. That event in turn unleashed Kristallnacht. The Feldmans were living history. It was history they would have preferred to avoid.

As the young Alfred Feldman fled south through France toward the Mediterranean and eventually settled with his family in a small town in the summer of 1940, he was caught up in many more dramatic events of World War II in Western Europe. The Franco-German armistice divided France into a northern, German-occupied zone that included Paris and Bordeaux, and a southern, smaller, unoccupied zone often referred to as Vichy, after the spa where the French government established its capital. The Feldmans were in the latter, so-called free zone. The reactionary, collaborationist Vichy regime, however, which had full authority in the southern zone and jurisdiction subject to German approval in the north, grew increasingly repressive. On July 9 and 10, a somewhat cowed rump parliament voted by an overwhelming majority to revoke the Third Republic Constitution of 1875 and award Pétain full powers to promulgate a new one. Pétain promptly declared himself chief of state with a "totality of government power" and adjourned the Senate and the Chamber of Deputies indefinitely. Anti-Jewish decrees issued by the Germans only for the north and by the "Vichyites" for both north and south soon affected all Jews in France—some 195,000 citizens and 135,000 foreigners. Among many other restrictions defined in Vichy's *Statut des Juifs* on October 3, 1940, and June 2, 1941, Jews lost the right to own property over a certain value and to participate in the legal and medical professions, public service, the officer corps of the armed forces, teaching, journalism, theater, radio, and cinema. A Vichy measure also abrogated the Daladier-Marchandeau decree of April 21, 1939, which had prohibited attacks on individuals in the press based on race or religion. An anti-Semitic press, often with covert Nazi funding, soon proliferated.

As refugees in France without employment or possessions, the Feldmans were not greatly affected by many of the French anti-Jewish laws of 1940 and 1941. Their major problem, however, involved the ever-present threat of internment. Already in September 1939, when France entered the war at the time of the invasion of Poland, French police throughout the country had rounded up and interned an estimated fifteen thousand enemy nationals, mostly men, both Jews and non-Jews. Most of these were released within a few months, only to be arrested again at the onset of the Battle of France. At that time, the French government ordered the internment of *all* male immigrants from the Third Reich between the ages of seventeen and fifty-five and all unmarried and childless married women. Initially these measures were not aimed specifically at Jews, but slowly that began to change.

During the confusion surrounding the French defeat, most enemy aliens were released or allowed to escape, but some, including a large proportion of Jews, continued to be held in internment camps under appalling conditions. Then on September 27, 1940, a Vichy decree gave prefects the power to intern male immigrants, both Jews and non-Jews, between the ages of eighteen and fifty-five who were judged to be "superfluous in the national economy." Again, this measure was not directed only against the Jews, but on October 4, another decree authorized prefects to intern, assign to supervised residence, or enroll in forced labor any foreign *Jews* in their departments as they saw fit. Thousands were affected. In this respect, if in no other, the parents of Alfred Feldman were fortunate. Paula was not interned or subjected to obligatory labor. Joachim was asked to present himself at an internment camp but was sent back after a week or two because he could not tolerate the food. As his son has commented, "The camp's administrator, in those early days, was still decent." The Feldmans were registered as foreign Jews in the small town of Montagnac, in the department of Hérault, about twenty miles southwest of Montpellier. The townspeople and even local officials were friendly, but more hostile national authorities knew exactly where they were. When times grew worse, Alfred and his family were terrifyingly vulnerable.

One of the great charms of Alfred Feldman's memoirs is his ability to reconstruct the small details of his flight and his daily life in exile. He remembers the Belgian radio playing the same musical piece over and over again as the Germans invaded, revealing that the station's technicians had joined the general exodus. He recalls the forlorn look of the family house in Antwerp as they left it forever. From his time in Montagnac, he conveys a sense of the hardship of daily farm work for a city lad with no experience on the land. He describes the autumn grape harvest, the cultivation of vines in the spring, the interminable search for wood for heat and cooking, the scarcities and rationing, the disappearance of automobiles, the growing anti-Semitic propaganda. But above all, he remembers his French friends and neighbors, who shared what little they had with the newcomers and revealed no traces of the proverbial French dislike of foreign Jews. Those friends and neighbors would soon be called upon to do much more.

Mass arrests of foreign Jewish men in the occupied zone began in Paris on May 9, 1941. In five days, French police rounded up 3,747 men and sent them to internment camps at Pithiviers and Beune. On or soon after August 20, they seized another 4,230 men, mostly foreigners but including about 200 highly educated French Jews, many of whom were prominent lawyers formerly with the Paris Court of Appeal and the Council of State, the highest administrative court in France. The German occupiers had specifically ordered their arrests. Then on December 12, German rather than French police arrested 734 French Jews, still all men. The first deportation train left France for Auschwitz on March 27, 1942, carrying 1,112 mostly foreign Jewish men. Other trains followed on June 5, 22, 25, 28, and July 17. Each train carried approximately a thousand Jews, still mostly men from the German-occupied zone. Of the more than six thousand passengers on the six convoys, about 257 survived.

While Jewish women and children were initially spared from arrest and deportation, the situation changed drastically on July 16, 1942. In Paris on that terrible day, French police carrying long lists of specific names and addresses of foreign Jews launched their first roundup of entire families. They arrested 12,884 men, women, and children and confined them either at Drancy just outside of Paris or at the Vélodrome d'Hiver, a sports stadium on rue Nelaton in the fifteenth arrondissement. Nearly all the prisoners were deported to Auschwitz during the next two months.

For a few more blissful weeks after the July 1942 roundup, Alfred Feldman and his co-religionists in the unoccupied zone remained free from such dangers. The Vichy authorities, however, had already agreed to deliver 10,000 foreign Jews in the unoccupied zone to the Germans in northern France for deportation by September 15 and several thousand more after that. Again, the French government acted to spare Jewish citizens at the expense of foreigners. Those eligible for delivery were individuals from the Third Reich and some of its occupied countries who had entered France after January 1, 1936. Some exceptions were made, mostly for age and health. To obtain their 10,000 victims, French police first combed internment camps throughout southern France, beginning on August 6. There they found Jewish refugees without appropriate documents, indigent and unemployed—those judged to be "superfluous in the national economy." Some of them had been languishing in camps for more than two years. Between August 6 and 13, some 3,436 foreign Jews were delivered from camps in the south to Drancy in the occupied zone. From there, at least 3,380 of them were shipped to Auschwitz within a few days.

During the next ten days, another 1,184 Jewish men, women, and children were assembled, brought in from small forced labor sites scattered throughout the unoccupied zone. They were sent to Drancy on August 25, and on to Auschwitz a few days later. But still the quota promised by the Vichy French to the Germans had not been met. A thoroughly planned roundup therefore ensued, beginning in the early morning hours of August 26 and continuing for several days. Throughout the unoccupied zone, French police raided the homes of Jewish refugees like Alfred Feldman—all residences registered with the authorities, in obedience to the law. About 7,293 people were arrested. Of these, some 6,392 were sent north by the end of October. From there they were crammed into cattle cars and transported to Auschwitz. Among them were Alfred Feldman's mother and three sisters. They did not return. In a few tender but understated words, as is his style, Alfred conveys the searing pain that has never left him.

French neighbors in Montagnac protected Alfred and his father, provided them with false identification papers, and saved their lives. These rescuers were not alone. Hundreds of other ordinary French men and women, in contrast to those who governed them, did the same. In November 1942, however, in the wake of the Allied landings in North Africa, the German army occupied most of the formerly unoccupied southern French zone. In eight departments east of the Rhône River, the Italians, partners of the Germans, did the same. Nazi pressure for the deportation of Jews from France mounted. Vichy authorities, still in place and anxious to maintain at least a semblance of autonomy throughout the country, complied by delivering still more foreign and, less often, French Jews. But when Vichy police tried to make arrests in the new Italian zone of occupation, the Italians balked. Thus ensued the bizarre phenomenon of Italian military and diplomatic personnel representing an officially anti-Semitic Fascist regime allied with the Third Reich but protecting Jews from Nazi and Vichy French demands for their deportation.

Rumors of safety in the Italian zone were soon circulating. Thousands of Jews in the former "free" zone fled into Italian-occupied territory. There they settled in residences that were supervised but quite comfortable. Many were housed in resort hotels and vacation homes in ski areas now empty of tourists. They could not travel outside their villages, had to obey a curfew, and were required to report to the Italian authorities twice a day. But those authorities were friendly. Some Italian officials even shared meals or coffee with the refugees and attended their parties and concerts.

After his narrow escape in Montagnac in August 1942, Alfred Feldman, now protected by his new false papers, worked for several months in a French labor brigade along with other mostly non-Jewish young men. With his customary subtle humor, he describes his experiences there—his first exposure, away from his sheltering and religiously observant family, to the bawdy language and aspirations, if not activities, of rough young men in any society. But in the late spring of 1943, Alfred's father contacted him from St. Martin-Vésubie, a village in the mountains about twenty-five miles north of Nice, in the Italian zone. Joachim had arrived there on or about March 28 and had been promptly placed in supervised residence. Joachim's elderly mother, Alfred's grandmother, who had been spared arrest in Montagnac because of her age, had fled with him to the Italian zone. She was settled in a nursing home. Jews were treated well in St. Martin-Vésubie, Joachim informed his son. Alfred should make every effort to move there. The rather skeptical young man did so.

Alfred travelled to Nice, also in the Italian-occupied zone. There he met with a delegate from the Comité Dubouchage, a group of courageous if perhaps shortsighted French Jews dedicated to helping their foreign brethren. He was given a new card stating his real name and place of birth, as confirmed by the committee. He was also instructed to destroy his precious, irreplaceable false identification papers before joining his father in St. Martin-Vésubie. False documents were illegal and, if discovered, would only get him into trouble. Along with four to five thousand other Jewish refugees similarly advised and similarly sent by the Italian authorities to the mountainous interior of southeastern France, he did so.

The idyll in the Italian-occupied zone was too good to last. During the summer of 1943, the situation in Italy itself deteriorated precipitously. After defeating the Germans and Italians in North

Africa, the Allies landed on the southern beaches of Sicily on July 9 and began their race for Palermo. On the night of July 24–25, the Fascist Grand Council subjected Benito Mussolini to a vote of no confidence. As previously arranged, King Vittorio Emanuele III dismissed him the following morning. Marshal Pietro Badoglio replaced the Duce as head of government, and the twenty-one-year-old Fascist regime dissolved without a whimper. Italy remained officially at war on the side of the Third Reich, however, and the situation of Jews in Italian-occupied territories in France, Croatia, and Greece, and indeed in Italy itself, did not change. In all these areas, they were subjected to anti-Jewish legislation, but they were not deported as long as the Italians remained fully in control. But Badoglio soon initiated secret negotiations with the Allies for a separate peace. On September 8, somewhat earlier than the Italians expected, General Dwight David Eisenhower announced that an armistice had been agreed upon. The Germans, not surprised by the developments, immediately invaded and occupied Italy, except for the southern tip already under Allied control. They invaded the Italian-occupied territories at the same time.

The result, in southeastern France as elsewhere, was chaos and tragedy. Some twenty-five to thirty thousand Jews had gathered in the coastal areas around Nice, in the expectation that Jewish leaders with help from the British and Americans would be able to provide ships for their escape to North Africa. Of these Jews, about fifteen thousand were foreigners. Many had no false identification documents because they had, like Alfred Feldman, destroyed them a few months earlier. Two days after the armistice, SS Captain Aloïs Brunner and a small specialized German SS unit made their move in Nice, arresting French and foreign Jews alike in one of the few roundups in France that did not involve lists compiled carefully with consideration for the citizenship of the victims. Searches were brutal. Informers and torture were frequent. But French non-Jews, angered by the arrests of French citizens and appalled by the sight of German, rather than French, police brutality, rallied to protect the helpless. About 1,800 Jews were caught in Nice and the surrounding area—a tragic figure, but a small proportion of the numbers actually present.

Further north in the former Italian-occupied zone, in French mountain towns like Chambéry, Vence, Mégève, St. Gervais, Barcelonnette, and St. Martin-Vésubie, similar ruthless manhunts occurred. Hundreds were arrested, especially the old, the sick, and the immobile, who could not flee. Among these was Alfred's eighty-four-year-old grandmother, who was transferred to Drancy and then to Auschwitz, where she was murdered. After September 1943, the Germans and their Vichy accomplices continued to search for Jews throughout France until the liberation. The final result was that at least 75,721 French and foreign Jews were deported from the entire country between 1942 and 1944. Of these, only about 2,800 survived. At least another 1,100 Jews were executed in France during the war, and an estimated 3,000 foreign Jews died from disease and deprivation in French internment camps. The death toll reached at least 77,021, or about 24 percent of the prewar Jewish community.

Despite such dangers and devastation, however, most Jews in the Italian-occupied zone were warned of the Italian retreat and the approach of the Germans after September 8, 1943. Most of them were able to escape into the countryside and find shelter with French families. Still others—perhaps a thousand or two in French villages closest to the border—decided that the safest course was to cross the Alps and enter Italy. After all, Italy had signed an armistice with the Allies. The war there, it seemed, was over. The border ran through steep mountains and was accessible only by rocky footpaths, but it was just a few miles away. Refugees who had been fleeing from the Germans for years set out yet again. Alfred Feldman and his father were among them. They arrived in the small town of Valdieri, in the province of Cuneo, southwest of Turin, only to find that the German army was occupying Italy as well.

Italian villagers, herdsmen, and peasants welcomed the refugees with open arms. Like the people of Montagnac, they provided shelter, food, clothing, and moral support. But on the morning of September 18, Italians and their Jewish guests were confronted with a poster ordering all refugees to turn themselves in to the German SS, on pain of death for themselves and all who sheltered them. What to do? Alfred's indomitable father nearly gave up. His son talked him out of it, and the two men decided to take their chances in the mountains. But many refugees, exhausted, impoverished, and demoralized, did as the poster bid them. Others tried to evade the SS but were caught. About 349 refugees were imprisoned in an old army barracks in nearby Borgo San Dalmazzo, from where, on November 21, 328 of them were sent back to Nice, then to Drancy, and then to Auschwitz. Ten are known to have survived.

Although Alfred and his father did not know it then, the war would continue in northern Italy for more than a year and a half. During that long period, the Germans and their Fascist collaborators in the newly established Italian Social Republic (the so-called Republic of Salò, under the now German puppet, Mussolini) would conduct fierce hunts for Jews of all nationalities, including Italian. Thousands of Jews would fall into their clutches, including 1,259 in Rome in a single day, the infamous "Black Sabbath," October 16, 1943. About 6,746 Jews were deported from Italy, mostly to Auschwitz, during the twenty months of the German occupation. They represented about 15 percent of a population of roughly 43,000 Italian and foreign Jews in the country in September 1943. Only a handful returned. Another 292 Jews were murdered in Italy itself. Among these, as Alfred Feldman notes, were six Jewish refugees seized by a group of Italian Fascist militiamen from a prison in Cuneo on April 25, 1945, just a few days before the end of the war. Like Alfred and his father, the victims—two from Vienna, two from Warsaw, one from Paris, and one from Luxembourg—had crossed the Alps from France into Italy at the time of the Italian armistice, hoping to find a safe haven. Instead they were arrested, thrown into prison, and then taken from it to be shot. Their bodies were thrown under a bridge.

Throughout the terrible year and a half of the German occupation of Italy, Alfred and his father survived, with other Jewish refugees, in mountain huts and stables in isolated, often snowbound hamlets linked only by footpaths. The hardy local residents all knew exactly where the fugitives were but never betrayed them. On the contrary, despite their meager resources they vied with each other to display the traditional Italian peasant hospitality toward strangers. Alfred knew them all. Courtesy demanded that he stop in at each hut he passed on his innumerable journeys for food. He tells us, however, that he often took detours to avoid such visits in order to spare the generous inhabitants from yet another drain on their supplies. Each day was an adventure. In the winter, it was an effort just to keep warm. Cleanliness was impossible. Spring brought fleas and German patrols looking for partisans. By September 1944, the sweeps were almost daily. Alfred, never certain whether the partisans protected the refugees or endangered them by attracting German attention, nevertheless helped them whenever he could. His story makes riveting reading.

There is much here that is new and fresh. Few survivors have chosen to write about the Vichy raids of August 26, 1942, the French labor brigades, the Comité Dubouchage, or life in supervised residence in France under the Italians. Few have described as vividly as in these pages the flight over the mountains in September 1943, or the struggle for survival in the Italian Alps. This book contains much of value to historians. It confirms, for example, that Jewish fugitives knew little and believed less about the fate of their deported loved ones. Feldman writes, also, of the priests who visited him and his father in the mountains, bringing small amounts of money indispensable for life. One priest told them of Cardinal Pietro Boetto, Archbishop of Genoa, and of his wish to be helpful. The money came, not from Rome, as Feldman believed, but from Genoa. It *was* "Jewish money," as he wrote, but it came from the American Jewish Joint Distribution Committee, via an Italian Jewish rescue organization known as Delasem, the *Delegazione Assistenza Emigranti Ebrei.* When Delasem was forced to go underground during the German occupation, its president, Lelio Vittorio Valobra, closed its central office in Genoa and asked Archbishop Boetto if he would accept its funds and continue the work of distributing them to foreign Jews throughout northern Italy. Boetto immediately agreed and recruited priests to perform the dangerous work. I have studied this rescue network at length, but Alfred Feldman's testimony confirms how far was Boetto's reach, and how effective.

There is, also, much here for the nonspecialist. This is the story of a family destroyed and a family reconstituted. It tells of a son who grew to protect the father and of a father whose wisdom and love inspired the son. And if it is a tale of the evil of a powerful few, it is also a tribute to the courageous simple people who refused to accept the anti-Semitic propaganda and rhetoric of their governments, continued to judge and decide for themselves, and enabled hundreds, perhaps thousands, to survive.

Acknowledgments

I DID NOT CONTEMPLATE WRITING a memoir. But of course, when Alberto Cavaglion, the son of my friend Enzo, solicited my recollection of the 1943 crossing of the Alps for a school project, I obliged. That school project, for which he gathered much more information than I supplied, eventually turned into a book that saw several editions and a translation. His book brought me in contact with Dr. Susan Zuccotti who, upon hearing about the rest of my war experiences, suggested that I write them down. Wagging her finger at me, she said, "You owe it to history." What could I do?

I had not kept a diary. To write this memoir, I had to supplement my memory with what I could extract from surviving relatives, friends, and helpful strangers and glean in libraries. I am indebted to my Aunt Betty for her recollections of what happened in Germany and Poland and to my Aunt Charlotte for what happened in Belgium and in France. Of others mentioned in my account, I thank my cousins Paula Nizan (née Beglückter), Goldine Teicher (née Ehrenfeld), Ruth Goldstein (née Feldman), Simon Knoll, Josi Rosenbaum, Ines Finkel (née Rosenbaum), and Willi Rosenbaum; my friends Enzo and Riccardo Cavaglion, Léon L. Kowarski, Rachel Rubinfeld (née Diamant), Charles A. Spirn, and Mala Wassner (née Weiss).

I owe much to my wife for her unflinching support and to my children, Suzanne and Philip, for their suggestions and critique. At the Library of Congress in Washington, I found a knowing, helping, and wonderful staff. In France, Mr. Pierre Grasset dedicatedly combed for me both literature and archives, even going to the cemetery to check the inscription on a tombstone. In Italy, Alberto Cavaglion connected me with Dr. Giovanni B. Varnier, who located the reports on the little Cilli as well as information about some of the Italian clerics under whose protection I had been. In Israel, Nadine Neiger (née Lustig) kept me informed of what she thought might be of interest to me and read her first book in Hebrew in order to translate some of it for me. When I expressed my thanks, she wrote, "But, Alfred, it is with the greatest pleasure that I do this, and whatever you need, I am always at your disposal. I find it so important to witness. Our generation is going, and then it will be too late."

I am indebted, furthermore, to François-Xavier Amprimoz, John Paul Abranches, Sergio Arneodo, Klaus Jochen Arnold, Benton M. Arnovitz, Fred Babbin, Ruth Babbin, Giorgio Bernardi, A. David Blum, Wolf Brafman, Lucien Bringuier, Battista Cesana, Richard Curtis, Leo Ehrenfeld, Rifka Ehrenfeld, Pierre Embry, Elaine Farbenbloom, Herbert Finkel, Louis Goldman, Carmen Granal, Monique Grasset, Victoria C. Hill, Meno Menashe Horowitz, Rivka Horowitz, Shoshana Kerewsky, Yvonne Kinkaid, Serge Klarsfeld, Ariel Koprov, Albina Malerba, Walter Marx, Renée Miro, André Nos, Patrick Ormea, Shlomo Porter, Charles M. Roman, Rina Rosenbaum, Marsha L. Rozenblit, Mary Doria Russell, Dorothea Scheimann, Georges Schnek, Vicki Sipe, Nell Stewart, Lucienne Trebosc, Gus Tyler, Albert Uziel, Charles E. Walker, Gerhard L. Weinberg, and Courtney B. Wilson.

Last but not least, I gratefully acknowledge the assistance of Alan Adelson, executive director of the Jewish Heritage Project in New York; of Baltimore's Jewish Historical Society; and of my editors at Southern Illinois University Press.

ONE
STEP
AHEAD

Genealogy of the Feldman Family

This genealogy includes members of Alfred's father's family. Only the final generation is complete. The descendants of Jakob Bezalel Rotenberg, however, who lived in the United States are not included. Family names are underlined, and persons whose names are shown in boldface died of deprivation or were killed by the Nazis. For some persons, nicknames (in quotes) or Jewish names appear in parentheses. Cousins Minna Feldman and Simon Rosenbaum are listed twice: once as progeny and again as each other's spouse.

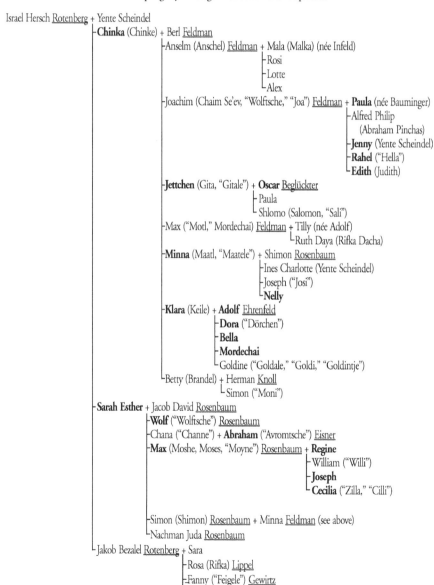

Israel Hersch <u>Rotenberg</u> + Yente Scheindel
- **Chinka** (Chinke) + Berl <u>Feldman</u>
  - Anselm (Anschel) <u>Feldman</u> + Mala (Malka) (née Infeld)
    - Rosi
    - Lotte
    - Alex
  - Joachim (Chaim Se'ev, "Wolftsche," "Joa") <u>Feldman</u> + **Paula** (née Bauminger)
    - Alfred Philip (Abraham Pinchas)
    - **Jenny** (Yente Scheindel)
    - **Rahel** ("Hella")
    - **Edith** (Judith)
  - **Jettchen** (Gita, "Gitale") + **Oscar** <u>Beglückter</u>
    - Paula
    - Shlomo (Salomon, "Sali")
  - Max ("Motl," Mordechai) <u>Feldman</u> + Tilly (née Adolf)
    - Ruth Daya (Rifka Dacha)
  - **Minna** (Maatl, "Maatele") + Shimon <u>Rosenbaum</u>
    - Ines Charlotte (Yente Scheindel)
    - Joseph ("Josi")
    - **Nelly**
  - **Klara** (Keile) + **Adolf** <u>Ehrenfeld</u>
    - **Dora** ("Dörchen")
    - **Bella**
    - **Mordechai**
    - Goldine ("Goldale," "Goldi," "Goldintje")
  - Betty (Brandel) + Herman <u>Knoll</u>
    - Simon ("Moni")
- **Sarah Esther** + Jacob David <u>Rosenbaum</u>
  - **Wolf** ("Wolftsche") <u>Rosenbaum</u>
  - Chana ("Channe") + **Abraham** ("Avromtsche") <u>Eisner</u>
  - **Max** (Moshe, Moses, "Moyne") <u>Rosenbaum</u> + **Regine**
    - William ("Willi")
    - **Joseph**
    - **Cecilia** ("Zilla," "Cilli")
  - Simon (Shimon) <u>Rosenbaum</u> + Minna <u>Feldman</u> (see above)
  - Nachman Juda <u>Rosenbaum</u>
- Jakob Bezalel <u>Rotenberg</u> + Sara
  - Rosa (Rifka) <u>Lippel</u>
  - Fanny ("Feigele") <u>Gewirtz</u>
  - Ida (Ita) <u>Lippel</u>

1
How We Arrived in Germany, and How We Left

In 1922, the value of the German mark fell from 162 M to the dollar to more than 7,000. The next year, the plunge accelerated until one dollar fetched 4.2 trillion marks. Exporters, whose costs vanished under such inflation, profited handsomely, and so did those who had debts to pay off. Understandably however, workers, the middle classes, and pensioners were devastated. Strikes and food riots ensued, providing a fertile ground for extremists to gain prominence—among them Communists and Hitler's still small National Socialist movement.[1] Such was the legacy of a war waged and lost.

My mother, back then, happened to be caught up in a curious event. On August 7, 1923, in Hamburg, a riot had delayed her way to the hospital. She made it safely inside, but outside the disturbance intensified. Suddenly, the staccato sound of a machine gun penetrated the maternity ward. Screams and pandemonium ensued. My mother and several women already in labor gave birth at once, adding their screams to those heard outside. Years later, when I misbehaved, my mother sometimes referred to this event, concluding that a boy who refused to eat his cauliflower could not possibly be her son. The panicking nurses must surely have mixed up the babies.

Anti-Semitism, another misery my parents had to cope with was, however, no joking matter. They kept quiet to us children about it, and so did, I think, most German Jews. Although I heard that word often enough, I let it languish along with other big words that a child's mind cannot comprehend.

Suppression of such knowledge was a troublesome task. It required intervention, for instance, even in our most beloved observance, the Seder. This ancient ritual is celebrated at home on the first and second nights of Passover. Then the table is resplendent with white linen, glowing candles, and tableware never touched by bread. Under the parents' prideful eyes, a child begins reading, in Hebrew, some well-rehearsed questions from the Haggada: "Why is this night different? . . ." The father answers at length chanting also from the Haggada: "Slaves were we to Pharaoh. . . ." A sumptuous meal follows, during which the children attempt to "steal" the afikomen, a piece of matzo required for the ritual that can be parlayed for a reward. That keeps their interest up on this long evening. Benedictions besprinkle all this, as well as ritual tastings and the filling of everyone's goblet of wine at four different times. One goblet, however, is filled only once. Placed at the center of the Seder plate, it is for a guest whose arrival we ache for. It is for Elijah, the prophet who, tradition has it, will usher in the Messiah on this night. The goblet is a vision of the future, a toast to a redeemed world.[2]

There are more benedictions after the meal. The ritual is not finished yet. It ends with happy, rousing songs. But before singing, it was my task to hold open the door to our apartment while my father intoned something that sounded important:

> Pour out Your wrath on the nations that do not know You,
> And on the kingdoms that do not call on Your name.
> For they have devoured Jacob,
> And laid waste his dwelling place.[3]
> Pour out Your indignation upon them,
> And let Your wrathful anger overtake them.[4]
> Pursue them in anger,
> And destroy them,
> From under the heavens of the Lord.[5]

Only years later, my Hebrew having considerably progressed, did I understand what was being said here, and only much later yet did I learn that this part of the ceremony originated in the Dark Ages, when the fiction was current that Jews prepare their matzoth with the blood of a Christian child. Credulity in this blood libel provoked gruesome massacres of Jews and offered murderers a convenient place for disposing of corpses. Jews opened their doors on Passover Eve to ascertain that no cadaver had been placed on their doorstep in the dark of that night.[6] The practice became part of the ritual.

But we children were told—and many others as well—that the door was opened to allow the prophet Elijah to enter for a sip of his wine. A little white lie, but it taints the engaging toast to a redeemed world.

With guile and luck, my parents were able to shield their children from a knowledge of anti-Semitism for many years. In 1931, my father's home office in Cologne sent him to open a branch office in the Belgian port city of Antwerp. He managed to bring us there the next year, eluding the beginning of the Nazi dominion in Germany.

The apartment into which we moved, on the rue Montebello, chanced to be across the street from a German school run by the German government. My parents enrolled me there, thinking that it would ease my transition into French. Indeed, the school, with small classes and excellent teachers, was ideal for me.

But while Germans, after Hitler's rise to power, all too eagerly boycotted Jewish businesses in Germany, expelled Jewish artists and teachers, and burned books by Jewish authors, my school remained undisturbed. German or not, my teachers remained invariably friendly.

My parents' friends and relatives were appalled that I should still attend a German school, and so I left at the end of the school year (which, according to German custom, is in March). On that occasion the principal presented me in a little ceremony with a certificate for completing fourth grade. I in turn gave him a souvenir, a drawing I had made, duly signed, my conception of a storm-tossed sailing ship. Amidst good-byes, the teachers invited me to come back to report about the Jewish school to which I was transferring. Months later when I did so, the first thing I noticed was my drawing, framed, prominently hanging in the principal's office. I had never shown much artistic promise, nor had this been my best work. The prominence given to the work of the school's only Jewish student was, I suspect, the faculty's defiant protest of what went on in Germany.

The occasional visitors from Cologne who were invited to our apartment usually avoided discussions about business or politics. Still, our guests could not repress all tales. I remember one of them relating how a Jewish colleague of his, driving a car, was stopped by a uniformed SA. The man, it turned out, wanted to hitch a ride.

"Are you a true Aryan?" the colleague asked him.

"Jawohl," the hitchhiker said proudly.

"Well then," the colleague said as he sped off, "you can stay right where you are."

We laughed, and our visitor had to remind us that his colleague's rebuff had not been without danger. This tale, the only instance that I recall in which a Jew defied a Nazi openly to his face, did nothing to clarify the meaning of anti-Semitism.

In 1935—I was eleven then—my father decided to take the entire family to visit his parents in Cologne. The nearer our departure date, the more my mother fretted, alarmed by the treatment of Jews in Germany. But my father, who frequently visited his home office, assured her that we had nothing to fear, that the Germans sought to ingratiate themselves with people from abroad, and that they had always been "utterly correct" toward him.

One traveled by train in those times and, with the beginning of each summer, I looked forward to our train ride to the seashore. How different, however, was our ride into Germany! Night had fallen when we reached the border. There, an additional steam locomotive was added to our train, coupled to the back to assist it up the grades in the hilly terrain beyond. Seated in the last car, we had been jolted by that noisy coupling, and now, as the train began to roll, the powerful laboring of that engine filled our car. Curious, I walked to its rear and opened the door to the enclosed platform. The noise there was hellish, penetrating my insides. Although through the darkness outside I could see nothing, I realized that I stood right in front of the engine. No baggage car separated us from it. Frantically it puffed, worrying the coupling, letting go a little, then ramming the bumpers from a running start. Under each impact, the platform clanked and shuddered, seemingly ready to give way. Outside, the occasional passing light, the glow of a flying ember, revealed nothing. I felt uneasy. I could sense the evil outside, the evil of which I had heard so much in recent years, the evil of the country through which the train rolled that night.

It took but a small, inconspicuous event to solidify my concept of evil. It happened a few days later in Cologne. I had arranged to meet Aunt Betty in a public square nearby where she was taking her little Moni for fresh air. When I arrived, she was not alone. A woman walked alongside the baby carriage, berating my aunt for having sat on a public bench. Aunt Betty angrily countered that she paid her taxes and had as much right to sit there as anyone else. The woman left in a huff, and we observed that, having reached the far side of the square, she talked to a policeman. Aunt Betty thought it prudent to leave the square.

As we passed a newsstand, she showed me, prominently displayed, an issue of *Der Stürmer*, its bold headlines proclaiming some outrage committed by Jews, caricatured there with large noses, devious eyes, and hairy profiles evoking the face of sheep.

Within me, feelings of indignation welled up at the malice, the insult, the calumny of the thing. It evoked a sense of being snubbed, of having been chastened that was not without fear. But I remember vividly as well the satisfaction I experienced for having come to comprehend so important a word as "anti-Semitism."

Rzeszów—Lancut—Przeworsk.

These names are familiar. Lancut, in the province of Galicia, which now is divided between Poland and Ukraine, was part of the Austrian empire when my paternal grandfather, Berl Feldman, was born there. A history of the Polish railways shows the dates on which the railway first reached these towns.[7] Lancut—which was Landshut then—was connected November 15, 1859. My grandfather, born about two years later, grew up with the railroad.

Over tracks as smooth as calm waters, the railroad hauled people and freight at stormy speeds, and in quantities akin not to what a horse-drawn wagon can carry but to what a ship can load. The ossified Galician economy, in which occupations were determined by ethnicity, custom, and discriminatory laws, was slow to adapt to this new technology. The non-Jewish population—mostly the peasantry—rarely rode the railways. The landed aristocracy traveled, of course, in first or second class. The Jews, however, traveled with such frequency that the third-class coaches became their virtually exclusive domain.[8]

My grandfather used the railroad to leave Galicia. In the late 1880s he boarded the train to Cracow, thence across the border to Berlin, and thence clear across Germany, all the way to Cologne. There he established a business. On German documents the profession of my venturesome, railroading grandfather was entered as peddler.[9]

Going from house to house in the better neighborhoods, he bought up discarded clothes that he resold. In time, he opened his own secondhand clothing store.

He had married before leaving for Germany, and from time to time he returned to visit Chinka, his wife, in Zolynia, which was a stone's throw from Landshut. In 1897, his business having prospered, he was ready to bring her and their four children to Cologne. She, however, with her youngest still a baby, was apprehensive about the journey and life in Germany. When her parents suggested that she leave her second child, Wolftsche, with them, she agreed.

Five years later, the boy, my father, rejoined his parents. How strange Cologne appeared to the ten-year-old! My father told me more than once of his astonishment at seeing a man talking loudly to a wall. He had not noticed the little wooden box attached to it and had never heard of a telephone. He had another surprise: three new sisters, Maatl, Keile, and Brandel. As for his older siblings, they had new names. At school, their teachers had Germanized Anschel to Anselm, Gitale to Jettchen, and Motl to Max. The new sisters, as they entered school, would become Minna, Klara, and Betty.

Their former names were not abandoned. They remained their real names. On her birth certificate, Aunt Betty was still registered as Brandel. These names were used on invitations to bar mitzvahs; in the ketubah, the Jewish marriage contract; and at the synagogue, to call a person to the Torah. But by the next generation already, secular names appeared on our birth certificates. These insured some anonymity in a factious world. I was registered as Alfred Philip, but my Hebrew names are Abraham Pinchas. Those of us who had only Jewish names were addressed by diminutive or nickname. Thus, Aunt Jettchen's son Salomon would be called Sali; Aunt Betty's son Simon, Moni; and my sister Rahel, Hella.

My father had not gone to school in Galicia but been taught by his grandfather. The boy read only Hebrew, spoke only Yiddish. Although German laws made education compulsory until age fourteen, my grandfather thought that it was too late to put his son into a German school. He could pass for a fourteen-year-old. But my father's older brother, Anschel, who still had to go to school, was unhappy with the unfairness of this arrangement. He let it be known that Wolftsche played hooky. The Jewish school, sensitive about infractions of German law, took action. In February 1903, at age eleven, his first name now "Joachim," my father went to school for the first time.

He was placed in a class with much younger children but by the end of the school year, had advanced to the fourth grade. By the end of the next year, he had caught up, and when he finished eighth grade two years later, he was, according to Aunt Betty, at the head of his class.

One of his teachers had mentioned his meteoric progress to two young entrepreneurs, the brothers Lissauer, who did a profitable business buying ores from Russia. They offered my father a job. My grandfather, however, would not hear of it.

In Galicia, Jews and Gentiles did not mix socially. They differed in their ways of life, and they differed in their manner of thought. Their religions stood them apart, and their languages, and their clothing, and their foods. For untold generations, those differences had engendered mistrust. Unlike the English word "Gentile," its Yiddish counterpart, the word "goy," carries derogatory connotations.

My grandfather, one of the first Eastern European Jews to settle in Cologne, held on to the only way of life he had ever known. He did not mix with the Germans or adopt any of their ways. He kept his house open to any of his Jewish countrymen newly arriving in town. There they could count on a meal, even a bed. His house served as a place of prayer until they established their own *shul*. Seven years after my grandfather's arrival in Cologne, the growth of this community justified the establishment of a kosher butcher. Until then my grandfather had had no meat on his table. His brother-in-law in Galicia, Jakob Bezalel Rothenberg, had to send him matzo for Passover. Living in such cultural isolation, he failed to realize that employment in industrialized Germany was not the rare, ill-paid occupation he remembered from Galicia, where no one in the family had ever worked for a non-Jew.

My father's teacher, however, was unfazed. He went to see my grandfather, pleaded with him, assured him that the Lissauers were proper Jewish boys, that their office was closed on Shabbos, that all their employees were Jewish, and that they were well paid. Only then did my grandfather consent to let his son take that job.

At the Lissauers' office, my father began the day by lighting the stove and making coffee. In time, he was entrusted with the delicate mission of carrying letters between one of the brothers, Meno Lissauer, and his bride-to-be. He also learned the exacting art of sampling ores, and his next promotion was to monitor shipments of ore from a certain mine to the nearest harbor. To the end of his life he could recite the serial number of the railroad car that shuttled between mine and harbor to haul "his" ore. As the Lissauers' business expanded, they sent my father to do similar work in Greece, Spain, North Africa, Italy, and other distant places. Then they asked him to open a branch office in Hamburg, and there he met and married my mother.

My uncle Max also married in Hamburg. He had come to visit my father and met his secretary who, in time, became my aunt Tilly.

Paula Bauminger, my mother, had come to Germany at an early age. In Cracow, her father's haberdashery had failed and his partner absconded with the cash. They moved to Hamburg, opening an upscale bakery that proved to be a success with the Jewish community. I remember my grandfather Isaac's distinguished presence, enhanced by a well-trimmed beard and a prosperous stoutness. He always wore a top hat to the synagogue and spoke, as did my grandmother, Scheindel Chaja, an impeccable German. They saw to it that their children—my mother and her younger brother, Jacob—received an excellent education. My mother learned French, played the piano, visited museums, and attended musical and theatrical performances. Still, assimilation had its limits. When my married mother decided to buy Dubnow's *World History of the Jewish People,*[10] whose ten-volume publication began in 1925 to great critical acclaim, my grandfather vehemently objected because the work accepted scientific evidence that was at variance with the biblical account. My mother bought it anyway, but the memory of this event bothered her enough that she mentioned it to me whenever we happened to look at these books.

My mother raised us children as she had been raised herself, as good little Germans. I was the first. Two sisters were born in Hamburg and one in Cologne. My mother encouraged hygiene, a secular education, and the speaking of a flawless German. The songs she taught us were German, and the tales she read to us came from the Brothers Grimm. In her mind, Germany was one of the most civilized of nations. I think that in admiring German culture, she thought of the Enlightenment. Seen through Jewish eyes, the Enlightenment denigrated religion, but obviously accommodations had been possible. Seen through German eyes, however, it redeemed us Jews. My parents often mentioned *Nathan the Wise,* a classic work approbatory of a Jew and his religion by the eighteenth-century German writer Lessing. My mother owned his collected works, as well as those of Goethe, Schiller, and Heine. Their thoughts, along with German notions about order, culture, and progress, accounted for the civilized state of their country. In that style she intended to bring up her children.

I learned to read Hebrew before learning to read German, our holidays were different from those of the Germans, we ate kosher, we sang Hebrew songs at table on Shabbos, we didn't switch electric lights on or off on that day, nor travel by train or car, and we were Polish citizens. Still, my mother made us understand that we were German. Only our religion was different.

We moved to Cologne about 1928, when Lissauer recalled my father to the home office. Now I got to know my father's parents. My grandfather Berl was then a frail old man, his long, snow-white beard made more dramatic by his slight stature. When my mother, in his presence, once decried the length of my fingernails, he offered to cut them, and he did so quickly and painlessly under my mother's alarmed gaze using his sharp pocketknife. My cousin Ruth, the daughter of Uncle Max and Aunt Tilly, remembers him on a visit to Hamburg taking her to the fish market, buying a carp on which later, at her house, he chopped away with a cleaver, preparing gefilte fish better than her mother's.

My paternal grandparents had bought their house before World War I. It was a solid house, four stories high, with a corner location and two small storefronts flanking its front entrance. I remember the darkness inside, the smells of cooking that always permeated it, and the constant bustle of women and children among whom my grandmother stood out so little that I am unable to picture her then. The male visitors to this house all spoke a poor German sprinkled with quotations from the Talmud. My grandparents still lived as they, their parents, and many preceding generations had lived in Poland.

Of the people who visited my grandparents' house, one intrigued even my father. He took me along to see that man because, he said,

I was not likely to encounter his kind again. He was a flagellant. I did not get to see much of his performance as a crowd pushed ahead of me, but in the gloomy room I heard the terrifying cracks of the leather whip with which the man was scourged, or scourged himself.

Not even after catching my mother crinkling up her nose at the mention of Yiddish, which she called "jargon," did I grasp the difference that separated our way of life from that of my grandparents. Nor was I aware, during the time that I remained in Cologne, that either we or my grandparents might be different from the Germans. There was no television then. I remember only two instances when I noticed such a difference. When I was seven, I went weekly to a heder where I and a few other boys were taught to read and translate from a large-print Hebrew Bible. I was old enough to walk there by myself but, to cross one particular street, my mother had told me always to accompany another person. That time, that person, a nice lady, talked to me while we were crossing. What was that big book that I was carrying? I told her. Having arrived on the other side, she asked me to see it. She opened it. Can you read this? Her voice was skeptical. So I proceeded to read from it then and there. The book had opened where the pages were most worn, where the text was familiar. The lady was utterly astonished. Oh, you really can read this! She made me feel like a genius.

And when a friend one day introduced me to his grandfather, a man without a beard, I was dumbfounded.

Thus our life in Germany might have continued. The differences between us and the Germans might, in time, have been accepted. The differences between generations might have worked themselves out. The girls would have been married off, the boys would have set themselves up in a business or even found employment. There might have been a black sheep among us or perhaps a genius. Somehow all would have made their accommodations with modern life. It was not to be. Change begets change. The next upheaval was to be far more unsettling than the coming of the railroad. But for this change, we Jews were woefully unprepared.

My family, as I have related already, left Germany shortly before the Nazis came to power. I recall nothing about our departure. My last memories of my life in Germany are of the vacation we took the preceding summer. My parents had been married close to ten years, and my mother had had a child every other year since then. But with my youngest sister, Edith, now a toddler, a vacation could be managed. A colleague of my father, who owned a car large enough to hold the whole family, drove us the thirty miles to Honnef, a resort on the Rhine, near Königswinter. There we shared a cottage with its owner. There was a garden and garden tools. To a city kid like me, raised in apartments, traversing mostly treeless streets, and taken to parks where walking on grass was strictly prohibited, these were marvels. I got permission to dig, but, improbably proficient, I soon was astir amidst the tender shoots planted by the daughter of the house. The matter was amicably resolved, and the next day, my father took the oldest of us to the Drachenfels, the Rock of the Dragon. He had to walk to the ruins of the castle that towered atop the mountain, but my sisters and I rode up on saddled and beribboned donkeys. It was my first ride on an animal, my first visit to a castle, my first ascent of a mountain, and my first view of the world from the top of one. I shall never forget the joy of it.

After we left and the Nazis came to power, there was no joy in Germany. My mother's brother, Uncle Jacob, left in 1934, a year after our departure. He dealt in graphite, which, used in industrial lubricants, shoe polishes, pencils, and more, is an international business that required travel. Outraged by official boycotts against Jewish businesses and anticipating travel difficulties if, as he heard, German Jews were to be stripped of their citizenship, he joined us in Antwerp. His business could be run from any country. He celebrated his getaway by courting and marrying a local girl who thus became my Aunt Charlotte.

With both their children in Antwerp, my maternal grandparents sold their bakery and retired to our city.

In Cologne, Uncle Anschel, more daring, more adventurous, or more foresighted perhaps than the rest of the family, was the first to make up his mind. In 1933 he left his little dairy shop in the capable hands of his wife, Aunt Mala, and went to Palestine, where he established an eatery near a construction site. He did well enough to allow his wife and children to follow him the next year. Aunt Klara and her husband then took over Uncle Anschel's dairy business.

By 1935, the outbreaks against the Jews lessened. The Nazis were seeking to curry favor with the world in anticipation of the

Olympic Games to be held the next year in Berlin. The anxiety of my relatives remaining in Germany abated. The ultrareligious Jewish community to which they belonged even approved the notorious Nuremberg laws, which were enacted in September of that year.[11] These laws forbade mixed marriages, and codified the place of the Jews in Germany. That seemed to remove any reason for arbitrary terror. My relatives were lulled into temporizing. No one opted to follow Uncle Anschel's example. The consensus, Aunt Betty told me long afterward, was that the Nazis wouldn't last any longer than previous governments. The next government could only be better.

But there would be no next government, and when the Olympics ended, the Nazis were quick to return to their mischief. In October 1936, Uncle Oscar staggered home one day, barely able to tell his wife, Aunt Jettchen, that some Nazis toughs, calling him a Jew, had hit him over the head. He went to bed and within two days was dead. His children had not been at home and were not told what had happened. His daughter Paula would become aware of the circumstances of his death only upon reading the first draft of these lines. She had been told that he had died of a sudden heart attack. Her brother Sali, age five, was kept ignorant even of the death of his father. For a while, he was "invited" to stay with a friend, away from home. But religious custom required that he recite the Kaddish for his dead father. Sali was told that, because of his nice voice, he would sing before a group of people. There, he imitated someone word for word, chanting the Kaddish unaware of its meaning.

Grandfather departed next. In April 1937, he died of cancer. He had little to show for a lifetime of enterprise and work. The runaway inflation that followed World War I had wiped out his savings. After the Nazis rose to power, the two stores downstairs could no longer be rented. Aunt Jettchen, a widow without means of support, lived in the house with her two children, unable to pay any rent. Without the rents, payments could not be maintained on a mortgage that had provided dowries to Aunts Klara and Betty. The house went into receivership. My grandfather had spent the last years of his life as a virtual prisoner in his house, having heard that Nazi thugs amused themselves on the street by jerking old Jews around by their beards.

Grandfather knew that things would not get better. On his deathbed, he said to Aunt Betty, quoting from the Book of Job: "The living shall envy the dead."

My cousin Ruth remembers two Jewish women entering her parents' dairy store in Hamburg, debating whether to buy two eggs, and deciding that it could wait. Shunned by Gentiles, supported by customers such as these, a Jewish business could not survive. Ruth's mother, Aunt Tilly, went to work as a secretary again but prepared to emigrate to the United States. She had relatives there, and the Great Depression could not be worse there than what faced them here in Germany.

There were some formalities. One of the few steps President Hoover had taken to cope with that depression[12] was a regulation requiring a would-be immigrant to prove that he would not become a public charge in the United States. The immigrant had to find a sponsor, an American citizen, with the resources to assume this obligation and willing to pledge his commitment under oath, by affidavit. When these documents were examined at the U.S. consulate, it was determined that Aunt Tilly's relatives, an uncle and a brother, lacked the means to sponsor the entire family.

Aunt Tilly departed with their daughter and her mother, expecting to sponsor her husband herself. A year would pass before Uncle Max could rejoin them.

Inadequate affidavits also tore Aunt Minna's family apart. Her husband, Uncle Shimon, had first sought to emigrate to Palestine but, as the British kept reducing the number of immigration permits, switched his destination. It took him until 1938 to obtain an affidavit, and then this proved adequate only for him. "We cried all night after he was gone," recalled my cousin Ines, his eldest. Aunt Minna could not run her husband's one-man delivery service. She and her three children would move into the foreclosed house, to live there with her mother and sister Jettchen.

Not long before Ines's father departed, the Hitler Jugend had burst into her school, the Jewish school that both my father and I had attended. Their leader, Ines told me, entered her classroom, shouting, "We are taking over," whereupon the German children—"children of our age," Ines said—beat up the Jewish children, tore up their books, and pursued them even as they fled the school.

Aunt Minna wrote my father, asking him to invite Ines to spend the summer of 1938 with us. For several years we had been inviting my cousin Paula, Aunt Jettchen's daughter, to spend the summer vacation with us. Now, Aunt Minna felt, it was her daughter's turn. My parents agreed. Aunt Minna got Ines a visitor's visa and a railroad ticket and, although the eleven-year-old girl had never made such a voyage, sent her off alone.

Ines would not see her mother again.

Aunt Betty's husband, after receiving in 1936 a letter from his supplier stating that he was no longer permitted to do business with Jews, had also decided to emigrate to Palestine. To immigrate as a capitalist, Uncle Herman had to show a deposit with a British bank equal to 15,000 German marks. He could come up with that sum. Germany, however, restricted the outflow of its currency. How was he to get the money into a British bank?

He had a relative who could help, a man who exchanged money on the black market. He happened to be arrested with Uncle Herman's money still in his possession. The police further found on him a booklet in which he had recorded the names of his customers. Uncle Herman had to leave Germany, and fast.

But where to? He had several cousins in the United States, but he had not been in touch with them and didn't know their addresses. He still had relatives in Poland, in the town of Kuty. Afraid to show himself, he sent his wife, who would not leave her three-year-old son behind. Aunt Betty's expedition into the Carpathian mountains, where some of her travel had to be made by horse carriage, proved memorable and successful. She found the relatives and obtained the addresses of those in the United States. Upon being contacted, the latter provided affidavits by 1938. These proved sufficient for my uncle only, and he left Germany that year leaving Aunt Betty and their son behind.

In March of that year, Germany had invaded and annexed a willing Austria. There, in one "spring cleaning," the Nazis inflicted on the Jews what it had taken them years to accomplish in Germany. In the first month of the occupation, more than five hundred Austrian Jewish people committed suicide.[13]

And now Germany had copycats. Rumania abrogated the rights of Jews, Hungary restricted their number in the liberal professions and in various enterprises, and Poland had already undertaken an official anti-Jewish boycott. Everywhere, Jews sought to emigrate.

One door remained open. But as the number of would-be immigrants rose to flood proportions, that door became difficult to reach. In 1924 the United States had enacted the National Origins Quota Law, which limited the numbers of immigrants by country of birth. Asians were barred altogether. Those born in Western Europe had no quota limitation. Poland's limit was 6,524 annually. Germany's, including Austria, was 27,370.[14] In 1938 these limits were attained.

When somewhat belatedly, Aunts Jettchen and Klara undertook the trip to the consulate in Stuttgart to apply for immigration to the United States, they were assigned quota numbers and told that they would be informed when their turn came up. And they must have been made to understand that, in the meantime, obtaining an affidavit was premature as these expire after six months.

In that same year, the Polish government ordered the revalidation of the passports of its citizens residing abroad. Those who failed to comply by October 29, 1938, would be barred from re-entering Poland.

My family, along with probably all Polish Jews in Germany, ignored this order. They knew that it was but an attempt to strip them of their citizenship.

Germany, under the pretext that it couldn't be stuck with these people, decided to send them back. Without warning, on the deadline's eve, before dawn, police in Germany and Austria invaded the homes of Polish Jews, rounded up the heads of family and, allowing no more than ten marks in their pockets, shipped them to Poland. A newspaper called it "perhaps [the] greatest mass deportation of recent times."[15]

Particularly woeful was the plight of divided families. Their husbands having emigrated, the wives were considered heads of family. Should they leave their children behind? Take them along?

In Cologne, the police handled the matter relatively decently. They invaded no homes. They merely notified those concerned to leave their passports at police stations and report by evening to an army barracks, from where they would depart the next day.

As head of family, Aunt Klara's husband, Uncle Adolf, reported. Aunt Jettchen also reported, her widowhood making her head of family. She took along her two children, Paula and Sali.

Aunt Betty had already surrendered her passport but then had second thoughts. She would not go to the barracks. She would not leave her seventy-eight-year-old mother at home alone. She would not leave Aunt Klara, whose husband had to leave, managing the business and her four small children alone. She decided to tell the authorities that she was about to leave Germany, not for Poland but to join her husband in America.

She attempted to convince Aunt Minna to do the same. Her husband was also in America. But Aunt Minna would not listen. She feared confronting the German authorities, and she did not want to separate herself, under the circumstances, from her widowed sister, Aunt Jettchen. Arguing that she might just as well wait for her American visa in Galicia, she and her two youngest children, Josi and Nelly, went to the barracks.

The next morning, the deportees were put on a train, which arrived at the border town of Zbaszyn before the deadline expired. There, Polish authorities examined passports so minutely that only a small number of the arrivals were admitted. Most of the 15,000 Jewish deportees remained trapped in a no-man's-land. The town had shelter for only a fortunate few hundred, among them my relatives. They lived packed nine to a room. The other refugees had to live in stables. Thus they remained through a long and bitter winter, surviving mainly on tea and bread.[16]

Poland forbade its Jewish press to report these events. Only an appeal for funds was permitted.

Aunt Betty, having said farewell to Aunt Minna at the barracks, went to get her mother who had been left alone in the foreclosed house. There, she packed only a few belongings to forestall any suspicion that she was taking away foreclosed property. Leaving with her mother for Aunt Klara's apartment, Aunt Betty left a light turned on to give the impression that she would soon return.

The next morning, she helped Aunt Klara close her business. They forwarded the entire inventory of perishable dairy products to the Jewish orphanage in Cologne, which had been a steady customer, and which lately had found it difficult to make ends meet. Also, since Aunt Klara's youngest child had been born a scant three months earlier, Aunt Betty requested a helper from the Jewish Home for Young Women. They obligingly sent Sarah,[17] a teenage girl.

Two days later, a policeman appeared at Aunt Betty's apartment to arrest "Branel Knoll," whose passport had been left unclaimed in Zbaszyn. The policeman thought he had come to arrest a man. Aunt Betty—whose first name was Brandel—told him that he must have been mistaken, that no such person lived here, and that anyway she couldn't leave her mother and her child at home alone. He agreed to go back to check on the matter. Aunt Betty did not wait. Once he had left, she packed the barest necessities and departed with her mother and child. Again she left a light burning, closed the door, and hurried to Aunt Klara's house.

Occasionally I still hear or read of someone critical of Jewish meekness in the face of Nazi abuse. Such people must not remember how the Nazis treated anyone who resisted them. They must have forgotten that in Paris, a Jewish teenager, outraged by the deportation of his parents to Zbaszyn, did get hold of a gun, got into the German embassy, and shot a German official. When, two days later, the official died, Germany exploded in the well-orchestrated nationwide pogrom that has since come to be known as the Kristallnacht.

In the middle of that night, Aunt Betty was awakened by someone banging like mad against the door of Aunt Klara's Jewish neighbor, yelling, in Yiddish, "Flee! Flee!" Then she heard the terrifying phrase that, since the Middle Ages, has so often chilled Jewish bones to the marrow: *"men harget yidn,"* they are killing Jews!

While Aunt Klara lay in bed, retching, Aunt Betty and Sarah quickly dressed the children. Then out into the dark night they went, three women and five children, frightened, bewildered, at their wit's end. They set out for the Jewish orphanage, the recipient of Aunt Klara's dairy largesse. Located on the outskirts of town, it would, they hoped, remain unmolested. They walked through the long night, keeping to back streets to avoid the mobs, reaching the orphanage as dawn broke. Grandmother, exhausted, stumbled on its doorsill, fell, and had to be taken to a hospital. The orphanage could accept only Aunt Klara's two oldest children. The Jewish Home for Young Women, to which Sarah was returned next, was more hospitable. There Aunt Klara and her two youngest children were allowed to stay. Aunt Betty, relieved of these responsibilities, took her son Moni back to her apartment, which, she figured, had stood empty long enough. The police must have given up finding her there. Indeed, she found her apartment untouched.

The Swiss consul in Cologne, reporting three days later on the events of the Kristallnacht, mentioned that "even today one can still see bedding hanging from trees and bushes" tossed from windows by organized parties who had moved from one Jewish apartment to another.[18]

My father obtained a Belgian visa for his mother, and in February 1939, having recovered from her fall, she came to live with us. Aunt Betty kissed her good-bye in Cologne, and my father welcomed her in Antwerp. With a visa, her trip was uneventful. How different, however, the trip would be for his remaining sisters!

Aunt Betty at first decided to stay in Germany. Her visa to the United States was due any time now. But Aunt Klara, who had to wait for her quota number, had to resort to rather desperate measures to get out of Germany.

Soon after the Kristallnacht, customs officials and conductors on the night train that crossed from Germany into Belgium began to encounter a new type of passenger. These were travelers they did not know how to deal with. These travelers were children, even babies, bundled up, soundly asleep, a bit drugged perhaps, traveling unaccompanied. Each had a railway ticket pinned to its togs and a label with a name, but no passport or other official document.[19]

Among these travelers one night were Aunt Klara's two oldest children, Dora, age six, and Bella, age four. Their mother and Aunt Betty had accompanied them to Aachen, the German border town. At Herbesthal, the next stop, on the Belgian side, my father and Aunt Charlotte were waiting. The operation proceeded without a hitch. I suppose the authorities were only too happy not to have any lost or abandoned children on their hands (see map 1).

Aunt Klara soon followed her two children. Weeks had gone by in futile efforts to get her a visa. Now Aunt Klara, an upright and law-abiding citizen, placed her two youngest children in the Jewish orphanage, then crossed the border—not by train, but like a criminal, at night, led by a smuggler.

She had to try it twice. The first time, a smuggler led the group of fugitives she had joined near the border all night through a forest, whereupon, declaring that they were in Belgium, he collected his

Map 1. Belgium and its prewar border with Germany, which Alfred's relatives crossed by various means

money and sent them walking "straight ahead." So they did until they ran into German border guards. Things could have been worse. They were merely sent back. On the second try, Aunt Klara succeeded.

Now it was the turn of Aunt Klara's two youngest children, Mordechai, a little over two years old, and Goldine, now seven months old. They would travel on the night train, alone, as their siblings had. This time, however, the trip proved to be more of an adventure.

Aunt Betty had heard of four Jewish teenagers who, having obtained visas to England, were about to travel there by way of Belgium. Though the teenagers would not take responsibility for the infants, she arranged to have them travel to the border in the compartment next to theirs. In Aachen, she pinned railway tickets on the children, then, wishing the teenagers Godspeed, left the train and proceeded to a telephone to report the children's location in the train to our house in Antwerp, which functioned as a relay station.

No sooner had Aunt Betty completed her call than she noticed German border guards escorting the four teenagers off the train and, to her dismay, Aunt Klara's children as well. "A guard carried the baby under his arm, like a package," Aunt Betty recalled. "They disappeared into the basement of a building. The train would leave without them. What would happen to the children? I was afraid they would kill them!" However, the train did not leave until all the children were back on board.

When the train arrived in Herbesthal, procedures there had changed as well. Clearly, the flow of unaccompanied children could not be allowed to go on. To their horror, my father and Aunt Charlotte, who had been waiting there, found access to the train to be barred. They watched helplessly as Belgian border guards removed some forty unaccompanied Jewish children from the train. Suddenly, Aunt Charlotte spotted two border guards carrying what seemed to be Aunt Klara's children. She made her way to the guards, asking to read the labels pinned to them.

Aunt Charlotte was the only Belgian citizen in our family. Now the wisdom of her coming to the border bore fruit.

"These are my relatives," she said to the guards.

"Where is their mother?" they wanted to know.

"In Antwerp," she replied.

"Why isn't she here?"

"She's afraid of being arrested!"

Such absurd talk made sense in those days. The guards believed Aunt Charlotte and surrendered the infants. Children whose mothers were in Germany were placed on the next returning train.

Aunt Betty delayed her departure from Germany. In New York, her husband had assembled all the papers necessary for her immigration and sent them to the American consulate in Stuttgart. With the immigration visa, she could leave Germany legally. She knew that if she went to Belgium without that visa, her papers would have to be transferred from the consulate in Stuttgart to the one in Antwerp. That was likely to cause a considerable delay.

Thus she had remained in Germany. She had moved into the foreclosed house in which she now lived alone with her son. As no Jewish stores were in business anymore, my father sent her weekly packages of kosher food: chicken, butter, and cheese. Then in February, the month that she had accompanied the last of Aunt Klara's children to the border, six German employees of the American consulate in Stuttgart were dismissed on charges of accepting bribes.[20]

My aunt was not involved in this affair, but the loss of manpower confused and delayed the consulate's operations. She could hold out no longer. She and her son Moni, not quite five years old, would be smuggled into Belgium.

It took two attempts. About the first one, my aunt is reticent, but of the second one she talked to me at length. She had planned it well. Though it was only July, she had paid her taxes for the full year. If apprehended at the border, she could not be prosecuted for evading her taxes. Further, she had contracted with a smuggler to bring her not only across the border but to Brussels.

On the day before, she and her son took the trolley to Bettstein. From the end of the line, they walked an hour to reach the Jewish cemetery for a last visit to her father's grave. "You were right, father," she said to him. "The living are envying the dead."

The next day—July 10, 1939—she locked the empty, foreclosed house once more, leaving a light turned on. She walked away, one hand holding her son's, the other an empty-looking bag, as if going to shop at the corner grocery.

Thus the last of my family left Germany.

2
The Halfway House

How DIFFERENT WE LIVED, during all these years in Belgium!

I remember in particular my ninth birthday, celebrated in 1932. Of all my birthdays, it was the most enjoyable. The evening before, having been sent to bed, I kept hearing the tearing and crinkling of paper, hushed talk, and suppressed giggles. That morning, I awoke early, and while everyone else was still asleep, I quietly went downstairs. There I saw our dining room table laden with toys of all kinds, with candies, goodies, and, I suppose, some useful things as well. All this was for me.

My parents must have intended to raise my spirits. Unlike my sisters, I had been slow to take to the French language. We had been in Belgium six months already, and I was not doing well at school. Even my mother's attempts to tutor me had proved to be little help. One's first foreign language is always the most difficult, especially if it is taught when new notions about grammar and spelling conflict with those, still shaky, learned about the mother tongue. It did not help that the first lesson in my French primer dealt with farm life, of which I had no experience at all.

Little did I suspect that I would learn not one but six new languages!

From the apartment across the street from the German school, we moved into a house nearer the Jewish school to which I transferred, on a street named after the constellation of Taurus, the bull. Both "rue du Taureau" and "Stierstraat" appeared on the street signs. The first was the French designation, the other its Flemish equivalent. All street signs showed two names. Belgium was a bilingual country.

Antwerp's indigenous population spoke Flemish. In many small stores only that language was understood. The maids my mother hired after we moved into that house spoke nothing but Flemish.

We all picked up that language very quickly, without having to use a book.

Like all Belgian elementary schools, my Jewish religious school provided instruction in either of the two national languages. My parents, doubting the utility of Flemish for my education, enrolled me in the French section.

As hardly any Orthodox Jew in Antwerp was qualified to teach in either French or Flemish, the school had two faculties: one Jewish and one Gentile. It had two principals as well. The Gentile faculty taught the secular classes. The Jewish classes were taught very differently. They were modeled, I discovered in time, after the heders of Eastern Europe.[1] Our Jewish teachers did not lecture, and we students took no notes. We studied the Torah by taking turns reading a sentence aloud in Hebrew, then translating it, word for word, into Yiddish. Our goal was to finish off a given segment of the Bible during the term. If a word thwarted a student, the teacher or another student would supply the translation. In the Jewish classes all discussions, as well as our teacher's comments, were in Yiddish. My classmates, in fact, normally spoke Yiddish among themselves. In time I gained a solid knowledge of the scriptures. I also learned Hebrew but not enough to speak it. Indeed, we did not study Hebrew grammar. But I quickly became fluent in Yiddish, long before I would be fluent in French.

The following year, studying in the same manner, we progressed to the Talmud, most of which is written not in Hebrew but in Aramaic. That was my fifth new language.

And one day, at the beginning of that school year, our Gentile teacher entered the classroom dramatically carrying a glass half-filled with water. As we sat in suspense, wondering what this was all about, he placed it on his desk and said slowly, in English, "The glass of water is on the table." Thus he introduced what was, according to the curriculum, our *first* foreign language.

History was Belgian history, of course. Our teacher lectured not about Mozart, Edison, or Shakespeare, but about André Modeste Grétry,[2] a Belgian composer, about Zénobe Gramme,[3] the Belgian inventor of the electric dynamo, and about Maurice Maeterlinck, the Belgian writer who won the Nobel prize. Though Belgium had gained its independence only in 1830, our history course opened with Julius Caesar's remark that of all the Gallic tribes, the Belgicae were the most courageous. Then followed snippets of the histories of other nations—Spain, Austria, France, or the Netherlands—while these ruled or subjugated the descendants of the Belgicae. It ended with the reign of the current king, Albert I, whose helmeted portrait looked at us from above the blackboard. In World War I he had held back the German onslaught at the Ypres River on the tiniest corner of his country.

With the Germans now rearming across the border, Belgian history became relevant. The German invasion that began the last war would not be allowed to recur. Like a shield, the Albert Canal now arched along our northeastern border, abutting on the fortress of Eben Emael, the most redoubtable on earth. Against these, any future German offensive would surely splinter itself.

Our own history, the history of the Jews, was not taught. The chronicle of the only people to have, as Dubnow noted, a world history,[4] must have affected the school board as it had my mother's father, who had objected to her acquiring these books. The Bible, we were told, was our history. And it was more than that: it encompassed all that God intended man to know. The Talmud had already explained the Bible fairly two thousand years ago. One could find in it whatever one needed. Its teachings were, of course, pertinent to the present.[5] I remember one of our teachers railing against the other Jewish school in town for burdening its students with the dates during which Talmudic sages flourished. "What Rabbi Akiba said is what matters," he insisted, "not when he said it nor what some historian may think about it."

One consequence of this attitude was an ignorance of pedagogy. While one student translated a Hebrew sentence, the others, having little to do, failed to remain quiet. Most of our religious teachers presided over noisy and unruly classes. I remember one of my Jewish teachers, utterly exasperated, once asking the class, "Why do you behave yourselves only with the *goyishe* [Gentile] teachers?"

It was one of our Gentile teachers who taught us "Oyfn Pripetshik," the only Yiddish song I learned there, and to which I shall return.

I pricked up my ears when a teacher with a bit of dramatic flair one day quoted Archimedes: "Give me a place to stand, and I shall move the earth." When he proceeded to show us how it could be done—by introducing the theorems of the lever—I was impressed. In fact, I can't recall anything learned at that school that impressed me as much. The capability to move our planet! What a vision! How it expanded my horizon! How it stirred my thoughts!

Mechanical things had always fascinated me. As a child, I recognized the makes of automobiles. The pictures of airplanes, battleships, and tanks were what induced me to read newspapers. In Cologne, I played with the iron wires that wrapped the kindling wood delivered for the kitchen range. One day I wound a wire around the base of a dead light bulb. I still remember the thrill of discovering that I could thread the light bulb in and out of this socket. I began constructing "machines" out of such wires, an interconnected, ever-growing jumble hanging from one of our window's hardware. I added not only dead light bulbs, but also paper cutouts, which I moved by means of levers for any visitor who happened by. Wisely, my parents bought me a Meccano set (a construction set with metallic parts). And I heard about Edison. I learned of his inventions and that he had, as a youngster, printed a newspaper aboard a railway car, whereupon a conductor had yanked him out by his ear, causing it to remain deaf for the rest of his life. I empathized. I knew that I, too, would be an inventor.

At school, after the theorems of the lever, the teacher went into plant life, and I lost interest. But we were also taken to historical places, to the Steen, the castle on the Scheldt around which Antwerp grew, whose basement bristled with medieval implements of torture. I could figure out how those things were used. We visited an early print shop, that of Plantin and Moretus, who, among many other books, published a famed polyglot Bible. A guide, explaining the paraphernalia used by these printers, contrasted the spoons that poured molten metal with those the printers used to eat soup. The former, with oval bowls, were modern looking; the latter retained inconvenient round bowls at the end of the handle. That was the sort of stuff that interested me.

We visited also the workshop of Antwerp's great painter, Peter Paul Rubens but not Antwerp's major art museum, with its collections of famed Flemish painters. I suspect an aversion on the part of my school to nudity.

Upon leaving Cologne, someone had given me the book *With*

Rocket Power Through the Universe.[6] I read it many times, managing to understand both the principle of rocket propulsion and the reason for using it in airless space. In Antwerp, I began to read popular science books on automobiles, radios, and science. I remember how thrilled I was upon understanding the function of the automobile radiator. However, when I attempted to deflect a magnetic needle with an electric current, as illustrated in a physics text, I got nowhere. I had failed to realize that the illustration was but a diagram. Instead of using a single wire, as shown, I should have used a coil whose windings, compounding the magnetic field, would have been strong enough to move the needle of the toy compass that I used.

Sometimes, ploddingly, I could overcome such difficulties. At other times I could not. Then I had no one to turn to for help. Not at school, not at home. Once, playing with my Meccano set, I stripped a screw. The nut could be turned but would not come off. No one could help me separate the two pieces that it held together. My father admitted being curious about science but found it beyond his comprehension. None of my teachers could answer my questions. Did, perhaps, any of my schoolmates have an inventor, or a scientist, or an engineer as a father? No. When a teacher asked the class about their fathers' professions, I was the only one who had difficulty explaining it. The only tangible evidence of my father's profession accumulated in a closet: sealed little glass bottles, all filled with grayish powder. The names impressed into their seals were often accompanied by crossed hammers. Did he sell them? my teacher asked. No, I replied, explaining that he tossed them out from time to time into the trash. At home that evening, my father explained to me that these bottles contained spare samples of ore shipments, kept as replacement for any that might get lost in the mail. My classmates, however, described their fathers' occupations easily. They needed no more than two words, one of which was "diamonds." Antwerp was a major center of the diamond trade.

I continued to read popularizations of science. Once I fancied that I had invented something. I had read of the explosive properties of mixtures of hydrogen and oxygen, known as *Knallgas* in German, for which "thunder gas" might be a suitable translation. I had also read that an electric current generates hydrogen and oxygen when passed through water. Well, I thought, Knallgas could certainly run a motor, the motor could certainly run a dynamo—the thing Zénobe Gramme had invented—and the current from the dynamo would generate more Knallgas to run the motor. No one to whom I talked about this idea could see anything wrong with it. I made a neat diagram of my idea and went, by bicycle, to a smelter to which I had once accompanied my father. There I informed the receptionist that I had an invention about which I wanted to see an engineer. In the formal conference room to which I was led, the engineer smiled. The diagram was clear, he said. I had invented a "perpetuum mobile." These don't work because, according to the second law of thermodynamics, no machine can produce more energy than it uses. That lit a light in my mind. I had understood a rather profound concept. The man suggested that I read up on perpetual motion machines, of which many had been tried in the past. Back home my parents, and even my sister Jenny, were disappointed. My mother suggested that I might consult with another engineer. No light had lit her mind.

In 1937, the effects of the Great Depression caused a severe stagnation in Antwerp's diamond business. Though these were also the years in which the Nazis disenfranchised the Jews in Germany, Lissauer prospered. His company traded in the ores that contained the metals that went into tanks, planes, submarines, and ammunition. Lissauer established an agent in London; a branch office, Associated Metals and Minerals Corp., in New York; and another, N. V. Oxyde, in the Netherlands that, although Lissauer remained in Germany, would become the company's headquarters. In Antwerp my father's office was incorporated under the name "Prominex S. A." My mother greatly admired this name, which, although derived from the words *Produits Miniers* (Mineral Products), also suggested "prominent." The office added rooms and employees, and Cologne rotated trainees to work in the branch offices, including Antwerp. We moved into a larger house on the Zurenborgstraat, and my father drove a car, a little Opel, his first, and only the second car on our street.

It was not pure bliss. More than once my father explained to me that to refrain from doing business with German firms would merely reward less principled competitors, of which there was no shortage. My father was not involved in arranging such deals, only in executing them. Still, it burdened his soul.

Neither these circumstances nor the events in Germany had affected us children thus far. School and homework kept us busy.

Sunday was our only day of leisure. When we were still little, my mother took us to a nearby park. As we grew older and Shirley Temple became a sensation, she also took us occasionally to the movies. My father, who usually went to his office on Sunday mornings, often invited me, and perhaps one of my sisters, to come along. No one else would be there, and we could do our homework on the office typewriters. Before leaving, my father would give us money for a bar of the excellent Belgian Côte d'Or chocolate, available at a little corner store down the street.

Occasionally he took me along to the harbor, where he had to meet the captain of a ship that had brought a cargo of ore. Once up the gangplank, he closeted himself with the captain while a ship's officer might show me around. Sometimes I was free to roam about the ship alone. How commanding was my view of the harbor from the bridge! How vertiginous the height! How easy it was, with my face whipped by the breeze, to imagine the ship at sea! I could identify the flags of most nations whose ships called in Antwerp and tell the company colors painted on the ships' funnels.

Rarely—because I could go only when school was out—my father invited me to come along to a smelter. These dark, fuming, sprawling plants vented pungent smells and reverberated with noisy hisses and roars. Danger was all about, so I had to remain close to my father. Once a worker was asked to take me in tow. I asked him some questions, but, to my surprise, the man replied that he had to check with someone else before he could answer, which, fussily, he did. Thus I became aware of trade secrets.

One place to which I always accompanied my father was our synagogue, the Eisenmann Shul. On Fridays, the eve of Shabbos, he left his office well before dark, met me at home, where we both changed into our good clothes, and went to shul. On our return, the smells of the traditional chicken soup and fresh challah, the glow of the Shabbos candles, and the festive white tablecloth greeted us, and we countered with a loud *"gut Shabbos."* Then my father intoned the song that welcomed the angels of the Lord and after that the paean to the virtuous wife who is worth more than rubies, is trusted by her husband, and is kind to the poor.[7] If my mother was still busy in the kitchen, he went there, and I remember how pleased she looked while he sang that paean to her. More songs followed during the intervals of the meal, songs written long ago in Hebrew or even Aramaic, songs of praise of the Almighty and of His blessings, one of which poetically compared the children arrayed around the table to a cluster of olives.[8] As in other Jewish households, the olives at our table lustily participated in these songs.

The next morning my father and I were again in shul. To my lasting envy, an unwritten tradition allowed the womenfolk to sleep late that day. They didn't even have to cook. "You shall kindle no fire" on this day, the Bible commands.[9] On the gas range, therefore, a couple of burners remained lit throughout the Shabbos. An asbestos screen covered each, ensuring the integrity of the flame when the vessel that sat on top of it was lifted. Thus we kept a kettle of water hot and food simmering. There are dishes such as cholent whose flavor improves the longer they cook. My mother rarely prepared cholent, but she had other recipes, and with such food and more songs the noon meal was as festive as that of the evening before.

On Shabbos, also, there always was cake. Pound cake, coffee cake, honey cake, and more. Before shul or after shul, late in the afternoon, anytime, one could walk into the empty, dimly lit kitchen, help oneself to some of these delights, and sip fresh hot tea.

In the afternoon, my mother, having made sure that we were presentable, took us to visit her parents where we would be served more goodies. Back home, in the increasing darkness, we played while my parents might take a nap. Shabbos departed with nightfall to the crackling flare of a braided candle doused in the overflow from my father's beaker of wine.

Our traditions were different from those of most Jews in Antwerp. We, and the German-speaking congregation at the Eisenmann Shul, pronounced Hebrew words differently than my teachers and schoolmates did. The traditional songs we sang had the lilt of German folk songs, not the lively rhythm favored by Eastern European Jews. For my family, these traditions were a recent acquisition. My father had not grown up with them. On my mother's side, they reached back one generation. We had adopted them in Germany, but now that we lived again amidst Eastern Jews, we did not revert back.

Such was life in Belgium. But a fire burned next door, and towards 1937, its embers began to scatter, reaching far and wide, igniting malcontents of various stripes: racists, misfits, renegades, jingoists, xenophobes, troublemakers, agitators, and all kinds of ruffians.

From many countries such people were now heard. I heard about the French author who, under the pen name Celine, argued that his country was occupied by Jews and could be liberated only by a German invasion. Poland and Hungary followed the Nazi example by enacting anti-Jewish laws. Nor was Belgium passed by. Rabid anti-Semitic literature appeared in our mailbox distributed by a pro-Fascist party, the Rexists. Venom was not all directed against the Jews: at night, Flemish nationalists painted out the French names on Antwerp's bilingual street signs.

At school, I heard rumors of students being beaten up on their way home. Because my classmates and I were in the eighth grade, the graduating class, we felt it our duty to accompany the younger students home.

One afternoon after classes, I joined the group of protectors instead of going home. I was surprised at our small number, and at the even smaller number of kids—just two or three—desiring protection. Still, we went ahead, leaderless, to drop off the younger kids. That done, and already somewhat dispersed on our way home, one of us saw the gang. Equally suddenly, I was alone, racing through empty streets, the gang in hot pursuit. I knew the neighborhood. My school's Gentile principal lived here. I had been at his house once, and now I headed for it. The gang was gaining on me, but I reached his street, turned the corner, and flattened myself inside his doorway, the third or fourth on the street. I hoped that the gang would run right past without noticing me as I had seen it happen in the movies. But they did notice me, and they formed a circle around the doorway. They talked to me, but I didn't answer. Surreptitiously I looked at the doorbell, still hesitating to ring it. A man walked by, stopped, and asked what was going on. The boys said, "Nothing." Still, the man persisted, asking me, specifically, what was the matter. Shrugging my shoulders, I said, "Oh, nothing," whereupon the man left. The gang also disbanded, and I went home. My mother would never know what had happened.

That year, just before my fourteenth birthday, I had to report to the police to obtain my first identity card. At the station, a policeman had me sit down next to his desk and asked the usual questions: my height, color of hair, color of eyes, and so on. Then he took an uncomfortably long look at me and asked in a changed voice: "Distinguishing characteristics?" I did not know what to say. After another long moment, he volunteered, "A large nose." After receiving my new identity card, my heart beating madly, I noted with relief that the space next to "distinguishing characteristics" was still blank.

The embers of hate stirred even at the seashore where we vacationed every summer, and where my father joined us on weekends. There, in the resort town of Knokke, we always lodged in the same apartment, a bright and cheerful place with freshly starched curtains fluttering in the sea breeze. We liked the landlady, who ran a grocery below, and she liked us and would not have rented her apartment to anyone else.

Her daughter, a few years older than I, liked to tease me about the whiteness of my skin, which, on my suntanned body, she could see only by playfully pushing down, ever so slightly, the waistband of my shorts. On the eve of Shabbos, she knew when to turn our electric lights off. We could not do this because one generates a spark when one interrupts a current. Therefore, our sages determined, the biblical prohibition against lighting a fire on Shabbos applies also to electrical appliances. In Antwerp, an electric timer—my father's pride—took care of the lights on that day.

One Sunday, the girl, looking upset, confided to me in a low but outraged voice that their priest, from the pulpit of their church, had damned all Jews for betraying Jesus to the Romans. "That can't be," she kept repeating, more to herself than for me. "That can't be!"

In the fall of 1937 I went to a new school, a trade school that specialized in commerce. My grades in the Jewish school had not been very good, and my parents had decided not to send me to the lyceum. Clearly, they thought it best for me to follow in my father's footsteps. I did not think of questioning their judgment.

I did not like that school. Only a few Jewish boys attended it, and we had little in common with our Flemish classmates. We cared little for the spectator sports that engaged them, and most of us spoke their language with a foreign accent. My sisters, who had always gone to public school, freely made friends with Gentile girls. We Jewish boys, however, were at a loss about how to deal with our classmates, and tended to stick together. The Gentile boys noticed it. At recess one day, one of them taunted me. "Look at that," he said, pointing with a display of disgust at a knot of Jewish boys talking among themselves. "That is a nest."

I did not report such petty anti-Semitic episodes to my parents. They, too, hid such accounts from us. When the Nazi goons had murdered Uncle Oscar the preceding year, my parents told us no more than that he had suddenly died.

My mother sensed yet another danger. Nazi militancy, she perceived, had begun to upset the Belgians, who feared a repetition of the German invasion of 1914. They remembered the barbarities the Germans had perpetrated on them. They began to view with suspicion, if not with animosity, anything that was German. Cautious, my mother insisted that we not speak German on the street, though we still used it at home. Perhaps she had witnessed violence against civilians during the past war. She knew that if there should be riots against Germans, nobody would first inquire whether they might be Jews.

I remember how far-fetched my mother's misgivings seemed to me at the time. Could we really incur the wrath of both Nazi admirers and their opponents? And yet, as it turned out, we were to be caught in exactly that double jeopardy.

I have been asked how I felt about the burgeoning anti-Semitism of those times. To me, it was just one of many difficulties that I had to cope with. At my Jewish school, my German upbringing had differentiated me from the other boys; thus the bigotry of my Gentile classmates at the trade school was nothing new. Being set apart in this manner put me in a league with grown-ups who, at the synagogue, often discussed similar experiences. What made me wince in the Gentile environment gave me a sense of importance in the Jewish one.

For some time, refugees had been arriving in Antwerp. In 1933, in the first trickle, my Uncle Jacob had arrived. He lodged with us and soon could be heard all over the house happily singing Papageno's aria from the opera *The Magic Flute*. He was courting the girl who, as I have related, would become my Aunt Charlotte.

My grandparents from Hamburg also arrived that year and rented an apartment near us. With relatives in town, Antwerp no longer felt like a foreign city. My grandparents also readily fitted into Antwerp's Jewish community. When my grandfather died in the fall of 1936, those attending his funeral went around his casket with lighted candles, dripping wax on it. This, my father said, was a signal honor, not done for everybody.

By then the trickle of refugees had swelled. It proved a boon to the town. The Eisenmann Shul gained prestige with the arrival of a rabbi of some renown, a refugee. My Jewish school acquired a new teacher, Mr. Ostersetzer, whose beard may have been too neatly trimmed, and whose Yiddish may have had a German accent, but who kept discipline in his classroom. After I graduated from that school, he became its principal.

My mother hired a nursemaid for us, Rita Buchholz, a refugee with a degree in early childhood education. She further engaged a talented dressmaker, also a refugee, to make dresses for my two oldest sisters. Jenny and Hella were atwitter with excitement at being fitted and, after they wore their sparingly decorated but well-cut dresses, didn't cease to admire them and be admired. Shopping became easier for my mother. She no longer had to go out of the house to buy fruits and vegetables. A greengrocer, a refugee, brought his wares to our door, displayed on a cart that he pulled with the assistance of a dog in harness underneath.

One refugee's adversity provided me with a memorable vacation. In 1938, a well-known lawyer had to leave Germany so suddenly that he and his family arrived in Antwerp short of cash. His son, about my age, had been scheduled to camp in the Alps with a troop of Boy Scouts; the trip had already been paid for, and the man now sought to recoup his outlays. My father heard of it, and came up with the money. Thus I took the boy's place.

To travel abroad, I had to obtain a Polish passport and a French visa. Both proved difficult to obtain, which, once more, gave me the satisfaction of talking importantly about my "difficulties" with the authorities. Still, my papers came through in time. I traveled to Paris with my father, who happened to be traveling there. He left me, a few days early, with the scoutmaster, whom I helped readying the tents in which I and about two dozen Jewish Boy Scouts camped that summer. We were in a meadow high over Lake Geneva, ate porridge for breakfast, did chores, climbed mountains, took a swing into Switzerland, and sang French songs around the campfire.

That fall, in Antwerp, I chanced on yet another incredible piece of good luck. I gained access to a fabulous country estate located within bicycling distance from home. A Zionist organization had obtained it to serve as a hachshara, a school to teach farming to Jewish boys. Farm workers, like capitalists, were permitted to immigrate to Palestine. The estate, named Hulgenrode, centered around a grand manor surrounded by a moat. It encompassed farmland, pastures, a little forest, and vast patches of blackberries. My father must have made a contribution, for we were invited to come back as often as we liked. I took liberal advantage of this invitation.

The leaking roof of the manor and the overgrown pastures provided the students with excellent teaching material. So did the fences that failed when, on the evening the cattle arrived, their homing instinct urged them to return to the farmer who had sold them. I made friends with the students, some twenty Jewish boys from Germany, and could do whatever I wanted at Hulgenrode. At first I picked blackberries, which I was allowed to take home; on later visits, wanting to be useful, I decided to clear the moat of logs and other debris that clogged it. From a bridge, I attempted to lasso a tree trunk and haul it to the edge of the moat. After much effort and despite the general opinion that I was wasting my time, I succeeded, and I was gratified to see an instructor telling the students to use the trunk to shore up an embankment. Thereafter, I continued to clear the moat, freeing a raft made of a wooden platform supported by four barrels. It still floated, and I had my own boat.

In 1938, the trickle of refugees turned into a flood. Our doorbell rang with increasing frequency. Most times, a schnorrer or two would be at the door, religious Eastern Jews with imposing beards, who made the circuit of Jewish homes to beg. We kept small change in the mailbox for them.

Early in July, I happened to open the door after the bell rang. Outside was a little girl who looked vaguely familiar and a taxi whose driver wanted to be paid. The girl was my cousin Ines who, not quite twelve years old, had come alone from Germany. She quickly became part of the family. She never mentioned the trauma she had recently undergone but enchanted everyone with her sunny disposition, her ready, pealing laughter and giggles. Our large house had impressed her, she told me recently, as well as our way of life. We had a maid. We spoke not only German, but also Flemish and French, and we all read Hebrew. We went swimming, rode bicycles, played the piano, and vacationed at the shore in summer. None of that, however, intimidated her.

As I went to camp in France with the Boy Scouts that summer, I missed Ines at the seashore. When I returned home by the end of August, I was happy to hear that she would not return to Cologne. My father feared that Germany was about to provoke a war to "liberate" the Sudetenland from Czechoslovakia. The Sudeten Germans were stirring up trouble. Hitler threatened action. France promised to come to the aid of the Czechs. The British navy held maneuvers in the North Sea. Hitler increased his demands. But even after British prime minister Neville Chamberlain returned from Munich that September, heralding his accord with Hitler as "peace in our time," Ines remained with us. Nor did she return when her visa expired. We now harbored an illegal alien in our house.

That October, as I have related, Ines's mother and Aunt Jettchen, their children, and Uncle Adolf were deported to Zbaszyn. While our house was abuzz with discussions of how to send them money and parcels, news came of the Kristallnacht. Those relatives who had remained in Germany were in peril as well.

My parents, with the connivance of Uncle Jacob and his wife, now mounted an international undercover operation. While outwardly my father and Uncle Jacob worked as business people and their wives ostensibly kept house, in their spare time they conducted illegal activities. They sprinkled some of their telephone conversation with unobtrusive code words, such as "noodles" that stood for dollars. On certain nights my father and Aunt Charlotte disappeared on surreptitious missions, coordinated from a bedroom that served as a communications center.

The recovery of Aunt Klara's two oldest children, whose odyssey across the German-Belgian border I have related, was this team's first exploit. We children had been told little about it, but I remember the phone ringing throughout the night, quickly picked up by my mother. Aunt Betty called from the German side of the border to report the children's compartment and car number. My father called from the Belgian side to obtain this information. When the train was delayed, he kept calling before my mother had any news, and thereafter Aunt Betty had to call several times before she could be reassured that the children had been found.

Before dawn, I was awakened once more, not by the phone but by a commotion at the door. I jumped out of bed, running into other pajama-clad shadows on the way downstairs. The front door opened and Aunt Charlotte entered, beaming, holding in her arms something tightly wrapped in a blanket. It was Bella, the second of Aunt Klara's girls, soundly asleep. Behind her, my father emerged into the light, holding the hand of Dora, the older sister.

Aunt Klara arrived next, then my paternal grandmother, then Aunt Klara's two youngest children, Mordechai and Goldine, whose harrowing border crossing I have related. Next came, one at a time, the children of a cousin of my father, Moyne Rosenbaum, who was among those deported to Zbaszyn. The first, Willi, a boy my age, crossed without mishap, but his younger brother Joseph was caught and sent back on his first attempt. He was successful on the second try. Then came their mother, Regine, with a toddler, a little girl called Cecilia whom we called Zilla. Then after the Germans overran what remained of Czechoslovakia, a young man, Simon Pappenheim, a relative on my mother's side, came from there. His parents followed.

Most of these people were smuggled in, were unfamiliar with the local languages, and had to be met at some location. Thereafter all were accommodated for some time in our house, whose occupancy tripled. Rita Buchholz, our nursemaid, had been offered a better job and departed. My mother persuaded our current cleaning lady, Mrs. Delphine Janssens, to give notice to her other employers and work for us full-time. Aunt Klara and Cousin Regine helped in the kitchen and with the kids. My grandmother, seeing that Aunt Klara had little time for her baby, took charge of it. The busying was good for her, gave her a purpose, an excuse to get in the way. She fed the baby, soothed it when it cried, swaddled it, carried it around. In Cologne, in the dark house with the many people, I had hardly noticed my grandmother. She had been just one of those people to whom I had to say *"guten Tag."* Now, however, I came to know her as a warm, outgoing person. When my mother, irritated by bickering among us older children, snapped at me, Grandmother was there to listen to my complaints and soothe my feelings with a piece of honey cake that she kept, unwrapped, in her ample purse. Although I ate it somewhat dubiously, it was the kind of gesture that warms a teenager's heart.

On Shabbos, we extended the main table with another one and added yet one more for the little children. With the entire cluster of olives singing, it was a Shabbos to be proud of. During the week, however, dinner was served in four installments: first the toddlers, then the schoolchildren, then the grown-ups, and last, my father, alone. His office had grown to nearly a dozen employees. He worked late and could not stand all the noise we children made. My mother served him herself. They enjoyed this little time they had to themselves.

One day, a ball bounced into our dining room, toppling a crystal decanter, the centerpiece of a set that graced our dining room. My father, in the early days of his marriage, had brought it from Bohemia. This decanter had survived a previous fall that had left a cleft in the upper part of its long, swanlike neck. As it could still hold its sparkling stopper, my mother had turned it with the cleft to the wall. Now the encounter with the ball had shattered it. It was a small tragedy, compared with so many others that I was aware of in those days. But as I watched my mother pick up the shards, I glimpsed grief in her face, and it stung.

My cousin Ines witnessed another drama. The new arrivals had displaced her from my sister's bedroom. She now slept on a cot at the foot of my parents' bed. From there she overheard many a squabble between them. These, Ines told me long afterwards, were always about money. The increased expenses of our household, the money and packages sent to our relatives in Zbaszyn and to those still in Germany, must have caused considerable financial strain.

In July 1939, the Polish authorities finally allowed the people in the no-man's-land around Zbaszyn to enter Poland. Aunts Jettchen and Minna traveled with their children to Przeworsk, there to stay with the families of Gita Locker and Chana Eisner, their cousins. Aunt Klara's husband, Uncle Adolf, obtained an authorization to return to Cologne to liquidate his business. Then he had himself smuggled into Belgium and rejoined his family in Antwerp. Cousin Moyne must have done likewise. Both obtained their own apartments, so that when Aunt Betty and her son, Moni, arrived that month, we had space for them.

None of our recently arrived relatives intended to remain here. All were at one stage or another of emigrating to the United States. Antwerp was but a way station, and our house but a halfway house. The immigration process remained slow and tedious. Governments, as well as the error-prone martinets that staffed the consulates, remained indifferent to the floods of refugees the Nazi outrage created.

On a nice spring Sunday in May 1939, visiting Hulgenrode, I found everyone sitting around instead of working. Glumly, they talked about a "White Paper" that British colonial secretary Malcolm MacDonald had issued. It restricted Jewish immigration into Palestine, prohibited the sale of land to Jews, even placed Palestinian Arabs in some governing positions. The students' efforts, and the hachshara itself, had been for naught. Their prospects for being admitted to Palestine had vanished.

Years later I read that MacDonald had defended this action on the grounds that, in the struggle against Hitler, the Jews would be on Britain's side no matter what, but not the Arab nations.[10] Afterwards, he did admit that this policy had been "one of my crashing failures in statecraft."[11]

In June 1939, the SS *St. Louis* berthed in Antwerp's harbor. The German passenger ship had returned from America, unable to discharge her Jewish passengers there. These passengers, having obtained Cuban visas with great effort, had boarded her in Germany.[12] Two weeks before their arrival in Cuba, that country had passed a law that rendered their visas invalid. They were not allowed to disembark. After two suicide attempts, the crew spread the false rumor on board that the United States might allow them to land. As long as possible, the captain delayed recrossing the Atlantic, but no other country would accept the passengers. Now Antwerp had opened its gates before the ship docked in Germany. When I saw the ship, the police had cordoned off a wide space dockside as if the vessel carried lepers. Belgium at least, and England, France, and the Netherlands, would allow some of its passengers to disembark.

This was the most notorious but not the only instance in which a country rejected refugees with valid visas.

My refugee relatives kept working on their visas, writing letters to their sponsors, obtaining documents, standing in lines, watching the days go by, worrying, hoping.

For Aunt Betty, there was a brief reprieve. No sooner out of Germany, she and her son were vacationing at the seashore. They had arrived in Antwerp in July just as we were preparing to leave for Knokke. Gallantly, my father had invited them to come along.

But the transfer of her papers from the American consulate in Stuttgart to the American consulate in Antwerp did, as she expected, take a long time and result in a serious error. Befuddled by the Belgian practice of retaining a woman's maiden name on official documents, someone at the consulate had transcribed my aunt's maiden name instead of her family name when entering her son's name on some document. The child, it seemed, was not her husband's, and the affidavit, therefore, did not cover him. More time was lost in correcting this error.

Then another delay. On the first day of September 1939, the German army invaded Poland. Two days later, Great Britain and France declared war on Germany. World War II had begun.

In our house, an unaccustomed quiet descended at the times that news was broadcast. We heard of the rapid disintegration of the Polish army and, two weeks later, of the Russian army joining the Germans in the occupation of Poland. "Blitzkrieg" became a familiar word. Not all the news was bad. When Russian armies attacked Finland, we gloated as plucky little Finland held them at bay.

In Antwerp, as in many other cities, rallies were organized in support of the gallant Finns. I attended one, watched a short movie, applauded the speakers, and contributed a little money. Excepting Finland, however, serious fighting had stopped. The newspapers began to write about the "phony war." Still, life did not quite return to normal.

Mail, even airmail, took longer. A letter between Antwerp and New York—both located in neutral countries—took from three to four weeks. With Poland, no mail service operated. We had received one telegram from Aunts Jettchen and Minna and nothing more. My father wrote to the Red Cross and to a Jewish committee in Berlin. Aunt Minna's immigration papers were ready. She had been summoned to the American consulate in Stuttgart.

When my father took me along to the harbor one Sunday, I spotted an anti-aircraft gun mounted on a British merchant vessel.

Belgium, though resolutely neutral, prepared itself for war. Occasionally a platoon of soldiers came down the middle of our street, one of them with a trumpet, blasting away with "Marching through Georgia." Ration coupons, though not yet needed, were distributed. For a week or so, my business school transformed itself into a coupon distribution center manned by students and faculty.

People who remembered World War I stocked up on food. The government printed instructions on how to store food. These were distributed to schoolchildren to take home. I still remember one warning: "Don't store foods in the bedroom, where they tend to pick up undesirable odors."

One day a truck dropped sandbags in front of each house on our street. These were to be emptied over the attic floor as a protection against incendiary bombs. A blue wash was distributed that, painted over outside lights, would make them invisible to enemy aircraft.

There was not much else we could do to prepare for war. My father could not abandon his office and take his family out of Belgium. He already had opened bank accounts in New York and in Switzerland and kept money there.

Our landlady from Knokke came to visit us with her husband, urging us to live with them in Knokke where, they assured us, we would be out of harm's way. But my father would have taken us much farther away had he only been able to shut down his office. We offered our guests tea and cookies, and when we heard that their return train would not leave for several hours, insisted that they wait in our parlor. They had to wait alone. My sisters and I had homework to do, my father business to attend to, and my mother dinner to prepare. Mr. Pappenheim, though he lived in his own apartment, came by, as he did most every afternoon, to use our radio to tune into a news broadcast from some neutral country—perhaps Switzerland—in a language—usually German—that he could understand. Radio reception, as usual, faded amidst a cacophony of whistles and squeals. It was not long before Moni, Aunt Betty's son, added to the commotion, yelling and crying in a spirited argument with his mother. Ponderously, my grandmother made her way downstairs to see what the trouble was. In between, one schnorrer or another rang the doorbell and had to be attended to. My mother barely managed to see that our guests' tea stayed hot. Then it was time for them to leave, and so ended their laudable rescue effort.

By year's end, Aunt Betty obtained her visa. She embarked with her son on December 8, 1939, from Rotterdam. Though the voyage, hampered by mines, took fifteen days instead of the usual five or six, they arrived safe and sound in New York.

A long-awaited telegram from Aunt Betty did not quite convince my grandmother. She could read only Yiddish, which is written in

Hebrew characters. Why was there no letter? Were we trying to hide something? That first letter from Aunt Betty took about a month to arrive.

Two months later, my grandmother, convinced that her daughter had become sufficiently accustomed to her new country, dictated a letter to her. She inquired about life in New York and old acquaintances who had emigrated to the United States. But the point of the letter was to ask Aunt Betty to prevail on relatives, "even if you don't have time," to provide immigration papers to Aunt Jettchen's children and her nephew Moyne, whose quota had come up. "Break walls," she urged her daughter. "My eyes no longer drip with tears, but with blood."

Another month went by before the American consulate agreed that all requirements for Ines's immigration visa had been satisfied. She was scheduled to embark by the end of April. She would travel during Passover, and my mother, concerned that she would be served bread aboard ship, laid in an eight-day supply of matzo for her. This precaution proved unnecessary. On April 9, the Germans suddenly invaded Norway and Denmark, and the British, reacting this time with force, landed troops on the shores of Norway. The ship on which Ines was to sail delayed its departure.

It was well past Passover when Ines finally embarked, loaded up with at least some of the matzo my mother had accumulated for her. May 8 was a Wednesday, a school day, and only my father and Aunts Charlotte and Klara accompanied her to the ship, the SS *Penland*. They remained at dockside until they saw the vessel cast off. That evening, my father came home so relieved that he bounced as if he were a younger man.

Two days later, I was awakened early in the morning by repeated blows of what at first I took to be our neighbor hammering nails into our common wall. More widely awake, I realized that these blows shook the entire house. Even after they stopped, the windows kept rattling for no apparent cause. From my window I saw the sleepy head of a neighbor across the street, calling to someone on our side asking what was going on. I looked up at the sky. There was nothing to be seen but a pale immaculate dawn that promised a sunny spring day. Downstairs, I found my family already up, as perplexed as I. My father fiddled with the radio, unable to get reception. Later we heard music. That was comforting until we noticed that the station played the same record over and over. There was no announcer. Outside, someone spotted the shimmer of tiny airplane wings high up in the sky. Everyone rushed to the windows. The Germans, a neighbor opined, are attacking England. It was only later, when the radio finally recovered from its paralysis, that we learned that it was we who were bombed.

The fire next door had spread. It was engulfing us.

3
Practice Makes Perfect

THAT MORNING WHILE WE LISTENED to the radio, my mother tried to get some breakfast into us. German planes, we heard, were swarming over the Low Countries, northern France, England, and the North Sea. Parachute troops had landed at various locations. In the Netherlands they had landed wearing Dutch uniforms. The Belgian radio summoned soldiers to join their units at once and exhorted the people to remain calm. The Dutch opened their dikes to turn their fertile land into vast moats.

A few hours of the same news from different stations mitigated the initial shock. We went about preparing for the war. My father went through various rooms collecting valuables and important papers. He elicited some trepidation amongst us when he announced that he was taking these to the safe deposit box rented at the bank. From there he went to the office to take care of what business needed attention. He called home a number of times to reassure us that everything seemed calm. My mother and sisters began gathering things to pack in case we should have to leave. I went to the attic and, as instructed, emptied the sandbags delivered months earlier by the municipality and spread the sand in a thick layer over the floor. Then I latticed our windows with adhesive tape to reduce injuries from splintered glass. Finally I daubed with blue wash any outside lights, any windows that could not be curtained, and, after my father returned, the headlights of his car.

Then, on the pretext that I needed something, I took my bicycle and rode downtown, a ride of about fifteen minutes. War was, after all, a fascinating experience, and I was not displeased that school was closed. My mind reverberated with recollections of dashing heroes, epic battles, and weapons of the future of which I had read. Now I would see for myself.

There was no panic, nor any other evidence of war as I imagined it. Clearly, like my family, everybody had made contingency plans. Calmly now, deliberately, these were carried out. The city seemed to be seething. The streets had more traffic than I expected, and on the sidewalks, pedestrians walked faster than usual. Air-raid sirens had finally begun to operate and now sounded an alert, the first of a dozen that day. I could see the silvery flashes of airplane wings high up, but nobody bothered to seek shelter. In the store where I went to make my purchase, the owner, whom I could see in the back busy with paperwork, ignored me at first and, after I called, served me brusquely, giving the impression that he would be happy had I left even without paying. Outside, a few people stood around reminiscing about World War I, which had been fought not much more than two decades earlier. No one knew where the bombs had fallen that awoke us that morning.

In the afternoon, I noticed something new in the sky: puffs of smoke, the first sign of anti-aircraft fire.

That evening, the eve of Shabbos, my mother did light the candles, but my father skipped going to shul. Dinner was as lugubrious as the blue gloom of occulted lights outside. Thereafter we did something that would not have been tolerated on Friday eve: we sat around the radio. It had become our link to the outside world. No newspapers had appeared that day.

On the radio we heard more talk about German parachutists, of "fifth column" saboteurs, and of the numbers of German planes shot down. At Antwerp, the airfield and a military hospital had been bombed. Along the German and Luxembourg frontiers, artillery fire was being heard. The king had instructed Belgium's ambassador in Berlin to lodge a protest.

Commentators began evaluating the situation. One opined that the German armies would meet far more effective opposition than they had encountered in the 1914 war. The defenses the Kaiser's armies encountered in 1914 were embryonic compared with the deep, strong, elaborate fortifications we had today. Should the Germans manage to get through to the French border, they would arrive a tired, battered force, much of their elaborate, costly equipment smashed.

On Saturday, the second day, we did not go to synagogue but listened to the radio that because of Shabbos we had not switched off the evening before. Brussels and Antwerp had been bombed, it reported. King Leopold was at the front. Despite the loss of Limburg Province in the northeast, the Belgian army resisted. The Dutch held the Germans back along the Yssel and Meuse Rivers. Parachutists who landed in Rotterdam had not succeeded in seizing the city, and the Dutch commander in chief had declared their surprise attack a failure. The French battled German troops on the banks of the Moselle.

The reassurances sounded hollow. If the Belgian army resisted, how was Limburg Province lost so quickly? And Rotterdam was deep inside the Netherlands. But my father had heard that Churchill had been made prime minister of Great Britain, and that, he said, reassured him greatly.

Sometime that morning, my mother began examining what each of us had assembled for packing. My sisters had gathered not only necessities but also many objects that were dear to them. Gently, my mother dissuaded them from taking these along. That gave me time to hide my harmonica—a recent acquisition—in my pocket.

Among my belongings was a gold embroidered, blue velvet satchel, which my father had given me some four years earlier, a month before my bar mitzvah. It contained a pair of phylacteries and a tallis. When he showed me how to wear these, my father had said, in an earnest voice, that after I died it was in this tallis that I would be buried. This had made a deep impression on me then. And now there was no question about taking the satchel along.

That afternoon, I took a little walk on which I saw a British truck driving down a street, a few soldiers, from under the canvas top, cheerfully raising their fingers in a V for victory sign. More trucks followed, all brand new, all racing ahead. This was no parade. Later I saw also a few French military vehicles. It was easy to tell them from the British because their trucks, dirty and weather-beaten, did not race, and their soldiers did not wave to the passersby. They clearly came from the front.

I counted more than a dozen air raids again that day.

On Sunday, the third day, the radio reported that the Allies were pouring large forces into the Low Countries and that a great battle was expected. The British reported bombing the Krupp Works along the Rhine. In the Netherlands, the Germans had forded the Yssel River; Rotterdam was ablaze, and Dutch troops there fought parachutists and fifth column infiltrators who sniped from the roofs of private houses.

A few hours later, the Belgian communiqué reported that the enemy had "gained a foothold in our defense line" in the Maastricht region, claimed the capture of Eben Emael, and that the king had ordered the army to retreat to a fallback line.

What a shock it was to hear that Eben Emael had fallen, the impregnable fortress that my teachers had so celebrated! Provided with every military artifice, dovetailing with felicitous natural obstacles, it was supposed to ward off any German invasion. It was located not far from Herbesthal, where my father had picked up Aunt Klara's children. After the war I learned how the Germans had prepared themselves for this assault. In the preceding four years, in utter secrecy, they had retraced the fort's layout on similar terrain and rehearsed landing gliders within. They had practiced sapping the casemates on the Beneš Line, abandoned when the Czechs surrendered the Sudetenland. On Friday, May 10, they were well prepared. Their gliders reached the fort as the sun rose behind them. Everything was quiet. The German armies, poised along a wide front, remained hidden. The gliders landed unnoticed. From them leapt seventy-eight men and, still unnoticed, they spread quickly, each to his assigned gun, casemate, observation cupola, or ventilation shaft, and blew them up. The fort was doomed. Only then were the German armies given the order to attack.[1] It was a daring tactic, but practice had made it succeed.

Antwerp, only seventy-five miles behind Eben Emael, was now in a precarious position. My father decided that it would be too risky to remain here. Although the bank was closed—it was Sunday—and he carried only small change, we could not delay our departure.

One traveled mostly by train in those days; but trains, we had heard already, were being mobbed. Were we to leave by train, we couldn't take much luggage with us, and worse, we risked being separated. We had a car, the four-seater Opel, which my father used for business. It could carry a lot of our belongings, but it could not hold the whole family.

So we split up. My father drove my mother and two youngest sisters to Uncle Jacob who, with a family of five and Grandma

Bauminger, had managed to rent a limousine large enough to accommodate them all. There were no good-byes, no hugs and kisses. It was as if we were not separating. It was as if they were traveling merely in another car. We would meet in Coxyde, a resort town near the French border.

After my father returned, I lashed two suitcases to the folding luggage rack at the back of the Opel. There was still more to take along but no way to stow more suitcases. We decided to repack our remaining belongings into the largest receptacle we had, a square laundry hamper, which I covered with a waxed tablecloth, lifted onto the roof of the car, and tied down with clotheslines strung to the car's window frames and bumpers.

We left around noon, me sitting next to my father, and Grandmother Feldman and Jenny in the rear. I had a last, apprehensive look at our house. Not so long ago, it had throbbed with people. It stood empty now. With my latticework over its windows and the blue-daubed pane over the door, it already had a war-weary look.

By car, travel was easy. The streets were empty. The city already looked deserted.

Barely outside Antwerp, we saw our first German soldier. He was a strapping fellow in a very green uniform escorted by police and a wave of very excited people that surged behind him across the road. "A parachutist," we guessed.

The road was familiar. It was the way to Knokke. On our last vacation, I had contrived to ride with my father in his car instead of going by train with my mother. But at Bruges, where we had turned north, we now swung south. Toward evening we crossed the Yser River where the Germans had been stopped in World War I. Once on a summer outing, we had visited the war museum there. Next to it a stretch of trenches had been preserved with their barbed wire, guns, bomb shelters, debris, grime, and lugubrious looks. Now, as we crossed the Yser, I experienced a great sense of relief on being behind a tried and true defense line.

Soon we reached Coxyde. My father had no difficulty finding us a nice apartment. We had more than doubled the distance separating us from Eben Emael.

The next morning he went to find my mother and my two youngest sisters. He located them around noon. The driver of their limousine, anxious to return to Antwerp, had taken them only to Ostend, where they had spent the night. This morning they had boarded the trolley that linked all the resorts along the Belgian coast and reached Coxyde around noon. My father spotted them at the trolley stop.

In our sunny dining room over quickly prepared lunch, they told of their experience. And in that cheerful little resort town, with its fresh paint, the sunshine, the sea breeze, the war for us became a vacation.

That day and the next, we walked around Coxyde's well-tended streets and public gardens, meeting many acquaintances and friends from Antwerp. Although there was no radio in our apartment, French newspapers could be bought in stores. We also got much of our news from people we talked with. Everybody sounded upbeat. The latest news was no longer so bad: the Germans had taken no more Belgian cities. I remember a story in a paper comparing the current refugees, traveling comfortably in modern automobiles or trucks, with the refugees of the earlier war, going in open horse carts or on foot. Someone pointed out to me a man in overalls standing atop a dump truck heaped with garbage. That was the town's mayor, he said. Caught unprepared by the sudden influx of refugees, he was doing what he could to keep the resort spotless. Coxyde would be a wonderful place to sit out the war.

My father bragged that he had been able to lock in the off-season rental of our apartment for the rest of the year.

Could it be that our departure had been premature?

The only disconcerting news was that the nearby French border was closed to us. Only French and Belgian citizens could cross.

On Wednesday, my father, having seen no reports of further German advances in Belgium, returned to Antwerp. He needed to pick up money at the bank and finish some other business. My mother, of course, was on tenterhooks until he returned. He arrived late, saying that, though his trip had been uneventful, the news was bad: the Netherlands had capitulated. Antwerp was quiet but half empty. Cousin Moyne had managed to buy a truck and, though able only to speak German, was about to depart from Antwerp with family and belongings. As for Aunt Klara and her family, they would move into our house. Burdened with their little children, speaking only German, they could not face the uncertainties of flight. Our house, at least, was amply provisioned. My father had paid the rent for several months and asked our cleaning lady, Delphine, to keep an eye on them.

On Thursday, my father was able to relax, but on Friday, he came home with the newspaper he had bought and told me that he was very worried. The papers still devoted much of their space to German attacks on the Belgian front, to threats to Brussels and Antwerp, to ships sunk off the Belgian and Dutch coasts, and to air raids by both sides. But what worried my father was that the Germans had managed to capture the French city of Sedan, to cross the Meuse, and to achieve a sizable bridgehead, all in just a few days. And now, the battle there, according to a French communiqué, "had assumed the character of a war of movement."

My father was familiar with this region. Here, in the First World War, the German advance had been checked, and here that conflict's major battles had been fought. My father had followed those events from the safety of the Netherlands, which remained a neutral country then. Thus he and his brother Anschel, who had followed him, had avoided having to fight for the Austro-Hungarian empire, which he had known as hardly more than an occupying force in Galicia.

Now my father explained to me that the Germans either had punched through or circumvented the impregnable Maginot Line, and that armored units capable of achieving this were not likely to be impeded by any makeshift French defenses beyond. Furthermore, these forces to the southeast were *below* us. Forthwith, he drove over to Uncle Jacob to warn him.

We also heard some good news. The French border would be open to everyone the next day. That, my father decided, was when we would leave.

The next day, however, would be Shabbos, the day on which it is prohibited to ride by car or train. We had never transgressed this law. I knew that it could be done only under life-threatening circumstances. Such a situation, my father judged, was now at hand.

All was quiet the next morning. Coxyde still showed no signs of the war. On the sleepy street, my father seated my mother and my two younger sisters in his car, and I lashed their suitcases to the folding rack on the back. Before we could leave, they had to be driven to Uncle Jacob with whose family they would travel by train. Again, there were no good-byes, no hugs and kisses. It was as if we were not separating. It was as if they were traveling merely in another car. It was as if we were not about to contend with armored German units racing ahead. And when my father turned on the ignition, it was as if he were not violating the Shabbos.

Upon my father's return, I lashed our suitcases on our car's folding rack, and again tied the laundry hamper onto the roof of the car. We planned to meet my mother in Bordeaux, a city some five hundred miles south, on the Atlantic coast near the Spanish border.

The road was deserted, but at one point we noticed an accident ahead: cars stopped, people standing around. It was not an accident. It was the end of a line of cars stretching to the French border. Talking to the nearest people, my father learned these were recent refugees who, unable to find lodgings in the resort towns, had had to go on. The line to the border stretched for miles, they said, and the border guards were utterly swamped. Somewhat later, word came up the line that an army convoy was arriving, that inspections at the border would be discontinued, and that any vehicle remaining on the road would be shoved into the ditch alongside. Soon, the cars ahead of us began to move, and we followed. At the border station, soldiers hurried us across.

In time, we encountered the convoy coming in the opposite direction. It stayed on its side of the road, we on ours. It consisted mostly of trucks, some carrying large pieces of equipment, among which I recognized awe-inspiring anti-aircraft guns. We waved to soldiers when they looked at us, and they flashed V signs in return. We did not have to reduce our speed, and no car needed to be shoved into the canal that here hugged our side of the road.

William Shirer, in his *Berlin Diary*, tells of the millions of refugees who fled Paris, clogging the roads along with troops, bombed and strafed by German planes, lying along the roadside without food, water, or shelter, starving, dying.[2] We had no such experience. For us, the shortest way to Bordeaux bypassed Paris by a wide margin. Our problem was mostly traffic creeping endlessly along two-lane roads, coming to a near standstill in every little town. Our car had no radio, and my father bought what papers were locally available.

But what was happening was all too obvious in the vacant, dazed stares of the local people beholding our endless procession. France, that proud country, the victor of World War I, whose army had been considered the mightiest in the world, was on her knees.

My father worried that we might run out of food and gas. At a grocery store where we stopped, he noticed cans of sweetened condensed milk and bought a good supply of them. The milk, which we ate undiluted with a spoon tasted good, and wherever we went, we kept buying it as long as it remained available. At a hardware store, my father stopped to buy a gasoline can, which we filled and lashed to the car's front bumper. That proved useless. The steady rattling caused the can to spring a leak, and it had to be emptied into the car's tank.

That day's newspaper mentioned that the German armored units coming from Sedan, were fighting at Rethel and had crossed the Oise river. Looking at my road map, I saw that Rethel was about thirty miles distant from Sedan. The Oise, however, was more than twice as far away, and not in the direction of Paris. Were the Germans attempting to circumvent some Parisian defenses? Or were they heading for the sea? If that is where they were headed, our paths would have to cross (see map 2). Unfamiliar with military developments, I did not make this connection. And my father, if he did, was wise enough not to mention it.

We encountered our worst traffic jams along the outskirts of Dunkirk, and again in a town called Abbeville, which we reached in the early afternoon. Since leaving Coxyde, we had covered little more than a hundred miles.

On my road map, I noticed some country roads leading south from Abbeville paralleling more or less the congested highway that we were on. When I showed these to my father, he decided to take them even though they ran east of our highway—closer, that is, to the Germans. The road was deserted, and we barreled along. Suddenly an airplane, coming from behind, swooped over us. It was so quick, and it was gone so fast, that we could not tell whether it was French or German. My father had time neither to pull to the side of the road nor to stop, and we went on as if nothing had happened. Still, this incident must have frightened me more than I was aware of. Try as I might, I cannot remember the rest of this trip to Bordeaux, which must have included an overnight stay.

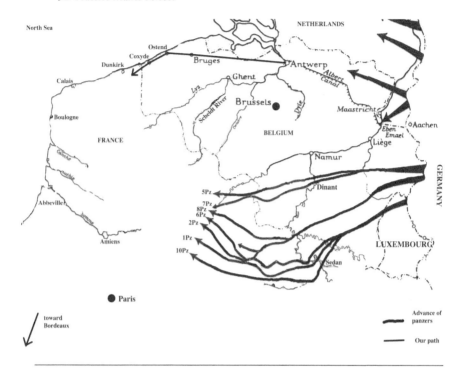

Map 2. *May 18, 1940 (Saturday). While the German panzer columns are heading not for Paris but the sea, the Feldman family leaves Coxyde for Bordeaux, in the southwest of France. Their paths must cross.*

After the war I read that the Germans reached Abbeville two days later. In that battle they leveled four-fifths of the town and cut off the French and British troops that had poured into Belgium. The Germans had purposefully refrained from advancing into Belgium, which their capture of Eben Emael had laid wide open. It was that respite that had allowed my father to dash to Antwerp, us to enjoy Coxyde for a few days, and the Allies to be drawn into Belgium. Hitler reportedly cried for joy when informed that the French and the British had, in fact, rushed into this trap.[3]

I do remember, however, our arrival in Bordeaux. Everybody it seemed had been fleeing toward that town, and traffic had stopped long before we arrived there. It was a roadblock, where police checked everyone's papers and stamped identity cards.[4] Though the road was clear thereafter, the respite was brief. Luck, however, was with us. Inching forward in the streets of Bordeaux, my father suddenly spotted a parking space opening up and managed to get into it. It was as good a place to stop as any since we had nowhere in particular to go. Leaving us in the car, he went to look around. After awhile he came back, looking pleased. He had found us an apartment! He just happened to ask someone coming out the door of a building. Yes, he had said, there was an empty apartment there. The concierge confirmed this, helpfully adding that it was newly furnished. It belonged to a doctor who just had married. Events had prevented the couple's return from their honeymoon. The concierge had called the doctor's parents, who allowed us to stay in it.

Neighbors brought us bedsheets and blankets, pots and tableware. Grandma fixed us something to eat, and we went to bed. When I awoke the next morning, my father was already up, sitting in the cheerful, sunny kitchen. "How did you sleep?" he inquired. Only then did I notice that I was itching all over. One of the blankets we had been given was infested with bedbugs.

My parents had agreed to write each other "poste restante" (general delivery) in Bordeaux and also to keep Aunt Betty in New York up to date. Every morning my father left the apartment alone, going first to the post office, where he joined the long line at the "will call" window. Every refugee, he told me, had his mail addressed poste restante.

After that, he took steps to get us out of France. That entailed obtaining a visa to some country—any country, in fact. With that, he could request transit visas to Spain and Portugal. As soon as we got out of France, we would be out of harm's way.

But obtaining that first visa, difficult enough even before the war, was virtually impossible now. My father heard that the Haitian Consulate would give visas. When he got there, it was mobbed by refugees. He could not even get near, he told me.

Only once did my father take me along on one of his errands. That happened after the government decreed that all refugees' cars be removed from the streets of Bordeaux and parked at a designated location outside the city. As our car, with Belgian license plates, could not be dissimulated, my father drove it out there. In a muddy field already filled with cars as far as the eye could see, officials directed us to the next available parking space, and there I had a last look at the bedraggled Opel with its somber blue headlights. We got a receipt and left by public transportation.

Soon thereafter, at the post office, the clerk handed my father a couple of postcards from my mother. One had been dropped in a mailbox at a station where her train had stopped, but the other had been mailed at Bordeaux. No refugee, she wrote on it, had been allowed to leave the station after her train had arrived here. All were to board a special refugee train bound for distant Marseilles. Thus the postcards left us both relieved and disappointed.

Had it been a week already since our arrival in Bordeaux? I whiled away the time by shopping occasionally for food and other necessities. Grandmother cooked and kept house, and Jenny helped her. When I had nothing to do, I read the papers, commenting patronizingly to the womenfolk about the news. I had no sense of impending peril but was bewildered by my mother's plight. I remember one night, in the bed that I shared with my father, fretting about what I should do were something to happen to him.

One evening my father brought a guest to our apartment. He had run into one of the Rotenberg boys, Maurice. During dinner the young man mentioned that he was running out of money and that the next morning he would go to the waterfront, to hire out as a day laborer. My father suggested that he take me with him.

The next day we joined a knot of workers at the waterfront. One contractor after another came by, announcing what work he had and how many workers he needed. When one contractor announced that he needed a single worker, Maurice raised his hand and was hired. I did not get a job and felt unhappy. With time to kill, I took a detour to explore some of the harbor. Looking down from a walkway I saw a small British man-of-war, trim, scrubbed, engine humming, pennants in the wind. It was some auxiliary vessel, carrying only a few small guns. A fellow onlooker informed me that it would depart by evening, and anyone who wanted could come along. Had my mother and sisters been with us, I would have had time to gather them. We could all have come on board. What a stroke of luck that would have been!

More mail came from my mother. She and the rest of the family had not reached Marseilles. With other refugees, they had been taken off the train, put onto busses, and dropped off in a small town named Montagnac. I located it on a map, found it to be within twenty miles from the Mediterranean and about eighty miles from the Spanish border. From Bordeaux, its distance was about three hundred miles (see map 3).

My father would have liked my mother to rejoin us in Bordeaux. Should he obtain the visas, we could all head immediately for the border. But what if my mother were to be denied, once more, entry into Bordeaux?

The possibility soon became moot. The Germans, after a pause, were on the move again. On June 3, two weeks after our arrival in Bordeaux, they reached Dunkirk. Two days later they launched an offensive against what remained of France. Italy declared war. In

Map 3. *May 1940 to November 1942. The lines show Alfred's path from Antwerp to Le Puy en Velay.*

Paris, the French government prepared to move to Bordeaux. To make room, it ordered all refugees to be expelled from that town. We were assigned to Lacanau, a resort on the Atlantic Ocean.

By June 10 we had registered there. Without a car, we had been unable to take all our possessions along. Our unknown hosts, upon their return to Bordeaux, would find in their apartment a somewhat battered hamper, still more than half full, but not with laundry. We left the bedbug-infested blanket spread over the balcony's railing. Its colors had begun to run after the first rain. Following that first night, we had not dared to touch it.

From Lacanau, my father commuted daily to Bordeaux, still intent on obtaining the Haitian visa. Why did it take so long? Why so many trips? I suspect that the visa required not only an application but also a bribe. In such times, my father would not have confided such things to his teenage son. But later, after he was in touch with Aunt Betty again, he asked her to repay several loans out of his American bank account.

The commute was too tedious, took too much time. Increasingly desperate for a visa, my father dashed my expectations of a languorous seaside summer by taking us all back to Bordeaux. This time we had only a dingy apartment, in a neighborhood of old, dank, and smelly buildings. We still had an address at Lacanau, he reasoned, and our identity cards had been stamped there,[5] and with the increasing confusion, we were not likely to be apprehended.

On June 14, the Germans entered Paris. Two days later, France sued for an armistice. Against the German onslaught mighty France had lasted hardly longer than Poland.

But for my father, there was a victory. On June 19, he obtained the Haitian visa.

With that he immediately went to the Portuguese consulate. There, while he waited at a desk, he witnessed a strange event. At another desk, applicants for visas, all refugees, all apparently Jewish, were processed much faster. One after another they got their visas, into their passports if they had them, otherwise on a piece of paper. One man alone wrote the visas, stamped them, handed them over, at no cost, "one after another," my father told me that evening. I sensed just a twinge of jealousy in him for having had to go to so much trouble to obtain what others were receiving so easily. He did not let this bother him. He had already telegraphed my mother. Could she meet us at Cerbère? Cerbère, on the Mediterranean side of the Franco-Spanish border, was closest to Montagnac.

What my father had witnessed at the Portuguese consulate was one of the greatest acts of courage performed in this war. The man who provided the free visas was the consul himself, Dr. Aristides de Sousa Mendes. He handed out thousands of them in direct contravention of orders from Portugal. His government quickly called him back, stripped him of his post, of the right to practice law, and blacklisted him. He died in poverty in 1954. Only because of persistent efforts by his sons in the United States, of pleas by members of the U.S. Congress and a grateful Jewish community, did Portugal rehabilitate him posthumously.[6]

The next day, my father received the Spanish transit visa[7] as well as a telegram from my mother that yes, she could meet us at Cerbère. We were ready to go.

My father sent another telegram to my mother instructing her to go ahead. Then, while Jenny began packing our belongings, I accompanied my father to retrieve our car.

The Opel was not at the location where we had surrendered it. After a lengthy inquiry, we were told it had been requisitioned by a French army officer. Why our car, instead of any other? He needed a small car, we were told. We left with another receipt.

Back in town we went to the railroad station. To our surprise, we found it under military guard and empty. No passenger traffic. Trains were running on schedule, my father was told, but were reserved for the military and officials. To the officer in charge, my father explained how he had become separated from wife and children and that he could not rejoin them because the army had just requisitioned his car. The least the army could do was to let him board the train. He argued, pleaded, produced the receipt for the car, showed that it had that day's date, all to no avail. No one could board without an official permit. Orders, the officer said, were orders. Suddenly my father remembered a paper the Polish consulate had given him, stating that he was a refugee in need of help. He showed it to the French officer. It was written in Polish. But it had an official, recognizably Polish stamp on it, and Poland was the reason France had declared war on Germany. The officer declared that "permit" OK. My father could board a train, along with anyone accompanying him. When was the next train? Tomorrow morning.

On the way back to our apartment, my father had to figure out how my mother might reach the Spanish border. She had no permit. She could not board a train.

He contemplated phoning her. That would have required both parties to be present simultaneously at separate post offices, and, were that accomplished, it was not at all certain that the operator would be able to make the connection. We had seen post offices crowded with people waiting for calls to come through. Instead, my father decided to send my mother another telegram, telling her to stay put, that he was coming to get her in Montagnac the next afternoon. Using his "permit," we would then travel to Spain together.

But all night long he tossed in bed next to me. "I could pull my hair out," he said, again and again.

Early the next morning we arrived at the station, found our train, and seated ourselves. The coach was empty but for two other passengers at the far end. My father admitted to having been worried that, with a different guard at the gate this morning, his "permit" might have been questioned. But this guard had casually waved us on. Presently the train departed, silently, without the customary whistle, without "all aboard" shouts or banging doors. It was an eerie ride. No conductor came to punch tickets or to announce stations. Silently the train slipped into a few deserted stations, and equally silently departed. In between, the train, an express, ran at a good clip. Looking out the window, I counted the wrecks of airplanes crashed along the track.

About noon we arrived in Béziers. From there, we were told, a local bus went to Montagnac. Travel restrictions did not apply to bus traffic, and the bus was crowded. It took us only about an hour to reach that town. My father had us sit in a café near the bus stop while he went in search of my mother.

In half an hour he returned, and I sensed that something terrible had happened. His face was ashen. He had located some Jewish refugees who knew my mother. From them he heard that she and my sisters had departed that very morning, by bus, going toward Béziers. My mother had received my father's first telegram. The second one must have arrived only after she had left.

No one in Montagnac knew that civilians were barred from traveling by train. My mother would have discovered that as soon as she arrived at the station in Béziers. She might have returned on the bus we had taken. She might return on the next day's bus. Could she, somehow, have managed to get on a train? Someone surmised that she might reach the border by traveling only on local busses. There was no way to confirm this.

There was nothing more we could do that day. The next morning, my father could either try to follow my mother or wait for her to come back.

We settled in my mother's lodgings and waited. Indeed, we could not do otherwise. What if she returned only to hear that we had just left? The days went by. The mails hardly moved anymore. The border to Spain was closed. Our visas expired. From my mother, we heard nothing.

We had come so close. My father's plans for our flight from Antwerp had been purposeful. He had taken various contingencies in stride and had adapted to change when this became necessary. We had not been blown about like feathers in the wind. But planning is not enough. To ensure that a plan will work, it must be tested. And unlike the Germans, who captured Eben Emael so easily, we had had no chance to practice.

4
A Crazy Summer

THE MOST CONGESTED CORNER in Montagnac was the bus stop. There, anyone who arrived was welcomed with cries and embraces like a long-lost child. Anyone who departed was bid a somber farewell as if he or she might never return. I would be there, perhaps my father and Jenny as well, perchance to see my mother return. But after the bus had arrived and she failed to alight from it, that corner became the most lonesome place in town.

One day, amidst the bustle and hubbub at that corner, I noticed a black-haired tomboy of a girl objecting to something her companion told her. She flared up, tossed back her hair, sparks in her black eyes. Instantly, I was smitten.

As the bus arrived, I lost sight of them. But I had overheard enough of their exchange to recognize them as Jewish refugees. I felt confident that I would see the girl again.

We had moved into my mother's lodgings, an old and narrow stone house on rue Badoc. What a strange sensation I felt there! Though I had never seen the place before, I could feel her presence. The rustic table looked as if she had just gotten up from it, the worn hutch as if she had just closed it, and the narrow little kitchen as if she was about to return to it.

One entered the house from a curving cobblestone street that seemed to run through rather than between houses. Just wide enough to let a cart pass through, the streets in the old town appeared narrower as the houses bordering them commonly rose three stories high. That kept the streets shaded from the intense Mediterranean sun. The small entrance to our new abode was always dark. Inside, the staircase on the left was virtually invisible, but to its right, a colorful curtain of stringed beads, the only decoration in this lodging, hung across a door that opened onto the room with the adjacent narrow kitchen. The staircase, of deeply worn stone, twisted steeply up to bedrooms on the upper floors. The house had electricity, and the kitchen had a small gas range and running water. But I soon discovered that the drainpipe from the sink ended outside the house wall. Every house, in fact, had a drainpipe protruding a foot or so above street level. From it, a sudden spurt of wastewater might surprise a passerby, splash onto the cobblestones, and meander toward a shallow gutter that ran down the middle of each street. Within that gutter flowed a steady rivulet of water, intended to dilute and carry off wastes. Alongside, a cat might chase a floating bit of garbage, or a dog pause for a drink. Every street in the old town sloped, and each channeled its rivulet of water. The streets were an open sewer. And yet, what a clever piece of civil engineering this was!

The house had no toilet, nor outhouse, nor cesspit. Upon inquiry, I was told to look for a blue enameled pail with lid. I found it in one of the bedrooms. Each morning, a tank cart stopped at the upper corner of our street, announced only by its pungent stench. If someone approached it carrying a blue pail, the carter pulled a lever that, as in salute, raised a lid at the far end of the tank, allowing the pail's owner to dump the contents into the tank. The cart, commonly referred to as *la tinette,* was the most modern horse-drawn vehicle seen in town: it rolled on automobile wheels with rubber tires.

Our house buzzed and crawled with flies. There were so many that every few hours I had to replace the flypaper spiraling below the light bulb. Glistening with the color of honey, it was irresistible to the flies, but once one had landed, a fly's every natural reaction, its attempts to clean its legs, to fly away, all led only to further trouble. This was a devilishly clever device. The bead curtain that rustled over the entrance to our living/dining room, I soon realized, was not just a quaint local decoration, but a device to keep flies out. Similar curtains covered the entrances of every house and shop in town. But it took a deft technique to walk through one and leave the flies behind.

Two further discoveries fascinated me. Next to our house, the collapse of two or three houses had created a space abutting on a half-crumbled wall. Above that wall, the third story of the next building was open like a doll house, revealing a green papered bedroom, its furniture still standing, the bed still made.

The other discovery lurked in the back of our kitchen, behind a door that resisted my attempts to pry it open. When I finally succeeded, it revealed a sight that I invited everyone who came to behold. It was a forest of dusty remains of spider webs. They hung like stalactites from an unseen ceiling, filling what must have been a stable or a barn. Pale daylight, vaguely filtering through from behind, illuminated all this. No one ventured inside.

My first occupation in Montagnac was repairing hot plates. Many refugees, having no access to a gas range, had bought them. But these were cheap appliances, whose electrical element quickly burned out. With a pair of needle-nosed pliers, I managed to twist the severed wires back together. Although my repairs didn't last very long, I was soon sought after. I didn't charge for my services but obtained something far more valuable. Through subtle inquiries among my customers, I had discovered the name of the girl who had caught my attention at the bus stop. She was the youngest of the Weiss family, four sisters living with their mother. Her name was Peshu.

In the agitation of our arrival in Montagnac, I had failed to notice that Uncle Jacob and his family were not there. Eventually, from the other refugees in Montagnac, we heard what had happened to them. On the bus that took the refugees from Béziers to Montagnac, papers were verified. This was done by Czech soldiers. The one who examined my uncle's identity card noticed an erasure. It had been made by the clerk who, long ago in Belgium, had issued this card. He had mistakenly entered "German" as my uncle's nationality. When my uncle pointed out that Germany had stripped all German Jews of their citizenship, the clerk had corrected his error. Now that erasure looked very suspicious. Uncle Jacob and his family were not allowed to remain in Montagnac. He was escorted to St. Pons, to an ancient prison that served as an internment camp. Aunt Charlotte and her three little children were interned in the camp at Gurs.

We read of another tragedy in the papers. Few even could talk about it. On June 22, the day after our arrival in Montagnac, France signed its surrender in the very railroad car in the forest of Compiègne in which, in 1918, the German surrender had been signed.

Montagnac had a town crier. He wore a uniform, carried a drum, stopped at street corner after street corner, and commanded attention with a peremptory drum roll, following which he announced local sales and events. He always ended by proclaiming that a film would be shown at the movie house but not what film: *"Ce soir, à huit heures, cinéma!"*—Tonight, at eight o'clock, movies!—What a spectacle it would have been, I mused, to see this man announcing a French victory! But the news at hand the town crier did not and could not voice.

And yet, things could have been worse. England was still fighting. The Germans did not occupy all of France and allowed the French to establish a government in Vichy, in the unoccupied zone. This was done to forestall the French fleet in the Mediterranean from joining the British fleet and France from continuing the war from its possessions in North Africa and elsewhere. Montagnac, as luck would have it, was located in the unoccupied zone.

Slowly, public services began to function again. Trains accepted passengers once more, mail began to arrive, and one day, one of the Jewish refugees in Montagnac received a letter from my mother, posted from a town near the Spanish border. She asked if they had heard from my father.

Soon my mother arrived in Montagnac with my two younger sisters and Grandmother Bauminger. Thus we learned of their odyssey. They and Uncle Jacob's family had crossed the Franco-Belgian border on foot, pushing a baby carriage that the Coxyde landlord had let them have. In Dunkirk, upon someone's advice, they had headed for the harbor to take a ship to England but, failing to locate it, had boarded a train south. Strafed by enemy planes, the train was switched from its Amiens destination to Rouen. That got them out of the path of the advancing Germans. From there they continued to Bordeaux and thence to Montagnac.

Jenny, asked to prepare some food for the hungry travelers, put some eggs in water to boil and forgot about them in the excitement until they were discovered roasting in the pot.

A few days later Aunt Charlotte and her children were released from Gurs and also returned to Montagnac. They were given the last remaining, and thus the scruffiest, accommodations. Uncle Jacob remained interned. Presently, the new Vichy government transferred him from St. Pons to Le Vernet, a camp for politically suspect foreigners. My mother had worried in Antwerp that we might be exposed to both anti-German as well as German reprisals.

Unlikely as this possibility had been seemed at the time, it now had happened. I remember Aunt Charlotte coming to my mother, crying.

"We reside here in a small place pretty much cut off from the world," my father wrote Aunt Betty on July 30, 1940.[1] More than a month had elapsed since the armistice, and we had adjusted to life in Montagnac. "We here are completely free, as in nicest peacetime. There is no censorship, only foodstuffs are turning scanty." But we needed money. My father must have telegraphed his sister for it. "It appears [from your letter] that money cannot be transferred to us from the USA," he wrote, "I would like to hear from you in detail the how and why. Do you think we can live here without money?" The problem was not only the jumble of regulations that impeded transfers of currency but also the official rate of exchange that, as yet, had not taken notice of the precipitous plunge in the value of the French franc. "Doubtlessly, there are other ways for sending money here," my father suggested. "Please talk with an experienced person, one that is not a dilettante," and, he cautioned, "don't fall into the hands of a swindler."

Aunt Charlotte had received mail from her brothers in New York before we heard from Aunt Betty. "According to the letter from the Rotenbergs," my father continued, "it would seem that I was either in Spain or in Portugal, which I do not understand, as I am still in France, in the *unoccupied* part. I hope that you haven't sent everything to Spain instead of to France. . . . I notice again and again that if one writes at the correct time, the letter arrives promptly. Why then does it not work with me? I hope I won't lose my patience before I receive news from you."

He had other errands for her. "Put constant pressure on Neuwirth to write me directly, because I must absolutely know what is happening on the business side," he wrote. "Could some close relative who is an American citizen request Mother? Who could pay for the voyage?" And "Please inquire whether there is a possibility that we all could come over there, as we dread a forced return to Belgium." He ended, "I hope that these lines opened your eyes somewhat, and made you recognize the situation in which we and all Israel are in. . . . Please write your brother, who has become impatient, as soon as possible, and who, in the meantime, sends you his heartfelt greetings."

My father had shown his exasperation also by beginning the letter not with the usual "Dear Betty," but with "Dear Sister and

Brother-in-law." The real bombshell, however, was the innocent looking postscript. It gave our return address. Fearing that, with so many refugees in town, the mailman might misdeliver our mail in the jumble of old houses, my father had arranged with a local store to have our mail delivered there. The establishment was "Peyrottes, Boucherie," a local butcher. Why a butcher? Aunt Betty might have mixed up Spain with France, but she well knew that no Jews lived in the small towns of southern France and that, therefore, no kosher butcher was to be found there. She certainly knew, also, that one cannot use a butcher's address if one is not his customer, and that our dietary laws may be violated only in desperate circumstances. Had my father selected the Gentile butcher's address to impress on his sister the desperation of our circumstances, which had forced us to contravene our dietary laws?

The war, however, seemed over for us, and that summer, most refugees were allowed to return home. Only the Jews did not return, and the hapless residents of the Alsace Lorraine, whose provinces Germany annexed. We took this opportunity to move out of the old town into the Maurel house, which had been vacated. We occupied the first story and Aunt Charlotte the basement. The spacious rooms of that house had colorful tiled floors, and its windows allowed cross ventilation. It even had a toilet, and there were no flies. The house was new; in fact, it had not quite been completed. Its stairway still lacked a banister, and the plumbing carried water only to the washroom in the basement. It was my job to go down there to draw water for our kitchen.

With space available, the municipality granted the more than seventy Jewish souls stranded in Montagnac a couple of rooms for a shul, where we put up a curtain to separate the women from the men. Occasionally Mr. Dreyfuss, a young Jewish Frenchman, would join us from the neighboring town of Pézenas. That was a walk of over one hour. He knew very little about Orthodox Judaism, and we were eager to enlighten him.

We met not only for prayers. The younger generation was invited for a "shalosh seudos" on Shabbos afternoons. We sang traditional Jewish songs and listened to some elderly people, Mr. Rosenberg perhaps, or Mr. Hirsch, or Mr. Rapoport, sharing some pearls of wisdom from the Talmud. At home in Antwerp, I rarely had joined a shalosh seudos. But in Montagnac it was considered important to pursue religious activities despite the war, and even more so because of it.

Shalosh seudos was for men. Women did not attend. Montagnac, however, had a more sociable meeting place, a handsome esplanade onto which almost everyone converged toward evening. A public promenade, shaded by two rows of stately plane trees and lined by benches, it stretched for about a quarter mile from the bus stop to the railway station. It was level. Past the halfway point, stone walls shored it up, rising over the sloping town, its end opening invitingly to the evening breeze.

There the buoyant Mr. Rosenberg, a full beard framing his face, his diminutive wife always at his side, never tired of talking about his two sons who, until the war began, ran their own businesses yet still sought his advice. Mr. Rapoport, his white goatee always trim, recounted his wheelings and dealings in the depression-ridden United States, where he had been as a fund-raiser for religious causes. His older son, who had been a construction worker in Palestine, related the chiseling and cheating practiced in that holy land by that trade. His younger son, Shulu, was my age, and we became good friends. Mr. Goldwasser, a crotchety old bachelor, his face, wrinkled and red, bereft of hair, a large tumor afflicting his forehead, was reported to have called my father *"ein Fisch Jude,"* a fish Jew, because of my father's efforts to obtain fish for us to eat.

My father would go to the esplanade by himself, and so did I, while my sisters usually went together. My mother, who had to clean the kitchen, often couldn't make it and neither could Aunt Charlotte. The Diamant family, with four youngsters, always came as a group, and Mr. Horowitz always arrived in the company of his pert wife and their ten-year-old son. His head occasionally jerked from a pronounced tic, a souvenir from his stay in the German concentration camp of Buchenwald, about which he would not talk. Occasionally one or another of the Weiss sisters would be there.

On the esplanade we mixed little with the local people. Had we been the only Jewish refugees there, I am sure that they would have drawn us in, but since there were many of us, we sought each other's company. The men usually congregated on one or two benches, discussing the news. The Battle of Britain began that August, a German invasion of England was anticipated, and the pro-German slant of the news reported by the thinning local newspapers could be argued over interminably.

The women met on different benches. There, my mother found out what foods were available at which store; picked up tips on preparing some of the exotic produce available locally, such as aubergine (eggplant) or salsifis (salsify, a root also known, because of its taste, as oyster plant); and learned of the advantages of espadrilles, a local shoe of canvas with a coiled-rope sole.

We younger folk had our own bench where several of us young men congregated around the two Hirsch girls, Olga and Lili. Several years my senior and originally from Hungary, they were warm, outgoing women, endowed with opulent "balconies" as someone once put it. They flirted a little with the older boys and we sang songs together, and I did not require much encouragement to whip out my harmonica. The girls clearly were a little giddy with the loosening of their traditional life. Still, everybody behaved very properly.

None of the Weiss girls joined our group. They usually associated with the other women. My mother admired Mala, the sister who had fussed at Peshu when I first saw them. A tall, comely blonde, scarcely two years my senior, she once thanked the mayor for some administrative favor by telling him for all to hear, "I could kiss you for this!" My mother, relating this bit of news to us, had added somewhat wistfully that she could never muster such courage.

One evening one of the Weiss sisters sat right across from my group. Next to her stood Peshu. There was no space left on their bench. Clearly bored, she stood first on one leg, then on the other. I wanted to invite her to join us, but, afraid of a public rebuff, I did not. Though I was about to turn seventeen, I was still unsure of how to approach a girl. After leaving the German school in Antwerp, I had attended only boys' schools. Dating was as unheard of in our house as it was in general among religious Jewish families. All my father's siblings had found their spouses through matchmakers. If a boy was seen with a girl, they knew that people would talk. I knew that, were I to ask one of my sisters to introduce me to Peshu, she would have tattled, to my everlasting embarrassment. It was an unspoken rule. In using the butcher's address, my father had flouted tradition. Now I discovered how difficult that could be.

In time, we had yet another social activity. Mr. Horowitz decided to create a youth group and expose its members to ideas broader than those absorbed in shul. Tradition, he felt, held us to the past. We needed to look to the future. Zionism was what he had in mind: meetings, skits performed for the other refugees, and perhaps a newspaper. At our first gathering, he taught us a Zionist song. Standing in front of us, his head jerked by his tic, he taught us its words: "Rest comes to the worker and respite to the laborer."[2] Studying the Bible had not familiarized me with the Hebrew synonyms for worker or rest nor with the poetic description of the valley of Jezreel glistening with dew in the moonlight. We had to apply ourselves.

I attended regularly, hoping that Peshu might show up. But she never did.

I learned not only Zionist songs. Although we were without a radio, my sisters picked up current hits, one of which rhapsodized about a Gypsy with black eyes and hair the color of evening. They also learned ancient French songs of love and troth, in one of which the girl chides her lover that he will forsake her the moment he sees another, but he assures her that he shall love her even after death, if this be granted to the deceased.

One song struck me as surprisingly irreverent. My sisters had learned it at school. "Cursed be thou, bell ringer," it went, "whom God created for my misfortune. From the crack of dawn he hitches himself to the bell, and evening still finds him there!" The melody, which imitated a swinging bell, descended an octave and slowed to a solemn cadence: "When will the death knell toll for the bell ringer?" It was fun, but, I thought, it poked fun at the Church. Wasn't this sacrilege? What school in Belgium or Germany would have taught such a song?

Among the songs I had learned at school in Belgium, I remember a ballad from the time of the buccaneers glorifying Piet Heyn, a Dutch admiral, for conquering the Spanish silver fleet. We also learned the song "Sarie Marijs" in the original Afrikaans because we could understand it and appreciate its difference from the Dutch. And of course, there was that Yiddish song "Oyfn Pripetshik" in which the teacher cajoles his little pupils into memorizing the letters of the Hebrew alphabet for which, he tells them, the Jews have suffered such tears and pain.

Among the children's songs I had learned in Germany, one advised him who wishes to be among the soldiers "that he must carry a gun, that he must load it with powder, and a heavy bullet." Another mourned a comrade "none better to be had." But

A bullet came a flying,
Was it intended for me or you?
It took him from my side . . .

I learned these in nursery school, years before the Nazis came to power!

Germany has many other songs, of course, some very lovely. My mother would sing Brahms' lullaby to her babies. One evening, when she sang it to my youngest sister, Edith, I asked her about the words in it: *"mit Rosen bedacht, mit Näglein besteckt. . . . "* In translations, the first three words are usually rendered as "with roses bedight" while the last three are paraphrased. My mother must have realized that she could not explain them to a six-year-old. Possibly sensing some jealousy, she sang the song just for me, looking at me as if I still were her baby. Oh how I wish I could have sung my own children to sleep with my mother's lullaby! But how could German words express love anymore? My first child was born in Columbus, Ohio. How could I sing a German lullaby to an American child? I went to a store, bought a record, and duly learned from it "Mary had a little lamb."

As for the French love songs that my sisters sang, they have remained unspoiled. They still evoke, in my mind, those summer days of 1940, when the war for us was over and yet not over, the danger clearly gone and yet not gone, when one inviolable tradition succumbed but another held fast, and when, in an old town splashed with sunshine, my heart so stirred with longing for a black-haired fourteen-year-old.

The two youngest of the Weiss girls, Frieda and Peshu, having been admitted to a children's transport bound for the United States, left Montagnac unexpectedly. Many of us refugees came to the bus stop to wish them Godspeed. As the bus arrived and the crowd surged, I lost sight of them. Then, fleetingly, I saw Peshu boarding the overloaded vehicle. That was my last glimpse of her.

Many years later I learned that Aunt Betty had kept some of my father's letters from the war years. Rereading them, I was dumbfounded to discover that they contradicted my memory. Though I had correctly retained the facts, I had reshuffled them. Peshu and her sister did not leave by the end of the summer, as I recalled. They departed in May 1941; the date was written in one of the letters in my own hand! As for the songs, I remember my sisters singing them that summer. They did not. They learned them in school. Going to different grades, each learned different songs, and they sang them to each other at home. But schools in Montagnac were closed in summer, and that fall they opened late.

It all had an air of unreality—the German invasion, our flight before it, the family separated and reunited, the unthinkable defeat of France, the poignancy of French love songs, and the presence of an alluring sprite in that quaint, sun-drenched town. Each of these clamored to be engraved, indelibly, in my memory. It was all too much. I remember a sense of detachment, as if I witnessed events from a theater seat. I felt involved in what I saw happening and yet not part of it. A sense of reality set in later, when life took on a darker cast. The delay seems to have played havoc with my memories. My poor, boggled mind must have separated events, shifting the pleasant ones into the earlier unreality, and leaving me with the recollection of a jumbled, crazy summer.

5
Time Turns Back

THE VINEYARDS BEGAN ON the street corner opposite our house. They enclosed Montagnac and undulated over the hilly countryside, reaching everywhere. They nearly obliterated the few olive trees scattered among them, the wooded bank of the Hérault River, and the lines of dark cypresses that shaded the approaches to manorial wineries. From a stretch along the road to Villeveyrac, a mile or so beyond our house, the view opened upon distant Mont St. Clair, rising between a lagoon and the blue Mediterranean. In the wide sweep of the intervening miles, one saw nothing but row upon row of grapevines, heavy with fruit, ripening under a cloudless sun.

All this and much more had to be harvested within a span of two weeks. All hands were needed. As the Germans had failed to release a million or so French prisoners of war, school opening was postponed until October so that the children could work, and even we refugees were eagerly bid for. My mother bought pruning shears and wide-brimmed straw hats. Our neighbor across the street, Madame Rose Granal, suggested whom we might work for. I signed up with one grower, my two oldest sisters with another. My mother, father, and Edith decided to work for the Granals. There would be singing and merrymaking in the fields, we were told; there would be wine to drink with one's lunch or simply to cool off; and yes, we could eat all the grapes we wanted. Two bottles of wine, furthermore, came as part of one's wages.

When the day was at hand to begin cutting the grapes, my employer lined me up along with my coworkers at the edge of a vineyard, and we advanced, each along a row of vines, each with a bucket to hold one's pickings. It was women's work. The men carried heavy wooden tubs, called "comportes," into which we emptied our buckets. It took a pair of men to lift a full comporte. They hooked a pair of poles under its handles then carried it over the rough terrain, the poles bending, the comporte bouncing. Out of the field, up a gangplank they went, and onto a makeshift platform where, with a deft movement of the poles, they overturned the comporte, dumping its contents into a waiting horse cart. Then they took the empty comporte, shimmering with fresh grape juice, to where it would be needed next.

All day long I snipped away for dear life, hot and miserable, fearing to lag behind, fearing to miss a bunch of grapes. From time to time, a kind-hearted lady would switch to my row, allowing me to catch up. The only gaffe I committed was to follow a woman with my eyes as she went a few steps out of line. What was she doing, standing still, her legs spread apart, gazing into the distance? To my surprise, something began to splash below her. The lady was not pleased with me. "What do you think you are doing?" she yelled, for all to hear.

I did eat grapes fresh from the vine and drank wine to quench my thirst. But there were no songs and there was no laughter. Still, the women occasionally had fun of a sort. When we cutters had advanced far afield, greatly lengthening the distance the comportes had to be carried, casual banter might suddenly cease. Nothing was heard but the rustle of hands rushing through the leaves and the splash of buckets being emptied. Then, about to run out of empty comportes, the women triumphantly cut loose with all manner of imprecation at the menfolk who couldn't keep up with them. What a commotion they caused! The men would rise to the challenge, charging through the vineyard with their comportes, snorting like horses, dripping with sweat, bespattered with grape-colored mud. Never had I imagined work to be this hard.

That evening, carrying my two bottles of wine, sore and tired, I made the long walk home. My mother was there, ready to look after me. She and Edith had decided to work only part time, and they had dinner ready for the rest of us. My father also had left work early in the day, concluding that he was not cut out for that sort of thing. But Jenny and Hella, in high spirits, recounted with relish their experiences that day. How did they do it?

My sisters and I persevered. Our only problem was to find enough bottles to hold the wine that was part of our wages. My mother and Edith did not bother to bring their share home.

After the vendange—the grape harvest—my father bought a dorade, a splendid fish that Mme. Granal offered to bake as we had no oven. When she returned the fish, with a slice of lemon on its golden brown crust, its aroma filling the house, it did honor to the Granals' fine kitchen. How well I remember this dorade! It was the last decent meal I would have for a long time.

Not long thereafter, my mother plunked a hunk of bread on the table in front of me when she returned from her shopping. I wish I had looked at the expression on her face, but I saw only the bread. Bread? It was scum gray, dense, and soggy, having hardly risen. It seemed to owe more to potatoes than to flour. "That," my mother said, "is your ration for the week." Then she surprised my sisters in like manner.

In stores, shelves had precipitously turned bare. The black market had siphoned off most nonrationed food. Upon news of a delivery to a store, a line quickly formed in front of it. Food became the major topic of conversation: what store might receive supplies and how to make palatable rutabaga and topinambour, erstwhile animal feeds now sold for people. The first of these, also called Swedish turnip, had purgative properties, and was laced with woody fibers that Edith said scratched her throat. Topinambour, a tuber known in the United States as Jerusalem artichoke, tasted better. It was cultivated in France despite having little nutritive value even for animals. Rations provided only 1,200 calories per day, half the normal requirements.[1]

Fish were not rationed but expensive, and my father bought what he could. For a while Mme. Granal brought us some produce from her kitchen garden. It didn't go far, for between us and Aunt Charlotte's brood, there were twelve mouths to feed. Mme. Granal had planted for only four. In December, we helped her harvest olives from a few trees she owned. Then the cold winter came.

"Paula," my father wrote Aunt Betty on December 8, 1940, "spends hours shopping each day, but most importantly, we eat our fill." He was too optimistic. Often, when going to bed, I was still hungry. It is a feeling one doesn't forget. But there was no use complaining. "The kids look healthy," my father continued, "and even gain weight, while we adults keep a negative balance-sheet. Paula has lost about 20 Kg. [44 pounds], and I have lost about 8 Kg.

[18 pounds]. Mornings we face the problem of what to eat," he went on, "yet evenings we go to bed satiated. The children, however, are voracious. Partly, this is caused by the healthy climate, but mainly, it is because the food is not nutritious."

Wistfully, my mother recalled a newspaper headline she had read as a young girl in Hamburg. "They are smiling again," it said. "They," were the owners of food stores. My mother told me of the food shortages in Germany during World War I. Food store owners with only small rations to sell and able to make little profit, turned irascible and churlish. With the war over and food plentiful again, they began to smile once more, and the newspaper took notice. Now she would have to live through that again. In Montagnac, food store owners, I noticed, no longer were friendly.

Local people took to the mountains with money or barrels of wine to barter and returned with edibles. We refugees, however, who needed a permit to travel, and whom the newspapers had begun to revile, as Jews, for black market activities, we could not venture into an unfamiliar locale to solicit for goods that normally were rationed.

We undertook, instead, to obtain food from America. "I hope," my father wrote Aunt Betty in January 1941, "that you have sent us, according to my last letter, a package of matzo, as well as matzo meal and fat. As I hear, packages do arrive here from the USA, and you should therefore endeavor to send us packages continuously. I am writing today, according to enclosure, to the firm [Associated], and believe that it will provide you the means to do this. Even if you should not hear from them right away, you must make a serious attempt, perhaps through a collection from the relatives, to send us something. You must ascertain, of course, that these shipments get through. Your relief organizations will inform you about this. The following items would be particularly desirable: semolina, Maizena, oat flakes, rice, legumes, flour, noodles, possibly sugar, kosher meat preserves, cocoa, soup cubes."

Money had joined food as a source of worry. In that same letter, my father had written his sister, "we worry a lot because no money reaches us. I hope that mail from you will soon arrive, and that you succeeded in transferring some money to us."

Life had taken on a sadder cast. Our money did run out, and my father had to apply for public welfare. This was one of the few errands on which he took me along. The municipal office to which we went was clean and friendly. We were the only visitors. My father had me read the document he had to sign. One paragraph, I remember, was a promise to repay the French government all funds obtained as soon as conditions would permit.

Being on welfare entitled us not only to money but also to clothing. From stores of unused French military uniforms, a social worker obtained a pair of pants for me. When I tried them on, they suddenly revealed to me why France had lost its war. The fabric and lining of the garment had been sewn together without a hem so that both would quickly unravel. What would a soldier think his life was worth, I wondered, given such wear? How courageously would he fight? Later I came to think that maybe these pants had been rejects. I did not wear them.

That winter was the coldest of the war. No snow fell, no water froze, and the sky remained sunny and clear. But the mistral, a cold and persevering wind, whipped noisily around our house stirring frigid drafts over its stone-tiled floors. When we left Antwerp, we had taken along summer clothing. As it became clear that we would remain in Montagnac, my father had written Aunt Klara in Antwerp to send us some of our winter clothes and bedding. These arrived around the beginning of January, barely in time, and we had the luxury of dressing warmly and sleeping comfortably. My father again wore a suit. He looked funny in it. His shirt collar was much too wide, a consequence of the weight he had lost.

A little stove stood in our dining room. To Aunt Betty, my father described it as a primitive heating setup, adding that we lacked the supplies for it. "We must seek our own wood," he wrote, "which doesn't yield much heat." I had started by gathering fallen branches along a tree-shaded road. They burned with amazing speed after I lit the stove. I had been accustomed to slow-burning coal.

One vintner offered my father the brindilles, the branches of vines that are pruned at winter's beginning, and promised to deliver them to our house. We arrived at his vineyard after an hour's walk. The day was cold and blustery; the brindilles, already cut, lay scattered through the vineyard. The man showed us how to assemble them into faggots. But after working all morning, we had assembled only a few faggots, and I felt faint. Perhaps my two-week vendange experience had not hardened me sufficiently for farm work, or perhaps it was the poor food, or perhaps it was an aftereffect of the jaundice that I, as well as a number of refugees, had contracted after arriving in Montagnac. My worried father had me rest, excused us, and we walked home. A few days later, as promised, the vintner drew up with a large horse cart to deliver a very small-looking load.

The brindilles burned well—too well in fact. They burned faster than I could cut them. My grandmother, bless her, who had chopped wood as a young girl in Poland, showed me how to do it. Common sense suggested that one kept one's hands clear of the chopping block. That is how I had cut the brindilles, one by one. Not so my grandmother. Grabbing several brindilles with her left hand, she slid them forward over the chopping block with one hand while chopping away with her right. That disposed quickly of the brindilles, but her fingers came perilously close to the swinging blade. I was not about to have an eighty-year-old woman best me. I took a bigger handful of brindilles and swung the hatchet wider. Miraculously, I still have my fingers.

It turned out that one didn't have to go far for brindilles. Every vintner would let you have them. But they burned too quickly, generated too much heat, and required one to constantly feed the stove. In our backyard, overgrown with weeds, was an ancient car with a wooden, tonneau-shaped rear. I pried off the wood from its iron frame, burnt it, burnt even the tires, and am horrified to this day that I did such a thing, because the wood was still good enough to have been restored.

Mme. Granal suggested that I cut some trees along the banks of the Hérault, about a mile away. She would let me borrow her mule and cart. Thus I, who had never owned a pet, learned to make the animal get up if it was lying down, harness it, attach it to the traces, lodge the bit into its mouth, and command it with the reins. The psyche of the animal was a more difficult problem. When it found something edible along the roadside, I could not make it go; when it came to a crossing, I could not make it stop. Fortunately, traffic on the roads had virtually disappeared by then, a result of the lack of fuel.

The wood that I brought back was green. After being sawed and split, it would not burn. It took the instant heat of the brindilles and constant attention to get a fire going. The other refugees had similar experiences. Mr. Horowitz's skit, which he got us to perform at this time, mentioned the "Dauerbrennholz"—wood that burns forever—of the Hérault:

Straight man: Dauerbrennholz?
His foil: Yes, everburn wood. It burns, and burns, and isn't consumed!

The few cars remaining on the roads sprouted a strange appendage. It was black, the shape and size of a hot water heater, and it was mounted outboard to the left, right, or aft. It gave a small car the appearance of the tail that wags the dog. Called a *gazogène*, it converted wood or coal into a "lean" gas on which a gasoline engine supposedly could run. It was a cantankerous and smelly thing, messy to fill, took a long time to get started, and frequently had to be cleaned of clinker or other deposits.[2]

Without fuel, the bus stopped running. From the old railway station at the foot of the esplanade, a locomotive that hadn't run for decades whistled once again. A couple of picturesque, antique railway cars with open platforms were refurbished. The old conductor dusted off his uniform. And I managed to contrive a purpose to take the train. It proved to be a memorable ride. As we were chugging along, I saw a passenger suddenly jump for the pull cord of the emergency brake. He jerked the cord harder and harder but nothing happened. Passengers looking out the windows on the opposite side had seen the conductor fall off the train. Now some of them stepped onto the car's open platform, attempting to hail the engineer. Their voices proved powerless against the steam locomotive's puffing and hissing. Presently one young man clambered from the lowest step of our car's platform to a similar step of the car ahead. That was how the conductor had lost his footing. But the young man managed to get onto the next car, whose emergency brake he then frantically pulled. Again, it proved to no avail. Then everyone's head leaned out the windows to see the young man jumping from the first car's front platform onto the roadbed. Thus ensued an epic contest between man and machine. The young man had to pass the baggage car to reach the locomotive, which puffed fiercely as it strained uphill. At one moment, he was gaining ground; at another, it was the train. Just as the engine was about to reach the top of the grade, the young man, with a last burst of energy, managed to race abreast of it. Only then did the engineer see him and stop the train. Looking back, we saw the conductor. He had gotten up already and was loping towards the train, his white shirt showing through a wide tear in his pants.

The bus eventually ran again. It had grown to twice its size. An immense, slug-like balloon had been fastened to its roof, inflated with household gas. I never saw the thing in all its glory because by the time it arrived in Montagnac it was already half deflated.

The vintners did not tinker with modern technology. They fell back, instead, onto older ways. Where the highway entered town, the farrier's business boomed, spreading wide the stench of burning hooves. The wheelwright's shop was across the road. Passing by one day, I saw three men standing around a ring of fire. From it they lifted a perfect circle of bright glowing heat with long iron tongs. They walked it a few steps to a large wooden cartwheel lying on the ground. As they dropped the ring over it, the wheel disappeared in a hiss of steam and smoke. In the blink of an eye, the men each grabbed a water-filled bucket and quenched the fire. In the brief turmoil of steam, the iron ring contracted, squeezing the wheel's woodwork in a permanent, vise-like grip. Not a nail was used, yet nothing now could dislodge that rim, not the rockiest road, not even the men who just had mounted it. The old-timers, satisfied, paused a moment to examine their work. I admired their handiwork much longer, noticing the perfection of the fit that admitted of no adjustment and the splotchy cover of black mud and rust that, once the wheel started rolling, would become bright metal.

The most common vehicles on the roads now were heavy horse carts balanced on two such huge iron-rimmed wheels. These carried the vintners and their supplies, ever so slowly, to and from the vineyards. Montagnac looked as it did at the beginning of the age of the automobile. Time had turned back.

The Vichy government pushed time back even further. It retreated past the French Revolution, past the glorious time when all men were declared free, equal, and brothers. It retreated deep into the Dark Ages, where Jews in particular were neither equal, nor brothers, nor free.

In what a hurry that government had been to get there! A mere two months after the armistice, in August 1940, it annulled a French law that prohibited attacks in the press based on race or religion.[3] A month later, it empowered prefects to intern all male immigrants between the ages of eighteen and fifty-five judged to be "superfluous in the national economy."[4] The next month it established special laws, the *"Statut des Juifs,"* that defined Jews, limited their civil rights, and subjected their property to despoilment, which is official plunder. Outdoing the Germans, Vichy's definition exceeded the Nuremberg laws, and the Statute was rushed through ahead of a similar German ordinance.[5] Next, Vichy bore down upon its foreign Jews. It passed a law authorizing prefects to assign them a forced residence, intern them, or constrain them to forced labor; and an ordinance requiring them to obtain a permit (sauf-conduit) to travel outside their community of residence.[6]

Two regional newspapers reached Montagnac, *L'Éclair* and *Le Petit Méridional.* The former, Pétainiste, reflected the views of the Vichy government while the latter was liberal. But under tight censorship and reduced to four pages each, there was little difference between them.[7] As I prepared to write these pages, I attempted without success to locate contemporary issues of these newspapers. I perused instead the 1941 issues of *Paris-Soir,* a national newspaper. Vividly, with the first page that I happened to see, the oppressive feeling of those times returned. I found diatribes against the Rothschilds, which I vaguely remember. I found a laudatory review of the movie *Jud Süss,* a sleazy piece of German propaganda that had been shown in Montagnac and that a few refugees even went to see. Even more disturbing were little notices such as this one that I translate here in its entirety: "Lyon, 11 February. A large number of black market traffickers have been apprehended by the Sûreté of Lyon. Stocks of cloth, clothing, furs, silks, shoes, and razor blades have been seized. Among those arrested were Joseph Maek, Fagne-Mendel, Abraham Finger, Moise Schlinber, Sucher Neustadt, Joachim Bloch, William Fresco, Edgar Lehmann, Robert Kaufmann, Anatole Airsch, etc."[8] This short item is surmounted by a headline more than an inch tall that screams, "ISRAEL DIRECTED THE BLACK MARKET OF LYON." It does not say "Black marketers," it does not say "Criminals," it says "ISRAEL," and that includes me. It stares me in the face, and it stared our neighbors in the face and everyone who read the paper. One cannot strike back, one cannot do anything at all.

Needless to say, important news, for us refugees, came neither from newspapers nor from the radio, to which we had no access. It came mostly by rumor. Thus we heard of *"rafles,"* of police arriving suddenly, cordoning off a street, examining the papers of everyone so trapped, and carrying off some hapless refugees. Thus we heard that in Béziers, the town from where, in the spring of 1940, we had boarded the bus to Montagnac, the word "Jew" was painted on certain shop windows.[9] Another time, Jewish stores had their windows broken and graffiti smeared on their walls: "All will go better when our knives are reddened by Jewish blood."[10] Mr. Dreyfuss, though he did not often undertake the long walk from Pézenas, was our source for much of such news.

One Shabbos afternoon, happening to drop in at shul at a time when the girls met for one of their social programs, I overheard one of them relating how a Jewish girl, dragged along a street during a pogrom, managed to hold down her dress with a nail that she jammed into her leg, thus protecting her modesty. The tale, presumably from Jewish folklore, sent an unforgettable chill down my spine. Still, I did not consider the story pertinent to our situation. The narrator, as it turned out, was more prescient.

In the spring of 1941, a well-meaning stranger, a young rabbi, visited Montagnac. Representing an organization called "Friends of the Jewish Tradition," he was about to restrict even more our scarce food, at least temporarily. He was there to help us to observe, under present circumstances, the biblical injunctions against consuming leavened bread during the upcoming Passover.

He brought leaflets that informed us, for example, that the ersatz coffee sold during the war, which contained grain substitutes, could not be used during Passover. Shortening could be used if obtained in a closed package, but if one's ration coupons did not suffice for a whole package, the surface cut by the merchant had to be scraped. And the local wine, despite its abundance, was not kosher for the Seder. "One may use," the leaflet advised, "a wine prepared from raisins. If the wine suffices only for four cups, it should be used the first evening of the Seder. Should it be impossible to obtain wine, one shall recite the Kiddush anyway, omitting, however, the blessing of the wine." In a similar manner, the leaflets "eased" the rules governing the kitchen utensils to be used during Passover.

About matzo, the most conspicuous Passover food, the pamphlet said nothing. Arrangements were being made to get us some, but the obligation to collect the necessary ration coupons beforehand caused some trouble. Also a Haggada, the book prescribing the ritual of the Seder, was being printed and could be ordered collect.

When he came to our house, we had a surprise for the rabbi. We already were on our way to having a Haggada. Weeks before I had borrowed one from a refugee. Some people are prepared for every eventuality! Now I was in the midst of copying its text into a notebook. The rabbi greatly admired it, but my father, unsure of whether I would complete my undertaking, ordered two of the Haggadas yet to be printed.

Word of my undertaking spread among the Jewish community of Montagnac. One by one, the more religious among the refugees—Mr. Diamant, Mr. Rosenberg, Mr. Hirsch—came to admire this work of patience, if not of art. They coached me in composing its title page. Written in Hebrew, it reflected consummate Talmudic tradition. The acronym of an invocation for God's blessing began the page; periods distinguished the Hebrew letters that stood for numerals. The title "the youth" preceded my surname, rendered not as "Alfred Philip" but as the Hebrew "Abraham Pinchas." Having read in a newspaper that methylene blue could serve as an ink substitute, I had obtained this dye from the druggist and used it for writing even though there was no shortage of ink. The Haggada survived the war, and when, in 1981, I donated it to Brandeis University,[11] its librarian declared it "an amazing piece of work."

The Haggadas that my father had ordered did arrive in time, so my work was not needed to save the Seder. That evening the white tablecloth, the glow of the candles, and the Seder plate with the goblet of wine filled for the prophet Elijah lent a festive air to the room. The table, presided over by my father, surrounded by my mother and sisters, the two grandmothers, and Aunt Charlotte and her children, all so neatly dressed, was like our Seders in Antwerp. The traditional questions were asked and the afikomen was stolen. The familiar songs and ceremonial evoked the past. When my mother got up to bring the first course from the kitchen, I unwittingly anticipated the familiar, sumptuous meal. Chicken soup with matzo balls is what used to start it. As she returned with a tray of steaming dishes, I believe I actually smelled it. But in the plates she placed in front of us there were only coarse, watery rutabagas, staring me in the face with malicious triumph as if it were one of the Egyptian plagues.

The war was on hold. A standoff had been reached. The British had not buckled under the relentless bombing known as the Blitz. The much anticipated German invasion of England had not materialized. But there was no peace, either. We were in for a protracted war.

For some time, my father, like every refugee in Montagnac, had begun to work on our emigration. We could not ignore the anti-Semitic laws. We had to get out of France.

At our shul or on the esplanade, wherever we refugees met, our possibilities for emigration were discussed. Most every one of us had relatives abroad with whom we corresponded. The information gathered was freely exchanged through an informal grapevine, then confirmed or questioned, discussed, analyzed, evaluated. On this topic, the expertise available in this remote and inconsequential town was second to none.

The best prospects, it appeared, were Cuba and the United States. Aunt Charlotte's brothers in New York endeavored to obtain Cuban visas for her and for Uncle Jacob. My father thought his chances were better with the United States. Both the German and Polish quotas, he argued, were wide open. While our relatives in America had already pledged their resources for earlier affidavits, there still remained Cousin Arthur Bernstein, who worked on the New York Stock Exchange. Then there was my father's employer, Associated, where someone with adequate means might be prevailed upon to sponsor us. There were still other possible sponsors. My father wrote to them all.

All that correspondence my father sent through Aunt Betty. She could see to it that it was received, and that it was replied to. The mail was still a problem. "We just received your dear letter of the 12th with footnote dated the 19," my father wrote her on December 8, 1940. "We too have waited almost five weeks for a letter from you, since we received your last letter, dated 19 October, on 3 November. Therefore, you did not write between 19 October and 19 November. Alfred keeps a precise accounting, and if his accounting is correct, you allowed four weeks to elapse before writing us. Nevertheless, I cannot understand why you have to wait more than four weeks for a letter from us. We sent you various letters during October, which predated Alfred's accounting. In November, we included a letter for you, dated the 1st, in a letter sent to Jos [Aunt Charlotte's brother]. On both the 4th and the 11th, we sent you letters directly and on the 21st we again included a letter for you in a letter sent to Jos."

Aunt Betty was busy. Life was not easy in an America still mired in the Great Depression. She and her husband, barely able to speak the language, were virtually unemployable. They planned to open a greengrocery. Still, she never complained nor rebuffed my father, never flagged in her efforts to help us. But in America she was a greenhorn, and her knowledge of her new country was scant. When she read in the newspapers of a proposal to use the Virgin Islands as a temporary haven for refugees,[12] she confused them with the similarly-named state. My father replied, "I was astonished to read, in your letter, that one can obtain a visa to Virginia. Since Virginia, to my knowledge, is a state of the union of the USA, this would be equivalent to a visa to the USA. Please inquire exactly under what circumstances such a visa is granted, and if you can, obtain an affidavit for us all."

My father had more for Aunt Betty to do. "In addition to the 'Affidavit of Support,'" my father explained in January of 1941, "one needs now also a so-called 'Affidavit of Morality.' You will learn all the details from the attached letter to Cousin Bernstein, to whom you will hopefully have transmitted also the enclosures to my letter of January 16. Additionally, I am enclosing a statement from my [New York] bank, so that it can be shown, in the Affidavit of Support, that I have about $2,000 in my account there. You must now convince yourselves that Bernstein will really undertake everything quickly, otherwise you must look for someone else. As I have mentioned, all depends on obtaining most speedily a good affidavit."

The next month, he followed up: "I have repeatedly given you all our data, and you must have them ready at any time. You should also know that the Affidavit of Support must be accompanied by the sponsor's tax return for the past year, and by a so-called Political and Moral affidavit, in which the American citizen confirms knowing us well with respect to morals and politics. It is advisable that that citizen also has a reputable person provide him with a similar attestation." The mark of the Montagnac grapevine is evident in this precision, this detail. My father continued: "I repeat all of this for safety's sake so that the affidavit, when finally issued, is unobjectionable in any way. A little error, and a further inquiry can result in a delay of six months. The affidavit, also, should be sent out in at least two copies, so that, if one letter is lost, the second one is immediately available. In addition, the affidavit should be prepared by experienced and competent people, and one must be careful not to be taken in by a dabbler. Not everyone who asserts that he can prepare an affidavit is up on the latest restrictions. That which was perhaps unobjectionable the year before, today may no longer be acceptable. You can imagine the picking and choosing, when today one pays less attention to the quota than the affidavit. I am disappointed that Arthur Bernstein hasn't accomplished anything yet. I have assumed that, among his acquaintances at the stock exchange, he would have quickly located a suitable person with sufficient means to do us this strictly perfunctory favor. If you do not have the time, you should ask important acquaintances to remind him of this as often as possible. If he tries, he will certainly have someone ready in short order. He should be told that one may not waste any time. Tomorrow, conditions may turn, perhaps, much worse."

My father's hopes that Associated would help had been in vain. "For some time already," he added, "the firm has refused, because of overload, to provide affidavits. But as you know, Dr. Rothschild has found, among his acquaintances, providers of affidavits for various colleagues." Not ready to give up, he added: "If, however, some important person could talk with them," he suggested, "I would be interested to see what their answer might be."

More successful were the efforts of a Jewish organization in France, the OSE (Œuvre de secours aux enfants).[13] They organized the children's convoys, on one of which Frieda and Peshu Weiss reached the United States. My sisters were registered for one of these. "We have the opportunity to send our three youngest children to your country, taking advantage of a children's transport," my father wrote several cousins of his in New York. He promised them that "Betty will arrange for their accommodation there; they will not become a burden to anyone. It is however required that American citizens accept the children." The effort came to naught, not for lack of cooperation from the family, but because the transport, in the end, did not materialize.

It has become well-known how reluctant the U.S. government was in those years to accept Jewish refugees. A fear had infected the country, a familiar fear, fifth column hysteria. The press had gone crazy with specious accounts of spies masquerading as refugees and of refugees forced into spying. "War by Refugee" was the title of a story appearing in the popular *Saturday Evening Post* in March 1941. President Roosevelt himself had talked about "a Trojan horse." A congressional committee, the Dies Committee, fueled the fire. Measures against aliens, a senator observed, had become "perhaps the best vote-getting argument in present day politics."[14]

At the State Department, a political appointee, Breckinridge Long, had become the assistant secretary who ruled on the granting of U.S. visas. An erstwhile ambassador to Rome, he had admired Mussolini and decorated one of his generals. Now, as naïvely, he was taken in by fifth column rumors. He listened to any spy story. He gave credence to any rumor linking refugees to radicals, communists, or just activists. To the author of "War by Refugee," he had allowed special access to dubious intelligence. He saw it as his duty to protect his country from refugee spies.[15]

Versed in the ways of government, he was effective. When, for example, the Virgin Islands were proposed as a haven for refugees— their governor had the authority to admit visitors without visas— Long called upon the chief of Naval Intelligence, suggesting that the Navy declare the islands a restricted area "for strictly naval reasons." In a time of war, there was no arguing with that.[16]

In June 1941, Breckinridge Long's conservative friends in the U.S. Congress passed the Russell Act, which excluded all immigrants "inimical to the public welfare." The State Department interpreted this to include immigrants who had close relatives living under the enemy's dominion.[17] The logic was that by threatening the latter, the enemy could coerce the former to steal America's military and technological secrets whether they wanted to or not.

Because of such policies, the U.S. immigration quota remained half unused during the war.[18]

Unexpectedly, in March 1941, Aunt Klara in Antwerp received a letter from the American consulate informing her that her quota number had been reached and that she and her family could travel to the United States as soon as they had a complete and valid affidavit as well as ship tickets. As already mentioned, she had applied for U.S. immigration before the war began. In the meantime, she had had an affidavit prepared for her family. It needed only to be renewed, and she foresaw no difficulty with that. Money for the tickets, however, was another matter. "Should it perhaps not be possible to meet the costs of the ship tickets for all of us," she wrote Aunt Betty, "then obtain them at least for Adolf and the boy." But the money could not be found, and three months later, in June, she wrote to her sister that "we are therefore unable to do anything with the affidavit, and we must, I think, have patience until the war is over."

In the meantime, my father's efforts to obtain visas had turned into a cliff-hanger. Aunt Betty had obtained the affidavits for us. He had an appointment with the consul in Marseilles for July 13. However, neither our political and moral certification nor his mother's affidavit had yet arrived. And now, on June 6, 1941, my father, being unemployed, had been sent to the work camp in Agde, a town about a dozen miles from Montagnac.

My mother wrote Aunt Betty, "Please spare no effort to get the missing papers here by the beginning of July. Who knows how long it may be before he [my father] can again obtain a notification. For us, all now depends on this notification. . . . The dear mother is quite depressed and spiritless. Remember that, when you stayed with us, I told you that we would always be there if someone needed help, but that, if we needed help, who would there be? This is, God forbid, no reproach to you, as I know that you exceed your strength in your efforts on our behalf. This is only to establish what bitter fate has befallen us."

As suddenly, bright sunshine dispersed the gloom. After only a week or two at the work camp, my father received a medical discharge. He had been unable to tolerate the food served there. And then all the missing immigration papers also arrived.

On the appointed day, my father traveled to Marseilles. There the consul informed him that, although his papers seemed to be in order, he had a sister—Aunt Klara—living under German occupation. The "close relatives" regulations, which had just been communicated to the consulate, prevented him from issuing us a visa. We could, of course, file an appeal, but regrettably, that would entail a lengthy procedure.

Of the refugees in Montagnac, only the Weiss girls, whom I have already mentioned, and the Spirn family managed to emigrate to the United States during the war. The latter, though granted U.S. visas in September 1942, were refused an exit visa by the French government. The Montagnac gendarmes nevertheless issued them a safe-conduct, a feat all the more admirable as it came after the cruel *rafles* of August, with which I shall deal in the next chapter. The safe-conduct got them to the Pyrénées, across which they had to be smuggled into Spain. They were arrested there and would have been returned to France had not the mother, injured and exhausted, been hospitalized. Thus they all gained a respite, and eventually managed to reach Portugal, where they picked up their U.S. visas. They crossed the ocean on a Portuguese passenger ship "that was half empty," Charles Spirn told me afterward.

Aunt Charlotte's brothers in New York managed to obtain two Cuban visas. One went to Uncle Jacob, who was thereupon released from the camp in January 1942 and safely reached Cuba.

The second went to Aunt Charlotte's brother Salomon Rotenberg. He had been caught in a *rafle* somewhere in France and been sent to the work camp at Vidauban. There, on a diet of thin soup and little bread he, along with other unfortunates, was made to carry telephone poles uphill. Unaccustomed to such work, his shoulders soon burst with oozing sores that remained untended.

At the time, a contract from a farmer sufficed to release an inmate from a work camp. Salomon's younger brother, Alexander, also a refugee in southern France, came to visit his sister in Montagnac to try to obtain a contract for their brother. Although the town depended on agriculture, it was not easy for a vintner to justify a contract to someone totally lacking in agricultural experience. Nevertheless, our neighbor, Jean Pierre Granal, assured that Salomon was about to receive a visa to Cuba, convinced one of his acquaintances to do just that. Montagnac's mayor, André Bringuier, then signed the necessary travel papers and, spurning official channels, dispatched his chief of police to fetch Salomon from the camp.[19]

Such, in an anti-Semitic France, was the disposition of Montagnac toward its Jewish refugees.

I shall not omit another act of uncommon kindness. It happened during our first winter in Montagnac. I needed to haul a load of firewood from the riverbank. The Granals' mule, which I had used before, was sick. It had worked itself loose one night and broken into its supply of oats. Its belly bloated, the vet had to be called, and the animal took a long time to recover. Most vintners owned horses, which I did not feel secure handling. I heard of a donkey owned by a local woman, Jeanne Babau, who lived in the old part of town. Her circumstances were not the best. I noticed with astonishment that the dress she wore was but a flour sack, plainly recognizable by its lettering. She had cut openings for her neck and arms and gathered it around her waist with a string. It was rather short, and she wore it with a chic that disguised its origin. Nor was she shy. When I attempted to pay for using her donkey and cart, she refused firmly. She could not take money from a refugee, she said, and that was that. There was no arguing.[20]

What prompted the people in Montagnac to be so kind to us, when elsewhere—in the Ariège, the Aude, the Creuse, the Lozère, the Saône-et-Loire, the Gers, or the Indre—Frenchmen did not hide their satisfaction when the Jews amongst them were deported?[21] I found what may be the answer when, in preparation for these pages, I explored Montagnac's history. I read that four centuries earlier, Montagnac had been a hotbed of sedition, participating in the first surge of the Reformation. Repeatedly the town had been besieged, taken, and pillaged.[22] Its Protestant inhabitants were hunted as heretics, burnt as witches.[23] The civil rights of those who remained were curtailed. Protestants were not allowed to bury their dead in daylight; their funerals were permitted only at dawn or dusk.[24] A variety of occupations remained closed to them.[25] Once they were given fifteen days to either convert or leave the country.[26] Thereafter, those who converted were scrutinized with suspicion.[27] How similar to ours was their past!

The French Revolution, establishing the Rights of Man, included freedom of religion, but the Restoration soon reestablished much of the old order. Montagnac, it so happened, remained in the grip of this order until the 1904 elections.[28]

When, four decades later, our hapless band of Jews took refuge in their town, the memory of the earlier persecutions must still have been alive among its people. They may have been strangers to us, but we were no strangers to them. Looking at us, Protestants and Catholics alike may have seen their own past staring them in the eye. Time had turned back.

6
The Warmth of a Mother's Love

Several times foreign diplomats had requested to know where the transports of Jews from the unoccupied territory were taken.

It was decided, on this request of President Laval, that he was to answer in the future that the Jews of the unoccupied territory who surrendered to the occupying authorities were transferred to the "General Government" for work.

—head of the SS and chief of the police in France,
September 4, 1942, from Serge Klarsfeld's *Memorial to the Jews Deported from France, 1942–1944*

DURING THAT CRAZY FIRST SUMMER in Montagnac, my seventeenth birthday slipped by unnoticed. I well remember, however, the next one. It entitled me to a tobacco ration, which I could sell for more than a day's wages, and it made me liable for service in work camps. Strange times, I mused, in which such regulations coincide.

Farm work, I knew, would keep me out of work camps. I had hired out as a farm hand well before that birthday—as soon, in fact, as emerging weeds in the vineyards signaled our first winter's passing. Most young refugee men in Montagnac had done likewise.

Déchaussage, the hoeing around the foot of each vine to remove the weeds, inaugurates the growing season. As with the vendange, a line of workers advances along rows of plants, and as with the vendange, I tended to fall behind. The vintners preferred seasoned workers, so I often was the sole refugee. Yet the work didn't require much practice. Was it inadequate food that made me a slow worker?

Was it my hoe that I could not keep sharp? The implements being sold now at the hardware store were no better than the heating wire of the hot plates that I used to repair. And I had to walk to work, usually an hour or so, and return that way, carrying, besides tool and lunch, three empty bottles in the morning filled with wine on the way back. Yes, I did a man's work.

After the leaves sprouted on the vines, they had to be sprayed. All day long I walked along rows of vines, a container strapped to my back, pumping with my left hand, waving the spout with my right, covering each leaf on both surfaces with a mist of copper sulfate solution. The whole countryside took on a bluish hue, and so did my clothes, my shoes, my hands. Work gloves were unknown. When I first encountered them in the United States, they struck me as an extravagant frill.

It was no steady work. Vintners hired for specific needs. We heard of jobs through the grapevine, so to speak, one refugee passing the word to another. Not all work was in the vineyards. Once some stables needed to be cleaned. We used pitchforks to remove the straw from the ground, then shovels to dig the dung beneath. That revealed a masonry drain, too narrow for shovels. The foreman wanted it cleared. "How do you do that?" I asked. "Use your hands!" he shouted. I did, but to this day, I wonder. Had it been a practical joke?

When the time came for the vendanges, the comportes were still too heavy for me. Once more I worked with the women. This did not bother me. It kept me out of work camp. Then it was winter, and no farm work to be done. For a few weeks, I joined a road gang, removing about half an inch of blacktop from a street. My pickax, like the hoe, needed frequent sharpening. The wind blew cold, and I tended to fall behind, and the pay did not include wine.

And yet that winter was not as cold as our first, and the news was so much better. That summer the Germans had invaded Russia, advancing at breakneck speed and taking hundreds of thousands of prisoners. Cold and snow, however, had surprised unprepared German armies. How gladly we braved the cold mistral that winter! The Russians, taking advantage of the invader's predicament, had mounted a counteroffensive. Avidly we tried to read between the lines of the censored newspapers. In North Africa the British also had bloodied the Germans' noses. And one day, we read about Pearl

Harbor, and a few days later about America joining the war against Germany. These were our happiest moments in a long time.

Russia, North Africa, and Pearl Harbor were far away, however. Nearer to us, evil still prospered. That winter, an ordinance was issued that required all Jewish refugees to register at the local police stations. Although the wording was polite—it referred not to "Jews," but to "Israelites"—we in Montagnac had concerned discussions about it. No consensus emerged. My father decided to register. He thought that we would be worse off by not doing so. Mr. Goldwasser, however, told anyone who would listen that he had not registered. Most others kept mum.

My mind had been made up well ahead of my father's. I would show "them" that I was not afraid. I registered in Montagnac, proudly I thought, but very fearfully as well.

That spring, despite the shortage of field hands, work in the vineyards would no longer keep a refugee out of work camps. There happened to be, however, an alternative. French law provided a deferment for foreigners attending a vocational school. Providentially, the year before, the Jewish organization ORT (customarily translated as Society for Trades and Agricultural Labor) had established a vocational school at Agde.[1] I enrolled in its course on agriculture.

Shulu Rapoport and I went together. Arriving in town, we self-consciously turned our backs to the work camp where my father had been and rented a furnished room in the opposite direction, near the building where our classes would be held. Our instructor, after some theory, took us to a leased field, already plowed, where he assigned a section to each student to be planted with corn. I was one of a very few with some agricultural experience, and my prowess in manipulating a hoe, I noticed, elicited some admiration. But the crop, as it rose under the Mediterranean sun, was uneven. At the end of the field, where my rows were located, my plants lagged. The soil there was too sandy.

The ORT offered courses other than agriculture. In particular it offered a course in photography taught by Mr. Zweigenthal, a renowned photo reporter, now also a refugee. I had seen his photos in the magazine *Match,* and recalled his pen name, Gental. One of his students took me to his domain where, ducking through film strips hanging from laundry pins, he showed me the darkroom and other equipment. Classwork included taking photos, he said, for which one checked out a Leica, the most advanced camera of the day. I watched a student removing enlargements from a bath and another critiquing a portrait photo. The fellows here impressed me as bright boys—the kind likely to be computer whizzes nowadays— much brighter than the students taking agriculture. I managed to talk to Mr. Zweigenthal, and although the class was already halfway through the course, he allowed me to join it.

What a difference this change would make! No hard work in the fields anymore! No dirt! No sweat! And as I left the building, I noticed that the street, the houses, the people looked different. The whole town had changed. The narrow crooked streets no longer appeared dirty but picturesque. How unaffected that woman carried a fish! How disdainful that man with the monocle! It had taken me but one visit to my new class to acquire the photographer's eye.

From then on, I saw nothing but opportunities for photographs. There was the procession that issued from the austere twelfth-century cathedral, robed prelates and women garbed in picturesque regional costumes, the path strewn with flowers. There were Indo-Chinese soldiers, unable to return home, whose betel-juice-blackened teeth rendered horrid their ready smiles. There was a canal, a seventeenth-century engineering marvel[2] still in operation, with a dam for water supply and a circular basin for turning barges around. In the Hérault River porpoises cavorted. Local fishing boats thrust up a rakish stem, a vestige, I fancied, of the Viking ships that had plied these waters a thousand years ago. There was the fish market with its display of fish ranging from electric eels to square-jawed, sharp-toothed monsters. There, one slow day, a fish monger unraveled for me with an impromptu dissection the amazingly complex sex organs of a shark.

Agde was not alone to offer amazing possibilities for pictures. Montagnac had the blacksmith, the wheelwright, and that antique train. And toward Pézenas, atop the highest of a trio of hills, was a Roman altar. My sister's teacher had mentioned it, and it hadn't taken me long to get up there and locate it. It was smaller than I had expected and hidden by grape vines. It was a single stone, with smooth faces along whose edges I could see Roman columns clearly incised.

Most of these fancied pictures I never took. Film, I quickly was made to understand, was scarce. Every frame counted. And it was not so much what one shot, but how one did it, and how one developed it, that made for a good photograph. I saw an exquisite example one day. David Blum, a student with whom I was to become friends, had made a photo of his grandfather's head. It showed every hair of his beard, every wrinkle of his skin. I realized that I had much to learn.

To catch up with the class, Mr. Zweigenthal gave me a book to read. In it I encountered sets of numbers that looked familiar. I had seen similar ones inscribed on the lens barrel of a Voigtlander, a camera with bellows that my mother had used in her maiden days. She didn't know the meaning of these numbers and had long since switched to a box camera. Now the book explained the purpose of these numbers. How sweet the satisfaction of suddenly comprehending what had eluded me for so long! Here, if I had a question, there always was someone to whom I could turn. How different this was from Antwerp where, if I stumbled at some point while reading a popular book on science, I seldom could find anyone to ask for help. Now, gradually, I mastered cameras, enlargers, light meters, and other superlative equipment that was at hand and exulted in a competence never experienced before.

But the war distorted everything. It made tobacco a treasure, had us rejoice at the Japanese attack on Pearl Harbor, and now, in the spring of 1942, it transmuted my enchantment with photography into a worry. For, given the times, might not agriculture have provided a safer alternative to work camps?

Classes recessed for the summer, and I returned to Montagnac. There the refugee community was abuzz with rumors about *rafles* everywhere in France. Then word came from Mala Weiss that there would be a *rafle* in Montagnac. A gendarme with whose daughter Peshu had gone to school had alerted her.

The Granals suggested that my father and I sleep in their "cellar," so called because it contained the vats used for storing wine. But it was really a hangar, built above ground next to their villa and serving also as storage for farm equipment and as stable for their mule. They piled some straw into one corner, and we laid on it, sleeping very little because of prickly and scratchy slivers of it creeping into our clothes. It was all for nothing; it had been a false alarm.

When Mala Weiss once more relayed a warning, another neighbor, Mr. Trébosc, offered us a spare bedroom in the back of his house, from which we could escape should the need arise. But again, nothing happened that night.

Instead, the police revoked my work release. I had to report to the work camp at Agde.

I departed about the same time as Edith. She was to take the place of Hella, who had just returned from a year's sojourn at a children's home for refugee children maintained by a Jewish philanthropic organization. It was no ordinary home. She went to live in a château, I to the work camp.

I arrived around noon, riding a borrowed bike. My sojourn in Agde had acquainted me with the town. As I reached the street that led to the camp, I noticed that something had changed. The bars, eateries, shops, and other establishments that had catered to the inmates showed no sign of life. The entrance to the camp at the end of that street was deserted as well. Gone were the casual knots of inmates who used to gather in the vicinity of the guardhouse. Coming closer, I saw that the gate itself, through which inmates used to pass rather informally, was barred. Gendarmes, carbines slung across their backs, helmets instead of képis on their heads, stood by. Had I not been familiar with this street, I might have pedaled innocently to the entrance. Instead, I panicked.

Instinctively I made a U-turn. My heart pounding, I already felt like a hunted animal. With a turn of the handlebars, I had become an outlaw, on the run, a shiftless clandestine evading the authorities.

Had the gendarmes noticed? Were they about to come after me?

No one in town had examined my papers on the way in, but now I saw in every shadow a gendarme or an informer. My permit did not allow me to travel away from the camp, and I knew that, the farther I got, the less credible would be an excuse that I had lost something. To leave town, I had to traverse the sole bridge across the Hérault, skirt the wharves along the Canal du Midi, cross the tracks of the main railway line at the edge of the station, then cross the Canal du Midi—all installations likely to be under surveillance. I had the presence of mind not to go too fast nor too slow. When finally I reached vineyards, which began on the far side of the canal, I decided to leave the road, though it was deserted, and make my way along the narrow, rutted byways by which vintners reach their plots.

The sky reflected my mood. The blackest cloud began spreading over it. The thunderstorm struck as I arrived below the hills on which stood the Roman altar. With no shelter in sight, I slogged on in the downpour. The desperation of my situation had fully sunk in. Were I to return to the camp, I would be punished, and what would that be like? Even if that didn't happen, how could I live in a camp under the watch of armed guards? But what would life be if I could be arrested, anywhere, any time?

Just before setting, the sun peeked out from beneath the rim of the black clouds, painting their chaotic underside a garish violet and raising a bright double rainbow. It had been hours since I had made that fateful U-turn. The panic had subsided, the pressure relented. I had regained hold of myself. I still contemplated, in awe, the enormity of what I had done. The savage sky, the thunder and lightning that had raged about me, the mud through which I struggled, and the vicinity of the mountain with the Roman altar, they all suggested, I fancied, the wrath of the gods.

Darkness had already fallen when I reached Montagnac. Circumventing town to avoid riding down the main street, I knocked on the back door of our house. My surprised mother, torn between relief and worry, toweled me dry and put me into clean clothes. My sisters, who normally wouldn't lift a finger on my behalf, hurried to fetch whatever was needed. In no time I had a warm meal and was tucked into bed, and even the light was switched off for me. It felt delicious. In my first night as an outlaw, I slept soundly and peacefully, without a worry in the world. Such is the warmth of a mother's love.

A letter arrived from Edith at the children's home, lyrical about the food they were served and about the evenings of songs and comradeship around the campfire. As for me, I began to take little walks after sunset when the road that passed our house was deserted. No one had come looking for me.

Unbeknownst to us, on August 16, the owners of some forty busses in various towns and villages of the Hérault were ordered to provide their vehicles at a yet undetermined date. They were threatened with severe sanctions should they fail to comply. Their service, they were informed, was of national character and therefore of absolute priority.

Their service was to be kept secret, but a few days later, an official in Béziers informed the underprefect that the intended measures against the Israelites had become known to them, so the effect of surprise would be lost.[3]

Charles Spirn, who had been studying in Montpellier, the provincial capital, relayed the rumors to my father when he rejoined his parents in Montagnac. And on August 25, the day Aunt Charlotte returned from the hospital with a new baby, the result of having visited Uncle Jacob before his departure for Cuba, Mala Weiss passed on a warning from the local gendarmerie that a *rafle* was planned that night.

My father, having obtained a certificate from the local doctor that he was too ill to work and still in possession of his release papers from the camp, decided he could remain home. I, of course, had to be hidden. No one imagined that the roundup might include women.

That evening, Mr. Granal led me into their "cellar"; then up a ladder to the top of a story-high wooden wine vat, thence over loose planks to the top of a concrete vat. There, among dusty discarded crates, he had arranged a hiding place for me.

Backtracking, he removed the loose planks that bridged the void between the two vats, explaining that the ones he was replacing them with were old and would not support a person's weight. Having gone down the ladder, he replaced it as well, using an old one with treacherous rungs. As he left, he took the good ladder with him. Convinced that I was safe, I slept soundly. Vaguely I remembered hearing a few shouts during the night, and the idling engine of a bus.

In the morning, I heard Mr. Granal's voice, then the sound of a ladder placed against my vat. The gendarmes, he said as his face appeared above the side, had come and gone, and all the Jewish refugees camped far out in the vineyards were safe. His tone was jovial. The gendarmes, he said, hadn't even attempted to search for them among the vines. Still, he cautioned, it would be best that I remain hidden until it was safe to come out. He poured some water into a pan for me to wash, then produced my breakfast, remarking on a particular delicacy his wife had included for me. With every meal thereafter—breakfast, lunch, or dinner—his wife included something special, and he, in his jovial tone, always pointed it out. As he left, he took the ladder down and hid it again.

I spent the next several days reading old illustrated magazines from a stack the Granals had placed up there for me. Some dated from the turn of the century. One issue had a story predicting life in 1950, which was now only eight years away. The illustrations showed modernistic buildings and vehicles, but the men in them still wore Edwardian suits and the women the hoop skirts popular at the turn of the century. I remember a telephone, the mouthpiece and earphone still separated, below which protruded a gloved hand that would transmit a handshake through a servo-mechanism. When not reading, I had another distraction: little mice that proved to be quite tame and willing to be fed.

After remaining atop the vat for perhaps a week, it was not Mr. Granal but his wife who came up the ladder one day. She brought no food and she looked distraught. She must have struggled long to get the terrible news off her chest. *"Ils ont pris ta maman,"* she said, referring to the night of the *rafle*. "They took your mummy." I clearly recall her using the word "mummy," which one uses in talking to children, not to a young man who had turned nineteen.

I remained speechless. What she said made no sense. My mother? Why her? Clearly Mme. Granal did not have the answer, and, seeing that I had nothing to say, she left.[4]

I thought long about what I had heard, but I could not comprehend it. Was my failure to report to the work camp the reason they had taken my mother? That is not done to even the worst criminal, and further, they had taken her in a *rafle* that encompassed all the refugees. But why her? It undoubtedly was an error. I had no reason to mistrust the gendarmes. It was one thing to search for shirkers evading forced labor, and quite another to hold an innocent person such as my mother in police custody. Police brutality had never been a headline in the newspapers that I had seen. I had been miffed at a policeman in Antwerp when, applying for my identity card, he had suggested "a large nose" as a distinguishing characteristic, but that had not been a serious matter. Thus I felt that I had no cause for concern. Whatever the reason for taking her, my mother would be safe under police protection.

Later, Mr. Granal came up to tell me that it was safe to go back home, and as soon as it was dark, he helped me down. I looked up and down the street and, seeing it deserted, crossed it. The door to our house was unlocked. The moment I stepped inside, I became conscious of an unaccustomed quiet. Climbing the stairs that still lacked the banister, I reached the landing to see my father, who must have heard me, come out of his bedroom, small in his oversize housecoat, looking unkempt and very old. We sat down in the living room where he showed me a letter he had already received from my mother, mailed from the camp of Rivesaltes.[5] She and my sisters were well, she wrote, giving details of the food they ate and bunks on which they slept. My sisters? Suddenly I realized why the house was so quiet. Mme. Granal had not told me everything.

Edith had joined them, my mother further wrote. Independently, my father had heard from the children's home that the police had come with orders to take her.[6] My mother must have revealed her whereabouts. "Why did she do that?" my father kept saying.

My father then told me what had happened on the night of the *rafle.* After repeated banging at the door, Aunt Charlotte had opened it. The gendarmes—they were gardes mobiles, Vichy police from out of town—wanted my family. Their commander shouted at everybody to get dressed, pack a few belongings, and be ready in a few minutes. A bus was waiting outside. My father showed him his release from camp and the certificate from the doctor. The commander agreed to let him remain at home, and my father thought that this had settled the matter. But no, the commander wanted the rest of the family, agreeing only to let the grandmothers remain. "Orders," he shouted.

My father told me that a couple of days after the *rafle,* two representatives of a Jewish organization, which my Aunt Charlotte believes was the HICEM (an alliance of groups who helped immigrants), had visited Montagnac, talking to its mayor and the gendarmes and visiting the remaining refugees. They told my father that I should come to Montpellier, where I would be given false identity papers and sent to a safe place. Presently, my father gave me the address to which I had to report. I was to take the bus to Montpellier the next day. Though I had no travel permit and was AWOL from the work camp, I would have to take the chance.

While my father and I were talking, Grandma Feldman came into the room, looking as unkempt as my father. Presently she fixed something for me to eat. I said that I didn't want to eat, but she insisted. It was perhaps the last thing she could do for me. What she prepared tasted vile. Her traditional Jewish cooking could not come to terms with the French rutabaga. Pitying my father whom I was leaving behind to eat such fare, I struggled with spoonful after spoonful. It was such a trivial event, but it stands stark in my memory.

The next day, my father bid me good-bye and gave me a kiss, something he had never done before. His last advice to me was, "Don't make any friends." I had packed but few belongings so as not to be obtrusive. Defiantly, however, I had included among these the blue velvet satchel, embroidered with a golden Star of David, given me for my bar mitzvah and containing my tallis and phylacteries. Thus I walked out of the house into the broad daylight, down the street, alone, in dread of being early, in dread of being late, daring to look neither left nor right. At the bus stop I had to wait. I was afraid of joining the small crowd there and equally afraid of attracting attention if I stood by myself. I dreaded merely being greeted. Thus I stood until the bus arrived, thus I boarded it, and thus I left Montagnac.

My mother fainted after having been taken to the local gendarmerie. A doctor was called and pronounced her unfit to be transported. She could go home, she was told. And my sisters? They would be sent to a camp. But my mother could not bring herself to abandon them. When the time came, she went with them of her own free will. Such is the warmth of a mother's love.

A young girl, Rachel Diamant (now Rubinfeld), was among those apprehended.[7] She escaped after Brigadier Cregut, a local gendarme whom she knew, told her as they were alone for a moment, "Go home, and don't show yourself again." She remembers that my mother attempted to place a long distance call from the gendarmerie to my sister Edith. She wanted to keep the family together. Did she fear that Edith would be deported independently? Aunt Charlotte may have been spared because of her newborn baby or because she was a Belgian citizen. In the early *rafles* mainly Polish, German, and stateless Jews were sought.[8] The Hirsch family were the only other people caught that night. The police released them because they were citizens of Hungary, a German ally. Mala Weiss (now Wassner) told me that she and her sister were not on the list of Jewish refugees to be deported. Their gendarme friend had seen to that. All other refugees had managed to hide. My mother and sisters were the only ones to be deported. Later, Aunt Charlotte heard from the gendarmes that had my mother consented to be sent home, they might have succeeded, as with Rachel Diamant, to save my sisters.

Convoy 31, the train on whose transport list the names of my mother and sisters appear, left Paris on September 11, 1942, carrying over a thousand deportees.[9] The French farewell, if similar to that for another recorded convoy, had "gendarmes [who] tore the women's clothing, . . . looking for jewels or money."[10] Did they suspect what the Germans were up to?

Their train arrived in Auschwitz on September 13. Of its passengers, the German jailers selected some to work; the rest were gassed immediately. Among those selected for work were seventy-eight women identified by the numbers 19530 through 19607 tattooed on their forearms. None survived.[11] They were worked to death or worse.

I have not checked further. I have gone far enough.

7
My Life as Somebody Else

WHEN I ARRIVED IN MONTPELLIER, I left the bus stop quickly. "That is where they are watching," my father had warned me. "That is where they are checking identifications." "They" were operatives and police such as those who had burst into our abode at night and now were on the alert for Jews on the run. My father had told me to walk unhesitatingly down the avenue and to hail a cab as soon as I saw one. He had given me the address of a safe house to which the cab was to take me. I was expected, he had assured me, and they would pay my fare.

I was lucky. I spotted a taxi almost immediately, and it stopped when I hailed it. But as I got in, a man followed me, pushed me over, and closed the door. Just another passenger trying to share a scarce cab, I thought. When the cabbie asked for our destinations, I, innocently, gave mine first. I realized the terrible mistake I had made as soon as the other passenger said, "That is where I go, too." He had been following me, I realized. He was no common passenger. He was an undercover policeman. And I was leading him to the safe house, betraying all inside.

As the cab rolled along, I risked a look at my pursuer. The man's eyes did not glint with the triumph of the sleuth cornering his quarry. They were downcast. He looked dispirited, as scared as I was. He must be a fellow refugee, I concluded, and we must have arrived on the same bus.

At our destination, the young woman who answered the door bell wasn't expecting two visitors. Despite our pleadings, she closed the door, saying only that she had to check. For what seemed an endless time we stood there, the two of us and the taxi driver, before she came back, paid the driver, and let us in.

I did not see my traveling companion again. The young woman led me along a corridor to a room with a bed and some furniture, pointed at a supply of reading materials, and suggested that I make myself comfortable. Later, another young woman, smiling reassuringly, entered the room and asked for my identity card. Hopefully by the end of the next day, a new identity card would be ready for me. That evening, yet another young woman led a man into the room to share it with me. Then she returned with some sandwiches, apologizing that this was all we would have for supper as food was scarce and they had no ration coupons for us.

My roommate and I hardly talked to each other. He ate his sandwich and made the couch into a bed, all the while humming a popular tune, always the same. I slept well that night, awakened next morning by my companion humming his song and a smiling young woman bringing us food.

That evening she took me to a corner of the corridor where my roommate could not hear us, told me that my identity card was ready, and that my name, henceforth, was Alfred Faubert. After the war I would learn that such identity cards had been produced by local Jewish Boy Scouts. According to my card, I was a native of Alsace, the region of France that the Germans had decided to annex. My story would be that, unable to go "home," I had enlisted in a "Groupement" of Young Workers[1] set up by the present government to accommodate dislocated French youths. This part of the story was true. A center for such workers located in the city of Le Puy en Velay had already accepted me (see map 3 in chap. 3). Its director, the young woman said, knew that he was harboring some Jewish boys, but the other boys would not be aware of this.

The next morning I was awakened before dawn. Escorted to the hallway, I met my traveling companion, introduced to me as Léon Roche. Someone who had been observing the outside through some curtains declared the street deserted, and out we went.

Roche knew the way to the train station, and we walked unhesitatingly through the empty streets. We tried to become acquainted, if that is possible when neither of us could reveal his real name or his real past. We were to discover only after the war that we had been in Agde at the same time, had both taken the photography course but somehow, with me registering late and students photographing independently and working alone in the darkroom, had either not met or failed to notice each other. That morning, on the way to the station, we talked about music. Roche, it turned out, liked jazz and was particularly enamored with the expatriate American singer Josephine Baker, who was then in her prime. I was no fan of jazz, didn't think much of Josephine Baker, and deemed Roche a shallow fellow.

Nearer the station, there was some traffic. Suddenly, as we were about to cross a street, a gendarme stopped his bicycle in front of us, blocking our way. "Your identification," he demanded.

Roche was first to produce his card. The gendarme asked, "Don't you know that a curfew is in effect?" Roche explained in a casual voice that we had enlisted in a Groupement of Young Workers and been assigned to the center in Le Puy, a hundred miles north of Montpellier, and were on our way to catch the train.

The gendarme replied that people spent the night at the station to board that train.

Roche, unperturbed, referred to the situation in France as it was, to the difficulty of our finding something to do, to our hopes with the Groupement, and so on. I noticed that as Roche chatted, the gendarme nodded in assent. I needed only to keep my mouth shut. In the end, he let us go, not even bothering to check my identity card.

I no longer thought of Roche as a shallow fellow.

At his home in Le Puy that afternoon, Mr. De Ridder was expecting us. We had come at the right time, he said, because supplies were to arrive at the "Hermitage"—the quarters where our Groupement would be lodged—and someone had to be there to receive and watch the goods.

Without further ado, he drove us some two miles out of town, stopping at an isolated building along the road. The Hermitage had formerly been a restaurant. De Ridder took us through what had been the main dining room, which would be our refectory, and to a private dining room behind it, our dormitory. The kitchen was on the other side of the entrance and above it two rooms that would serve as living quarters for the cook and our chief. In the meantime they would be ours. He left us some food and keys and drove off.

For a week or two, we loafed, cooked our meals, and talked. I learned a lot about jazz, as well as Josephine Baker's song, *"J'ai deux amours, mon pays et Paris."* Supplies arrived, among them a shipment of dark blue uniforms. These turned out to be virtually identical—down to the shoulder patches and the Gallic rooster on the bérets—to the uniforms of another creation of the Vichy government, the *Compagnons de France.* We also had time to walk to Le Puy—there was no public transportation. There, Roche decided to stop at a bar at the edge of town, the Café Bonnet. As he paid the bill, he struck up a conversation with the proprietress, told her where we stayed, and asked if we could have our mail addressed to her establishment. She readily agreed. He had done that, he told me on the way back, so that our mail would not be seen by our fellows in our Groupement.

After the supplies, the people arrived. The cook, Mr. Cartal, came first. He was to occupy our bedroom, and Roche and I moved to the dormitory. Every day a few new boys joined us. Several chiefs also arrived. One, who slept with us in the dormitory, had a Lithuanian name so unpronounceable that we called him Stanis, the only one of us to go by his first name. The rest of us went by our last names, as in the army. The next chief to arrive was Jacques Oudot. He lodged in the other upstairs bedroom. Then one day, when our number had reached its full complement of about two dozen boys, yet another chief arrived, one who did not lodge at the Hermitage. He assembled us, introduced himself as Albert Louis Bernard, and explained what had been planned for us. We would soon be sent out on work details, repairing roads, clearing land, cutting wood, and performing other public utility projects. Then he checked our uniforms, gave us tips as to how to wear them correctly, and taught us the salute. He would call, *"Jeunesse!"*[2] to which we would reply with the shout, *"France!"* We practiced that salute two or three times.

I worried about how my new identity would wear in close daily contact with the French boys. A number of these Roche and I recognized immediately as Jewish despite their French names. One of them, David Blum, I had met at the ORT in Agde. He arrived with his younger brother, Jacques, and their last name now was Rèche.

All the Jewish boys were circumcised, none of the French boys were likely to be. How would we explain that to them? The lack of hot water and showers took care of this concern. Mornings, each boy washed himself as he saw fit at a cold-water faucet in the toilets of the former restaurant. And it was not long afterward that Roche and I walked the streets of Le Puy, from barbershop to barbershop, until we found one willing to administer us a shampoo to kill head lice.

We didn't undress even when going to bed. Unaware of this custom, two Jewish boys, the brothers Peloux, innocently donned their pajamas before laying down on their first evening. Observing them from the next bunk, a French boy, Piquet, asked them what it was that they were wearing.

"Pajamas," the older one answered dubiously.

"Pajamas?"

Piquet had never seen such attire nor heard the word. On the spot, from a slang word meaning "dig that," he coined the pun, *"Pige-moi-ça!"* Wisely, the Peloux brothers slept in their underwear thereafter.

Another close call came when Piquet, having been assigned to help the chief with the paper work, noticed that a number of boys had failed to turn in their ration cards upon arrival. These must have been the Jewish boys. "That is very fishy," Piquet proclaimed loudly at mealtime after mentioning his discovery. Nobody said a word, and the matter was not mentioned again.

Having left Montagnac with my phylacteries and tallis, I occasionally slipped away early in the morning, walked unobserved past the two newly installed, open-air shower stalls, and disappeared behind the partition that screened them. There I would don my tallis, prop up my sleeve, slip the black leather noose of one of the phylacteries up my arm, and place the little black box with the scriptural passages next to my heart as the Bible commands. I would secure the box by tightening the noose, and wind the black leather thong seven times around my arm. Then I would strap the other phylactery to my forehead, close to my brain. Then back to the thong of the first phylactery, which had to be wound around my hand and fingers in a pattern recognizable as the Hebrew letters spelling *shadai,* meaning God. In this traditional attire I recited my prayers, as I had done since the age of thirteen.

I did not do this often. But why did I do it at all? I was not desperate for divine succor; I was not in imminent trouble. My prayers were, I think, a refusal to relinquish more than necessary of what was left of my normal life. They amounted also, perhaps, to a bit of defiance, an affirmation that I would not be subdued.

This could not go on for long. One morning someone discovered me. Luckily it was Roche. He remembers putting "very energetically" a stop to my prayers. He remembers also that it hurt him a long time afterwards.

A contemporary described the youths in organizations such as ours as "idle fellows, badly looked after, badly fed, not to mention [their] exploits—thefts, burglaries, etc."[3] That was, I think, because the work that had been anticipated failed to materialize. The little that turned up was not enough to keep all of us busy, and Stanis, to please those who gave us what little employment we had, did not rotate his work crew but picked always the best he had, always the same boys. That did not include me.

Our chiefs did not occupy us with busywork. Occasionally, however, they gave us lessons. Thus Chief Bernard taught us first aid. That proved handy when one evening a cyclist took a spill and came to our door for help. I was the one who doctored him, scratch by scratch, with peroxide. We were also taken sightseeing. We visited the eleventh-century chapel of St. Michel, perched atop a natural 260-foot obelisk—the core of a volcano—and reached by a stairway hewn into its solid rock. Another excursion was in the opposite direction, to the medieval keep of Polignac, erected atop an impregnable butte of basalt, another volcanic core. The region offered an inexhaustible supply of such excursions. The bizarre remainders of age-old volcanic torment had promoted pagan worship, which had mutated into destinations for Christian pilgrimages and stimulated the creation of churches, castles, and crafts. But for us, lack of transportation and the limited interests of my comrades restricted our options.

Most of the time we sat around the large potbellied stove that heated the Hermitage's refectory. One could roast chestnuts on it. If, as was more likely, one had a potato, one would slice it with a pocket knife and stick the slices against the hot metal, removing them as soon as the potato chips were done.

The first casualty of this idleness was our salute. Its practice ceased after a few mornings.

Idle hours promoted horseplay. The ladle that filled our cups with ersatz coffee at breakfast came up, one morning, with a dripping sock. It didn't stop anyone from drinking the brew. Another prank began to bedevil our nights. It had been discovered that our top-heavy bunks tipped over easily. Some boy, unable to sleep, might then entertain himself and his friends by turning over someone else's bunk. In the dark, this could be done quickly and without revealing the perpetrator, and everyone guffawed with delight as the victim had to get up in the dark, set up his bunk, pick up his things, and straighten them out. "If that should happen to me," Roche once said, "I would turn over Stanis's bunk."

And that is what I did when, one evening, I arrived at the Hermitage past bedtime. I had to find my bunk in the dark, discovered that it had been unmade, and the blanket tied in knots. Patiently, amidst snickerings in the dark, I unmade the mess. But no sooner had I laid down than someone overturned my bunk. I got up and, instead of making my bed once more, remembered Roche's advice. I overturned Stanis's bunk. No one had dared do that before. He immediately had the lights switched on, glared at me, and declared that there would be no more of this. He made his bed while I made mine, switched the lights off, and that was the end of that. He did not hold a grudge against me. We even became friends after that.

Life in our Groupement held other surprises. One day, accompanied by two of my comrades, I bought something in a small store, paying with a bill for which the merchant had to go into the back room for change. Once outside, my comrades showed me what they had pocketed during the proprietor's brief absence. Innocently, they offered to share their loot with me.

Another time, a comrade and I bought some food from a small farmer. Here there were no vineyards; here farmers had food. Before leaving, we asked the farmer for some water. In the pigsty to which he directed us, my companion was amazed to see potatoes in the slop fed to the sow. The potatoes were pea sized, but they were potatoes nonetheless, and the boy, obviously familiar with farm animals, proceeded to fight the sow for them. She was equally determined to defend her food. I was astonished at the viciousness with which he kicked her in the snout. The fight netted us a handful of the tiny potatoes.

I met not only farmers. I even met Jews. These lived in a little house in Polignac. The lady of the house happened to be outside one day as I passed by. Had she any food for sale? I inquired. No, she said, looking apprehensively at my uniform. That sufficed to make me realize that she was a stranger and probably Jewish. Not wanting to embarrass her, I walked away, but she called me back. She must have suspected that I, too, was Jewish. We talked a little, pussyfooting, afraid to come out with it. It ended with her asking me in and introducing me to a son and his friend. Thereafter, I visited them from time to time, but I never learned their true identity.

Many of the French boys at the Hermitage had problems. Malfant, on the day he came, asked me for some money. With his large, well-proportioned frame, he might have been a handsome youth, but he walked with a pronounced limp, and heavy black circles under his eyes gave his sunken face an ugly, baleful expression. He urgently needed some cash, he said, to buy some medicine that he had forgotten, along with his money, at home. How could I refuse? He promised to pay me back the next day. He didn't, of course, and I soon found out that he had tried to borrow money from the others as well. Day after day, I kept pressing him to pay me back, but he always had some excuse, always assured me not to worry, that he would pay me back. Then one day, unexpectedly, he invited me to his parents' home for dinner. His family lived in a small apartment in a working-class neighborhood. To accommodate the large family, the long table extended from the dining room almost into the kitchen. He introduced me to his parents, and everybody sat down and said grace. They all looked like very decent people and behaved nicely to me. The only person they didn't seem to care about was Malfant, who had invited me. I can only surmise that he had invited me to impress on his family that he had nice friends. I never again asked him to repay me.

Lebon was the first to leave the Hermitage. He didn't say good-bye. We heard of it only afterwards. He had transferred to some other youth center, and some of the boys went to visit him there. I joined them on subsequent visits. The center, though located in the old part of town, had quarters that were spacious and clean. I went to see him several times until I was accosted by a man whom I had seen before but to whom I had never been introduced. He was a warden, and he grilled me about Lebon's whereabouts. That youth center, I learned only then, was a correctional institution, and my friend was AWOL.

One day at that center, I had a conversation with an elderly gentleman who expressed an interest when I mentioned that I had studied photography. He invited me to lunch and afterwards showed me his business, a shop with some microfilming equipment. He microfilmed legal records for the courts, he said. It was a good business, but he was getting along in years and was looking for a capable young man to learn the business and take it over. But when he heard that I hailed from Alsace, he lost interest in me. You will return there after the war, he said. He wanted a local boy. He was ready to take his chances even with a youthful offender.

Chiaccu had been the last to arrive at the Hermitage. He was a secretive fellow who tended to sit in the back of the refectory, talk out of earshot, and stop when someone approached. But in our close quarters, the content of his conversations did not remain hidden for long. His talk was about underworld figures, his heroes. The underworld organization was particularly strong in Algeria and, he assured his listeners, getting stronger. It had its own mystique, even its own songs, and soon I knew snatches of them. Here is one that I still remember:

> After my judgment, they committed me to Cayenne
> That's where I suffered my torments and my pains
> Youth of today, don't live it up,
> As all those whores lead you to Biribi.
> *Refrain:*
> Death to the Vaches, death to the Condés
> Long live the children of Cayenne, down those of the Security.

Cayenne was a notorious penal colony. *Vaches* (cows) were gendarmes. What *Condés* referred to I never fathomed. Many were the slang expressions the boys used. *Rabiot,* for example, was a second helping at a meal. *Boulot* was work. *Piger* translates to "get it," as in Piquet's *pige-moi-ça* pun. And *putain* was one of their most frequently used expressions. It is a whore. I had never heard such language before.

This leads me to the topic that, more than any other, pervaded our conversations. During the many hours spent around the potbellied stove, on the long walks to Le Puy or Polignac, and even during the infrequent talks we boys might have in private, much of our talk centered around sex. At my home, this topic was not mentioned. As a child in Germany, I had been told that it was the stork who brought babies. I had not given the matter much thought since then. One day in Montagnac, however, this matter happened to come up in a discussion with my sister Jenny. I was horrified to hear her say that a woman had a baby by going to the toilet. That didn't seem possible to me, and we went to my mother to whom my sister repeated her statement. To my astonishment, my mother remained strangely silent.

At the Hermitage, my deficient sex education was quickly remedied. Without having to open my mouth, and with everything vouchsafed by detailed accounts of the narrator's prowess, I was introduced to the difficulties of arousing orgasm in a woman, the details of foreplay, the diverse mating positions; I learned of the use of bromides to deaden the sex drive of soldiers; I heard titillating stories about newlyweds meeting in bed for the first time, and so on and on.

My face bloomed with acne at the time, which made me doubt that I could lead a maiden to her downfall. Given our lack of privacy, I doubted that many of my comrades did. But one evening, word spread that a couple of girls had come to visit Chief Oudot and the cook. That night, we were very quiet. In the morning, we saw the girls leaving, alone, on foot. I expected that the boys would make much fun of this, but no one did.

I don't recall seeing a newspaper at the Hermitage, nor was there a radio. Still, when on November 8 the United States landed an expeditionary force in North Africa, we heard of it. Morocco and Algeria, the invasion sites, were French colonies.

A few nights later before dawn,[4] the sound of traffic awoke us. Normally a motor car was a rare occurrence here. Now we heard the rumble of wave after wave of vehicles. Some boys, who had gone to the windows to see what they could in the darkness outside, came back, saying they were German. The rest of us listened in disbelief. What was up?

After dawn, we could see them: now and then a few trucks, then a group of motorcycles, then perhaps a single car, then more motorcycles, then more trucks, often with long intervals in between. They all drove in the same direction, toward Le Puy. As the light increased, we could distinguish the telltale shape of their helmets and the green of their uniforms. They were indeed German. The French would have worn khaki.

The traffic continued all day and the next. Chief Bernard, who had been able to come by, told us not to worry, that the Germans had come only to prevent the Allies, advancing in North Africa, from landing on the French Mediterranean coast.

Other people came by. There were rumors galore. Roche heard that the Germans, arriving in Le Puy, had found an American flag draping the statue of the Marquis de Lafayette, a native of this region. He also heard of tracks being found in a farmer's fields made by American aircraft that must have landed there. The only rumor that I could subsequently verify was that Lafayette's bronze statue was unfastened and hidden one night to prevent the Germans from melting it down.[5]

When Roche asked me to teach him a few German words, I was utterly surprised when this quintessential Frenchman with his flawless speech, his Gallic manner, could repeat my German words only with a thick Polish accent. I warned him never to try that again. After the war, I learned that his real name was Kowarski.

He then told me that Stanis had approached him one morning, saying, "You talked in a funny language in your sleep." Roche's quickly contrived explanation failed to persuade Stanis, who replied, *"Mon vieux*—buddy—I know that you talked in Polish!" Then he had added, "but don't worry, I won't tell anyone." And he kept his word.

From my father I received a letter, picked up at the Café Bonnet, relating that all nonpermanent residents had been barred from a twenty-mile-wide strip[6] along the Mediterranean and that a German detachment was to be quartered in Montagnac. Every Jewish refugee in town had to find a place elsewhere to hide and quickly.

Though the Germans had also been stationed in Le Puy, I felt safe. I nonchalantly walked its streets, past parked German military cars, sizing them up and glancing at the colorful little insignia painted on their bumpers. I ignored a troop of German soldiers marching by singing. Later, I also ignored their military band as it performed to an empty public square. Never had I been so close to the feared German army. And what gave me this feeling of safety? It was this miraculous little piece of paper that I carried with me. My new identity was wearing very well.

Not long thereafter, the French people were ordered to surrender all firearms in their possession, and we in the Groupement were enlisted to assist with the collection.

Early one morning off we went, marching to Le Puy, the first time we in the Groupement had turned out in full force for work. Marching? It was, rather, a ragged, inconstant drift. Some of us straddled the road, others held to its side, some looked where they were going, others not, some talked to each other, others walked in silence. The distances among us steadily increased. I spotted a condom on the road, tossed no doubt, from a German military vehicle. I had never seen one. A few months earlier I would not have known what it was and might have picked it up. My recent education thus saved me a great embarrassment. Presently we passed by a dramatic fluted rock formation with a little souvenir shop at its base. From here the road descended into the basin from which, in the crisp, cold morning light, rose the city of Le Puy, enveloped by an immense brownish cocoon, the result of the numerous wood fires that kept its residents warm. We were headed for its municipal museum.

Inside the museum, long tables had been set up at which the guns were exchanged for receipts. We were there to carry the rifles from the tables to the halls above, empty now, their walls protected by a rough wooden wainscoting. We were not trusted with handguns or ammunition. The museum staff or the police locked these up.

The weapons ranged from ancient flintlocks to self-loading Winchesters, from hunting rifles to military ordnance, from weapons of French issue to those captured by French soldiers from the Germans and other nationalities. Some rifles had bayonets still mounted on them, some dated from the Napoleonic wars. An elderly curator who hovered around us seemed to have a thorough knowledge of weapons. Spotting me carrying some particularly handsome weapon, he would approach me, mumble that it was too valuable to surrender to the Germans, whereupon, around some out-of-sight corner, I would turn the item over to him.

After a few days, the rate of submissions began to slacken, and most of my comrades disappeared. I with nothing to do and the curator without visitors had leisure to talk. He explained to me the workings of the various firearms and then—I must have said something right—opened the museum's displays to me.

I remember only one hall. A paltry light entered through its untidily shrouded, tall windows. But once I gazed inside the staid, burnished display cases that filled the hall, nothing else mattered. Never before had I seen what I saw inside them. The cases exhibited ideas.

A rifle such as I had handled in the preceding days is so packed with inventions that it is difficult to notice them individually. This is true for just about any machine. A half century before my visit, however, a local engineer had isolated the ideas behind such inventions, stripped them of extraneous detail, and constructed for each a working mechanical model. That is what the display cases contained. Some of these models, for example, showed "rapid return" linkages. Able to follow their workings, I was fascinated by the ingenuity that had contrived to link two wheels so that while the first steadily turns, the second at first slows down, then catches up quickly before the end of the cycle. I further found it remarkable that even the simplest linkage, the translation of the linear motion of a piston into the circular motion of a wheel, had a number of implementations. One involved the use of a slide, others involved gearing, others yet depended on levers. I was surprised even more to see that each of these was known by its inventor's name. They were the Lahire and the Cartwright gears, and the Watts and Evans and Peaucellier parallelograms.[7] I could almost see the inventors in the flesh.

It had been my childhood dream to become an inventor. What a pleasure it must be, I thought, to puzzle out such things as I saw, to see one's ideas realized in gleaming metal, with jewel-like precision, and perhaps even to have them, as here, enshrined in a museum. How I would have liked to leave my mark on science! And yet how unattainable my dream seemed! I lacked a technical education, having started business school instead of college. My present pursuits were irrelevant. I performed work at which I did not excel and consorted with fellows with whom I had little in common. And my most cherished possession was a false identity card.

After the interlude at the museum, the rumor spread that our Groupement would be sent to work in Germany. Indeed, in the spring of 1943, the Hermitage closed.

Our Groupement scattered. Somehow I was boarded at a trade school, and when that didn't work out, I was appointed assistant cook at a monastery. Our kitchen served students, and my boss, it turned out, was Cartal, our cook from the Hermitage.

The monastery was an isolated place, where I learned little of what went on outside. For that matter, the Hermitage had been equally isolated. All that time I did not know, for instance, that a scant thirty miles from Le Puy there was another heaven, a small village called Le Chambon-sur-Lignon, whose three thousand inhabitants managed to hide roughly five thousand Jews,[8] most of whom did not even possess false identity cards.

Nor did I know what my erstwhile companions at the Groupement were doing. After the war, I learned that Chiaccu had not gone to Germany but joined the French Pétainiste militia. "What harm he could have caused you," Chief Bernard wrote me then. David Blum and Léon Kowarski, alias Roche, joined the Resistance. Blum had already been in contact with them while at the Hermitage. He kept the secret well. The Germans did not play games.

The father of my Montagnac friend Henri Monheit perished when the Germans came into the village into which he had moved from Montagnac, rounded up all males, and shot them in front of their wives and families.

The Resistance was not for amateurs. Its efforts had to be coordinated, its participants trained. The majority of Frenchmen with military experience were prisoners in Germany. Would-be partisans such as David Blum and Léon Kowarski lacked weapons training. The Resistance had a long and difficult task ahead.

And there were the two Weiss sisters who had remained in France. They did not join the Resistance. Yet they found themselves in a position to save lives and were not afraid to do so. Having left Montagnac, they chanced to be engaged as part-time nursemaids to the children of Mr. Racine, a French Jew and well-to-do publisher who lived then in the resort town of Aix-les-Bains. As this town happens to be located not far from the Swiss border, talk there was often about refugees attempting to sneak into Switzerland. One day Mr. Racine told Mala Weiss that to be smuggled into Switzerland was only a matter of price, but the real problem was to get near enough to the border to reach the smugglers. He had a sister and other relatives in Paris who could not even get their children out of that city. Mala talked the matter over with her sister Tilla, and the two offered to fetch the children. They traveled to Paris, talked their way out of several police checks, and brought the children to Aix-les-Bains, where the smugglers took over.

Having been successful once, they repeated their exploit several times until a gendarme became so suspicious that it was decided that the Weiss girls better cross the border with the children. They departed from Aix-les-Bains at night, by car, "packed with as many people as it could hold," Mala remembers. They rode unchallenged. When the car stopped, it was still night. They could see lights and soldiers. The driver told them that the soldiers were Swiss, that they should walk up to them and request asylum. Mala and her sister had to claim as their own the children they had brought, for the Swiss, even then, turned away Jews unless they were either over the age of sixty or had children under the age of seven.

The Weiss girls' enterprise was not as foolhardy as it may seem. An identity card like mine, which showed its owner to be a resident of the inaccessible Alsace, might have aroused by then the suspicions of a sophisticated gendarme. But the Weiss sisters could flaunt identity cards showing that they hailed from Montagnac. These showed, too, that their family name was Bringuier. That was the mayor's family name. He had issued these cards to the girls when they left Montagnac. Mala Weiss became Juliette Bringuier, and Tilla Weiss became Madeleine Bringuier. The mayor was ready to head off any inquiry by confirming that they were indeed his daughters.[9]

Still in the spring of 1943, I received a letter from my father. It was postmarked in Nice, the center of the Riviera, near the Italian border. The Germans had not occupied the entire southern zone of France. A part of it, along the Italian border, had been occupied by their allies the Italians. Unbelievably, my father urged me to join him there. The Italians, he wrote in veiled terms, protected the Jews from both the French police and the Germans!

Next he wrote me from St. Martin-Vésubie, a small town high in the Alps. The Italian military had placed him there in forced residence. Still he urged me to come.

Map 4. *November 11, 1942, to September 8, 1943. The lines show Alfred's path from Le Puy en Velay to Gorrè. France was divided into German and Italian occupied zones in this time period.*

Feeling quite safe at the monastery, I was not eager to leave. But when Roche informed me that he was going to Grenoble, also in the Italian zone, I decided to come along (see map 4).

To be nearer the railway station in the morning, Chief Bernard offered to put us up for our last night at the Hotel du Chapon Rouge, which his in-laws owned in Le Puy. The manager gave each of us a room on a floor reserved for the Germans. Only one officer stayed there, he said, and it wasn't likely that we would meet him. What we did meet in the bedrooms were bedbugs, so many that I kept my lights on all night, unable to get much sleep.

We went to Grenoble not by train but by bus, on which searches were less likely. We arrived without incident. Grenoble was a much larger city than Le Puy and much busier. Its streets were full of people and of crowded streetcars and buses. Everywhere Italian soldiers mixed with the people or, at least, were not shunned. And what uniforms they had! Their military police, the carabinieri, wore bicornes, the Alpini had feathers in their mountaineers' hats, and the Bersaglieri, the soldiers of their crack rifle corps, roared off on motorcycles, a sheaf of black cockerel feathers tossing over their helmets. These were their field uniforms, I was told. Their regular outfits were even more splendid.

The French police were also busy. I was on an overcrowded trolley car when they stopped it to check identities. I overheard a lady next to me confiding to her companion that, on another such police action, someone had ducked behind her to avoid the police. He must have been a criminal, she said, but she had not betrayed him. A criminal? I wondered how people could still be that naïve? My identity card got but a cursory glance.

An aunt of Roche put us up on our first night in Grenoble. She lived in an upscale hotel whose management obliged her by setting up two cots for us in an adjoining pavilion. The next night the pavilion was rented for a party. But Roche's aunt knew of a rabbi who ran an orphanage about a dozen miles outside Grenoble, in the village of Voiron. She arranged for me to stay there.

The orphanage was in a beautiful villa. The rabbi—it was Zalman Chneerson—had his office in a sunny, high-ceilinged, well-appointed room, with an attractive secretary. But I had nothing to do, and after a few days, I was made to understand that my stay there could be permanent only if I joined the rabbi's organization. That I was not prepared to do. The secretary offered to take me back to Grenoble and put me up temporarily at her apartment, which she shared with a girlfriend. I actually spent one night there, but the woman's boyfriend, coming for a visit, was not pleased. I went back to the hotel where Roche's aunt lodged. She was not there, nor was Roche, and the management said, sorry, but their pavilion was rented for a party that evening. Then, not wanting to leave me out in the cold, they contacted the renter, a group of medical students celebrating their graduation. They had no objection to my sleeping beside the entrance, and I fell asleep amidst the noise and bawdy songs of the party.

In my attempts to find another lodging, I remember going to a cloister that, I heard, offered a bed to anyone who came. It was out in the countryside. I was admitted into the entrance hall in which a partition similar to that used in old-style banks separated the nuns from the visitors. Yes, one said, they could accommodate me. Soon a nun took me to a building and up some stairs and showed me a room with a bed, looking much like a hospital room, crisp and clean. In the morning, she said, all I had to do was close the door after I left. There were no other guests, and in the morning I left as directed, without encountering anyone. I did not return to this place.

Weary of the struggle for a place to sleep, I succumbed to my father's entreaties to join him at St. Martin-Vésubie. He had given me detailed instructions. Don't take the train to Nice, he had warned me, because it stops in Marseilles, outside the Italian zone of occupation, and one's papers are examined very thoroughly there. Instead I was to go by tour bus that followed a road through the mountains that remained entirely in the Italian zone. And so I did. The trip was spectacular. To take the hairpin turns, the bus had to back up, which more than once brought the back of the vehicle over an abyss, to the screams of the passengers looking out the windows there. The driver, however, knew his business and got us to Nice by evening, safely and on time.

The next morning, following my father's instructions, I went to see a Mr. Weinstein, who would assist me in surrendering to the Italian authorities. In his small office, he informed me that the Italians were swamped with people begging to be interned. He would place me on a waiting list.

He asked for my current identification, then filled in a mimeographed receipt that, as paper was scarce in France, used but a third of a sheet. It read:

> I, the undersigned, WEINSTEIN Georges, Delegate of the Welcoming Committee for Israelite Refugees, 24 Boulevard Dubouchage, Nice, state herewith of having accepted today Mr. Feldman Alfred, born August 7, 1923, in Hamburg, who is inscribed on our lists of departures No. XXXI and who will receive in the future his convocation for forced residence assigned by the Italian Authorities.
>
> This certificate is valid until July 5, 1943.
>
> Nice, the June 25, 1943
> Signed: G. Weinstein

It was stamped with the seal of the Israelite Cultural Association of the Ashkenazic Rite, in Nice.

Mr. Weinstein said, "This can be renewed, and it suffices to remove you from French jurisdiction."

I asked him for the identity card that I had handed him. This was not the card the Boy Scouts had made for me in Montpellier. This was not a falsified piece of paper but a duly registered document. "National" identity cards were introduced while we were in Le Puy, and Roche had determined to get these. Our best ploy, he had decided, was to present ourselves at the mairie of a small town, which would have little experience with them. Indeed, when the two of us showed up at the mairie of Brives-Charensac, the young employee there had the new cards issued to us without even asking for supporting documents. Roche wonders to this day whether she was just lax or whether, on the contrary, she helped because she recognized us for what we were.

It was this card that Mr. Weinstein now refused to return to me, explaining that running around with two different identities would be very dangerous. "That would make you a criminal," he said, "subject to arrest by the French police." From that card, he peeled off my photograph, and handed it to me. Then he dropped the card into a drawer, and thus ended my life as somebody else.

By an absurd quirk of fate, it was safer now to be a Jew.

Left to right: Alfred's father, Joachim Feldman; Alfred's mother, Paula; her mother, Scheindel Chaja Bauminger; and her husband, Isaac Bauminger. Hamburg, Germany, 1920s. Author's collection.

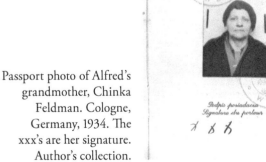

Passport photo of Alfred's grandmother, Chinka Feldman. Cologne, Germany, 1934. The xxx's are her signature. Author's collection.

Aunt Betty Knoll and her son Simon. Cologne, Germany, 1935. Author's collection.

Left to right: Alfred's sisters Jenny and Hella, Alfred's cousin Ines Rosenbaum, and Alfred's sister Edith at the beach. Knokke, Belgium, summer 1938. Author's collection.

Left to right, and top to bottom: Alfred's sisters Edith, Hella, and Jenny and Alfred's mother. Antwerp, Belgium, ca. 1939. Author's collection.

Jewish refugee children. *Front row, left to right*: Max Schiff, David Bauminger, Eve Bauminger, Rachel Bauminger, Hélène Schiff; *Second row, left to right*: Peshu Weiss, Sarah Diamant, Edith Feldman, Ernestine Spirn; *Third row, left to righ*t: Edith Schiff, Israel Diamant, Menachem Horowitz, Jacques Schiff, Jérôme Hirsch; *Last row, left to right*: Alfred Feldman, Rahel (Hella) Feldman, Taubé Spirn, Jenny Feldman, Rachel Diamant. Montagnac, France, ca. 1941. Photo taken by a representative of the Œuvre de secours aux enfants.

Title page of the hand-written Passover Haggada. Montagnac, France, 1941. Author's collection.

CARTE D'IDENTITÉ
8e Groupe de Travailleurs Étrangers

Card identifying
Alfred as a member
of the Eighth Group
of Foreign Workers.
Montagnac, France,
1942. Author's
collection.

Alfred and his father.
St. Martin-Vésubie,
France, summer 1943.
Author's collection.

View of the French side from the Cherry Pass. Photo by Patrick Ormea.

View of the Italian side from the Cherry Pass. The fog in the valley in September 1943 was much higher. Photo by Patrick Ormea.

The valley of the Bial, toward Rittana, Italy. The buildings at the bottom of the valley are in Tanara. The cave of San Mauro is in the cliff above and to the right. Author's collection, photo taken after the war.

The mule path from Rittana, Italy, to Gorrè, before it was paved after the war. Author's collection, photo taken after the war.

Second story entrance to the drying shed in Gorrè Sottano, Italy. The two stone steps leading to the door are missing. The building to the right was built after the war. Author's collection.

Basement entrance to the drying shed in Gorrè Sottano, Italy. Author's collection, photo taken after the war.

Nationalsozialistische Deutsche Arbeiterpartei

Parteigenossen!

Der Feind ist in Deutschland eingebrochen und die Horden der bolschewistischen Plutokraten-Söldlinge besudeln den heiligen Boden des Vaterlandes. Es ist derzeit unmöglich, sie zu vertreiben, aber das darf nicht das Ende des Krieges bedeuten.

Solange es uns nicht gelingt, den Feind restlos und für immer zu besiegen, solange muss der Krieg eben andauern. Gewiss, es wird der feindlichen Soldateska infolge ihrer feigen Uebermacht an Menschen und Material auch weiter gelingen, unsere Städte und Dörfer zu besetzen; aber was bedeutet das? Die Berge und Wälder müssen unser bleiben, dann können wir den Kampf noch Jahrelang fortsetzen. Der Feind kann ja nicht an jede Brücke, hinter jeden Felsen einen Wachtposten stellen und kann nicht jede Almhütte oder jeden Kohlenweiler besetzen.

Im Geiste der alten Germanen, Florian Geyers, Andeas Hofers und Schlageters muss die kämpfende Volksgemeinschaft den Widerstand bis aufs Messer fortsetzen. Auch unsere Frauen und Kinder müssen lernen, nicht nur mit sicheren Schüssen die Feinde niederzustrecken, sondern auch mit gut geführten Messerstössen sich zur Wehr zu setzen, wenn feindliche Patrouillen sich ihnen nähern.

Kein deutsches Mädchen würde sich so weit erniedrigen, einem Soldaten der Feindmächte auch nur zu antworten. Da hat unsere ganze Ausbildung einzusetzen. Wenige Wochen Schulung werden jedes tapfere deutsche Mädchen lehren, wie man scheinbar den Werbungen dieser geilen Burschen nachgibt und sie im entscheidenden Augenblick mit einem geschickten Handgriff oder einem schnellen Scherenschnitt entmannt.

Wenige Jahre eines solchen zielbewussten, verzweifelten Widerstandes werden den Gegnern jede Lust nehmen, weiter auf deutschem Boden zu verweilen.

All diese Pläne bedürfen natürlich genauer Vorbereitung. Schon heute muss jeder Parteigenosse beginnen, Handwaffen und Lebensmittel an versteckten Plätzen in Wald und Feld zu vergraben, er muss sich einsame Bergalmen oder eine Höhle unwegsamem Gelände aussuchen, wo er halbwegs gegen die Unbilden des kommenden Winters geschützt sein wird, er muss wieder das bodenständige Wissen unserer Ahnen erlernen, sich der Beeren und Kräuter des Waldes für seinen Unterhalt zu bedienen, um so und seine Kinder wenigstens notdürftig vor Hunger und Kälte zu bewahren. Weitere Anweisungen folgen.

Im Geiste des Trutzliedes aus den Bauernkriegen:

Geschlagen ziehen wir nach Haus,
Unsere Söhne fechten's besser aus!

Heil Hitler!
NSDAP Ausbildungsleitung Buschkrieg

München, im Dezember 1944.

Although the writing is in German and the emblem the Nazi swastika, this is a propaganda leaflet dropped by Allied planes near Gorrè, Italy, ca. 1945. Author's collection.

Hector and Delphine Janssens. Antwerp, Belgium, 1940s. Author's collection.

Clockwise: Leon and Maria Janssens, their daughter Gilberte, and Goldine Ehrenfeld. Bruges, Belgium, ca. 1944. Author's collection.

Alfred Feldman and his father, Joachim, toward the end of 1945. Author's collection.

Goldine Ehrenfeld.
Antwerp, Belgium, 1947.
Author's collection.

Left to right: Lt. Gen. A. W. Betts; Philip, Suzanne, Frances, and Alfred Feldman, at the presentation of an award for invention. Washington, D.C., 1970. Author's collection.

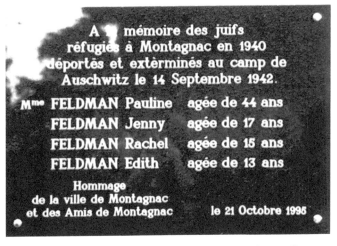

Memorial plaque, unveiled in Montagnac, 1995. Author's collection.

8
A Biblical Migration

A STEEP RISE OF THE ROAD, just before St. Martin-Vésubie, forced the bus driver to downshift so that the little bus entered town with a roar. But that road had yet another distinction, which I did not become aware of until two months later. The road did not extend beyond the town. At St. Martin-Vésubie, it reached a dead end.

Upon my arrival I was relieved to find my father looking fit again. During our yearlong separation, I had been haunted by my last sight of him in our silent and empty residence in Montagnac. Now, however, he seemed himself again, sociable and argumentative, and with plenty of people to talk to.

The number of people in St. Martin-Vésubie surprised me. They walked in the streets, stood around the bus stop, sat in outdoor cafés, or whiled away the time on the benches of the little park. I heard them speaking in French, German, even Yiddish. They all were Jews.

Their influx had begun the previous November, as soon as the Italian army had occupied the French Riviera. Why did we Jews trust them? Was Italy not one side of the Nazi-Fascist Axis? Had it not promulgated racial laws?[1] Barred Jewish children from public schools? Dismissed Jews from its army and the civil service? And now, like Germany, it interned Jews—albeit, for the time being, only foreign Jews? Yet like everyone else, I knew that there was a difference. We did not know the nature of this difference. Nor did we know how ceaselessly the Germans pressured their Italian allies to surrender the Jews in their occupied territories in France and Yugoslavia. Unable to persuade the Italian army, they pressed Mussolini. Whereupon his deputy in the Foreign Ministry, Giuseppe Bastianini, confided to the dictator: "Our people know what fate awaits the Jews consigned to the Germans. . . . our people will never permit such atrocities to take place with their connivance. And you,

Duce," he advised, "may not give your consent. Why do you want to assume a responsibility which will fall on you entirely?"[2]

That was the spirit that made the difference. That was the spirit of which we had become aware. Though everyone in forced residence, my father included, had to report at the carabinieri headquarters twice a day, Jews surged into the Italian-occupied sector. Mussolini had to appoint a special delegate to manage this "biblical exodus," as he called it.[3, 4] Even so, the authorities could not keep up with the influx, which is why I had been placed on a waiting list in Nice.

It took me one week to get a seat on the little bus to St. Martin-Vésubie. According to records, this town had 225 persons in enforced residence. Four or five times that many refugees actually stayed there, like me, illegally.

The slip of paper Mr. Weinstein had given me in Nice soon expired. It could not be renewed in St. Martin-Vésubie. My father assured me that it didn't matter. When in the past, the French police had attempted to check the identities of people in enforced residence, or even to arrest them for black marketeering, the Italian military had warned them not to overstep their authority. Thereafter the French police had avoided contact with any refugee. They had no way of knowing who was and who was not in enforced residence.

Despite the crowding, or perhaps in response to it, the Jewish community was well organized.[5] It operated a refectory, where my father and I ate our meals even though the tiny walk-up efficiency apartment that I now shared with him had a small kitchen range.

The community also maintained a synagogue, a school for children, and, in the nearby town of Berthemont, a nursing home for the aged. An American Jewish organization, informally called the "Joint,"[6] distributed an allowance to those in need. An elected committee represented the refugees before the Italian carabinieri and saw to the implementation of the latter's ordinances. This committee further functioned as an information center. With press and radio censored, with foreign broadcasts jammed and few people having access to radio anyway, the tidbits of information the committee obtained from the carabinieri were invaluable.

My father had taken his mother with him when he left Montagnac. She was now sheltered in the Jewish nursing home. I visited her regularly, sometimes with my father, sometimes alone. A spacious wooden deck extended from the building. Furnished with comfortable easy chairs, it was open to the cool air and offered a great view of the valley. That is where Grandmother and I would sit and talk.

One crisis that had her up in arms was about a vacant bed to which Mr. and Mrs. Kahn, the couple managing the nursing home, wanted to reassign one of their charges. Every resident objected as that bed's former occupant had recently died in it. My grandmother regaled me with a running account of the Byzantine politics played out in this contest. But she also talked about her past, about which she found me an attentive listener. She recalled events from her girlhood, one of which was the signing of the Triple Alliance. People had danced in the streets then, she remembered, because there would be no more wars. She may have been talking of the pact signed in 1882 (when she was twenty-two) by Germany, Austria, and Italy that placed the two remaining continental powers, France and Russia, at such military disadvantage as to make war inconceivable.

On that deck I heard also for the first time that my mother was my father's second wife. His first wife had died in childbirth, with the child.

All that summer, a fire burned in the valley. It was not put out. Perhaps it burned in places too inaccessible; perhaps firefighters were not available. On some days it remained unnoticed, brooding in some unnoticed crevices. But it might flare up unexpectedly. Smoke and even flames could then be seen. Occasionally a hazy pall covered the entire valley, and on some afternoons that haze advanced the sunset, prematurely decorating the sky with brilliant reds. Sitting on the deck, looking at this glow, my grandmother would insist that it was the sign of a terrible battle being fought, and she worried for her children.

Had she once seen the sky redden in the course of a battle? Had she once heard an account of such an event? My attempts to enlighten her of the real cause of our red sunsets were to no avail.

My father rarely reported to me the bits of news he gathered during his visits at the committee. But one day he reported that two Jews who had managed to escape from a German concentration camp in Poland had arrived in Nice. They warned everyone that in that camp, the Germans killed Jews. This information, he said, was absolutely dependable. He said no more, but after the war I learned that these two had been caught in Nice in the *rafles* of 1942, sent to Auschwitz, from where they managed to escape, and returned to Nice.[7] What they reported about Auschwitz was as unimaginable as their odyssey.

I still remember the vision this news evoked in my mind. It was of captives fighting for their lives in Roman arenas. Of course, I immediately dismissed the thought of gladiator games in Poland, yet I couldn't imagine the nature of the German killings. Indeed, without some hint, only a very sick mind would conjure up visions of individuals stripped of their clothing and gassed with industrial efficiency, trainload after trainload after trainload.

The world outside already knew this truth. Six months earlier, on March 1, 1943, nearly forty thousand people agitated at Madison Square Garden, in New York, for some way to stop Hitler's massacres.[8] But for such news to reach us, it had to penetrate the Nazi occupation, bypass censored press and mails, avoid the jamming that foreign radio broadcasts were subjected to, and withstand our natural suspicion of blatant war propaganda. Not even living eyewitnesses could convey such depravity. Trusting that the absence of mail from my mother and sisters was due to the disruptions of the war, I did not relate their fate to the escapees' report, to which I gave no further thought.

Nor could I have known that Aunt Klara and her three oldest children had been rounded up in Antwerp at about the same time as my mother,[9] nor that my Aunts Jettchen and Minna and Minna's youngest child, Nelly, had died of malnutrition and exposure in Siberia. Guilelessly, I kept reassuring my grandmother that the blood red sunsets were no cause for worry. But she knew better.

Who should I encounter in town but David Blum and his brother! Even more surprising, Cousin Moyne and his wife Regine had made it to St. Martin-Vésubie. Ever resourceful, he had bought a truck as the Germans approached Antwerp in 1940, leaving not only with his family and belongings but also taking Aunt Klara and her family along. They had left too late, however. The German advance to the sea had cut them off. About four weeks later they were back in Antwerp. Nevertheless, eventually he had managed to bring his family to France, where he had made arrangements to hide his three children. Now he resided with his wife in a luxurious villa that offered a breathtaking view of the valley. The Chalet Reseda was a bit crowded; they had to share it with other refugees. They had a bedroom, one corner of the drawing room, and access to the kitchen. The villa's expensive furniture included a player piano, an unusually ornate, splendid thing that stood in the middle of the drawing room. And it was loud. Before I could play it, I had to get permission from all the families sharing the chalet. It had been a long time since I had listened to music, and I enjoyed operating the thing. But it also takes a receptive mood to enjoy music. And that mood we owed to the news of the war.

What a difference a year can make! When I left Montagnac at the end of the summer of 1942, the Germans' breakneck advance in the south of Russia had brought them almost within smelling distance of the Caucasus oil fields. In North Africa, Rommel had entered Egypt, pushing into El Alamein, a mere sixty miles from the Suez Canal. Had he reached the canal, he would have disrupted the supply lines of the British Empire, made the Mediterranean a German sea, opened up a sea link with Japan, and fanned Arab revolts seething in Palestine and elsewhere. Since then, instead, the Russians had encircled the Germans in Stalingrad, obtained their surrender, and regained much of their territory. The Americans and the British had cleared Africa of German troops. Here in France no amount of prevarications by the censored press could minimize the enormity of these German defeats. And no sooner had I arrived in St. Martin-Vésubie than Anglo-American forces invaded Sicily. Sicily! They were getting close to us!

What a difference, also, in how people now took to the news! For the first two years of the war, one had feared to look at a newspaper's headlines. Reading the war communiqués had become self-inflicted pain. But now news was eagerly awaited. Whomever I encountered commented gleefully about the latest saturation air raid over Germany, or about the town most recently taken in Sicily, or about the German summer offensive in Russia, which had been stopped in a single week.

The lusty clangor of the player piano was not just music to be enjoyed after a long deprivation. It was a celebration of these wonderful events.

As the summer progressed, further evidence accumulated about the irremediable change in the tide of war. On July 24, Mussolini was deposed and arrested. The next day, Marshal Pietro Badoglio, appointed to run the Italian government, abolished the Fascist regime. My father spent almost the entire day at the committee.

Some surprising news was heard there. Angelo Donati, a banker in Nice with contacts among the higher Italian authorities, had chartered four ships to transport Jewish refugees from Nice to liberated North Africa. These ships, already painted with Red Cross colors, had been used earlier to transport Italian civilians from East Africa back to Italy. From the various forced residences in the region, refugees already were beginning to converge on Nice.[10] My father, however, did not mention any of this to me.

Cousin Moyne now decided that his six-year-old daughter Zilla should come to St. Martin-Vésubie. He wrote to the teacher who was hiding her and gave me the letter to mail. A few days later, he changed his mind, and asked me if, perchance, I still had the letter. Only then did I remember that it was still in my pocket. Loath to admit this, having no idea what the letter was about, I mailed it the same day. In due time, Zilla arrived. Had I stuck with the truth, her fate, as I shall relate, would have been very different. Such could be the consequences in those times of a teenager's conceit.

The news that reached us gave no intimation of such consequences. On August 17, Allied troops entered Messina, completing the conquest of Sicily. On September 3, they crossed the Straits of Messina to the mainland of Italy, encountering little resistance. Five days later, on September 9, the news spread like wildfire that Italy had surrendered.

And the very next day, we were fleeing before the advancing Germans.

As soon as we heard of Italy's surrender, my father, like virtually every refugee, had gone to the committee. When he returned for lunch, he told me that the Italian army was withdrawing from France and that it was clear that their place would be taken by the Germans. The committee had recommended unanimously that we should follow the Italians. "Pack our belongings," my father said before returning to the crowd that besieged the committee.

Returning home that evening, my father told me that already people were leaving.

I made a knapsack out of a blanket, folding it and tying its corners with the strings that would serve as shoulder straps, but keeping the blanket whole so that it could be used again. Camping with the Boy Scouts above Lake Geneva that summer before the war, I had gained some experience with backpacks and mountains.

The next morning, September 10, I packed the knapsack with all the food we had, packed the blue velvet satchel that held my tallis and phylacteries, packed my father's as well, added a prayer book and a Hebrew Bible, filled what space remained with some warm clothing, and tied another blanket over the top. My father sought to inform my grandmother of what we were about to do. Wanting to remain within earshot of the committee, he attempted to do this by phone. In the end, I believe, he managed to bid her farewell only by letter.

About noon, my father returned from the committee with the news that the Germans were already on their way to St. Martin-Vésubie. I immediately shouldered my backpack, and we left, abandoning the suitcases and boxes into which I had packed the bedding, my father's suits and things, all labeled and neatly stacked against the wall in my father's apartment.

How different this flight was from our flight from Belgium when the Germans attacked it in 1940! Then we rode by car and spent days tied up in traffic. Now we walked, taking along only what I could carry. My father, wearing his usual suit, overcoat, shoes, and a French béret that had replaced his hat years ago, looked as if he were going for a little walk into town.

We had no leader, no directions. The Jewish organization had collapsed literally overnight. A remnant of the committee hung in there as long as the carabinieri remained. Still, there was no panic. As my father and I crossed the stone bridge over the Vésubie that led out of town, trying to decide where to go next, we saw a refugee waiting there for someone. "It's everyone for himself," he said. It was a sentence I was to hear several times that day. Beyond we saw scattered groups of package-toting people walking along a dirt road. We followed them. We didn't know that from St. Martin-Vésubie two trails led into Italy over two different passes. The one we happened to take crossed the *Colle di Ciriegia*, the Cherry Pass. It didn't matter; both crossings were of comparable difficulty (see map 5).

The road was level and wide enough to accommodate cars, of which, however, there weren't any. My father and I walked alongside each other. Now that we were on our way, the impatience and the fretting were over. The walk seemed no more than an ordinary hike. We talked to each other. My father said that Cousin Moyne and he had agreed to proceed independently. It was truly everyone for himself. I asked him about Italy. As a young man, he had often traveled to that country. He even remembered a little of its language. Could he teach me some? I recall that he mentioned the word *bambino,* which means "child." What a lovely word, I thought, so similar to the French *bambin,* and yet how much bounce and play it evoked just because of the extra *o.* Next, I got a little grammar.

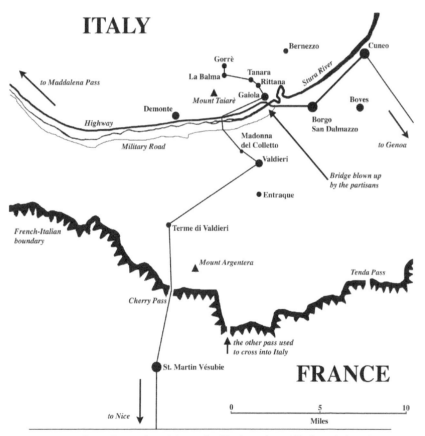

Map 5. *September 1943 to May 1945. The lines show Alfred's path from St. Martin-Vésubie to Gorrè, all done on foot.*

The letter *o,* my father pointed out, ends all masculine words in the singular, the letter *a* all feminine words. Thus *bambino* refers to a small boy, *bambina* to a small girl. Similarly, the letter *i* ends all masculine words in the plural, and the letter *e* all feminine words. Therefore *bambini* denotes small boys, and *bambine* small girls. None of the languages I knew had so simple a grammar. How many languages, I tried to determine, would I know after I learned Italian?

Here and there along the roadside, mountain folk, whose houses could be glimpsed through the trees, had set up makeshift tables from which they sold refreshments and food. Wanderers stopped there and put down their baggage, resting for a while. The refreshments sold "at outrageous prices," said the tired ones. Yet the road, still flat, had not even reached the trail that would lead us across the mountain.

The trail began inconspicuously from the side of the dirt road. It was unmarked and half hidden by underbrush. Had we not seen the group walking ahead of us turn off the road, we would have missed it. A couple of men standing at that spot saw to it, however, that we would not. Yes, they said, this path led to the trail. Access to it farther on, was not possible because a bridge down the road was impassable. This path was a detour. It would cross another path, and there we should turn left. I do not know whether these men had been posted there or whether they stayed only until someone else agreed to relay these instructions.

Nothing about this trail was unusual. Nothing betrayed its antiquity. Only much later did I learn that mountain paths, hemmed in by slopes, streams, and rocks, change little over the years. In particular, the trails that cross the Alps, already mentioned in the writings of ancient Rome,[11] have endured since time immemorial. The movement of animals perpetuates their trace as well as the traffic of occasional migrants, of merchants in bygone days, of smugglers in more recent times, and presently of an incongruous, scattered throng of men and women, young and old, with children, even babes in arms. All had traveled under risky circumstances before, eluding the French police and evading their German pursuers. But of the mountains surrounding St. Martin-Vésubie, few had any knowledge. Those in forced residence had not ventured outside the small restricted area to which they had been confined, and those

who, like me, were illegals had, of course, behaved likewise. Few
had any familiarity with mountain climbing.

Suddenly evidence of this unpreparedness stared at me. Our
path, upon leaving the dirt road, started to climb sharply, and there,
abandoned in the underbrush, I saw one suitcase and then another,
this one half open, still fully packed. Suddenly this path felt like no
other I had ever walked upon.

I had forgotten to watch for the crossing, but my father, walking
behind me, noticed it. Unsure whether the cleared underbrush was
really a path, we stopped, turning into it after we heard voices from
that direction. The new path was broader and more level, and we
walked on it all afternoon, hardly ever out of earshot of other people
walking. Now and then a band of Italian soldiers overtook us. They
carried neither backpacks nor weapons, and no officer commanded
them. It was obvious that the Italian army had disbanded. *"Passi
lunghi e piani,"* they exhorted us, "Take long and slow steps."
Occasionally we encountered soldiers who had joined a group of
refugees, carrying their suitcases and even their children.

"It was almost a biblical migration," one of our fellow refugees
recorded later.[12]

Unexpectedly, I encountered David Blum, the only person walking in the opposite direction. I was incredulous. Were they aware
of the Germans at St. Martin-Vésubie? David said only something
about being responsible for some people left behind and went on.
I never expected to see him again. But fifty years later, he told me
that the Resistance had sent them to reconnoiter the path, to make
sure that the rest of us could get through.

It was nearly dark when the forest opened up onto a clearing. A
huge campfire lit a wide circle of huddled and exhausted bodies.
The clearing was evidently a collection point for a logging operation,
for to one side I saw several soldiers removing a tree trunk from a
stack. With much effort, they carried it toward the fire that, fed by
whole tree trunks, gave off a heat so intense as to keep the soldiers
from approaching it. I wanted to watch how they would place their
tree trunk atop this fire, but my father insisted that we couldn't stay
here, that the fire was too bright, that the Germans would surely see
it from afar. I shouldered my knapsack, whose strings, unmindful
of the padding arrangements that I had tried, cut into my sore flesh.
We trudged along in the increasing darkness and came upon another

fire of similar size. Again my father said, "The Germans will surely see it," and again we trudged on. Then we reached yet another fire, and there we collapsed.

In St. Martin-Vésubie, at that time, not every Jew had departed. Bronka Halpern, with whom we would become acquainted later, was one of these. Walking past a local inn that evening, she was surprised to see all its windows lit up. Then she noticed an armed German soldier standing guard at its entrance. Full of fear, she went to her house, woke up the children, and dressed them. "Although we feared that the Germans might begin a roundup anytime," she recalled, " . . . it took us until half past one o'clock in the morning before we were ready." Walking in the dark, striking a match from time to time, they found the path no less dangerous than the Germans.[13]

All that was fear, only fear. The man whom Bronka had perceived as a sentinel could not have been a German. The German military did not arrive in St. Martin-Vésubie until a week or so later.[14]

It was not the gray dawn but the cold that woke me early the next morning. Never having slept under an open sky before, I felt stiff and forlorn. My father, already awake, seemed to hover over me. Were we alone? No. The people around us had moved closer to the fire as it subsided. Most of them already had departed. The few who remained seemed far away. Still asleep, they appeared to be scattered heaps of clothing. It had rained during the night, my father said, but I had slept right through it. As we made ready to leave, my father discovered that his wedding ring was missing. The cold must have shrunk his finger, he surmised. In the feeble morning light he began searching through the low bramble that covered the ground. Nothing. By the remains of the fire, a heap of clothing stirred, then some next to it, and soon the people rose and ponderously walked off. My father was still searching. I mentioned that since we had left so much behind already, what difference did a ring make? But my father persisted and did recover his ring. Our spirits raised, we were off.

Abruptly we reached the end of the woods. Here a steep, barren slope stood in our way. Our path turned sideways, seemingly avoiding it but actually zigzagging up. Looking upward, the path was not visible beyond the first switchback; its zigzags, however, could be inferred from the locations and directions of the groups of people scattered over that slope. The distance to be climbed was evident from the small size of the people near its top.

The first couple of switchbacks raised us above the trees, taking us from the confinement of the woods into the openness of the heights. The view encompassed immense distances and tall peaks under a wide sky. Watching my steps, fending off the smarting straps of my knapsack, I paid it little attention. The ascent must have taken an hour. Only when, finally, we cleared the top and rested did I take in the view. Then I looked at the path ahead. Punctuated by groups of walking people, it could be discerned for some distance. It followed the crest of a ridge that dipped disconcertingly, losing some of our hard-won height, only to rise yet higher beyond. The next height too was followed by a dip and a yet higher ascent, and so it went. I had no will left to look after my father, who followed me without a complaint. I determined never to go near mountains again.

As we moved higher, the surrounding mountains seemed to rise as well. It gave the scenery an imposing, even alarming appearance. I became aware of this only about noon when, ahead, the relatively gentle ridge that we had been following met the wide sweep of a jagged wall of rocks. It stretched for a considerable distance, all along which our path could be seen hanging halfway up. Had I not been reassured by the sight of scattered groups of refugees progressing there, I might have been reluctant to venture onto this stretch, hewn into sheer rock, where the cliff to our right offered little to hold on to, where one didn't dare to look down, and where anyone coming from the opposite direction would have no room to pass. I had seen nothing like this with the Boy Scouts. My father and I kept walking, not uttering a word. After a while we passed a lugubrious casemate incongruously protruding from the rocks. Then, unexpectedly, the path widened, turned sharply right around some hulking rocks, and abutted on a precipice. We had reached the pass.

Fellow refugees rested here and armed soldiers offered us water and canned army rations. Again and again they assured new arrivals that they could keep any Germans at bay. Indeed, behind the pass a small but trim military post was tucked into the rocks, complete with a bit of parade ground and a flag flapping in the breeze. Obviously some well-camouflaged guns must have been trained on that dizzying path. We refugees, no longer in fear of Germans in pursuit, had time to dawdle, to talk, and, from this altitude of about 8,000 feet, to open our eyes to the new scenery that had replaced the one familiar from our long ascent. A soldier came up to me, and speaking French, pointed at the peaks and told me their names.

It was the time of year when the color of the fall foliage reaches its peak. It was a panorama in which a botanist earlier in the century admired the "stern hostility and magnificence," the "tumbled and wild . . . mountains," and the "gaunt spars and precipices and pinnacles of naked granite" of the Argentera,[15] the Maritime Alps' tallest peak, which, seen through a gap in the rocks, rose straight out of a blue mist that filled the valley, contending with my fresh recollections of the fear that had propelled us to the pass, the huge campfires, and the abandoned suitcases.

Our descent took but a few hours. Soon we were among trees, and before dark we walked on a road bordered, here and there, by houses. These too had makeshift tables in front of them; here too people offered us water and food, mostly canned army rations. But here the people did not ask for money.

They directed us to a resort hotel nearby. So many of us arrived there, and so exhausted were we, that its staff assigned us rooms immediately, leaving the "guests" to register the next day. That night, my father and I slept in comfortable beds, between clean white sheets.

The hotel was the Terme di Valdieri, a fancy resort with sitting rooms, verandas, and a dining room that that day offered its patrons canned army rations from the abandoned army barracks nearby. I soon heard that it had thermal baths. There, in clear indoor pools where the Romans had once immersed themselves, we novice mountain climbers leisurely soothed our bruised feet and I, my sore back and shoulders.

We would have enjoyed these amenities more had we not been deprived so distressingly of news. Radio reception in this deep valley was difficult, and there were no newspapers. I remember the commotion an Italian soldier caused when he arrived on a motorcycle. He was mobbed by news seekers, yet nobody learned a thing—first, because of the language barrier, and second, because the man didn't know much. How nice it would have been had a jeep with a couple of GIs aboard suddenly driven up.

Hitler, unwilling to concede the defeat of his Axis partner, had hurriedly depleted his embattled Russian front of enough troops to secure Italy. We listened with disbelief to scraps of news trickling in: instead of the Allies, it was the Germans who were in Italy. The Allied advance in the south had come to a standstill.

Some refugees began to walk away, then more. Again, scattered groups of package-toting people walked into the unknown. Again, it was everyone for himself. The hotel did not bother to bill us.

We walked with Cousin Moyne, his wife, and Zilla, who also had landed at the hotel. We all walked down the valley. No one, as far as I know, returned to France. The road here was paved, and we all had recovered from crossing the mountains. There was no other road, and if it dispersed us, it was only because we did not all leave at the same time.

The distance to Valdieri, the nearest town, was about ten miles. Along the way, the road from Entraque merged with ours, and there a scattering of people looking just like us, laden with packages, joined our march. They were also from St. Martin-Vésubie and had crossed the mountains by the alternative trail.

Approaching Valdieri, we heard at regular intervals the sound of explosions, once every two seconds or so. These clearly were not the sounds of warfare. But what could they be?

In Valdieri, it was not only the refugees but also local people who filled the streets. I saw one local man carry a stovepipe, some others pieces of furniture, and others boxes. The town's inhabitants were plundering the local barracks, abandoned by the army. Carabinieri stood by, watching. One carabiniere destroyed the supply of hand grenades, one by one. That accounted for the explosions we heard.

It was impossible to find lodging in this crowded town. We followed a side road uphill out of town. Here the valley widened and was cultivated. We saw a hayloft in the distance and a refugee leaving it. When we met him, he told us that its owner allowed refugees to sleep there and that there was plenty of space. There we stayed for the next several days.

We did not have to worry about food. Cans of military rations, taken from the barracks, were freely available in Valdieri. But to decide what to do next, where to go from here, was not so easy. The next day, my father and Cousin Moyne went to town to see what information they might gather. The news they returned with was that the Germans were already in Cuneo, the provincial capital. Then the Germans were reported in Borgo San Dalmazzo, the first town on the road out of Valdieri. That was a mere six miles away. The Germans had us cornered like mice in a trap.

We remained in the hayloft. Early each morning, one or two of us would go to Valdieri for army rations and news. One morning, refugees coming from that town reported somberly that the Germans had arrived there. Not just any Germans but German storm troopers, the SS. They knew about our flight from St. Martin-Vésubie, and they had come for us. In town, they had posted the following proclamation:

The German Command of Borgo S. Dalmazzo

By 18:00 hours today, all strangers present in the territory of Borgo S. Dalmazzo and nearby communities must report to the German Command in Borgo S. Dalmazzo, at the Alpini Barracks.

After this deadline, all strangers who fail to report will be shot.

The same punishment will be meted out to those on whose premises these strangers will be found.

Borgo S. Dalmazzo, 18 September 1943.
The German Commander of the SS
Captain Müller

After the war, the original draft of this proclamation was recovered. Instead of "strangers," it said "Jews." The commander had changed the word because, in this region, nobody would have known what was meant by a Jew.[16]

The biblical migration had reached its end. In Valdieri, two pistol-brandishing SS troopers single-handedly rounded up some 350 weary and dispirited wretches of the chosen people.[17] There was no Moses to stretch his arms to heaven, no pillar of fire to interpose itself between the Jews and their pursuers, and no waves of water to close over the pursuers' heads.

9
Vogelfrei

THE DAY THE POSTER APPEARED in Valdieri, I encountered a refugee who told me about it. I happened to be first to leave our hayloft. I returned immediately to warn everyone there.

As I had not actually seen this poster, my father and Moyne, somewhat dubious, decided to go see it for themselves. On the way to Valdieri, we met other refugees. Each confirmed the news though none had actually seen the poster. Nor did anyone know that two German SS were already in town rounding up any refugees they encountered.

A sturdy bit of fence stood at the edge of town, inviting us to lean against it. There we stopped, agreeing that the poster was not just a rumor, and that this was as good a place as any to come to a decision. Indeed it was. Had we gone a few steps further, where our road met a street that descended to the center of town, we might have caught a glimpse of the SS and they of us.

My father felt that we had no choice but to surrender. Calmly, point by point, he made his case. Where would we hide? Where would we find food? The war was not about to end. The season was advancing. The snow would be high. Where would we find warmth? We owned no more than the clothes on our backs. We had little money, no identity cards, no ration coupons. We knew no one here. We did not speak the language. We could not pretend to be Italians. And the Italians, German allies in the past, were on notice that they would be shot should they shelter us. Surely they would not risk their lives for strangers. The Germans, despite their difficulties at the eastern front, had seen fit to send their storm troopers to capture us. Would they forget us? And now my father, who had endeavored in St. Martin-Vésubie to stamp in my mind the eyewitness report of Germans killing Jews in Polish concentration camps, drew these conclusions: the worst that could happen if we surrendered to the Germans was forced labor. The worst that could happen if we did not was to be shot.

I was flabbergasted. I could not believe what my father had said. Surrender? To the Germans? In a tone that I tried to keep as measured as his, I pointed out that on our trek, we had seen how vast the mountains were. The Germans would find it difficult to catch us there. As for the local people on whom we would have to depend for food and shelter, we had found them to be nice to us. Wouldn't it be better to trust them than the Germans?

Moyne broke the silence that followed, saying only that he believed that I was right. My father, who always respected Moyne's opinions, did not argue.

Retracing our steps, we walked in silence. A familiar feeling had returned. I had experienced it in Agde after making that U-turn on my bicycle. I had experienced it in Montagnac when I had to leave that town without papers. Then, however, that feeling had been short-lived. The first time it had abated as soon as I had reached home and the second time, as soon as I was in the safe house at Montpellier. Now I wondered how long I would have to live with it.

But I was aware of another feeling as well. It was a sense of pride. No rite of passage celebrates the transition between the period when a parent takes care of a child and the period when the child takes care of the parent. The duration of this transition usually mitigates its uncertainty and discomfort. But here, on this little road, it took me by surprise. Three years ago, on our flight from Belgium, my greatest worry had been about what to do should something happen to my father. I had always followed his advice unquestioningly. Now, so suddenly and in a matter of such crucial consequence, it was my counsel that had prevailed. I was both elated and terribly scared.

At the hayloft we repacked our belongings. We felt safe for the time being, the deadline being 6 P.M. Then we felt that we need not depart until the next morning since our hayloft was some distance from Valdieri.

That night we slept little, and the next morning we were off before dawn. Once again, my blanket had become a knapsack. Once again,

Moyne, with determined mien, lifted his two suitcases, followed
by wife and child. An unattended lady who had befriended Regine
came along.

Walking through the cultivated upland above Valdieri, we missed
the forests that had surrounded us on our way in. Now that we needed
a forest to hide in, we could see none. The road we followed mean-
dered up across undulating fields, approaching, in a tangential way,
the steep and barren mountain spurs that bordered the valley. The
only noticeable woods nestled between these spurs. In our judgment,
they were too small to offer us cover. Daylight turned brighter and we
walked on, looking back every so often with increasing apprehension.
The road steadily approached one spur, and as we rounded it, a more
sizable forest actually bordered the road, and we entered it.

Fallen trees here and there offered a seat for everyone, but we
passed them up until we judged that we had gone deep enough
into the woods. Next to a depression filled with brambles where we
hid our belongings, we settled on one tree trunk that kept our feet
off the damp soil. Facing the direction from which we had come,
keeping quiet, avoiding any movement, I had the leisure to mull
over the consequences of our defiance.

What, I wondered, were the Germans doing? Where did they
search? Would they converge on us, yelling, "Come out, we have seen
you"? Could they creep up behind us, unnoticed? A whirl of panic
attended the crack of any branch, the rustling of any leaf. One of
the women got up without an explanation, without a whisper, and
walked aside as quietly as she could to relieve herself. The noises
she made must have been audible from afar.

Suddenly, unmistakably, footsteps. People were coming. To run
now would have betrayed our presence. Hypnotized, we looked in
the direction of the approaching steps. Their sound was not that
of tramping soldiers but of the timid trudging of fellow refugees.
Then we saw them—a man and a woman carrying a baby—and
they saw us. Without saying a word, they sat down on a fallen tree
that we had passed by.

It was disconcerting that, in this pathless wood, they came so
easily upon us. Should we move? What place would be preferable?
Better not to make unnecessary noises.

Around noon, very quietly, Regine fed her daughter and passed
some ration tins around. I forced myself to eat. I might need a full

stomach. But not everyone ate. The silence returned. We listened. At times, the occasional cracks of branches and the rustling of leaves seemed connected. Did these denote the halting, stealthy progress of an individual? I also fretted about the baby who, I feared, would betray our presence by crying at the most inopportune moment. But the baby, perhaps sensing the tension, did not utter a sound all day long.

Evening finally approached. Nothing untoward having happened, one of us began to stretch a little, and then the others, and we began to whisper and then to talk about what to do next. Clearly, the Germans would not come anymore this day. Cautiously we filed toward the road. Everything was quiet; there was no movement at all.

Up the road beyond the forest, there was a farm. Perhaps they were abreast of the day's happenings? My father decided to go there accompanied by Moyne. They came back with news that the Germans, marching off several hundred refugees, had left Valdieri the day before. Furthermore, the farmer had a hayloft in which he allowed us to spend the night. His wife had even given my father and Moyne some food to take back to us.

We went back into the woods to retrieve our luggage. But search as we might, we could find no trace of it. Darkness was falling, and my father had to return to the farmhouse to ask for help. I watched him go up the road and disappear into the house. Within minutes, a little boy ran out of it, toward us, and past us into the forest. In a few minutes we heard him shouting. He had found our belongings. The people in the farmhouse had known our whereabouts all along. In all likelihood, the farmer and his little boy had come into the woods. Not all my suspicions about what caused branches to crack and leaves to rustle had been fantasy.

Not until after the war did I learn that only two SS had come to Valdieri to round up the Jewish refugees. They belonged to the fearsome division "Leibstandarte SS Adolf Hitler," Hitler's body guard. Fighting under Hitler's direct authority, that division was among those hurriedly withdrawn from the Russian front to prevent the defection of Italy.[1] These troops had freed Mussolini, reestablished a Fascist government, captured thousands of disbanded Italian soldiers—their former allies—and sent them as slave laborers to Germany.[2] We refugees, without newspapers, without radio, without even a bilingual dictionary, learned little of this. Ignorance is sometimes a good thing.

The day after the SS left Valdieri—the day we sat cowering in the woods—a company of them entered the little town of Boves, just eight miles away. Two of its men went to the local military depot to requisition what usable materials still remained there. There they met some partisans, Italians who had decided to stand up to the Germans. Most were soldiers who had escaped the German net and who, joined by a few civilians, had taken to the mountains and armed themselves. Of weapons, at least, there was no shortage.

Presently the partisans at the depot arrested the SS. The latter's comrades attempted to free them. In the shoot-out, the SS suffered one casualty and several wounded. Armored reinforcements then arrived and occupied positions from which they could block escape from the town. They asked the curate and a local businessman to intercede with the partisans for the release of the prisoners, promising to forgo reprisals in exchange. But once the prisoners had returned, the SS set the town on fire and blocked arriving fire fighting equipment. Three hundred and fifty houses were incinerated. Among the twenty-three victims burned alive were the curate and the businessman.[3]

We soon heard of this massacre, but vaguely. None of our informants mastered a passable French. *Strage* is the Italian word that describes what had happened, and *Tedeschi* is the word that denotes Germans. Still, we understood enough to feel sorry for the Italian victims and to realize that this event had rendered our situation even more precarious.

Yet as none of us refugees knew what to do, nothing changed. As the owners of haylofts did not prevent us from sleeping in them, we remained there. Day followed day. Whenever two of us refugees met, we eagerly discussed our perplexing situation. We all agreed with each other that this could not go on, that we ought to disperse, that the Germans were bound to return, that our welcome would wear out, and that winter was on its way. In such exchanges, the German word *Vogelfrei* was freely bandied about. Its literal meaning is "free as a bird." It evokes colorful plumage, warbling song, and unfettered flight under a wide sky. It strikes one as charming. In fact the word's real meaning, which I had not fathomed before, is sinister. It indicates the status of outlaws who may be shot at will.

I returned to Valdieri. Our army rations were about to run out, and I had heard that those tins were still available there. I got there by evening. I had been afraid to arrive sooner. My mission, however, was quickly completed. The first person I spoke to directed me to a particular person who provided me with a goodly supply. Did I have to pay? I do not remember. Did we have any Italian currency, or did people accept French francs? I do not know.

I had a long way to go back in the dark. Nearby was the hayloft in which we had slept until the arrival of the SS. I decided to spend the night there. When I arrived, I saw that the hayloft was occupied. The people there, several families of refugees, seemed to be already asleep. There was plenty of space, and there I laid down away from them. My fellow refugees slept rather noisily. Drowsing off, I heard a scurrying and rustling and whispering. Then all was quiet. Too quiet. I was alone. My presence had driven my fellow refugees into the cold mountain night. Such is the power of fear.

A rumor took us by surprise and ended our irresolution. Word spread that the Germans or the Fascist police were returning. We left immediately. Following the advice given us at the farmhouse, we went into the next valley, the valley of the Stura. We had to cross a mountain pass, the Madonna del Colletto, and although this one was not nearly as high as the one we crossed coming from France, we walked well into the night before finding a place level enough to sleep in the open. It had come to that again.

What I saw the next morning, as I awoke, was not reassuring. We were lying on a slope among majestic, widely spaced trees. Later I was to notice that such trees grew wherever the mountain slopes eased, and I learned that these were chestnut trees, which provided the mountain people with their major cash crop. But at the moment I was astonished to see other groups of refugees settled down among these trees. We had not dispersed. More disturbing, a man who did not look at all like a refugee was standing over the group lying nearest to us. He was talking to them. That is what had awakened me. What was he saying? What did he want?

Now the stranger approached us, brandishing a thick wad of dirty bills. He asked whether we had any gold. My father said yes, removed his wedding ring from his finger, and sold it for some of the man's money. My father then asked him where we might find an abode. Following an exchange in which gesticulations with arms and hands were as eloquent as my father's limited Italian and the stranger's broken French, the latter produced a dirty, crinkled little piece of paper on which he wrote, in a painful scrawl, the name "Brondello Giovanni." This man, he indicated with a wide wave of his arm, owned many houses across the valley, some unoccupied and high enough up the mountain to be safe. He gave us directions to Rittana, a village across the valley where the man lived.

Could we trust this stranger? My father was absolutely sure. He was even certain that he had received a fair price for his ring. The man, he said, could easily have taken it by force. Instead of bank notes, he could have brandished a gun. And he could have come with a gang.

Thus I gained a better understanding of the meaning of *Vogelfrei* and came to realize, as well, how far I still was from attaining my father's wisdom.

It took us two days to cover the six miles to Rittana. To reach the other side of the valley, we had to cross a major highway that went into France, as well as a military road, a railway line, and the Stura River. We contrived to do this early the next morning. The stranger had given us not only the necessary directions but even the time when the train passed, so we could avoid being seen. The highway was absolutely deserted. We used byways to reach Gaiola, a town astride that highway, wound our way through the back of that town, then turned left into the valley of the Bial.[4] Here we felt safe enough to walk on the road.

Having reached Rittana, we continued for a while beyond the town. The road, no longer paved, continued along the narrowing valley bottom between the fast-moving waters of the Bial and a few farms. Then, blocked by a mountain spur, the road branched into two rocky mule paths, each leading up a narrow, rapidly rising valley. Here, at a small footbridge, we stopped. The scenery beyond, bereft of any flat surface, looked stark and wild. The women and I stretched out on the last flat bit of land. My father and Moyne went off to locate Signor Brondello.

We had seen no one as we crossed the main highway. But over the footbridge next to which we sat, there was traffic, albeit at infrequent intervals. People came by, some alone, some in small groups. Oddly, they all went in the same direction, up the left valley. These were neither fellow refugees nor local farmers. Hirsute, wearing uniforms, their jackets unbuttoned, military insignia removed, they carried weapons of some sort, a rifle, a pistol, and usually a hand grenade or two tucked in their belt. They were partisans.

Of these, one young man took notice of us. He was shaven, wore a well-tailored sports outfit and carried his carbine rather stiffly. He asked us in passable French whether we were refugees from St. Martin-Vésubie. Upon the affirmative, he said that he too was Jewish. His name was Riccardo Cavaglion. He hailed from the provincial capital, Cuneo. When he and his family had heard of the inrush of Jewish refugees across the French border, his brother Enzo had gone to Valdieri to be of assistance. There he first had to convince the refugees that he was Jewish, which he did by speaking a few Hebrew words. Even then, however, what could he do? Now Riccardo was on his way to join the partisans in the mountains. Life under German occupation had become too dangerous.

Several hours later, my father and Moyne returned accompanied, to our relief, by Signor Brondello. Then all of us ascended the left mule path that led us, after about an hour's walk, to La Balma, two rows of small houses, some pressed together between path and mountain, the others between path and abyss. Only the houses on the right were inhabited. Those on the left, Mr. Brondello said, were for us. Each had no more than one or two small rooms, each with a tiny window, an open fireplace, and a vaulted ceiling. I admired the stonework and the cleanliness of their whitewashed interiors. To me, who had not set foot in a house for weeks, they looked downright palatial.

From across the path, our new neighbors brought a table and chairs, arranged them in one of the rooms, and pitched some clean straw into each of the others. Next they brought an oil lamp, as night was falling, and then wine and food. They were as curious about us as we were about them. They talked in Italian, we mostly in French. Laughter replaced what could not be understood, and there was much of it. The later it became, the more the spirits rose. The women were going strong well after I had gone to sleep atop one pile of fresh-smelling straw. How comfortably I lay, how euphoric I felt! How far from my mind the prickly straw in the Granals' stable! My last awareness, before falling asleep, was of Regine telling our new neighbors about a cake she had made. She used the French word *gâteau,* but pronounced it as German speakers do, by stressing the first syllable. To our new neighbors, it sounded like *gatto,* which in Italian means "cat." Months later, after I had become conversant in Italian, one of those neighbors recalled that evening, still pitying the hungry refugees who had deemed cat meat such a delicacy.

10
A Failed Rescue

THE NEXT MORNING, WHEN I OPENED the door of my room in La Balma, I saw two mules standing in front of it loaded with bags of flour. The evening before, in the darkness, I had not noticed the water-powered mill tucked into the side of the road. Presently the miller, wisps of flour dangling from his mustache and the brim of his hat, emerged from this structure followed by the owner of the mules. *"Buon giorno,"* we said to each other. To be living next to a friendly miller, when flour and bread were so scarce, was an incredible bit of good luck.

Or was it? From far and wide people come to a mill. There they have to wait while their grain is being ground. They would notice us, hear about us. Would they learn that we were Jews?

At least we had scattered. But what would we have thought had we known that no more that another mile uphill, at the tip of the valley, was Paralup, a long-abandoned hamlet in which a band of partisans now installed themselves.[1] That was where the partisans were heading whom we had seen crossing the bridge yesterday.

There was a small general store in the village of Gorrè, located farther up the road. Our neighbors said that had little to offer. They suggested we go to Rittana instead. We needed everything, and our army rations were about to give out. But my father had money now. At the bakery we did not have to introduce ourselves. Word of our arrival had already spread, and the baker's wife, who tended the store, assured us that we needn't worry about ration coupons. The tobacconist, whom we visited next, ran a sort of general store. Pointing at empty shelves, she lamented the dearth of goods. But she had the Turin newspaper, which paper shortages had reduced to a single sheet. My father bought it, happy to be able to catch up on the news. The girl—her name was Tersilla Chiocchia—suggested that anyone going up our way would gladly carry it to us so he could read it regularly. Then, upon hearing that my father smoked cigars, she sold him, without coupons, a Toscano, at the official, not the black market, price. "A Toscano!" my father exclaimed. He knew the brand from his previous travels in Italy.

On the street, we encountered a group of children walking with their schoolmistress and singing. How well they sang, how clear their voices, how assured their tune . . . and how long since I had heard anyone sing!

The town had two churches and two trattorie, or taverns. It may have had other stores, and we may have visited them, but I no longer remember. On the way back, in a hamlet called Tanara, we met the local barber—who was also the local cobbler—shearing his customer, towel around neck, astride a chair in the middle of the road. We reached La Balma after darkness had already fallen. On the step to our "dining" room, we were surprised to find a pitcher of milk and a small bag of flour. No gift has ever been so welcome.

We settled into our new abode. Regine and her friend did the cooking. Neither had cooked on an open fire before. They found it difficult to control the wood fire. They could not see or hear what happened inside the cauldron, which hung from a chain and required both hands for stirring. They lacked the skill to steady that heavy thing, which must be jammed against the back wall of the fireplace with one's knee using a split log between knee and cauldron to avoid the flames. Vehement arguments and anguished cries emanated from that kitchen, as well as frequent calls for my help.

My father, meanwhile, would sit calmly on a chair, studying the newspaper and puffing on a Toscano, or go for a walk with Moyne.

My job was to keep the kitchenware clean. I scoured the cauldron on the side of the road, using spring water that flowed there from a pipe and sand that had accumulated below it. One day, some city people, watching me work, remarked that Allied bombing had deprived them of running water as well as of gas for heating and cooking. And to buy food they had to come this far. To listen to them, I lived in the lap of luxury.

In the days that followed, I became better acquainted with Massimo Borgogno, our neighbor the miller. He had served in the Italian army during the World War I and loaned me the ample cape of his uniform to use as cover at night. But it was his mill, in particular, that fascinated me. Inside, huge beams powered by the great waterwheel outside turned a heavy millstone. And all this formidable machinery produced only a tiny rivulet of flour. Still, as long as there was water in the millpond, the flour flowed steadily, and in time would fill a bag. It must have flowed that way for a very long time. Millstones more or less buried bordered the mill, and it was obvious that by just digging a little or removing some weeds, one would find more of them. A millstone lasted a lifetime, Massimo said, and before taking over the mill, he had, according to custom, chiseled his own millstone, a labor that had taken him a year. He showed me his father's millstone and his grandfather's, and a wave of his hand encompassed the millstones of generations upon generations of Borgognos.

On our shopping expeditions to Rittana, we became acquainted also with the people who lived along the way. They obtained their foodstuffs not from the local stores but laid them in wholesale upon selling their harvest of chestnuts. They also produced their own milk and eggs. When they saw us come by, they would chitchat with us and not allow us to leave without taking some food along. Soon we obtained more food from these people than from the few stores with their empty shelves.

Once, having already walked though a little hamlet, I heard someone calling me. It was a little old lady, hurrying to catch up with me. I had never seen her before. She wanted to give me a potato.

Along the path to Rittana there was also a free-standing, vaulted masonry structure. It was an oven in which families took turns baking bread. Baking was an all-day affair. The men arrived early, filled the oven with wood, lit it, and allowed it to burn out. By then the women had arrived with their dough already shaped into loaves. One man, wielding a long-handled wooden shovel, quickly filled the oven with them. After a suitable length of time, he emptied the oven in the same manner and then filled it once more, not as tightly, with pies and other goodies. Rich people, I was told, baked white bread, which kept two weeks. Poor people baked dark bread, which kept a week longer. I soon learned the baking schedules and managed to pass by as the bread was taken out. The people never failed to offer me a loaf.

These were good-hearted folk. But just to make sure, the local curate, Don Giovanni Martini, exhorted his flock, *ex cathedra,* to offer us assistance.

Now everybody knew that we were *ebrei,* Jews!

One day when I returned home, my father told me that the curate had come by. It was not to convert us to Catholicism, as I feared. Nor was it just a social call. He had come to bring us money, Jewish money, as we learned after the war, from America.[2] Here we were, hidden in the mountains, cut off from the outside world, unable to send or receive mail, and yet that money reached us. It came, in a roundabout way, from Jewish communities in the United States. The Catholic clergy had undertaken to distribute it. There would be more. The curate expected to return regularly.

Soon he was back with even more astonishing news. The archdiocese of Genoa offered to arrange our departure to the south of Italy, where the advancing Allied armies, in all likelihood, would soon liberate us. Here in the mountains, life was too risky for us. Too many strangers moved about. Everyone knew of our whereabouts. The Nazis could not fail to become aware of us if they were not already. Most of all, we were unprepared for the winter that, up here, was severe. Already an emissary was shuttling back and forth, escorting small groups of Jewish refugees to Genoa.

Both my father and Moyne agreed to go.

Not long afterward, the emissary came to see us. He brought us some kind of documentation. These were not regular identification cards, he cautioned, and it would be best not to have to show them. He also brought several pairs of used shoes. Down in the plain, he said, our tattered footwear might tip off the police. None of the shoes really fit me, and I settled for a pair that was a tad large.

It was the end of October. We had lived nearly two months in the mountains. What an implausible adventure it had been!

The train, running on the tracks we had crossed coming from Valdieri to Rittana, arrived in Gaiola virtually empty. We sat down in separate groups, as if we had never met. The emissary from Genoa sat by himself, ahead of everybody, where we all could see him. He had told us to look out the window or to feign sleep. Any talk would betray us. Observing our group, I worried about our ill-assorted clothes. Would anyone really take us for locals? Only my father, in suit and overcoat, looked respectable. He even wore his tie.

In Cuneo, we followed the emissary as he changed trains and did so again in Savona. Here the trains were overcrowded and so were the stations. Nor did the train arrive on time. But we did make it to Genoa, moved with the crowd outside the station past many a uniformed minion scrutinizing the passersby. Outside the station we had to wait while the emissary disappeared to phone the archdiocese. We scattered some, so as not to attract attention, and when another guide arrived, the emissary split us up. We would walk, he said, as the police frequently inspected trolley cars. Five or so would follow the other guide. He would take charge of the rest. My father and I were in the first group, which was all male; Moyne and his family were assigned to the latter. We had no chance to say good-bye.

Walking along fairly busy streets, carrying our belongings in an inconspicuous bag, my father and I followed well behind our guide. When we lost sight of him, we focused on some other person in our group. There was no one to haul up the rear. Stopping at a fairly busy intersection, my father and I saw our guide entering an imposing building,[3] and when we reached its door, it opened quickly. Inside, a cleric in a black cassock, effusive and friendly, greeted us in a passable French. After everybody had arrived, he led us up a marble staircase to our rooms. He was the seminary's rector. The students, he explained, had been sent into the country after the heavy bombings in the autumn of 1942. We had their quarters.

Later, we were taken to a well-appointed faculty dining room where three or four refugees already sat at the table. They had arrived a few days earlier. Their appearance struck me as mangy, their behavior as lethargic—out of place in this room. It occurred to me that our group looked no better.

Someone came from the kitchen to serve us and, later, to clear the table. We could talk to each other in German, but there was not much to say. Still tired from the trip, we went to bed early. Cleaner than in a long time, I enjoyed sleeping between white sheets.

The food, I noted, was scarcer here than in the mountains. In Genoa, ration cards still mattered, and since we had none, the cook must have scoured every recess in his pantry. Our dinner, one night, was a puree of peas, served with toasted bread cubes. But the bread cubes had been toasted long ago. Poured atop the puree, its heat drove wriggly maggots out. Watching them flounder in the puree for awhile, I declared that I couldn't possibly eat it. But my father, taking his glasses off, said, "I don't see anything," and proceeded to eat his puree. Hungry we may have been, and concerned about hurting the cook's sensibilities, but only a few of us followed his example.

While waiting for dinner on our second evening, air-raid sirens sounded an alert. It was the first time that I heard them in more than three years. Looking out the window, I saw people scurrying across the street. As we wondered what to do, a staff member burst into our room and hustled us across the street into an air-raid shelter.

In this cavernous place, two blinding lights hanging in the dark void above proved unable to lift the gloom on the crowded floor. Here people had quickly arranged themselves to sleep as best they could. Obviously they had done this before. Then we heard the rattle of anti-aircraft fire, and the silence in the shelter became palpable. Next, we both heard and felt a big concussion, then another, and another. It seemed that each bomb landed precisely on top of us. A particularly heavy blow elicited knowing comments among my neighbors. Presently the clamor turned into an almost unremitting thunder. Slowly, a wisp of dust—or was it smoke?—drifted into the light beam overhead. In brief and ominous periods of calm, one could hear children cry. But when we were let out of the shelter later that night, I was surprised to see no apparent damage to the surrounding buildings. At the seminary, no one could tell me where the bombs had fallen.

That was our only visit to the air-raid shelter. The rector told us the next day that the Fascist police had been checking identities in the shelters. It was safer for us to risk Allied bombs.

Again, it was only after the war that I learned that the Germans, assisted by local Fascists and spies, began rounding up the Jews of Genoa at this time. That small Jewish community, having withstood the Fascist government's anti-Semitic edicts for years, misjudged the vigor with which the Germans would go after them. Hundreds were caught.[4]

On our very first day at the seminary, the rector had taken us on a tour of the premises, which consisted of several interconnected buildings erected at different times, occupying what seemed like an entire city block. The Germans had already come once to search it. Effusively the rector related how he had taken them around, up some staircases, down others, opening any doors they wanted. They had left thanking him for his courtesy, unaware that he had skipped entire sections of the complex.

Thereafter, the rector took us to the library, which filled several rooms. Pointing to a door that opened onto a small room, he suggested that it could be masked with shelves. That room had no other entrance and could serve us as a hiding place. We went to work forthwith, rearranging shelves and books, leaving an opening that someone would have to fill up after us. Even with the Germans already in the building, the rector said, we would have time to reach that hiding place.

Air raids continued almost nightly and sometimes occurred even in daytime. At first it felt strange to sit calmly at the window while sirens screamed and the street emptied itself, watching, in the ominous silence that followed, a laggard or two running to the shelter, their hands clasped over their heads. However, we got used to this. Once, having discovered a stairway that led to the roof, I got a bit reckless and climbed up there after the alert had sounded. The door at the top opened onto a catwalk that covered the ridge of the roof. From here, the view was unimpeded. In the darkness, I could hear the droning of the approaching bombers. In one corner of the sky, searchlights played against the clouds. There, suddenly, streams of tracer bullets arched gracefully into a flickering sky, and the staccato of anti-aircraft guns reverberated. Judging by their roar, the planes now were everywhere. Presently the horizon, beyond the fireworks, reddened in a blotchy glow. Had a plane been downed? A gasoline depot hit? Or just the effect of carpet bombing? Quite a spectacle, but my father suggested that once was enough.

I managed to see the bombings from yet another angle. That happened several weeks later, when our confinement in the seminary began weighing on some of us. When we mentioned this to the rector, he suggested a part of town where a small group might walk safely.

The area was nearby. We encountered only a few people on the street, and after turning a corner, as instructed, we saw no one anymore. The street was clean with no litter. Every window was shuttered, but now and then, a loose shutter in an upper story disclosed a window through which gaped the sky. We began to pass stores, their iron shutters all rolled down. Further along, the shutters bulged. I noticed that they all bulged in one direction, out on the left side of the street, in on the right side. Now some shutters had been torn loose, and upstairs, unshuttered windows revealed the open sky. When we turned a corner, the street ahead was much

brighter than ours and filled with rubble. Here, the buildings had
ceased to exist.

Genoa had been bombarded both from the air and by the guns
of the British fleet. We came across several impact sites, and I was
able to deduce that the iron shutters, pushed out by the explosion,
are sucked in the opposite direction by the returning air, and thus
bulged in the direction of ground zero. Our spirits revived by the
outing, we returned safely to the seminary.

Our prospects of going to Rome had dimmed. The Allied advance
had stalled after the capture of Naples. The Germans held firm in
fortified positions near the town of Cassino. In the meantime, Rome
had become a cauldron of the Nazi-Fascisti. Our rector mentioned
that instead of going south, we might be smuggled into Switzerland.

It was not to be. On Sunday, December 3, the rector burst into
our dining room and, very agitated, reported that the Germans
had captured a group of refugees and their escort on their way to
Switzerland. One of the escorting clerics had been able to escape
and managed to alert the archdiocese.[5] The Germans, knowing
where their captives had come from, might already be headed for
the seminary. We had to depart immediately. Our best hope was
to return to the mountains. There was no time to furnish us with
identification papers. Someone would take us to the station and buy
our railway tickets. From then on, we would be on our own. The
next train would leave in a few hours.

Reaching Savona, we learned that there were no further
connections to Cuneo that day. We had to spend the night here.
The waiting room, dim because of the blackout, was already full
of people and their baggage. Only a narrow, circular path threaded
through this mass. I inserted myself and my suitcase at one spot, and
my father at another. Then, like so many others there, I fell asleep.

Sometime during the night, loud voices awoke me. An identity
check was in progress. Opening my eyes, I saw that my father was
not where he had been. I also saw the police, German and Italian. I
was lying on their path; they could not miss me. What to do now?
Could I still slip out unobserved? I decided that it was too late for
that. I kept my eyes closed, pretending to sleep.

Fear raises a person's heart rate and blood pressure, stimulates the
brain, and stretches the duration of time. But it also focuses attention

on the present. I did not think of what might happen, only not to bat an eyelash, not to twitch a muscle. *"Documenti!"* Slowly the voices approached. I heard paper being fingered, then again, *"Documenti!"* Presently they stood at my feet. *Documenti!*

I didn't move. *Documenti!* they shouted. *Documenti!* They seemed to stay forever. Then I heard their *"Documenti!"* a little farther away. I was safe.

Long after the Germans and the carabinieri had gone, my father returned. He and the other refugees had gone outside the station, defying the curfew, hiding in some nooks or crannies under the cover of night. My father had stood the cold as long as he could and returned not quite sure whether it was safe. Later, when we had a chance to talk, he related how artfully the carabinieri had gulled the Germans. They had gone to the remotest corner of the waiting room, beginning their identity check by loudly awakening some girls who, they must have known, had nothing to fear. Their voices, and the girls' curses they provoked, alerted everyone. Starting where they did, they left the exit open. Yet the Germans had seemed pleased to have such cooperative carabinieri. So I laughed as well. But oh, how I longed to be back in the mountains already!

The remainder of our voyage was uneventful, except that rolling along on the train from Savona to Cuneo, we began to see patches of snow that, further along, became a continuous cover. Cuneo was white. We changed trains, our fellow refugees going their different ways. In Gaiola, my father and I were the only refugees to leave the train. Stepping off the car, I noticed that the snow, only partially removed, was deep.

We knew our way to Rittana, and my father and I were quickly off, following a narrow path cleared through the snow that covered the road. We were alone. Gaiola had disappeared after a bend in the road. No one followed us. Nothing moved, not in the valley that stretched to our right nor on the mountain that filled the horizon ahead. About halfway to Rittana, the cleared path veered away from the road, disappearing in the woods that there covered the mountain. We stopped. Ahead, the outline of the road, etched in virgin snow, evidenced no trace of traffic. And the snow was deep, more than knee deep. Never before had I seen so much snow.

To get to Rittana, we had to follow the road. Gingerly, I lifted my right foot, placed it on the snow, and put my weight on it. My foot seemed to descend forever before it met resistance. I removed my foot, and was astonished to see it come up shoeless, naked, a bright pink. The shoe, of course, had been a tad large. And it had been some time since I last wore socks. They had worn out quickly in the mountains. When my socks developed holes at the heels, I tucked my socks deeper into each shoe, continuing this procedure as new holes appeared. In the end, the socks literally vanished.

Now, perched precariously on one leg, propped up by my father, my naked foot held high, I looked at it, not knowing what to do. Neither of us laughed. Seemingly, our plight was desperate, as dire as my father had anticipated when, in Valdieri, I had dissuaded him from surrendering to the German SS. And yet, we were not worried. We were back in the mountains. We were among friends.

11
The Cave of San Mauro

I RECOVERED MY OVERSIZED SHOE, put my foot into it, and there we stood. Should we return to Gaiola or proceed along the unknown path? Around us in the picture-postcard winter landscape, nothing stirred, no one to ask for directions. Surmising that the cleared path detoured to link settlements along the way to Rittana, we followed it.

Our progress was arduous. The path had been cleared not by removing the snow but by tamping it down. The resulting bow-shaped surface, rising from the paved road, suggested a toboggan chute.

It was still early in the afternoon. We reached a farmhouse where a man cleaning the stable confirmed that our path led to Rittana. It was good to see him standing amidst a heap of steaming and stinking straw; to see that, in this white frozen world, life continued as usual.

We continued on the slippery path until we reached Rittana. "The Germans would not venture here," my father said. We would try lodging here. We needed go no farther.

We found a room not in Rittana but in the hamlet Tanara, on the way to the footbridge that I had crossed many times on my way up and down from La Balma. We arrived while it was still light. On the ground floor of the brick-and-concrete industrial structure that we were shown, a shuttered store had a neglected appearance. It was used only as a warehouse, the landlord said. Our room was over the store. We reached it by an exterior staircase and a balcony. A small iron stove, a table, and some chairs furnished it; there was some crockery as well as a bed that still had some straw in it. A farmhand had recently lived here, the landlord informed us. Outside, he showed us the hygienic facilities, an open cesspit the man had dug. That was providential for I could not have dug one in the frozen ground.

The landlord sold us a couple of army blankets and threw some utensils into the bargain: a pot, an oil lamp, and a hatchet. Soon we had a fire in the stove, sat at our table, drank hot ersatz coffee, and ate what food remained from the seminary. It was a happy ending to so ominous a day.

That night we discovered how cold it could get in the mountains. We had gone to bed fully clothed. We had used one blanket to cover the straw, the other to cover ourselves, then spread my father's overcoat on top of it. Still we were cold. The heat of the little stove did not reach the bed, and anyway, the former tenant had not left enough firewood to see us through the night. In front of the fading fire, we donned all the clothes remaining in our bag. We snuggled close to each other. Still we were cold.

The next morning we sought to become acquainted with our neighbors. In the house next to ours lived a young woman and her three young children, one of them still a baby. Her husband had been drafted into the Italian army, our landlord had said, and was at the Russian front. She did not answer when we knocked at her door. We were about to leave when she emerged from the stable, her slim figure slimmer for being cloaked in black, a habit of all married women here. We introduced ourselves, but she did not ask us into the house. She talked about her husband, who had written her how the German soldiers, in their retreat from the Russian front, had used the butts of their rifles to prevent Italian soldiers from climbing aboard their trucks. She was lucky, she said, looking very distraught, that this letter had passed the censor. Standing out in the open, we kept talking for awhile, ill at ease, attempting to say something to comfort her.

One other family lived in Tanara. At their house, again no one answered our knocks, but someone came from the stable. He introduced himself as Cuni Giovanni—he gave his last name first—and invited us to his stable. Before he closed the door on us, I briefly glimpsed two white cows, and then for awhile I could see no more than a small window. Signor Cuni introduced us to the signora, his wife, who sat at a small table next to that window. He offered my father a chair, me a three-legged stool, and we began to tell them a little about ourselves. My eyes had become accustomed to the dim light, and even my body began to feel comfortably warm. At some point I noticed that the stable had no stove. The cows gave off enough heat, Signora Cuni explained. In these parts, in winter, people lived in their stables. She left the stable only to cook. Indeed, beyond her chair, against the wall, I distinguished a bed. In this stable, the animals had far more space than that allocated to people. Their straw-covered berth was separated from us but by a dip in the beaten-earth floor. The signora admitted that the younger generation—their daughter Bettina—preferred sleeping by herself, in a cold bedroom.

As we readied ourselves to leave, she and her husband invited us to return soon and to stay as long as we wished, as winters were lonely. We left with some food, some old clothes, and I with some straw in my oversized shoes. That would keep my feet warm.

Likewise, we became acquainted with the sole inhabitants of Tetto Ponte, the next hamlet. Signor Brondello was relatively well-to-do. In addition to his stands of chestnut trees, he owned tracts of timber for logging. He had three cows in his stable where, in the winter, he and his wife lived with their animals. Their two daughters also lived with them. One, Lucia, had recently returned with her two young children. Her husband, too, was at the Russian front.

Deep winter was now upon us. Seen from our balcony, the sun rose only around 11 A.M., disappeared behind a peak by noon, and reappeared but briefly in the afternoon. As snow piled upon snow, the walls along the paths rose chest high. If one slipped, one slipped sideways, into the walls of soft snow. It was not difficult to get out, but everyone knew that only I made those holes. Our room was always cold. My father and I never undressed, washing no more than our faces and hands. Squatting on the ice-covered split log halves that straddled the cesspit, I noticed that the skin of my legs had turned gray, flaking here and there, each flake uncovering a soft pink spot. It was not frostbite. It was the natural sloughing off of dead skin, rendered visible by its grime.

The curate, Don Martini, came by to bring us money. He expected to bring us some every month. From our neighbor the barber and shoemaker, I now bought a pair of well-fitting boots. Although we did not have to depend on the charity of the valley's inhabitants, our neighbors insisted on giving us some food. Signora Brondello, remarking that she could sell her eggs for a price so high that she hardly dared eat them, always slipped me one or two. Our other neighbors were equally obliging.

As in Montagnac, firewood could not be bought. Though woods were nearby, the snow was too deep, and any trees felled now would have been too green to burn. Our neighbors, having laid in their supplies before the winter, had little to spare. They let me gather up all their previously disdained snags and knotted logs, to hone on these my skill as a lumberjack. It allowed me to cook but was insufficient to keep us warm.

Our neighbors, however, meant it when they invited us to their stables. The inside of a stable, even in daytime, was too dim to do much reading. Company thus was always welcome. And toward us refugees, with whom there was so much to talk about, and who spoke already a passable Italian, the welcome was genuine. Our visits became quite informal. Arriving at the stable door, one shouted *"permesso"*—"Can I come in?"—which elicited *"avanti"* in response. If the cold was intense, a vortex of snow formed in the open doorway as the cold air rushed in with the visitor. Quickly one closed the door. Inside, it was always warm. There, the man of the house might busy himself whittling some wood to make a leg for a stool, sharpening the saw, or cleaning the stable. As for the woman, talking to visitors did not interfere with her spinning. Yes, spinning, of which I shall have more to say. My father and Signor Brondello quickly took to each other. They discussed the predicament of the Allied advance up the Italian boot that remained stuck before Monte Cassino all that winter. The attempt to break the stalemate by landing at Anzio had not gone well; the Allied force remained pinned down on its beachhead. My father and Signor Brondello discussed their businesses as well. The Brondellos' daughter, Lucia, a pert and energetic woman, a teacher by profession, engaged me in literary conversations. We discovered that we both had read Axel Munthe's *The Story of San Michele,* albeit in different languages. And our other neighbors, the Cunis, listened with interest, if somewhat dubiously, as I held forth on the possibilities of space travel or tried to explain how a rocket works.

No one was afraid to discuss politics. The local people cursed the Fascist regime and freely heaped scorn on party officials. It had never been more than pretense and bungling. And now that Mussolini had fallen from power and been reinstated by the Germans, they utterly despised him. As for the Germans, they hated them.

In the evening it was difficult to leave. Outside, the cold was bitter. If the snow had settled, one could walk over it and take a shortcut. I remember how it squeaked underfoot and how, overhead, the stars twinkled brightly. Climbing the stairs to our room was dangerous. There was always ice. Then into bed, removing only our shoes, and my father his overcoat, which he draped atop the blanket.

We did not hear from Moyne and his family. They had not returned to Rittana. Don Martini inquired about them but to no avail. We also heard that the several hundred Jewish refugees whom the German SS in Valdieri had marched off to army barracks in Borgo San Dalmazzo had been deported.

Spring, when it finally came, was full of surprises. It arrived unevenly. Already by the end of February, patches of brown and green erupted on the valley's northern slope while its southern side remained inviolate. There, Signor Cuni sprinkled ashes on his ice-covered field to promote melting.

At our abode, spring arrived suddenly. One morning, it was in the air so plainly that before even lighting the stove, I succumbed to an urge to open our door. Outside, a warm breeze and birdsongs bid me welcome. And when my father got up, he decided to shed some of the clothes he had worn all winter. He removed a jacket, a sweater, whatever. Suddenly, he uttered a loud guffaw. He had just noticed the tie he had worn on the return trip from Genoa. He was still wearing it.

In the Rittana Valley, spring was cherry time. Many farmers grew cherry trees. Such was the tenor of the times that, try as I may, I do not recall any cherry blossoms. But the cherries I remember well. It was too difficult to bring these fresh to market, so anyone could eat, or take away, as many as he pleased. Picking them was no easy job. The trees were grown not for their fruit but for their wood, which was esteemed by nearby furniture makers. The lowest branch of the cherry trees, trained to grow tall, could be reached only from the topmost rung of the tallest ladder. I climbed one once under Signora Brondello's dismayed gaze. After that, she saw to it that we were given all the cherries we could eat.

The warmer weather gave me leisure to read. I had found some German magazines distributed as propaganda, but I would rather have studied. I asked Don Martini. Yes, he had some books from his time as seminarian. Though most were about theology, he had also taken a number of secular subjects. At the sacristy, we found a book on crystallography that I thought might interest me. "But don't ask me any questions," he said. "It's been too long."

Lucia, the Brondello's daughter, was intent on perfecting my Italian. First she gave me Munthe's *San Michele* to read. It would be easiest since I had already read it in a French translation. Thereafter she introduced me to an Italian classic, Manzoni's *I Promessi Sposi,* the story of a betrothed pair who, surviving an insurrection, a war, and a plague, had many adventures similar to mine, she said. Thus I fell in love with the Italian language. I admired its simple grammar, its sound, its lilt, and its warmth—the more so as, in the nearly two years that we hid in those mountains, no one ever sullied it by betraying our presence.

That spring brought yet another surprise. It had become warm enough to take a bath, a sponge bath without sponge, using water heated in a pot. That was indescribable luxury. But after the baths, our skin began to itch at night. In the morning, my father and I noticed reddish spots on it. The culprits, we soon discovered, were fleas. Everybody had them. They came with spring, jumped from person to person, hid in the seams of clothing and blankets. There, one by one, I could break their hard little bodies with my fingernail. But when I next looked, the little critters had filled the seams again, end to end, no space wasted. Our local friends opined that we washed too often. It made our skin too soft.

After the fleas came the Germans. My father and I encountered them one morning walking to Gaiola, using the paved road now free of snow. We happened to follow, at some distance, a small group of local women and children. We lost sight of them at a bend in the road. After we too had rounded that bend, we saw them again, as well as, in the distance, a bulky, odd-shaped vehicle surmounted by a turret. Presently that vehicle came to a stop on what must have been the main highway outside Gaiola. And then we heard several reports, loud and sharp. The women ran screaming into the nearest bushes. I wanted to see what was going on. The vehicle, I reasoned, had shot its cannon, and therefore had not taken aim either at us nor at the women, but my father insisted that we return forthwith.

Past the bend in the road and out of the vehicle's line of sight, we were safe.

No sooner home, we heard that the Germans were on the offensive against the partisans. When I discussed with Signor Cuni what we should do if the Germans came to Rittana, he had a surprising solution. Directly over Tanara, he said, in the cliffs rising on the other side of the stream, there was a cave. When Napoleon's army had occupied the Piedmont, the statue of San Mauro, in Rittana's church, had been concealed there. It was an excellent place to hide.

I lost no time seeking that cave. Though nearby, it was difficult to reach. One had to approach it not from below but from above the rugged cliff. I climbed up in a roundabout way and, following Signor Cuni's directions, located a gnarled little tree that protruded over the abyss. I then lowered myself as much as I dared. Now I was supposed to let go and lean forward as soon as my feet hit the ledge of the cave. I should fall but very little. But as I hung there, my feet dangling in midair, seeing nothing but the sheer height of the cliff, I didn't dare let go. I hoisted myself back up, went to see Signor Cuni, verified the directions, then suggested a rope. Not necessary, he reassured me; you let go and lean forward. I went back, tried again, berated myself for lack of courage, tried again, and did this a number of times, with no better result.

Next we heard rumors of Germans roaming through nearby valleys. My father and I prepared a few belongings to take with us. Did we need to take a lamp? I inquired. No, Signor Cuni assured us. A day or two later, Signor Cuni alerted us that the Germans had been spotted in our valley. They had, obviously, not come up from the highway but by mountain paths from adjacent valleys. Exactly where they were, no one knew.

Hurriedly, my father and I headed for the cave. Knowing the way well by now, I led my father up where the ascent was easiest, then through the wooded slope that capped the cliff. We were not aware that right then, the Germans, rushing in from the next valley, were advancing toward the rim of the cliff. Suddenly, ahead of us and quite nearby, a machine gun opened up. There was no going back. I dashed forward. The gnarled tree was not far away. Reaching it, I lowered myself, and, at the point of having to muster my courage once more, a second burst of machine-gun fire caused my hands to let go all by themselves. I landed on the ledge of the cave, told my father that I was all right, grabbed him in midfall as he followed, and pulled him in.

Then, to our consternation, we saw that the cave offered no possibility for hiding. Its shape suggested the inside of a human ear, except that, at the level of the ear canal, it abutted onto a ledge. It was on this ledge that we now stood, and it was into this "canal" that San Mauro's statue must have been inserted. Plugged with a stone, no one would suspect its presence. But that channel was too narrow for a person. The cave, foreshortened when seen from a distance, was unnoticeable. But the cliff dominated the valley, and we were exposed to view as on a stage. Signor Cuni quite likely had never looked through binoculars. For us, there was no way out. I arranged the few stones and branches that littered the ledge so as to conceal our heads somewhat. My father insisted on lying closest to the edge, shielding my body with his. There we lay as motionless as we could, listening to the bursts of the machine gun overhead.

We did not see the Germans. We heard later that, from the rim of the cliff, they fired into Rittana. Had they seen us? Who could know? After awhile the machine gun overhead fell silent, but firing continued elsewhere all day long. That night Signor Cuni came to the gnarled tree to slip us some food and advise us that the Germans were everywhere. This engagement was part, if I am correct, of Operation Tübingen, which lasted from April 23 to 27, 1944, and in which the Germans reported killing forty-nine partisans, wounding thirty-three, and capturing ten.[1] Had but one German trained his binoculars in our direction, we might have raised those statistics.

A half century later, life in the valley has changed. The road now is paved all the way up to Gorrè. People have cars, the younger generation commutes to work, chestnuts are no longer gathered, cows are no longer kept. A wealth of opulent flowers spills over walls and fences that surround the new construction that has expanded the old houses, making them spacious and comfortable. I had to search for the stables that, where they still exist, are used as storage places and appear unbelievably small. When I arrived there recently, with my wife and grown children in tow, people still remembered me. There was Caterina, the younger of Brondello's daughters, and Margherita, the lady in Tanara whose husband had not returned from the Russian front. And there were younger people as well, born after the war. These too must have heard of me, for each, amidst the shouting and laughter at the moment of recognition, raised an arm, hand pointing at the cave.

My father and I remained in that cave for three days. I never asked him what thoughts occupied his mind while he lay by its rim. As for me, I had prepared myself to while away time by bringing along the curate's book on crystallography. I had opened it once before, seen that it was difficult, and put it aside. That is why I had taken it along now. Confined here, I would be forced to read it. And so I did, despite even the occasional burst of gunfire. The book was filled with diagrams, tables, formulas, and unfamiliar technical jargon. I struggled even with the introductory chapter. But in those few pages, I sensed an astonishing fact. I had seen crystals in museums, admired their beauty, but considered them no more than broken rocks. Ah, but the edges! My book seemed to imply that, however the sides happen, the angles formed at their edges are constant, and specific for each type of crystal! How, I wondered, could that be? Or had I misread the text? I read and reread it. Frustrated, I closed the book and lay back, but kept puzzling about what I had read. Time and again, a possible interpretation of a particular word would strike my mind. Quickly, I reopened the book, perused the text once more. So it went for the three days that I spent in the cave, my immediate fate of less concern than this bewildering enigma.

At the end of the third day, I spotted what looked like a handkerchief lying on the grass outside the Cuni's home. It was, in fact, a bed sheet, a prearranged signal telling us that the Germans had left, and presently we heard Signor Cuni above us, coming to help us out of the cave.

Many years later, I learned the secret of crystals. They are atoms or molecules, all of one kind, arrayed next to each other, adhering so tightly that crystals grow without losing their original shapes. Looking at a crystal, we can glimpse the invisible atoms.

12
The Privilege to Be Shot as a Partisan

AFTER OUR ADVENTURE IN THE CAVE, we inquired about a place higher up in the mountains—higher even than La Balma, our former abode, which we deemed too close to the mule path and its traffic. We located such a place in Gorrè and, within days, moved in.

Gorrè was not accessible by vehicle. Although ruts left by wheels could be discerned along the mule path leading up to this village, I had seen a cart only once. It was a two-wheeled cart, much smaller than those used in Montagnac. A man and mule pulled it, the mule first, the man narrowly behind in the same traces. I saw the mule's hind leg slipping, kicking up stones that by a sheer miracle missed the man. Only thus could the carter negotiate the hairpin turns. Only thus could a little iron stove be brought up the mountain. German vehicles, at least, could not venture beyond the footbridge at Tetto Ponte.

Gorrè was a split village. The main village, Gorrè Soprano, a double tier of houses surmounted by a bell tower, was visible from afar. But the lodging we found was in the lower part, Gorrè Sottano. It was easily missed. A stranger coming up the mule path past La Balma and the mill would skirt a border of dense scrub, not suspecting that this scrub grew amidst the ruins of houses. Passing by a fountain—a stone trough, dug into the slope, catching dribbles from an iron pipe—the path turns, revealing a wicked stretch of road ahead, steep and straight, hollowed by runoff and bygone traffic. This is the final ascent to Gorrè. The stranger, bracing himself for the ascent, will fail to notice the little path leading from the fountain into the scrub, and will remain unaware of having just bypassed the lower part of the village.

Only one of the original inhabitants remained in Gorrè Sottano. He was an old man, a recluse, his presence manifested only by the presence of his chickens, his cat, and his dog. On our rare encounters, he never returned my greeting. Recently, however, a family had moved into the last stable that remained standing there: Ferdinand Gorges, his wife Annelise, and their daughter Lieserl, a radiant young girl with long, golden hair. They were refugees from Vienna. We quickly became friends.

Among the structures still standing, a few were still in use: one as a hayloft, and another, whose door clearly had not been opened for some time, to store tools and other discards. A house, still in good shape, had crutches extending from its rafters, a sign that its inhabitants had died of tuberculosis of the bones. No one ever entered it. The structure we were permitted to occupy was a drying shed, a stone building whose main room had a ceiling of wattle blackened by smoke. In bygone days, chestnuts had been spread out in it to dry. An iron stove was still in that room. Below was a low, vaulted basement, its entrance downhill around the corner. The basement had a fireplace and even a tiny window, but its floor was earthen. It had sheltered those minding the chestnuts. We moved into the upper room, airy despite its miniscule window, a benefit of the wattle ceiling. All that past smoke, I hoped, had conferred some insecticidal properties to the place. Alas, nothing interfered with the fleas' enjoyment of our presence.

Though unseen, our new location was an excellent listening post. Every sound in the valley was heard here. The slopes, dominated by a nearby peak, the Taiarè,[1] reverberated with them. On weekend evenings I could listen to the village boys singing at the trattoria in Gorrè Soprano. They might sing about a cruel hunter and a maiden and what he did to her. Or about a homesick soldier, imagining coming home, convincing his mother that he is back for good. Or about a captain of the Alpini who, about to die, longed to see his men once more. But they send word that they have no shoes, whereupon he orders, *"O colle scarpe, o senza scarpe, I miei Alpini, gli voglio qua."* "With or without shoes, I want my Alpini here!" I would have loved to join the boys had this not meant drinking away a bit of that small allowance received through the curate.

From up here one could follow, just by listening, the progress of some young man walking down in the valley. That was because they tended to sing at the top of their voices to while the time away. There was one in particular that we listened to. As likely as not, he would sing an aria from an opera. His favorite was "Una furtiva lagrima" from *The Elixir of Love,* which has the words "She loves me!" in it. The young man would give it all he had. Mr. Gorges assured me that he was a serious singer. Mr. Gorges should have known. He had been an impresario and mentioned once, offhandedly, that he had booked the Swedish diva Zarah Leander. His wife had been a concert pianist. He diverted us occasionally with arias from Viennese operettas. He kept his voice in shape by practicing scales every morning.

Beyond Gorrè, in the hamlet of Bric, we met some refugees from St. Martin-Vésubie: Bronka Halpern, her brother and his wife, and a couple of small children. Though a pediatrician, Bronka happened to be the only doctor a partisan could see without venturing into the valley. We understood that she was busy. Besides saying "hello" when I happened to come that way, I didn't see much of her. They left in April, shortly after our arrival, and reached Rome after some hair-raising adventures.[2]

In Gorrè Soprano, Riccardo Cavaglion and his brother Enzo had rented a room. We had seen them off and on since I first met Riccardo at the footbridge near Tetto Ponte. Their parents and sister lived there as well. Along with other Italian Jews in the region, they had been arrested and transferred to the barracks in Borgo San Dalmazzo, joining the captured refugees from St. Martin-Vésubie. Inexplicably, a week before the latter were deported, the Italian Jews had been released. Enzo and Riccardo lost no time bringing their parents and Miranda to Gorrè.

We visited them often. They lived in the village in a room almost identical to the one we had in Tanara, also entered from a balcony accessed by an outdoor stairway. But their room was bright inside. Their table was large and covered with a cloth, and a curtain hid the beds in the back. From them, we heard much of their life in Cuneo where, on its main street, Via Roma, they had a shop that sold cloth. From them we heard many a story about the Fascists but little about the partisans. Yet I sensed that Enzo and Riccardo were in contact with them. That, in all likelihood, was the reason for their silence. Only after the war did I learn that both had belonged to the small circle that, as the Germans occupied their country, had launched this province's partisan movement.[3] They had left to take care of their parents and sister, but they retained their contacts with the partisans in Paralup, whose presence remained unknown to me.

For our provisions I still had to go to Rittana. The small general store in Gorrè had little food to sell. On the way, I stopped, of course, at the places where I was known. To have done otherwise would have been unbecoming. The people were glad to see me, wanted to know how we were doing, and would not allow me to leave without some food to take back.

Not wanting to wear out my welcome by becoming too frequent a visitor, I went on excursions in new directions. Gorrè, though reached only by mule paths, was yet a crossroads. Here the path rising from Rittana abutted on a fairly level path that, clinging to the slopes, connected with the adjacent valleys. I began to explore this path. Wherever I went, I was no stranger. People knew who I was and where I lived. If someone was at home, I would be invited in. My Italian had become fairly fluent, and I picked up a few words of Piedmontese, the local dialect. We would exchange some bit of local news and bemoan the terrible times. When I was about to leave, the lady of the house, or her husband, would run into kitchen or pantry and return with something for me to take back: perhaps some lentils, an egg or two, or bread. And always they would invite me to come again.

In time, my wanderings turned into all-day affairs, as up here much greater distances separated hamlets than in the valley. Once I consumed the entire loaf of bread I had been given on my return walk. The high paths offered some memorable views. One time, having been delayed, I returned after dark. The night was clear, and the moon shone over a cloud that filled the valley. The path descended toward the cloud, then ran alongside it, the cloud so smooth, so calm, so bright, it appeared to be a lake. And once, after a storm, I looked upon a rainbow in the valley, its span closed, a shimmering double circle.

On my wanderings, I had become acquainted with a teacher, a middle-aged woman who, as was often done, was quartered in a schoolhouse. This was a one-room schoolhouse, the classroom below, the teacher's room above. One day when I came knocking at her door, she opened it still wearing her negligee. Come in, she said, I'll be dressed in a minute. The room was arranged much like the one we had in Tanara, a table and stove near the entrance, the bed in the back, and no partition in between. Averting my eyes, I sat at the table. After what seemed a long time, I looked up, only to see her lying in bed, one knee up, uncovered, naked. Seeing my gaze, she smiled at me. I was not prepared for this and looked away once more. Soon she was dressed. We chatted a little and I departed. The visit showered me with sex fantasies, but I never returned.

Although I was busy, my father had little to do. Up here he had not found local people such as those at Tetto Ponte or Tanara with whom he could have long conversations. But there were the Cavaglions and the Gorges. He might walk to the table that stood outside the latter's stable, a picnic table with parallel benches attached to it. There was more light there to read the single sheet newspaper, which still reached him. He studied it intently every day. Without access to a map, he attempted to infer to where in Russia the German troops had retreated. He also tried to read between the lines, to divine what really went on. It would not be long before Mrs. Gorges would come out, offering him a cup of the brew that passed for coffee. Mr. Gorges might join him to discuss the world situation, and one or the other of the Cavaglion boys might come by. Once, after listening to my father expound on the day's events, Enzo, not quite in agreement, took a look at the paper and discovered that it was an old paper, printed a couple of months ago.

I did all the cooking, which entailed fetching water in an army canvas bucket from the fountain and steadying a rickety pot atop the smoking stove. My father insisted, however, on a modicum of decor: we had to eat from plates, and our little table had to be covered, during meals, with a clean newspaper, which afterwards did duty as toilet paper. As I was the one doing all these chores and providing us with food, I had imperceptibly come to be in charge. I became aware of this only after the war ended for us, and our world changed. Then my father was in his element again, and I was totally out of mine.

I did not have to forage for food every day. I would stay home if the weather was bad, and if, after a rain, the Cavaglions came down, we would take Lieserl along and walk through the woods to collect mushrooms. I was not very good at it. Once, with great laughter, Enzo located a mushroom right next to where I had sat down. I needed eyeglasses and did not yet know it.

In Gorrè Sottano, without a nearby stable to go to for warmth, we would need wood for the winter. We computed that I would need to stack wood clear around our drying shed to supply our little stove. Lieserl and her parents needed as much, and so did the Cavaglions. We agreed to combine our efforts.

Enzo and Riccardo assembled an impressive panoply of woodsman's tools: saws for one man and saws for two, hatchets, axes, and mauls. Iron was a scarce commodity here, tediously husbanded, forever sharpened, made to last. The homemade handles of these tools required attention. One secured an axe head by banging a wedge into its handle and soaking it in water before use. One tensioned the blade of a bucksaw using a rope tourniquet, the very mechanism, I discerned, the ancient Romans had used in their catapults.

Off and on, we worked all summer long, felling trees, carrying them, cutting them up, and splitting the wood.

I did not cut any trees in or near Gorrè Sottano, particularly not trees sprouting from the rubble of collapsed buildings. Thus I hoped to minimize any signs of our presence. Instead, I went to the bottom of a nearby ravine. There, I once heard myself being called. Coming up, I met a man who introduced himself as the owner of this patch of woods. What could I say? Politely, I replied that I tried to limit myself to misshapen trees. The man grumbled that I could go on cutting, but perhaps I could cut a little higher up the ravine. Why? That patch belonged to someone else.

Sawing that wood was a more sociable affair. After I had accumulated a sufficient supply, Enzo and Riccardo would come down. Lieserl was invited to steady the log atop the sawhorse by sitting on it. She obliged, thereby eclipsing our panoply of tools, and turning hard work into banter and laughter as well as a cherished memory.

I would have liked to have had Lieserl as my girlfriend. Riccardo, however, had a crush on her. Lately, though, she and Riccardo had been at odds. Lieserl, in fact, began to confide her troubles to me, telling me how nice it was that she had me to talk to. I kept trying to comfort her while at the same time silently railing at fate for not having made this lovely girl fall for me. I still had much to learn.

Once, when I saw a piece of cardboard, a rarity in a place where nothing came in boxes, I asked its owner if I could make a toy from it for his kid. The toy was a jumping jack. The *"cicciu"* (pronounced

TCHIT'choo) was an instant success. Children in these parts did not have mechanical toys. Presently parents everywhere rummaged for cardboard. With the experience I gained, my jumping jacks increased in complexity, not only kicking up their legs but flailing their arms, rolling their eyes, sticking out their tongues, and doffing their hats. I was glad to reciprocate in this manner for the kindness these people had shown me. Twenty years later, on a visit, one father would still show me the *cicciu* I had made for his kids.

Convinced of my mechanical talents, people began asking me for help with their technical problems. One man had bought a small electric generator, salvaged from some bombed-out factory or shop. Such things could be obtained cheaply then. He wanted to generate electricity from a little creek running through his property. He had already constructed a small waterwheel that, as he demonstrated, turned merrily as long as it was not connected to the dynamo. How much larger did he have to make the wheel to turn the dynamo? I didn't know. Another person took me to his newly built house, constructed, as all the houses there, without the help of an architect. He burned some paper in its fireplace and asked me why there was no draft. Looking up the chimney, I saw the smoke go up and curl without finding the way out. It was sobering to find out how little I knew. This particular problem plagued me until, long after the war, I discovered that Count Rumford had solved it in 1796 by inventing a "smoke shelf" that has become the standard in constructing fireplaces.[4]

Beset by fleas, living in stables, and sleeping on straw, I considered the mountain people to be poor, and those living on this side of the footbridge to be the poorest among them. Up here, the owner of three cows was a rarity. Some possessed only one cow, with a mule sharing the stable with her. Up here, stables also tended to be smaller. Inside, a table was smaller as well, and one could not sit at either end: one end abutted the wall, and the other was too close to the animals. With the cows' heads tethered to a crib on the opposite wall, their tails were closest to the cramped living quarters. Sitting at the table, talking with farmer and family, I would suddenly see them jump up and, with much shouting and forceful shoving, prevent the animal, about to defecate, from shooting at the table.

Yet these people did not behave like poor people. Social distinctions were noticeable here as everywhere. The Brondellos at Tetto Ponte and the Cesanas at Frazione Battaglia were clearly patrician families. The young man who, with his sister, owned the small general store in Gorrè was obviously an up-and-coming business man. There were a few eccentrics. Our recluse neighbor at Gorrè Sottano was one; others were the bachelor miller, Massimo Borgogno, and a man in Butta who went by the nickname of *"disertur."*[5] He had been a deserter, I believe, in World War I. Most inhabitants behaved like solid, middle-class citizens, self-sufficient, owners of their homes and their land. Particularly in these times of shortages, their produce fetched undreamed-of prices. When I heard them complain, it was about the war, never about their material condition. We refugees were the ones who deserved charity.

I kept comparing living conditions here with those in Montagnac. There, to cope with the shortages of war, people had fallen back on an older technology, shifting, for example, from automobiles back to horse carts. But here, the old technology had never been relinquished. This technology, furthermore, was immensely older than the one Montagnac had fallen back upon.

Here the women washed their laundry on the side of the brook, kneeling on a flat stone about which the current eddied, scrubbing in ice-cold water, their arms bare and red. In the meadow, after the men had cut the hay, the women gathered it, wrapped it in a sheet, balanced it on their heads, and thus, over tricky mountain paths, carried it to the stable. And they cooked, as I have already described, over an open fire in a cauldron hanging from a chain, steadied with one's knee when stirring.

Their work was too much and too hard. "Once they reach thirty, they already look old," remarked my father. It didn't help that they wore black after they married. It occurred to me that Helen of Troy, whose beauty triggered the Trojan War, lived in an age when women worked like these. Was Helen so beautiful only because she didn't have to work?

That the women looked old was my father's opinion. To me, they radiated the aura of fairy tales. That was because of the work they did—more work yet—when their hands were free. Then they busied themselves with spinning. I knew about spinning. My mother had raised us children on the folk tales collected by the Brothers Grimm. I knew that the miller's daughter in Rumpelstiltskin had spun straw into gold. I knew that Sleeping Beauty had pricked her finger on a spindle. And I had seen spinning wheels in museums along with other carefully preserved objects that bespoke an immemorial past. Yet here I saw living people spin, spin like the miller's daughter in Rumpelstiltskin, in a tradition uninterrupted since fairy-tale times! I lacked the judgment to deplore such backwardness. Instead I was utterly captivated. Nothing ever had fascinated me as much.

Unlike the miller's daughter, who is usually depicted with a spinning wheel, the women here did not use such an implement. With what wonder did I gape at the equipment they used instead! It consisted simply of a long stick and a short one. The thread was formed on the way from the one to the other. To the top of the long stick, or distaff, that a woman held with her arm against her body, a bundle of fibers was bound. From it she drew out some fibers, a pinch at a time. With each pinch, the short stick, or spindle, which dangled and twirled alongside her robe, descended an inch or two. Just before the spindle reached the floor, the woman would grab it, quickly wind a finished length of thread onto it and, with a snap of her fingers, set it to twirl again.

One evening, in a stable, I asked the women to let me spin. Much merriment greeted the idea, as well as my awkward efforts. But I won't forget the surprise and awe of sensing the fibers come to life between my fingers, twisted by the spindle that spun and swayed more than a yard below.

I did, of course, ask the women why they didn't use a spinning wheel. They had never heard of one. The reason, I thought, was that a wheel makes spinning a sedentary occupation. Here, the women spun not only while sitting but also while walking and particularly while taking their cows to pasture. Indeed, the parklike appearance of the chestnut groves was a result of grazing. Feeding around the trees, cattle kept vegetation low, which facilitated gathering the chestnuts. Cows are, however, no mountain goats and might break a leg should they stray. A woman, therefore, always accompanied them, spinning all the while. Long afterwards, I learned that my theory about the absence of spinning wheels was wrong. That device produces too uneven a thread with hemp, which is what these women spun.[6]

The sheets in which women carried hay on their heads were homespun. Signor Cuni had a pair of pants made of homespun cloth. When they were new, he said laughingly, they had stood up by themselves. Few men wore them anymore. At a bend along the path to Cesana, there was a murky little pit flooded by a feeble creek. One noticed it only in the fall because of the putrid stench that surrounded it then. That was where harvested hemp stalks were soaked to rot. Afterwards, the fibers were removed from their straw for the women to spin. And in Cesana itself, there was a loom where a weaver made the spun yarn into cloth.

I went to see it. As I approached the stable that housed it, an intense and familiar odor struck me. It was the smell of grated raw potatoes, from which my mother used to make potato latkes, the traditional Jewish pancakes. Puzzled, I opened the door. There was the loom, a heavy, homemade frame, filling the space from ceiling to floor and from wall to the rump of the cows. It was sturdy enough to withstand the tension of thousands of threads. Strung from one end of the frame to the other, all in one plane, these lay so close together that already they looked like a sheet. One sheet? No, two, not quite parallel, that passed magically back and forth through each other. Raw potatoes mixed with butter lubricated their passage, the weaver explained. He sat at the end of the frame, on a worn, uneven board, pumping two pedals that, through a connection of ropes, rods, and beams, pulled two narrow, rectangular sails in opposite directions. These sails, called heddles, also intersected the sheets and were, in fact, the cause of their improbable intermeshing. Just when the distance between the two illusory sheets was widest, the weaver, with one hand, flung the shuttle between them. Then, while the sheets intermeshed once more, he jerked with the other hand a frame holding a comb that clapped the newly laid thread tightly against its predecessor. Then he threw the shuttle with the other hand, and thus the man went on, a-creaking and a-banging, heedless of my presence, carrying on with both hands, both arms, and both feet. Occasionally, he interrupted his work to make some adjustment and to examine his progress. I couldn't see any. Indeed, it would take him some eighty throws of the shuttle to produce just one inch of cloth.[7]

What a difference, I thought, between the miller and the weaver. The latter had been too busy to say more than but a few words to me. Massimo, however, had been eager to take me around his mill and talk about it. As he sat there and talked, around us the wooden axles and gears and millstone turned and groaned and even the walls quaked under the exertion of the water wheel. And all the while, without human intervention, the grain was ground.

Water power had been harnessed to grind corn in ancient Rome. Mechanical power had been applied to looms in England late in the eighteenth century. It was the event that ushered in the Industrial Revolution. Clearly, it had not arrived here yet.

The war changed that. Unbidden, metal had invaded the mountains. Steel machined to close tolerances, parts interacting precisely with each other, complex mechanisms in which neither wood nor string nor stone had a place. These novelties could be seen all around us: Sten guns, hand guns, hand grenades, even anti-tank rockets.

And one day we were treated to the most spectacular display of modern technology I ever saw. It occurred on the expiration date of an amnesty that the Fascist government had widely advertised by leaflets and in newspapers. Partisans who surrendered by the deadline, the government promised, would be allowed to return home. They would not be deported to Germany; they would not have to serve in the military; they would be rehabilitated. Those, however, who did not turn themselves in would be rooted out. Massive operations supported by artillery and other means would be launched against them immediately upon the expiration of the deadline. In anticipation, the name of every occupant of each house had to be posted prominently on its door. Anyone unable to explain his presence would be considered a partisan.

A number of partisans, grown weary, heeded the offer, but in the fastness of the mountains the disaffection was minimal. Still, as the deadline approached and the threats intensified, apprehension spread.

Without papers to confirm our identity, neither my father nor I nor any Jewish refugee could post a name on a door. Still, no small police force nor SS squad would risk roaming the mountains to surprise a few Jews. Our fate, henceforth, was intertwined with that of the partisans. "It will be our privilege," my father said philosophically, "to be shot as partisans."

On the day following the deadline, May 26, 1944, we were up at dawn, watching for any signs, ready to run or hide. The Gorges were up, and soon Enzo and Riccardo joined us. Suddenly we became very quiet, to hear better a faint and distant noise. It was the rumble of an engine. That was disquieting. It had to be Fascist or German, since no one else in these parts owned a motorized vehicle. The noise intensified. Once we could hear it better, we realized that it was the sound not of one but several engines and then that it was too steady to come from vehicles negotiating mountains. More likely, these were planes. The Germans had airfields in the valley and had used planes against the partisans before. What were they up to now? They couldn't check identities with planes. We were deadly afraid. Was this to be an indiscriminate massacre? Then we saw the planes. They were high up in the sky, very small, and those with keener eyes than mine could make out four engines on each. One after another they caught the sun, glistening golden in the pale sky, a fleet on the move. We counted the planes by their formations, each in the shape of an unevenly sided *V*. We counted ten, twenty, thirty formations and kept counting. Fear had turned into jubilation. This many could not possibly be German. These had to be American. Enzo jumped on the picnic table in front of the Gorges' stable, tore his shirt off, waved it wildly at the thundering sky. Each formation consisted of nine planes, and when we stopped counting, our total was more than a hundred. That was a thousand bombers, all of them in our field of view, roaring with four thousand engines, full throttled and unmuffled. It was a spectacle few people would ever witness. *"Farfalle d'oro,"* golden butterflies, somebody called them later.

Once they were gone, elation gave way to awe as we contemplated the fate about to befall the Germans. But later, when the planes returned, there were not that many, and our hearts now bled for them. The formations, however, had only scattered, some coming back earlier than others. We assured ourselves that each still had nine planes. As far as we could tell, not one plane was missing.

Checking up on this raid as I was writing these pages, I learned that its target was not Germany but marshaling yards in southern France. The bombers belonged to the U.S. Fifteenth Air Force, based in southern Italy.[8] Safe there from German air raids, its replacement bombers were no longer painted.[9] This unburdened each plane of several hundred pounds while the polished aluminum skin, flashing for us in the sunlight, added fifteen miles per hour to its speed. According to my source, there were seven hundred planes. We must have counted some formations more than once. But we were not alone in making this mistake. A partisan leader who later described this raid also mentions a thousand planes.[10] It seemed to be even more than that.

13
The Oldest Instinct

The Partisan war was a complete violation of international law and contradicted every principle of clean soldierly fighting . . . the [partisan's] southern temperament could run riot, their "patriotic mission" combined with vicious instincts leaving few loopholes for compunctions . . . To the work of these bands must be ascribed most of the many acts of sabotage . . . and the equally frequent crimes against humanity. In the whole calendar of crimes—from ambushing, hanging, drowning, burning, freezing, crucifying and every kind of torture, not forgetting the poisoning of wells and the repeated abuse of the Red Cross—there is not one which was not an everyday occurrence . . .

In consequence there was considerable irritation on our side, for the German soldier in the infested areas could not help seeing in every civilian of either sex a fanatical assassin or expecting to be fired at from every house.

—Field-Marshal Kesselring, commander, Italian theater of war, 1953, from *The Memoirs of Field Marshal Kesselring*

THE OVERFLIGHT OF THE AMERICAN planes presaged the Allied invasion of France, which everyone had anticipated for some time. People speculated about it, tried to guess when it might happen and how it would develop. Jokes made the rounds. One was about a city dweller who spent his meager ration of electricity attempting to tune in on the BBC. After years of trying, an interruption in the jamming finally allowed him to catch a broadcast, and, with his electricity ration running out, he just managed to hear, "Patience,

patience, we'll be coming soon!" Enzo had mastered the German translation of this punch line, and I still can hear the ring of his voice joshing my father with *"Geduld, Geduld, wir kommen bald!"* Enzo had many opportunities for joshing as, time and again, events flouted my father's prognostications.

We began to see more Allied bombers although never again in such large numbers. Once they bombed one of our valleys. As I stood watching their formations advancing in the sky, I saw them turn around. What had happened? For minutes, I wondered why. Then in the distance, I happened to notice a curious phenomenon: a mountain ridge darker and higher than I remembered it. It was no ridge. It grew as I looked on. It was black smoke, rising up the length of a valley. The planes had bombed it, then turned back. Of the explosions, I had heard no sound.

Sweeps continued, now here, now there, always carried out by German soldiers. They did not bother to examine the names posted on the doors of houses. The ink on such lists faded and the paper shriveled.

One evening, a sweep was reported in a neighboring valley. A column of partisans who were evading the Germans walked past our hamlet. They confirmed the report. After night had fallen, I noticed a fire flickering on the mountainside. Then I saw more such fires scattered about. German campfires, I realized. The sweep was not finished. They were combing our valley.

I had not heard of a night sweep before and decided to leave immediately. I figured that the partisans who had passed by earlier would know how to avoid German night patrols, and I hastened to catch up with them. That proved easy. At any fork along the path, I found people who could tell me which direction the partisans had taken. I located them in the next valley, already settled in an empty stable and ready to bed down.

I reported the German campfires to a partisan standing at the door. They had seen them, he said. No further questions being asked, I made myself a place in a straw pile among others already asleep.

On a table at the far side of the stable, a single oil lamp still shed a little light. Around it sat several partisans, still talking. Presently, one of them, whom I took to be their commander, turned around and asked for volunteers for a patrol.

No one answered.

"Come now," said the man. "We can't sit here and be surprised."
He coaxed and pleaded but to no avail.
I finally got up and went to him.
"I want to volunteer," I said.
Dubiously, he asked me who I was. A refugee, I replied, adding that I lived around here and knew all the paths. He nodded, saying that he had heard about the Jewish refugees, and asked about my military experience. To that, I had no answer, and he no comment. But he turned to his men, ever so mildly chiding them, the partisans, for not coming forward, for letting an inexperienced refugee put them to shame.

Several men now came forward, and I went back to sleep.

The next morning, the commander got us up early and out into a cold fog, in which one could see only a few feet ahead. After climbing for some distance, we unexpectedly came out of this fog. In broad daylight now, on a barren mountainside bereft of cover, our pace quickened. Even I could grasp that the Germans, seeing a column of partisans thus exposed, would have a heyday. The path ascended diagonally a steep slope, in and out of shallow, incipient ravines. Within these snow still lingered, old and icy, hiding the path. Here, I had only the footprints of my predecessors as a guide. I happened to look ahead just as a man missed his footing on this ice. Horrified, I saw him slide down. He made no sound and instantly was out of sight. No one stopped. No one as much as slowed down. Nor did I as I reached the footstep that bore the trace of his slip. I did not even glance sideways down the ravine, lest I, too, lose my footing.

Out of breath, I reached the top of the mountain, the peak of the Taiarè. From here, one could look down in every direction and see anyone approaching. Unless strafed by a plane, this small, uneven plateau, strewn with huge boulders, was easily defensible. Lying on the thick, old snow that covered everything, I relaxed. My tongue was completely dry, unfeeling when I bit it.

As I recovered, I began to look around. Nearby, a partisan motioned me to come. When I reached him he told me that the man I had lain next to was a Russian. I learned later that he was a deserter from Vlasov's army,[1] a "Liberation Army" made up of Russian soldiers who had defected to the Germans. Now they had defected to the partisans. "Don't get too close to him," the partisan cautioned me. "They have lice."

I asked him about the man who had missed his step. He was one of the Russians, he replied. What happened to him? He didn't know. I spent the rest of the day lolling on the ice, warmed by the sunshine, safe from lice and the Germans. By evening, I returned to my father.

On June 4, 1944, the Allies, having broken the five-month-long stalemate before Cassino, liberated Rome. Two days later the long-awaited landing took place in Normandy. Day after day, our censored paper reported the imminent failure of those landings, and day after day we agonized over the obvious difficulties experienced by the invasion forces, first on the beaches and then in their confined bridgehead. Quietly, I despaired that there might be some truth to what the paper reported, that our deductions and the rumors we heard were but wishful thinking. Most every day now, my father and I were in Gorrè to discuss the news with the Cavaglions. Short of real news, we spent much time arguing about the correct pronunciation of "Caen," the name of a key city the Allies had to take.

Those who could fight, however, did not stand idly by. Now partisans everywhere went on the offensive. Though here in the Alps they were far from any front, they still could pin down German forces.

Allied aircraft came in for support. Although they had to come a long way, these were not large bombers that remained high in the sky but fighter bombers that dove so near Gorrè that those with better eyesight than mine could distinguish their pilots' heads inside their canopy and their bombs detach as each plane pulled up.

Their target was a bridge outside Gaiola, where the valley widens and the river embraces the incipient plain with a giddy oxbow. A stone bridge carried the highway over the chasm the river created there, and an adjoining trestle carried the railway tracks. The nearness of the mountains, however, caused capricious drafts to buffet the planes. Their bombs, as rumor had it, hit a hospital and a school but never the bridge. In the end, partisan sappers, showing their mettle, blew it up.[2]

That was on July 13. How life changed thereafter!

"The partisan war, mobile, agile, heedless of fighting order," wrote a partisan commander, "was transformed into a war of position and into garrison life."[3] Securely ensconced behind the chasm, the partisans now held more than thirty miles of the Stura Valley, all the way to the Maddalena Pass on the border with France. The territory included a highway and train that connected nearly a dozen townships and many secondary valleys. Everywhere along this stretch, it was as if we had already been liberated.

I could safely go down to Gaiola, pause at the chasm, and stand in awe before the breathtaking footbridge, made entirely of rope, that the partisans had suspended over it. I watched as a couple of them coaxed an old woman carrying a large basket over its narrow, swaying gangway. Far below, half in water, rested the twisted skeleton of the former span. The footbridge was mined, I was told, just in case the Germans should give it a try.

Then I went into town, in broad daylight, and joined some other people in a living room vibrating with the crackling, fading, and squealing of a short-wave set, whose owner fiddled with its buttons. Eventually the Trumpet Voluntary, the signature of the BBC, came through. Reverently we listened to the litany of coded messages that preceded the news. Gleefully, we cheered the reports of Allied victories and German reverses. There was mention also of incredible atrocities committed by the Germans. Knowingly, we smiled. We were well aware that there had to be some war propaganda in such broadcasts.

And on my return, as I approached Gorrè, the air vibrated with songs shouted out with gusto from the trattoria.

Life outside our thirty-mile heaven, however, was wretched. We heard of severe food shortages, of harassment by the Fascist government, and of ambushes and retaliations.[4] These tribulations sent more and more people to seek refuge in our valley. People came from as far away as Turin and the Liguria. The number of partisans kept increasing.

The partisans did not sit passively in their domain but made forays into the surrounding countryside. In one of these I was asked to participate. In the town of Bernezzo, the partisans had arranged with a sympathetic Italian jailer to liberate their imprisoned comrades and supporters. As they would risk recapture if released all at once in an unfamiliar locale, guides were needed to escort them to safety. As a large group might attract attention, each guide would escort only a few of the inmates. Enzo asked me to be an escort.

I knew the territory well enough to reach the back road that led me to Bernezzo. Arriving in the town on the night of the release, I found the designated parking lot without difficulty, located as it was across the street from a church and next to a café. Out of the darkness, a shadowy figure approached me and, after an exchange of a few words, introduced me to another man. Quickly and silently the two of us were on our way.

Dawn broke as we hurried along a path atop a low ridge. Here we could be seen from afar, but I had to slow down and wait for my charge who, after his time in prison, had difficulty keeping up with me. Finally, the path reached cover and I stopped for a rest. It was time to become acquainted. I asked my charge the obvious question: How had he been captured?

I expected a tale of courage and daring, but I should have known better than that the partisans would entrust me with one of their heroes. The man I was leading to safety was a common murderer. His victim had been either his girlfriend or her lover, I no longer remember who. When the prisoners were liberated, no questions had been asked.

On August 15, two months after their landings on the beaches of Normandy and one month after the partisans' capture of the Stura Valley, the Allies carried out a second landing in France, this one on its Mediterranean coast. Their first objective was to seize the ports of Marseilles and Toulon, which would greatly facilitate supplying their armies in the north.

Those armies had finally broken out of their narrow bridgehead and were advancing on Paris. But while the German armies in France came apart, here in the Alps they went on the offensive. Two days after the Allied landings began in southern France, columns of German infantry and an armored regiment arrived at the abutments of the Stura Bridge. Advancing both on the highway and the military road, they punched their way to the Maddalena Pass. Neither the partisans nor Allied aircraft, who flew in support, could stop them.[5] The other valleys fared no better. A week later, on August 24, the German war communiqué reported: "In the Franco-Italian Alps region our battle groups advanced against stubbornly resisting terrorists across pass-roads to the west. Maddalena Pass is again in our hands following hard fighting."

If the Germans had been worried that the Allied troops pouring into southern France intended to use the partisan-held valleys to irrupt in the back of the Germans fighting in the Italian boot, then they had averted that danger. But if the Germans had hoped to interfere with the landings, they had come too late. By the time they reached the Maddalena Pass, these Allied forces were well established and rapidly fanning out.

Indeed, it must have been in preparation for this second landing that the Allies sought to plug all road exits from Italy. The twisted remains of the bridge that rested on the floor of the Stura River was one of the plugs that shielded the Allies' arrival, and the partisans' terrific defense of the valley held that shield up during the landing's critical stages.

Thereafter, the Allied armies, with excellent harbors assuring a steady flow of supplies, advanced as on wings. They entered Paris on August 25 to a delirious welcome, they liberated Antwerp, my home town, nine days later, and a week after that, not far from Cologne, they crossed the border into Germany.

In the Italian Alps, however, the Allies neglected the new front they had established, leaving but minimal forces to man it. The Germans, on the other hand, consolidated their positions, refitting the old fortifications along the Franco-Italian border. They brought in the Fascist Black Brigade to deal with the local population. The Black Brigade searched for partisans, relatives of partisans, and sympathizers of partisans. They confiscated property, impressed labor, penalized for specious infractions, and in general conducted themselves like the contemptible lot they were.[6] But they remained in the main valley. They did not venture onto the heights.

There the partisans still roamed, attacking the long and vulnerable roads in the valley that connected the front to the plain. Although their reign in the Stura Valley had lasted no longer than a month, they had not been vanquished. They had only reverted to their hit-and-run tactics.

The German army had to deal with them. The SS had long since gone, and the armored regiment left quickly. The German forces now consisted mostly of Austrian mountain troops. Well-trained and well-equipped, they accelerated the sweeps. At the Alpine front, most of the fighting took place in the rear of the German lines.

I debated with Enzo and Riccardo the best tactic to survive the anticipated sweeps. We agreed that neither the older folks nor the women needed to worry. The Germans looked only for men who might be partisans. That included the three of us. We had to decide whether it was safer to hide or to try to outrun the Germans. The local boys tended to conceal themselves, the partisans to retreat.

We had heard of one man's wife covering his hideaway with a heap of dung. He was asked, "Didn't it drip?" "Yes," the man acknowledged, "but it was warm." Another man, hurt by an exploding hand grenade, managed to hide in the nick of time in his grandmother's bed, the old lady lying right on top of him. Such was the potential of a straw bed.

Despite the lesson of the wood above Valdieri, I still considered hiding. Running around in the open seemed even more scary. Enzo and Riccardo, however, favored the tactic of the partisans. They argued that since we were familiar with the area and knew the people, we too could evade the Germans. Dubiously, I acquiesced.

The opportunity to test our strategy came quickly. News reached me that the Germans had been seen nearby. It was too late to coordinate with Enzo and Riccardo. When it was all over I had seen no Germans, but Enzo returned with a bullet hole in his sleeve. He and his brother had been seen and shot at, had jumped into a ravine while being fired upon, and then, out of sight, had managed to climb up behind a rock. Thus German pursuers searching the bottom of the ravine missed them.

While Enzo and Riccardo reconsidered their options, we heard that the Germans carried out sweeps even at night. Enzo obtained the owner's permission, and then he, his brother, and I rearranged a barn half full of hay so as to look full and had Lieserl cover the hole through which we entered. Much banter accompanied this undertaking, with many wishes of good night and pleasant dreams. We acted like kids on a holiday, and so it was the next evening again. Then these lovely nights in the hay ended. We heard that the Germans tended to set fire to suspected hideouts.

And I saw them do it. A sweep having been rumored, I had hurried to a ridge separating two valleys, ready to go from one into the other should the Germans show up in one of them. Nothing had happened, though, and I suspected a false alarm when a young man with whom I had passed the time, called me in a low voice, motioning me to come. The Germans are right here, he whispered as I reached him. You can see them. We crept up on our bellies to some bushes at the crest of the ridge. From there, a meadow swept down and then up to the next ridge on which stood a farmhouse and, in front of it, several German soldiers. All of this was so near that I clearly heard the shouted commands to torch the building. As flames quickly enveloped it, I could hear their crackling. My last view, before quietly retreating, was of German silhouettes outlined against the flames, their weapons pointed, ready to shoot anyone who might emerge.

Although Paralup was no longer a partisan headquarters then, the day came when the Germans strode through Gorrè Sottano. Alerted, I had hastened off. They did not bother my father when they saw him in bed. His worries were enough to make him look sick. Not understanding Italian, they did not bother to check papers. They could tell a partisan when they saw one.

When they opened the door to the Gorges' stable, they took but one look and went away. But Mr. Gorges was not content to see them go. He called them back. In German! He told them that he was an Austrian citizen, up here because he had been bombed out, and was glad to see them. The soldiers reported this encounter to their commander. Before long, several officers came to call on Mr. Gorges. His wife who, despite food scarcities, had on occasion regaled us with *Palatschinken,* a Viennese pancake, served them hot ersatz coffee and homemade sweets. They remained there for several hours, talking not about the war but of old times, of their families, and of what each had done as a civilian before the war. I am sure that Mr. Gorges mentioned, offhandedly, that he had booked Zarah Leander in Vienna. The officers, undoubtedly, had seen some of the German movies in which she starred, and may have known that she had entertained Hitler. Before leaving, the officers warned Mr. Gorges to beware of the partisans. He replied, with a straight face, that he had never seen any.

Afterward, Mr. Gorges justified his action to us: his papers identified him and his wife as Austrians. He had managed to learn no more than a few words of Italian. To be perceived as non-Jewish Austrians, they had to be affable to the Germans.

How life had changed! The dogs in the valley no longer alerted us of the presence of Germans. The sound of soldiers tramping by cowed them. They failed to bark. At such times also, people living down there feared to call up the mountain, so the vaunted acoustics of Gorrè proved to no avail to us. Sounds that frightened everybody might, on the other hand, turn out to be innocuous. More than once, a hungry partisan tried fishing the Bial with a hand grenade. Another partisan, hungry, cold, and tired, fired a burst of his machine gun as he approached Gorrè late at night, so that when he arrived, he found everybody up, eager to feed him and to learn what had happened. Even a cuckoo could be terrifying, piping up just as Riccardo, hidden nearby, thought he heard Germans approaching. The retelling of such events occasioned great hilarity. *"Oh, la paura!"*—"oh, the fear!"—I recall Lucia, the schoolmistress, exclaim in a great peal of laughter.

Laughter, however, was becoming rare. Tales of narrow escapes had ceased to be funny. Again and again we heard of some strapping young fellow whom we had met as he passed through being killed in an encounter. No one, anymore, brought me cardboard to make a *cicciu*.

Life, nevertheless, had to go on. We had not finished preparing wood for the winter. I still went foraging for food. The fleas did not relent. Other woes added to the trouble. One morning my father awoke with the left side of his face swollen. He diagnosed his illness a *"giftige Rose,"* which he knew to be fatal. He kept his head wrapped in a blanket while I went to the Cavaglions to send for a doctor. Indeed, before long a doctor came up on foot all the way from Gaiola, gave my father some medicine, and told him not to worry.

Not always can the doctor come to the patient. When I experienced an awful toothache, Enzo accompanied me to the nearest dentist, whose office was in Gaiola, now under German and Fascist control. Arriving ahead of the other patients, we were quickly ushered in. The dentist examined me and declared that I needed root canal work. He seemed nervous, afraid to be caught tending a partisan, I suppose. Nevertheless, he proceeded with the operation, working fast. I fainted. As I came to, Enzo was holding my legs up. The doctor continued with the procedure while Enzo stood by holding my legs, raising them when he thought I might pass out again. When we left, the waiting room was crowded and the people upset because a man lay twitching on the floor, brown liquid oozing from his eyes and mouth. He was suffering an epileptic seizure. Upset and unsteady, I made the long ascent to Gorrè.

Next there was a fire in the Gorges' stable. Convinced that smoke was bad for his singing voice, Mr. Gorges kept firewood stacked around their stove to dry before burning it. One day, the stove must have been too hot, and the wood too near, and it suddenly burst into flames. Hearing screams and seeing the red glow in their window, I ran up to Gorrè, calling the alarm. Quickly the boys of the village were on their way, overtaking me on the way down, each already carrying a bucket, each scooping it full of water as he ran past the fountain. They quickly quenched the fire. The Gorges' landlord, arriving before long, summarily evicted them. But then, the stable having cooled some, he examined the blackened tie beam. Finding that its integrity had not been affected, he let them stay.

There were some quiet days as well. On one such day, my father and I happened to be walking leisurely up to Gorrè. Some leaves had changed color and some already littered the path. Fall was in the air. "It is Yom Kippur," my father said unexpectedly.[7] How did he know? I wondered. We had no Jewish calendar. He may have counted ten days from the new moon in September. But I did not ask. We continued to walk in silence, I very surprised to feel the solemnity of this holy day.

Earlier that year, the Cavaglions, the Gorges, and we had celebrated the Passover Seder in Gorrè. We had neither matzo nor a Haggada, but I still had the Hebrew Bible brought along from St. Martin-Vésubie. From it my father made me translate a few passages relating to the exodus from Egypt. "I stretch out my hand over Egypt and bring out the children of Israel from their midst."[8] Our imminent deliverance could be glimpsed in such sentences. There was hope in the air. There was hope everywhere.

Indeed, it was following that Passover that the Allies landed in Normandy. But though their troops had reached the approaches of the Maddalena and the Cherry Passes well before Yom Kippur, it had become clear that they would not advance further. The solemnity I sensed on this Yom Kippur owed much to the foundering of the promise of that Passover.

One man remained unperturbed by the gloomy turn of events. His name was Don Raimondo Viale. He was someone of whom I had never heard. He was the curate of Borgo San Dalmazzo, a curate like so many other curates in the small towns, villages, and hamlets that had suddenly found themselves with helpless Jewish refugees on their hands. Unlike the other curates, however, he had better grasped the dangers to which we would be exposed, and he had urged the archdiocese in Genoa to action. That had launched the attempts to get us out of the mountains, as well as the allocation of our stipends. Don Viale thereafter distributed these moneys to the curates of the hamlets that harbored Jews. Never seen, he maintained a secret but meticulous accounting and, should he be arrested, had concocted explanations as to why he, an ordinary curate, had to carry so much money so far from his parish. He was particularly at risk because he had been jailed before the war for anti-Fascist activities that included veiled condemnations of the anti-Jewish laws of 1938. His four-year sentence had been reduced only through the personal intervention of the Bishop of Cuneo. And now Don Viale kept up his lone deliveries, month after month. He would not allow the intensified fighting to interfere.

The snow arrived unexpectedly. One morning, as I opened the door of our airy smoke room, it was already more than knee deep, obliterating the two stone steps that led to our door and much else. As I stood there looking, not quite knowing what to do, my unbelieving eyes saw a trench in the snow that, curiously, crumbled forward in my direction. Not until it nearly reached me did I see inside the recluse neighbor's dog, paddling ahead as if swimming in water.

I moved our bed and table into the basement, where I replaced the missing window pane with shards of glass that I wedged into the frame. I began to cook in the cauldron hanging in the open fireplace, whose fire kept the basement comfortably warm. And although the basement's low tie beams left an occasional bump on my head, its door opened on the splendid view of a snowy meadow gently sloping down as if bowing before the majestic peak of the Taiarè, glorying in all its whiteness in the sunshine.

I never tired of watching Taiarè's moods as it tousled with clouds, or trailed a plume of snow, or sparkled with ice.

Enzo and Riccardo, both accomplished skiers, decided that I needed a pair of skis. They got someone to make me a pair and, what proved more difficult, obtained the metal fasteners. They also had strips of seal pelt that, strapped to the underside of my skis, allowed me to go uphill. I practiced as much as I could, in part to gain experience, in part to confound any Germans attempting to follow my tracks. Because that winter the snow did not spare us German incursions.

Living in a suburb of Washington, D.C., I note with bemusement the slow removal of paltry amounts of snow. In the Italian Alps, the local boys never took more than half a day to reopen the paths linking the villages. In each village, they assembled following a snowfall and went downhill over the snow-covered path, the first in line donning snowshoes with which he tamped down the snow. As he got tired, the next in line spelled him, and so on, until they reached the next village. From there, the path had already been opened in a like manner.

One day the Germans came up these cleared paths all the way to Gorrè and beyond.

We had been alerted in time, and I left our house, going first to Gorrè, then sideways toward the Taiarè. I stopped at a stable to exchange news. It was well that I did, for the people inside had spotted in the distance Germans coming up the path to their house from the very direction into which I was heading. I had to leave immediately and hide.

Where? No woods were nearby. But a ravine ran parallel to the path, not too far away. That was my only chance. I jumped on the snow bordering the path. The settled snow supported my weight but retained my footprints. What could I do? I kept going. On the ravine's edge, I spotted a withered tree, its root undercut and exposed. Dark amidst the snowy whiteness, it would conceal me. But reaching the root, I found nothing underneath to support me. I tucked my legs into its ramifications, held on with arms and hands, and hung there.

It was in the nick of time. To my right, I could see out over the ravine, and there, emerging from behind a turn, three German soldiers advanced on the path. I could make out their helmets, their packs, their weapons. Had they seen me? The path remained level as it rimmed the sloping ravine. To follow the soldiers with my eyes, I had to twist my neck more and more, and soon I had to give this up. After what seemed a suitable length of time, I twisted my neck once more to make sure that the soldiers were gone. They were not. They stood no more than fifty feet beyond my hideout, their black silhouettes sharp against the snow, one man raising his arms to his face. He is aiming a gun at me, I thought. Not wanting to see more, I slowly turned my head back. Somehow, that motion dislodged a dark clump of frozen soil and rocks. I watched it tumble over the snowy slope toward the middle of the ravine, hesitatingly, like a pinwheel ending its spin. It seemed to take forever. But no shot came, and after another minute, I dared turn my neck once more, just in time to see the only remaining soldier putting away not a gun but a pair of binoculars. Had he not looked only into the distance, I think, he could not have failed to notice me.

From their window, the people in the stable had observed all this. When I stopped by later, they looked at me as if I were a ghost.

By the fall of 1944, I had seen partisans wearing British battle jackets and colorful silken headbands. The latter had been made from parachutes that had brought the former. One cold winter evening, I was asked to help carry away an anticipated parachute drop. Though the night was clear, I never got a good look at the half dozen mummified fellows I fell in with and followed over a considerable distance, quietly but for the squeaking snow underfoot. At an open field, our leader declared that we had arrived. There we waited for many hours. We even heard a distant plane again and again, but the drop never came. It must have fallen into German hands, I was told. Since then, however, I have learned that different partisan bands, desperate for weapons, managed to appropriate each other's signals. "This may seem incorrect, and disloyal, and illegal," wrote one partisan, "but he who lives in the partisan ambiance, and participates in its exigencies and practices, is not overly scandalized. The truth is that for a partisan commander, the *porro unum necessarium* are weapons. To obtain weapons for his formation, a partisan commander will stop at nothing, even if it means selling his soul to the devil. Consequently, he will not think twice at 'blowing' an airdrop from others."[9]

Hours later, back in our basement in the dark morning hours, I attempted to thaw the canvas leggings—hand-me-downs of a uniform of World War I—in front of the fire. Progress was very slow. My father had gotten out of bed, concerned. I could feel neither my legs nor my feet. It all felt like a block of ice, and I feared severe frostbite. For some time already, my footwear had been in a sorry state. Wet straw, collecting in the toe of my boots, had turned into a miniature compost pile, rotting the leather. The shoemaker had despaired of sewing toe cap to sole again. Another pair of boots was not to be had. Unwrapping the icy leggings, unraveling the frozen puttees underneath, seemed to take hours. All that was forgotten, however, when I saw that I could still wiggle my toes.

Among the supplies dropped by Allied planes there were occasionally propaganda leaflets, intended, I think, to be distributed surreptitiously to German troops. These usually depicted some fat and ugly Nazi graphically forcing his attention on some pretty but helpless woman—the wife, according to the caption, of a soldier away at the front. But one leaflet was different and caught my attention. Nothing indicated its true origin. It flaunted the logo of the Nazi party and the imprint of the "NSDAP Command for the Development of Bush Warfare." It exhorted German soldiers to fight on, even after "the cowardly enemy's superiority in men and materiel" had allowed its soldiery to occupy the cities and hamlets of Germany. "Already today," the leaflet insisted, "each party member must begin to bury food and weapons in secret places in wood and field, must seek a lonely hut in pathless terrain that will protect him at least halfway against the hardships of the coming winter. He must recapture the native wisdom of our ancestors, to use the herbs and berries of the forest for his sustenance."[10] As psychological warfare, this leaflet seemed flawed to me. It reflected the way we were living. And if we could live like that, might not the Germans, too?

What if the Germans got stuck here, among us? The Allied forces, having come up the Italian boot, were about to irrupt into the Po Valley, cutting off the German armies still in Italy. What if they didn't retreat in time?

It was inconceivable that the Germans would surrender to the partisans. They knew that no quarter would be given them. On my wanderings I had seen German posters showing photos of German soldiers, bludgeoned to death and their ears cut off, ostensibly by partisans.[11] The Germans knew that their safety here depended entirely on the force of arms and the fear of brutality. They could not disband. Any breach of discipline, any relaxation on their part, would be their undoing. Beaten everywhere else, the Germans remained unassailable here in Italy, their very last corner of Europe outside Germany.

I remember leaning against an escarpment, looking down our valley. Once more I was on the run. Once more I did not know whether the rumored sweep was real or not. During these long hours of waiting, I did not cower in fear. I tried to be comfortable, keep dry, and remain hidden. I listened. Did I hear voices? Whose were they? I was alert to any crack. Would it be followed by a second? As usual, I had chosen a hideout with a wide view. After nearly two years in these parts, I felt at home here. I admired the scenery. Many features in it were associated with some particular event. Below me in the distance rose the cliffs that harbored the cave of San Mauro, to my right loomed the Taiarè, in between was the ravine from which I had watched a German soldier seemingly taking aim at me. I remember my thoughts. The scenery before me, would I ever admire it in peace? How often had I been disappointed! Our flight from Antwerp had provided only temporary salvation, and so had Montagnac, Agde, the Hermitage, St. Martin-Vésubie, the crossing of the Alps, Genoa, and the Stura Valley under the partisans. I had been lucky. I had wriggled out of the labor camp in France, avoided the *rafle* that had claimed my mother and sisters, foiled the gendarmes in Montpellier, eluded the SS in Valdieri, been lucky at the railroad station in Savona, and thus far, evaded the Germans in these mountains. How much longer could this last? How much longer could my luck hold? This one and that one had been killed, this one and that one had been captured and taken away. The odds against me were stacked too high.

Leaning against the escarpment, looking down the valley, I resolved to make my capture as difficult as possible. With all hope lost, my prospects had come down to the dark and raw imperatives of self-preservation, the oldest instinct.

I remember distinctly the peace of mind that came with that resolve. I felt no more despair. My life, I noted, had taken on a dreamlike quality.

As spring approached and patches of earth protruded through the thinning snow, the Germans redoubled the frequency of their sweeps.

A distraught woman came to me one day, showing me a piece of paper. German soldiers had tendered it to her as they made off with her cow. German soldiers used the sweeps not only to hunt partisans but also to forage. Food must have been sparse at their barracks. They commonly picked up food at farms: bread, chestnuts, eggs. But a cow? For people owning no more than two animals, the loss of one was devastating. The "receipt" was but an obscenity scrawled on a piece of paper.

Another day, Signora Cesana came by from Battaglia, accompanied by the curate. She was always most generous when I dropped in on my foraging calls. Now she was terribly upset. The Germans, sweeping through her valley, had taken her son, Battista. But she had not come to see me. She had come to see Lieserl, the only person who could safely speak German. Lieserl left with them, a Jewish girl attempting to save a Christian boy from the Germans. Lieserl's parents were on tenterhooks until well after dark when their daughter returned. They had located the German command and pleaded with them, but to no avail. A few days later, however, the boy, quite familiar with the territory, was able to escape.

I remember the date: the third day of March, 1945. Once again someone had alerted us that the Germans were in our valley. I left Gorrè Sottano from the rear, by a path that, from behind the Gorges' stable, descended into the ravine from which I hauled our firewood. Emerging on the far side of that ravine, the path disappeared in a sloping meadow that I crossed, aiming for some trees on the other side. One of these had its roots undercut and, lying in that cavity, I could observe the valley.

Ice that lingered within that root began to drip on me. When I saw a man emerging from his hideout not far from me, I took the opportunity to leave my unpleasant cover. He was a disbanded soldier, still wearing parts of his uniform. The valley, we agreed, was remarkably calm; nothing seemed to be amiss. Was there really a sweep?

Suddenly the man uttered a subdued warning and disappeared into his hideout. Turning around, I saw, in the distance, three men running down a slope toward our meadow, accompanied by the glint of rifles.

I saw that I could not return unnoticed to my undercut root. Instead, I dashed in the opposite direction, hoping for the curvature of the meadow to conceal me. I saw a clump of trees. Did their roots hang over? I reached them too late to find out. A quick look backward had revealed the Germans already in view. At the base of the clump of trees before me, plenty of brambles and leaves had accumulated.

I dove into them, tried to disappear in them. I remained absolutely still, my face buried in leaves. I listened.

I heard them stop. *"Auf! Auf!"* one of them shouted in German. Had they noticed me? I didn't move. Maybe it was the disbanded soldier they had seen. I clearly heard one soldier say to the others: "I would shoot if I wasn't carrying these eggs." I realized what my life was presently worth. There was no further use pretending.

Slowly I got up. My arms surprised me by rising of themselves, just as I had seen it done by outlaws surrendering in the movies.

I walked toward them, three soldiers, their guns pointing at me. One of them quickly frisked me, taking my billfold and a small notebook, and smelling them—to detect the odor of gunpowder, I suppose.

"No weapons," he told the others.

A soldier, whom I took to be their sergeant, asked me:

"Partisan?"

"No."

He rummaged through my billfold. Tucked away in its deepest recess was the propaganda leaflet from the presumed NSDAP Command for Bush Warfare. He did not find it. Then he went through my notebook, studying page after page. On one I had drawn a diagram to explain to someone how a lens focuses an image. All three soldiers took turns looking at it. What was it?

I did not let on that I understood German. The sergeant repeated the question several times. Finally, I answered in Italian:

"Studente."

That answer seemed to produce a change of attitude. He handed me back my billfold and notebook. Next he wanted to know where my friends were. *"Amici,"* he said. His Italian vocabulary was modest. To make sure that I understood what he meant, he shoved me against a tree while his men unburdened themselves of their various pouches. Once more they pointed their guns at me.

"Amici," the sergeant said, threateningly.

Keeping an eye on his watch, he added, *"Due minuti,"* two minutes.

An officer happened by, all alone. He watched us for a moment and then asked the sergeant whether he had interrogated the prisoner, quoting the regulation that required this.

The sergeant replied that he would. The officer walked on, and the men lowered their rifles. I wondered: had they really been about to shoot me?

Only the Gorges could get me out of my predicament. My arms still up, I signaled with a wave of my head, said *"amici,"* and walked toward and then through the ravine by which I had come. Worried, the soldiers following me kept their weapons pointed at me, fingers on their triggers, stopping me every so often while their sergeant scanned the environs through his binoculars.

At the Gorges' stable, which we reached from the side, they must have noticed something that had escaped me, for the sergeant suddenly stopped, saying, in a puzzled voice: *"Nanu, was haben wir denn hier? Ein Generalhauptquartier?"* "Well, what have we here, general headquarters?"

But I did not stop. Shouting *"permesso,"* I opened the door and entered, followed closely by my captors.

In the dimness inside, we caused a brief commotion. I noticed several German officers who, presently, fussily returned their handguns to their holsters. The sergeant reported my capture to one of them. He, pointing at me, asked Mr. Gorges, "Do you know this man?"

In German, Mr. Gorges answered, "yes," and gave him my false name, getting it wrong. He assured them that I lived here, and that I was not a partisan.

"Why then was he hiding?" asked the officer.

Mr. Gorges cleverly avoided admitting that I had failed to report for military service that, as an Italian, I would have been obliged to do.

"All the boys do it," he replied, shrugging his shoulders.

His wife added that I was their daughter's fiancé.

Thereupon the sergeant asked the officer whether he should release me.

"He is your prisoner," the officer replied, emphasizing "your."

The sergeant had Mr. Gorges translate to me that I should get ready to leave with the Germans. We would depart in the afternoon. Then a soldier escorted me to our basement, where he left me.

My father laid there in bed, unaware of these events. It now occurred to both of us that the sergeant, leaving me unguarded, wanted me to escape. But I was reluctant to do so. German soldiers were coming and going, and I did not want to be caught again nor cause the Gorges any trouble. I told my father that I probably could escape later. He didn't disagree.

Around noon I fixed myself something to eat when a soldier came by to check on me. On his way back, we could hear him shout: *"Er isst seinen Galgenschmaus!"* He is eating his last meal. That killed my appetite.

Now I hoped that the Germans might just "forget" me. But that was not to be. In the afternoon we heard the clatter of a German column coming down from Gorrè. As it passed us by, the soldier returned to fetch me. After a somber good-bye to my father, I returned to the Gorges'. The officers, the sergeant, and his men stood already outside the stable, Mr. Gorges admonishing them to take care of me. I said good-bye to them, and then it was Lieserl's turn. She stood a little apart, pert, beautiful, her golden hair flowing over her shoulders. She hugged and kissed me, simply, without making a show of it. Thus I received my first kiss from a girl.

We had put on an act, and I think the soldiers suspected it. And yet, there they stood, watching us, hushed, none saying a word, and after Lieserl and I separated, they remained standing there, their eyes averted until, by ones and twos, they ambled silently toward the fountain, where the column still tramped by. The sergeant was the last to leave. How I hoped he would let me remain! But no. He told me to come. I walked behind him, haltingly, dispirited. Just before falling in with the column, he turned around, waved me away, and I blew him a kiss—it was an impulse, there was no time to think—and he was gone.

That was not the end of it. I remained standing where I was, watching the soldiers file by, afraid to turn and leave lest someone shoot me in the back. Towards the end of the column, a group of captured partisans filed by. Our eyes met but briefly. I shall never forget them. Their looks pierced me with spite and hatred. Standing there, free and unmolested, they must have thought me a traitor.

After the Germans let me go, I fancied that I would no longer have to hide. Already before the next sweep came, though, I had changed my mind. I also changed my ideas about the merits of running away before the Germans. I began constructing a hideaway in Gorrè Sottano. Among the collapsed houses, some walls still remained standing. Next to one of these were the cavities of what had been two small rooms. I cleared these to a depth of several feet, cut enough tree trunks to cover them, then collapsed the wall over these. From the inside, through the interstices that remained, I could look out. I could crawl from one room into the other. Should someone discover the entrance and toss a hand grenade into it, I might still be safe.

Finally, I obtained an Italian identity card. Enzo and Riccardo, requiring some official document, had gone to the municipality of the nearby town of Vignolo. When the secretary went to see the mayor, they noticed that her desk, with an array of official stamps, remained unattended. They contrived to return, carrying photographs that I and some others had peeled off some earlier documents. At the municipality, Enzo accompanied the secretary to the mayor and entertained them with his adventures in the mountains while Riccardo laid each photograph, one after the other, on a blank identity card and stamped them. Later, we glued the pictures to the cards so that the seal appeared unbroken. Next someone filled in the required information. Henceforth I was Alfredo Fondi, nineteen years old. The first entry under "profession" was scratched out and replaced by *"studente."* That, Enzo commented, gave the thing a look of indisputable authenticity: a forger would not have done that. My birthplace was Brindisi, a city in southern Italy that had long been liberated. No checking was possible there.

Unlike the false identity card that I so cherished in France, this one failed to raise my spirits. Times had changed. The Germans who captured me had not asked for my identification. So I still had to hide. My fancy shelter, however, was not completed. Increasingly frequent German sweeps kept me from finishing it. Always I was on the run, utterly miserable. France, within walking distance, had been freed for almost a year. The Allied forces that had landed there were fighting in Germany now. Those who had come up the Italian boot had reached the Po Valley and had only a plain to cross to dash to the Brenner Pass, cutting off the retreat of the Germans who surrounded us. Would it ever end?

Passover, that spring, slipped by unnoticed.

There was a lull in the sweeps. Were the Germans gone? No, said everyone. Why then the quiet? Receiving no answer, I went to see for myself.

I intended to reach a path that ran high above the Stura Valley in an area that had been logged. From there, I thought, I might catch a glimpse into the valley. As I walked through the logged area, I suddenly heard the ping of bullets all around me and their impacts as they hit trees. I thought of lying down on the path, but as it was narrow and ran along a steep slope, it offered little protection. So I remained standing behind a tree much narrower than I was. Curiously, I did not hear the shots that fired these bullets. Nor did I hear the shots that produced, overhead, the deep organ sounds of howitzer rounds. But I had my answer: the Germans were still here.

The partisans everywhere, in conjunction with French Gaullist forces from beyond the Maddalena Pass, had gone on a final offensive against the Germans.

That night, or perhaps it was the next night, I was awakened twice. The first disturbance had a familiar sound, though I had never heard it in the mountains. It was the gallop of a horse. The second occurred in the early dawn. It had a singular sound, so far away and so faint that, had I lost it then, I would have doubted ever having heard it at all. And so I strained my ears, hardly daring to breathe, not moving a muscle. The sound was that of a church bell, rung not in the ordinary, slow cadence, but in a mad, rapid-fire sort of way that I had never heard before. Very softly, I asked my father: "Did you hear that?" He was awake, and he answered "yes," and nothing more was said. Lying there, together, motionless, we now heard another bell joining the first, and then another, and another, all ringing away in the same, rapid, searing staccato. Now, from below, much louder, yet not drowning out the others, the bells of Rittana joined the clamor, and lastly, from above, the shrill and tinny bell of Gorrè Soprano.

Thus, on Wednesday, April 25, 1945, broke the dawn.

14
A Voyage of Discovery

LIBERATION, SO LONG AWAITED, had caught me nevertheless by surprise. Still, I felt no urge to shout, to cry, nor to whoop it up that morning. My father and I remained in bed, savoring the moment, stretching it, listening silently to the staccato of church bells that filled the heavens. The new reality felt fragile, dreamlike.

When we did get up and go outside, the sun shone festively from a smiling sky. The Gorges smiled when they came out of their stable, and we congratulated each other. The Cavaglion boys smiled when they came by, and we congratulated each other. Others came down the path, smiling, congratulating. There was not much to say, nothing that the bells did not express far more convincingly.

Or did they? My attempts, years later, to either confirm or refute an alternative interpretation proved futile. It had occurred to me that the sound of the bells was not the sound of deliverance nor the sound of peace. Their rabid staccato suggested the tocsin, the hoary alert of disaster and mayhem. The Germans, though retreating, were still in the Stura Valley, attacked by partisans surging from the mountains and pursued by French Gaullist forces advancing from the Alpine front. The next day, unknown to us, the German rear guard was still in Demonte, six miles up that valley, blowing up a bridge. Had the bells been recruited to compel urgency and terror on the retreating Germans? Did the war, which had distorted so much, play a trick one more time masquerading an act of war as a sign of peace?

No such thoughts, however, disturbed our bliss that morning in Gorrè. People stopping on their way down to Rittana talked about the carousing that was hatching there. They mentioned a player piano hoisted on a cart, shuttling between the two trattorias of Rittana, where wine was being dispensed in unlimited amounts, free to all. But I declined to go. What celebration could possibly befit the present occasion?

Perhaps, instead of going down, I should have climbed up, joining those who rang the bell in Gorrè. It was done with two hammers, rapidly alternating. Enzo and Riccardo, when they came by, had already taken their turn. You had to wait in line for it. Before ascending the belfry, you wrapped your head in as many blankets as available. Then, a hammer in each hand, you kept your footing next to the fellow currently beating the bell, watching him, absorbing the rhythm and jumping in as he tired, at full speed, without missing a beat. No one asked why the bell had to be rung in this particular way.

But I did not go to the bell tower. By early afternoon, I laid dreamily in the grass, apart from everyone else, allowing my mind to wander. Shreds of thoughts intruded, a tumult of scenes surged up, crowding each other out, insubordinate, returning again and again. I became aware that I could not stop them, not even when talking to people.

I decided to join the carousing in Rittana. That would certainly dissipate this inner turmoil. But it was already too late. The long descent proved an ordeal. I barely made it to the first house in town. That was where the baker lived. His wife was at home. Women did not participate in carousing, even on an occasion such as this. A worried soul, she put me to bed. But neither the bells of Rittana's two churches, almost overhead, nor the sounds of revelry outside could prevail over the roiling inside my head. I was conscious of it, my faculties remained intact, but all I could do was to stare, helplessly, at the room's vaulted ceiling. Now and then the baker's wife came by with some herbal tea or soup, but I declined.

By evening, the chaos in my head had relented somewhat. I undertook the long trek back to Gorrè, feeling miserable all the way. The day ended as incredibly as it had started.

A night's sleep cleared out my inner turmoil but left me feeling drained. I went outside the next morning, propping myself up comfortably against a log. From here I could look down the valley and dream. Signor Goletto came by, carrying a scythe. He barely gave me a nod and continued downhill, stopping where his meadow started. He had work to do, work neglected while roving German soldiery burned and killed. He dropped a small bag of tools, then began to swing the scythe into the overly tall grass. His wide, rhythmic strokes crisply felled it. After progressing downhill a little, he stopped, returned to his tool bag to sharpen the blade, then back to his wide, rhythmic strokes. Sweat began to taint his clothing under his arms, around his collar, and along his belt. The dark stains spread, widened, until his shirt and pants were dripping wet. But he kept going, his scythe swinging as resolutely as before, without letup, like the bells whose staccato still filled the sky.

They had kept ringing without interruption, all through the previous day, and all night long, and still this morning, as tempestuously as the day before. About noon they stopped, some a little sooner, some a little later, petering out quickly. Then all was quiet.

The quiet persisted. A wonderful quiet. A festive quiet. The fresh smell of cut hay filled the sunny air. The day looked so new, so pure, so full of promise. No dangers lurked about. All this was really true. The past was past. The future was here. It was pure enchantment. And the next day would be just like this one, and so would the next . . . and the next . . . and the next . . . and the next . . .

Our entry into this new life proceeded by stages. In the first stage, nothing happened. We remained right where we had been all along as Enzo and Riccardo deemed it unsafe for us to venture to Cuneo. We had been set free not by a conquering army, but by the withdrawal of German troops whose retreat, by way of Austria, threatened to be cut off. Their sudden departure left the Italian Piedmont with a disintegrating Fascist government. The partisans, belonging to different groups, were not firmly in control. We heard of fleeing Fascists who posed as refugees, of partisan roadblocks that could not reliably distinguish friend from foe, and of accounts being settled. Enzo and Riccardo told us to stay put. They would venture down first. They would keep us informed.

I felt no urge to leave. Our days were bliss and smiles. The fear gone, I saw our abode in a new light. I had become used to life up here. The local people were friendly and helpful. We were strangers no more. Where else could we find so warm a fellowship as our common tribulations had forged? Add the spectacular scenery, the bracing climate. What more had the world to offer?

Nothing could have upset the serenity of those days, and nothing did. Only later did I learn that on the very day of our liberation, members of the Italian Fascist militia, abandoned by the retreating Germans, had driven up to a prison in Cuneo. There, in a dastardly act of vengefulness, they had removed six Jews who had been caught in anti-partisan actions and, under the clamor of the bells, executed them.[1] That day, too, American and Russian forces had joined at the Elbe River and Russian armies had encircled Berlin. Three days later, near the Swiss border, Italian partisans had captured Mussolini and his mistress and shot them. And two days later, in a bunker in Berlin, Hitler and his mistress had committed suicide.

The retreating Germans in the Stura Valley had so thoroughly destroyed the roads behind them that their French pursuers lagged about a week behind. One day, from Gorrè, we saw an airplane circling low over the valley, releasing a parachute from time to time. It was supplying the unseen French soldiers who advanced on foot. This was our first view of our liberators.

When the Cavaglion boys returned from Cuneo, they brought each of us a small, mimeographed sheet of paper, a pass, signed by the chief constable of the "Corpo Volontario della Libertà," the partisan group that had taken over the local government. The photo stapled to my paper had been lifted from my French identification card. Duly signed across it was my false French name, Faubert. The passes identified each of us as a Jewish refugee, in need of every moral and material assistance, and allowed us to freely circulate in the province.

The time had come to say good-bye to the people who had helped us in these mountains. Once more I retraced my foraging treks. At each place, there were embraces and joy, laughter and tears. Despite the persisting food shortages, almost every household had a bottle of Marsala on hand for special occasions. My protestations that I had already drunk many glasses of Marsala along the way carried no weight. I remember one host pouring it right through my fingers, as I held them over my glass. Of all my foraging treks, this was the most perilous one.

In Cuneo, schools were closed. In a classroom, cots had been prepared for us. We were also given money. It was enough to allow us refugees to lodge in private rooms.

We went about the city without fear, sat in an outdoor café, a waiter fussing and bustling about us. News about the war hardly interested us anymore. What did it matter to us when we heard, a week late, of the surrender of the German troops that had hounded us in the mountains? What did it matter to us when we heard, next, that Germany had capitulated! My father and I happened to be sitting in a sidewalk café sipping ersatz coffee. We continued to sip. And no one else seemed to be particularly excited.

A newspaper kiosk displayed the paper with the photo of Mussolini and his mistress hanging by their feet from a piece of timber in Milan's Piazza Loreto. The paper was more than a week old. More recent newspapers did not replace it. Such was the news that interested people.

Occasionally I came upon a crowd surrounding some young woman seated on a chair in the middle of the street. While she kept a stony silence and an impassive face, someone sheared off her hair to a barrage of obscenities shouted from the surrounding crowd. I did not have to ask what she had done. Such poor things had been girlfriends to German soldiers.

Dark moments such as these were rare. More frequently, pleasant events surprised me. Girls, taking me for a partisan, cheered me as I rode a bicycle along a street. An acquaintance of the Cavaglions, seeing me walking in boots that gaped at both ends and trailed straw, wanted them as a souvenir. He offered to replace them with a new pair of shoes, then available only at exorbitant prices. And I was invited to the many parties given for the partisans, their girls, and their friends. These were crowded affairs, where now and then excited cries overcame the general din as people who had met before under some ghastly circumstance or other suddenly discovered each other again. But as almost everyone was washed and shaven now, and supplied amply with drinks, such recognitions occasionally turned out to be in error. But that only added to the general hilarity.

One did not see, in those days, the people who had suffered losses. Only later, after all that joy had abated, would they be noticed and their lost ones remembered. By then, however, my father and I were no longer in Italy.

We managed to see a little of Cuneo's history. One day, Enzo took us down Via Roma, the main street whose sidewalks are sheltered by arcades. In the newer part of the town, these are two stories high, but as one walks toward the older part, they become lower and the street narrower. One walks discernibly into the past. When one reaches the Middle Ages, which takes no more than ten minutes, there is a side street, also with arcades, that skirts what had been the Jewish ghetto, an area still enclosed, still accessible only through a couple of covered passageways. There, facing the street, the synagogue still stood. Though the building looked neglected, the war had done damage only to its alms boxes, which had been pried open. That was less than the Napoleonic war, which had left a cannon ball encased in its inside wall. Nor had the Torah scrolls and other sacred articles been in any danger. The local branch of the Banca d'Italia, Italy's National Bank, had hidden them in its vaults.

I happened to be present when Mrs. Gorges, a former concert pianist, encountered, for the first time after all these years, a piano.

The French Gaullist troops we had seen being supplied by air were stationed in Cuneo now. Their officers invited us and all other Jewish refugees in Cuneo to a party. We received formal invitations, and my father suggested that we dress up. He still had a suit and tie. I managed to borrow some togs but could find no decent tie. Mr. Gorges assured me that I looked fine without one.

The party was held in the Palazzo del Barra di Ferro, the best hotel in town. There we met the other guests of honor—no more than half a dozen—hollow, shadowy characters in mangy, ill-fitting clothes. As in Genoa, I realized that we ourselves didn't look any better. The exception was Mr. Gorges who, urbane and confident despite his poor command of French, soon engaged some officers in a conversation at the cocktail buffet. Lieserl too disappeared quickly amidst a group of officers.

Somewhat intimidated, I found myself with Mrs. Gorges. I remarked about the ostentatious splendor of the halls, whereupon, like museum goers, we walked from one to the next. We encountered no one but came upon a piano. Diffidently, she approached it, tried lifting the lid, and when it opened, she sat down and hesitatingly depressed a few keys. Pronouncing the instrument a little out of tune, she nevertheless tried a few scales, complaining about the stiffness of her fingers. How many years, she wondered, since she had last sat at a piano? But her fingers had not stopped, and soon she was into Chopin. She needed no sheet music.

My musical education had been limited to folk songs, operatic arias, and the brassy player piano in St. Martin-Vésubie. I was not acquainted with Chopin nor attuned to his music, so Mrs. Gorges' playing proved unfathomable to me. Still, I watched her hands flying over the keyboard, stopping suddenly, deftly timing a single tap, then another, then banging away all over the keyboard again, the piano quaking in waves of thunder. Up in Gorrè, I once overheard a discussion between her and her husband about an artist's "presence." A good performance, they had agreed, must include theatrics. The artist must toss his head, his facial expression must reflect the music's moods, and so on. But now, Mrs. Gorges ignored these precepts. She sat virtually motionless; only her arms and fingers moved. But how they moved! As I watched, it seemed incredible that the piano was not moving as well and that her hair was not whipped by gusts of wind. An officer came by, a cocktail glass in his hand, and remained there, watching. Another came, and another, and soon there was a small group of them. Dinner was being served, but no one dared to interrupt her. Had her husband not come to escort her, who knows how long she might have gone on.

The banquet was unlike any I ever attended. We all fitted comfortably at one table. Wine and delicacies were served that only high officers of a victorious army could have procured in those times of dearth. The service had a solicitude that only a hotel contrite for past chumminess with the Fascist regime would entertain. And yet the party did not quite come to life. Among us refugees, it seemed that only the timid ones knew French. Mostly it was Mr. Gorges who entertained the company, pushing his few French words recklessly beyond their intended meanings. My father, switching back and forth between French and Italian, at one point became confused and switched, of all things, to German. Unaware that he had done so, he failed to comprehend the astonished looks of his audience. All this was taken into stride with good humor. Still, the party achieved merely a forced gaiety. Only Mrs. Gorges' happiness did not seem forced. She hardly participated in the conversation. She sat on the last chair at the table, apart from it all, absorbed in her thoughts, radiant.

Like Mrs. Gorges, I had an experience that marked the watershed between past and future. It occurred, improbably, as I obtained my first pair of eyeglasses.

I had noticed an optician's shop under the arcades of Cuneo's main street. I entered it one day, telling the owner of my difficulty in seeing mushrooms in the forest and of my inability to read the dial on the belfry at Gorrè. He explained that first I needed a prescription from an ophthalmologist and suggested that I go to the hospital to get it.

The hospital's lobby was so crowded that I despaired of getting to see a doctor at all. I need not have worried. A nurse approached me, asked what I wanted, and then escorted me to a desk. There, I heard her asking permission to take me upstairs. A quick nod granted her request. I followed her up the elevator, down a corridor, and through a room packed with more people. There, she knocked at the doctor's door. He had me wait only until his current patient left and then called me in. Whoever had come down from the mountains, I gathered, was a hero, and was treated accordingly.

The doctor examined my eyes and then placed an open frame on my nose, into which he placed various lenses, one after another, and tested my vision. When he was satisfied that he had the correct lenses, he had me get up, still wearing the clumsy frame, and took me by the hand to steady me as, all around, everything appeared to be swimming. He led me through the roomful of waiting patients, down another corridor, and out onto a balcony. Before me, stretching the width of the horizon, rimming a broad plain, were the mountains.

Like a rampart they stood. Never before had I seen the jumble of their snowy peaks so crisply etched against the blue sky. The brilliance of their colors surprised me as well. In the past, my blurred vision had dulled them with a grayish cast.

I looked in the direction of Rittana, but I, who knew every path below the Taiarè, failed to locate that familiar peak. The mountains, distant now, seen in a new light and from a different perspective, had become strangers already. Soon I too would be gone and see them no more.

Reality was replacing the long enchantment. There on the balcony, with the doctor standing patiently at my side, I felt a sudden sense of loss. And for the first time, it occurred to me that the end of the war was not the end of everything, and that a great, mysterious, inscrutable future loomed ahead.

It dawned on me that, if I really intended to become a scientist and an inventor, the time was almost at hand. As yet, I had no idea on how to proceed.

Also, the time was almost at hand that we would be reunited with my mother and sisters. How would we find them and where? I tried to imagine how they might have changed in these three years. That too laid in the inscrutable future.

I still believed them resettled in Poland. The reports related in St. Martin-Vésubie from the two escapees from Auschwitz had, as I have mentioned, raised more bafflement than alarm in my mind. And what I had heard later on the BBC about German atrocities I still considered to be war propaganda.

Allied forces had entered Buchenwald a month earlier. Newspaper reports about what they discovered were scant and did not make the front page. A perplexed BBC even delayed its broadcast. But it was no longer because the evidence was in doubt. Now it was because the BBC feared that its reports would not be credible. It temporized for a number of days until it received an account from Edward R. Murrow, who was widely known and highly respected.[2] Eisenhower and Churchill had congressmen and members of parliament tour the camp. Next Bergen-Belsen was liberated. Now, hundreds of reporters rushed there, described the men and women lying in heaps on both sides of the railroad track, the ten thousand bodies still unburied, the living skeletons that ambled aimlessly about.[3] Only then did the world know.

But this occurred mid-April 1945, ten days still before the bells rang for us. The Fascist-censored newspapers to which we had access printed none of this. By the time I arrived in Cuneo, Germany had been overrun. No further German camps remained to be liberated. Only occasionally were new atrocities coming to light now and making news.

In Cuneo, Fascist newspapers had been replaced by a free press with access to the news reports from the free world. Paper shortages, however, still constrained them to cram everything onto a single sheet, and their current staffs, which had so recently replaced their Fascist predecessors, could do little more than keep abreast of current news—the turmoil in Italy, the war that was still being fought against Japan. What the Fascist press had suppressed would have to wait. If anyone in Cuneo knew what that had been, they kept quiet about such things to me. Despite a free press, I remained utterly ignorant of the Holocaust.

There was now talk of a long voyage. It had a name. It was called "repatriation." It intimated mystery and adventure, and generated apprehensions as well. What would we find? What would my mother and sisters have to tell? It would be a voyage of discovery.

The French military were preparing the first stage of this voyage, our transport to Nice. Its entire schedule, however, was already fixed in my father's mind. Although neither the postal service nor the telephone nor the telegraph were yet functioning in Italy, he posted mail to Aunt Betty and Associated. In France, which had been liberated more than a year ago, he would write again. And on our way to Antwerp, we would stop at all the places where we had been, to see what we might find there.

When would we leave? The road to France was still impassable, an official told us with a shrug. Likely, little would be done about it; the war effort was shifting to Japan. But one afternoon, I saw a military convoy, jeeps and trucks, moving slowly through town. People stopped on the sidewalks and began to clap their hands, and soon there were cheers as well. They were American, people said. The soldiers, all black, smiled broadly and waved at us. I noted that the convoy was coming from Borgo San Dalmazzo. It must have gotten there from France. The road was open.

Some days later, we were informed of the place, date, and time on which we were to meet a truck. Once more we spent the day preceding our departure in bittersweet farewells. Early the next morning, we surrendered our room, but in the evening, sheepishly, we were back: the truck had not shown up. Several days later, we once more said good-bye to everybody and, if memory serves me right, we repeated this ritual once more. Finally, on May 28, more than a month after the bells had rung out over the mountains, a truck appeared.

A heavy machine gun, installed over a manhole in the roof of its cab, pointed aimlessly at the sky. The truck's canvas covering had been removed. We would travel under an open sky. Seeing his passengers, the driver got out to help us climb onto the back of his truck. No more than half a dozen, we accommodated ourselves with room to spare on the two benches that paralleled the truck's side panels. The little baggage we brought, consisting mostly of food people had given us for the journey, was piled in the middle of the floor.

A shorter route to France over the Tenda Pass was still impassable. Our truck headed for the Maddalena Pass instead. Thus I was granted one last view of the Stura Valley.

The military road resolutely avoided all the bridges that crossed the Stura. Our truck descended to this road shortly before Gaiola, and from down here I had an eye-level glimpse into the chasm at the bottom of which rested the crashed trestlework of the bridge that the partisans had blown up a year earlier. We passed Gaiola, which could not be seen even from atop our truck. That was how the Germans had mostly seen it. By the time the road climbed above the river, the landscape had become unfamiliar. The road kept rising. The few villages we passed had been flattened, not a wall left standing. From time to time we noticed, past the edge of the road, far down the slope, the upended chassis of some truck. From atop our vehicle, pitching and bouncing over the rough, unpaved road, it seemed that we would soon find ourselves down there as well.

Dusty and weary, we arrived in Nice after nightfall. The truck stopped in front of a small hotel, the Hotel Washington. It had been converted into a refugee processing center. People welcomed us there, and others fumigated us with a new miracle chemical, one said, called DDT. Next, we were shown to our rooms. Tired, and having munched on food all day long, most of us skipped dinner. Before going to bed, I looked out the window at the dark street below where nothing moved. What light there was came from the neon sign over a bar across the street. I could hear music coming from there. I kept hearing it all the time that we stayed at this hotel. One particular tune was played more often than any others. I got to know it well. Years later, watching the film *The Wizard of Oz,* I heard it again and learned that it was "Over the Rainbow."

After breakfast the next morning, I had to fill out some questionnaires and was then unexpectedly subjected to lengthy interrogations by civilian officials and police officers. They wanted to reassure themselves that we were not Nazis in disguise. After that, we were provided with new identity papers, passes for free railway travel, and, still, ration cards. Camp inmates, the lady in that office said, were entitled to extra rations. Had I been in a camp? she asked.

Innocently I mentioned Agde, whereupon she roundly chided me for shamelessly trying to cheat. It did not occur to her that I might not have heard, as yet, of what the advancing Allied armies had discovered in Germany.

Aunt Charlotte had remained in Montagnac when my father left for St. Martin-Vésubie in 1942. With a happy face, he told me the next day that she was still there and that he had gotten hold of her by phone. She was in contact with her husband in Cuba and with her brothers in New York. From them she had heard that Goldine, Aunt Klara's youngest daughter, was safe and well in Antwerp. Our former cleaning lady, Delphine Janssens, had hidden her. About the rest of the family, she had heard nothing so far.

We stayed at the Hotel Washington about a week during which we sent letters to relatives and friends whose addresses we could remember. My father also took the bus to St. Martin-Vésubie, where he had left his mother. He returned with some laundry. He had gone to the establishment, presented the nearly two-year-old tickets, got the laundry, and paid the owner, no questions asked. Our other belongings, which I had so neatly stacked before leaving, were gone. Many years later, we learned that it was not the local inhabitants, but rather, the German occupiers, who had taken everything. As for my grandmother, she had been deported along with all the other residents of the nursing home a few days after the Germans had arrived.

Aunt Charlotte met us at the station in Montpellier, and we rode together on the bus to Montagnac. On the way, she told us that we had come just in time. She was about to rejoin her husband in Cuba. She still had to obtain a passport in Toulouse and tickets for the passage in Paris. We decided to make the trip together and to remain a few days in Montagnac to accommodate her schedule.

Montagnac had a new town crier who blew a trumpet instead of beating a drum. A new delicacy, grape sugar, delicious when spread on bread or eaten by the spoonful, was plentiful and popular. I enjoyed it and soon could feel my teeth crumbling in my mouth. Other food was still scarce and most required ration coupons. People were happy to see us. Inevitably, they asked about my mother and sisters. What could we say?

Aunt Charlotte had remained in Montagnac in defiance of the 1942 eviction of non-permanent residents.[4] How could she have traveled alone with four children, of whom the last was a newly born baby? In addition, she had an aged mother-in-law. She remained in the apartment above the fire station into which she had moved after leaving the Maurel house. She hid only briefly after the Germans occupied Montagnac. The whole town had become her accomplice. The Germans did not suspect anything even though Grandmother, who had become somewhat disoriented, could speak only German. She died in Montagnac and was buried in the cemetery there.[5] At the funeral, the undertaker, having misgivings about carrying her remains in a hearse surmounted by a cross and yet fearing to cover it up, twisted it just a little askew.

In Aunt Charlotte's apartment was a wicker hamper, the size of a steamer trunk, containing what belongings of ours had remained in Montagnac. It looked sturdy enough, so I tied it with some rope and shipped it to Antwerp, in care of a stevedoring company with whom my father had transacted much of his business before the war.

On a train once more, we headed for Paris. I managed to sit by the window. Watching the telegraph poles run by alongside the tracks, I noted with amazement that all their wires had been cut between every pair of poles. Just before a pole passed by the window, the wires rose from the ground, reached their insulators atop the pole's crossbeams, and then fell back to the ground. This went on for miles on end. It was a vivid illustration of the enormous amount of work needed to repair the war's damage.

We arrived in Paris early the next morning. We didn't have to worry about where to lodge or how to get there. A waiting police van picked us up and, racing down the empty boulevards with siren screaming, took us to a refugee center. It happened to be, I learned much later, the Vélodrome d'Hiver, the very place from which the Germans deported the Jews from France, including, in all likelihood, my mother and sisters.

We remained several days in Paris. This metropolis, my father thought, was the best place to locate missing relatives and to find out what had happened and what lay ahead. He was right. Although I had seen in the papers, since our arrival in France, several disturbing snatches of new discoveries of German atrocities against Jews, it was here in Paris, through people we met, that I heard more of what the Germans had done in their camps. We even heard what had happened to my grandmother. My father happened to encounter the Kahns, the couple who had managed the nursing home near St. Martin-Vésubie. Though seized with their wards, some snafu had kept them in Paris. They told us that my grandmother had been in good health upon reaching Paris but had then been sent on to the camps with the other inmates of the nursing home.

It was not until I had read a couple of books by survivors of the camps that I really understood what was being done there. In Paris I did not hear the term "death factory."[6] And although I heard there many a tale of hairbreadth escapes, I did not meet a single camp survivor. What I heard about the camps was all hearsay, generating but a welter of disorganized, incoherent, troublesome thoughts.

We arrived in Antwerp by the end of July—nearly two months after leaving Italy. We arrived in the evening and spent the night in an immense dormitory. Belgium was close to Germany, and refugees arrived here in far greater numbers than in Nice. The next morning most everyone left, but my father asked me to remain at the refugee center, and so I did. He returned early that evening and told me to pick up what luggage we had. We did not need to spend another night here. He had found his office almost intact. The concierge would not allow my father's spending another night at the refugee center. She would have two cots in my father's office by the time we returned.

For a week or so we lived in that office and ate breakfast at the concierge's table. Although no rent had been paid for the past several years, the landlord had refrained from leasing two rooms of the suite and had moved important items into them, in particular the filing cabinets. The most valuable items, however, proved to be the typewriters. Quickly, my father sold one of these. Scarce at the time, it fetched enough to tide us over for weeks.

Every day my father visited the Jewish committee where the names of displaced persons were posted and constantly updated. He never took me along. Perhaps he wanted to spare me the pain of the revelations of the Nazi death camps. Perhaps he simply had to be alone.

When my father contacted the stevedoring company to whom I had addressed the wicker hamper shipped from Montagnac, he was told that it had arrived, and he sent me to fetch it. At the warehouse, a man came to greet me and told me how glad he was that my father had returned and that it would be his pleasure to have someone deliver our belongings. A tractor pulled up, towing a sturdy, low-slung trailer such as the company used to haul cargoes alongside ships. The hamper was hefted onto its end, where it looked small, puny, and battered. I seated myself on top and, throbbing and clattering, the rig plodded out of the harbor, then along the genteel boulevards of Antwerp to my father's office.

Opening the hamper, my father and I unpacked some bedding as well as clothing belonging to my mother and sisters. Among these, I recognized with a shock the two dresses a refugee dressmaker had made before the war. Vividly I recalled how my sisters had tried them on and their delight with the understated chic of these dresses. Suddenly, the troublesome thoughts that had plagued me since Paris fell into place. I knew then that my sisters would never wear those clothes again.

My father must have felt the same. We never explicitly admitted to each other that we had lost hope. For a long time yet, he would go to peruse the lists of survivors. But the next day, when I looked for the dresses, they were gone. My father must have quickly given them away.

15
Aftershocks

ABOUT A MONTH AFTER OUR ARRIVAL in Antwerp, we received a letter. Our first mail from America since the attack on Pearl Harbor, some four years earlier, it was from Aunt Betty. We had written her repeatedly after our liberation, but until we wrote her from Antwerp, we could not give her an address to which to reply.

I no longer have this letter, but Aunt Betty saved our reply, dated August 20, 1945. "Today we received your letter of August 8," my father had written, "and I am pleased to learn from it something about which I have been totally in the dark for the past four years. You have forgotten that we never heard from our sisters in Siberia. Only in the beginning did you send us a card from them, indicating that they had been taken to Siberia. I hear now for the first time since our liberation that Josi and Shlomo are in Palestine." Josi was Aunt Minna's son, and Shlomo, called Sali in Germany and now using the Hebrew version of his name, was Aunt Jettchen's. My father continued: "You also write that clothing is being sent to Paula, from which I deduce, with joy, that also Paula is alive, and in Siberia. Now begins for me the guessing game of what happened to Jettchen and Minna and the little child. . . ." He next inquired about other relatives and concluded: "Even if the news may be very sad at times, it is still preferable to the uncertainty that has accompanied us all these years."

I contributed a page. Something had struck me as strange in my aunt's letter. It read like a letter of condolence. She commiserated with us, tried to comfort us, assured us of her sympathy and love. This was not to console us for the loss of my mother and sisters, whose fate was not certain yet. What she bemoaned was the life we must have led under the German boot.

I wrote: "We were very amused by your letter. You are amazed? But it is not your fault. Your intentions are good, but you interpret our situation incorrectly, and that is what has amused us. You pity us 'for what we have endured,' but that, we have long since forgotten, we must go on, we have no time to look back; what is past is past, we must go on." Clearly, I had something to learn about tact. But my father, who read this, let it pass. He too had been dumbfounded by the tone of his sister's letter; he too was looking ahead. He must have figured that my way was as good as any to communicate this to his sister.

And what was the future we were looking forward to? My father squarely addressed this question: "We urgently need clothing," he wrote. "We have had to discard the rags and tatters that we wore in Italy, and have nothing to replace them . . . If you think that the prices of clothing have risen too high, I can tell you only that here a suit for $40 would seem ridiculously cheap. . . ." He added that he had already sent her our measurements and had asked Meno Lissauer to put $300 at her disposal.

I added some vivid details: "Upon being liberated, in Italy, we were in such rags that we were given field gray (German or Italian) uniforms. That was temporary. You must understand that it is not particularly agreeable to run around like this. In France, we could finally buy ourselves some civilian garb, it was but a little, and so shoddy that it is almost worn out already. In half a day the socks have holes, and the yarn used to mend them tears already during mending. Furthermore, we have no one to mend or sew for us, and so it is with everything. I am still wearing a military shirt, and have worn the same underpants all this time, unable to wash them. Only now have I obtained another pair. It is much too large, but I finally have a change. It is the same with papa." I promised to describe our adventures and mentioned our weekly visits to Goldine.

Our first social call had been to our former cleaning lady, Delphine Janssens. One reached her house by taking a ferry across the Scheldt River and then walking for some time along a road that traversed a barren, sandy stretch. Here the American army had set up Camp Top Hat. Skirting a barbed wire fence, we walked past long rows of precisely parked Sherman tanks. With reverence I sized up these veterans of the campaigns that had crushed the Nazis, noting their emblems and wondering why some of the turrets were hung with pieces of track. Was it for additional protection or as spares?

Having passed the tanks, we walked past sundry military vehicles and then past tents amidst which we saw American soldiers as well as German prisoners of war. Beyond was Zwijndrecht, a depressing town of old brick houses, small and sooty, jammed together along drab, treeless streets. This was the housing the Industrial Revolution had bestowed on its working class. In one of these, Delphine and her husband welcomed us warmly. Inside, the house was spotless if rather crowded. The cause surprised us: it contained some of our furniture, overly large for these small rooms. Delphine explained that she had moved the furniture here because, after Aunt Klara was gone, she had no money to pay for its continued storage. Her own things, requiring less space, could be stowed elsewhere. A little girl entered, about six years old, in a trim little dress, a little shy in front of us strangers. It took me a moment to realize that this was my cousin Goldine, whom I remembered as the baby who had come with her brother, unaccompanied, from Germany.

Oh, how incongruous the coffee and cookies that Delphine served on her best china as she and her husband related how Goldine had been kept out of German reach! Aunt Klara, summoned for deportation in the summer of 1942, had mentioned to Delphine that without a husband she could not manage four little children. Delphine agreed to take the youngest. She then applied for support at the Jewish committee. That was a mistake. Just in time she learned of the danger to which that had exposed herself. So when the Germans came knocking at her door, the child was with her sister-in-law in Bruges. Persistent, the Germans looked there, too, but once more the child had been removed before they arrived. Six years old then, she was boarded at a convent school.

The Germans missed something else as well. Leon Janssens, Delphine's brother-in-law, was a railroad man who, with a railroad crew, interfered to their utmost with what the Germans had them transport. His most spectacular feat occurred at the end of August 1944. He had been ordered to bring a special train, consisting of three passenger cars, a boxcar, and two flat cars, from the coast to the city of Brugge. Two German railroad men joined Mr. Janssens in the cab. The passengers, they informed him, were an SS-detachment and its equipment. Assuring them that nothing unusual was expected, Janssens ran the train at high speed. Coming in view of Brugge, a bascule bridge ahead was open. Only Janssens had known that. The train could not be stopped in time. The engine crashed into the water, followed by several cars. Instantly the canal was blocked, the railroad tracks cut, and many of the SS injured or dead. But Janssens, at the last moment, had jumped from the engine, and so had his two German companions, he from one side, they from another. Fellow railroad men, who had plotted this disaster, quickly removed him from the scene. Janssens proved to be unharmed. Arriving home, his wife informed him of the railroad disaster of which she had just heard. He managed to look very surprised.[1]

Brugge was liberated a few days later, and so was Antwerp. Our cleaning lady was there in jail, fearing to be deported to a German concentration camp.

Goldine's stay at the convent school had left its mark. During that first visit already, she had mentioned "little Jesus." We had to find a Jewish home for the little girl.

We had to find a home for ourselves as well. In the days after our arrival, while my father made the rounds of his acquaintances, I diligently perused classified advertisements, made a list of available apartments, and my father and I went to look at them. At one of these, a young woman opened the door. As I stated the purpose of our visit in a Flemish somewhat out of practice, her pretty face contorted into a grimace of deep disgust. She made no attempt to hide her repugnance at seeing Jews returning.

I was flabbergasted. I had survived the entire war without ever facing an overt anti-Semite. Now that the war was over, now that the Nazis had been exposed for what they were, how could anyone still be swayed by their hate? I almost pitied that poor girl. What an accursed life hers would be! For her, the glorious day of deliverance would never arrive. Our presence would irk her forever.

This, I ardently wished, was a thing of the past.

I heard of many more instances of lingering anti-Semitism. An acquaintance of mine, Sidney Finkel, returned to Poland in 1944 as a member of the Red Army. He intended to visit Toporow, the town where his family had remained when he left in 1941. Before reaching that town, he met an acquaintance from whom he heard that his brother, the sole survivor of his family, had been killed there two weeks after the Germans had left. By Ukrainians. Sidney eventually entered that town under the protection of two NKVD men, angry at having to risk their lives on his account.[2] Until 1947 and possibly beyond, Jews were still being killed in Poland.[3]

I recall that one day after our return to Antwerp, the radio stations of many European countries hooked up together to broadcast a single program simultaneously from several locations. Everywhere, simultaneously, local choirs were singing Beethoven's chorale, which contains Schiller's words: *"Seid umschlungen, Millionen!"*—embrace, you millions. If I remember correctly, a million singers were on the air. Radio not being what it is today, there was noticeable fading during the performance, and the singing was not quite in unison. Still, so many people did try and did accomplish something together, and it was wonderful.

This, I ardently hoped, was the future.

It was not a classified advertisement that obtained us a place to live; it was my father's chance encounter with Mr. Beumers, the father of Denise, a Gentile girlfriend of my sister Jenny. Hearing that we slept in an office, he insisted that we stay with them. My father accepted, and when we arrived, we were shown into a small bedroom, extravagantly appointed with lace and knickknacks. The bed was rather high, requiring a footstool to climb into it. Mr. Beumers confided that, having only a bathroom to spare, he had steadied a mattress atop the bathtub and used lace to hide the carpentry. Once again, but for the last time now, my father and I would share a bed.

Then my father happened to run into Mr. Lustig. My father had become acquainted with him and his family while in Nice. They had managed to reach Switzerland. Having returned to Antwerp and the diamond business, Mr. Lustig was doing well. He had a spacious apartment to which he invited us for dinner on Shabbos eve.

Silver candelabras spread the glow of candles over the crisp white tablecloth. The evening was ushered in with the traditional paean to the virtuous wife. The benedictions over wine and challah followed. Mr. Lustig presided over a festive table around which we joined his wife, her mother (who, I understood, had a hand in the cooking), and, arrayed like a cluster of olives, the children: Nadine, a good-looking and sprightly teenager, and twin boys, Maurice and Bernard. The first course was carp in jelled broth followed by chicken soup with noodles. Roast chicken was served next, with *chrain* (horseradish), and last, a compote and cake. Between courses we all sang the traditional songs. Except for the chrain, which elsewhere is served with the fish, it was like my home long ago, so much so that once or twice I had to strain to forget what must be forgotten.

From then on, we had a standing invitation for both the eve of Shabbos and Shabbos noon.

When the package of cloth arrived from Aunt Betty, we went to a tailor. Then, wearing the suits he made for us, we went to a photographer and sent the pictures to all our relatives abroad. But to Goldine we went in person to amaze her with our impeccable finery.

Sunday was the day we usually visited the little girl. All week I looked forward to this day. A Jewish orphanage had been set up for children such as she. Located in Mariaburg, one had to travel by suburban trolley to reach it. The children were housed in a spacious villa tucked in amidst trees. When first my father and I arrived there, we were surprised to see two grim looking military trucks in its driveway. When we approached, we noticed that the group of soldiers, busying themselves around the vehicles, wore British uniforms with a blue-white-blue shoulder patch over which was applied a yellow Star of David. They were members of the Jewish Brigade, Palestinian Jews fighting with the British army under their own flag. I heard that the color of the star had been chosen to match the yellow star that the Germans had forced Jews to wear. That badge of shame now was a sign of victory. Presently the soldiers unloaded boxes of canned food scrounged from military supplies. They made themselves useful in other ways as well, even taking the children on outings in their vehicles.

Though Goldine made lasting friendships at the orphanage, she was never as happy there as at Delphine's. She hadn't wanted to leave. She wanted to go "home." When, some fifty years later, I sent her a draft of this chapter, she disagreed with my description of Zwijndrecht. She did not remember it as a "depressing town of old brick houses. . . ." She recalled it as a wonderful place, with flowers, trees, and sunshine, evidently Delphine's well-tended backyard. She must have complained once too often about the orphanage, for she still resents my father having said to her, "Do you want to clean houses like Delphine when you grow up?"

Delphine would have dearly liked to keep "Goldintje." She would not have asked for a centime in that event. But if we took her away, it was only fair that she be reimbursed for her expenses.

Heaven itself intervened in returning Goldine to her faith. Someone to whom Aunt Betty mentioned this money problem suggested that she contact in New York a brotherhood of former residents of the region from which my paternal grandparents hailed. She went to that brotherhood's next meeting, stood up in front of them, and told them in entreating words, so eloquent in Yiddish, about the little girl, the only surviving child of one of Yente Scheindel's grandchildren, saved by a *goye*. She added that the *goye* had endured prison and had nearly been deported for what she had done, and now the little girl needed to be redeemed so that she might grow up Jewish. Could the brotherhood help?

Several of the listeners remembered Yente Scheindel, my grandmother's mother. They voted to contribute $100 and immediately took up a collection. One man, Aunt Betty noticed, contributed $20. "A *proster* working man," she told me. "For him, $20 must have been a day's wages, and maybe more." She learned from him that he and his brother had grown up orphans. Every Thursday evening, Yente Scheindel had taken them into her house, bathed them and washed their clothes, so that they would be clean for Shabbos. "Bathing," Aunt Betty explained to me, "was difficult in those days. People had no running water, no drain, no bathtub. One had to go downstairs to fetch water, always carrying two buckets, one for the wastewater to be poured out, one for the fresh water to be fetched. The water had to be heated, wood was needed for that, and so on. Giving those orphans a weekly bath had been no mean task."

Aunt Betty collected another $300 from relatives. Delphine, I know, received more than that, the balance, I suppose, from my father.

Years later, in a solemn ceremony reported in the local newspapers, Delphine was honored with the Israeli Medal of the Righteous among the Nations. Her husband and Marie, her sister-in-law in Bruges, were similarly honored.[4]

"Lissauer, unfortunately, has not declared himself ready to assist me financially, nor to participate in any manner in my expenses here," my father wrote his brother in Israel on November 4, 1945. Associated[5]—now the headquarters of Lissauer's company—would not reopen the branch office in Antwerp. Nor had they another job to offer him.

Knowing people in the shipping business, my father chanced to hear that one could buy shipments of shell casings collected from sundry battlefields. Since they were made of brass, they were valuable. My father knew the smelters that could process such materials, and he knew how to finance their shipment. He set himself up in business. I went with him to the docks to examine arriving shipments. I remember one coming from North Africa. Among the casings I found fragments of memorial plaques made of brass, whose Italian inscriptions, which I had no difficulty reading, proclaimed Fascist victories.

We had our own lodgings by then, combined with an office. It was not, actually, an apartment. It was a conference room, surrounded by office and kitchen facilities and connected to a synagogue that stood empty now. The elderly concierge had an apartment next to us, and above us was an apartment to which the cantor and his wife were soon to return. The synagogue, built by Dutch Jews, the earliest to settle in Antwerp, was a monumental building, and the conference room had a grandiose ceiling of bold and colorful stuccowork.

Alas, within minutes after I opened the main water valve to our new quarters, I noticed a dark stain expanding over this stuccowork. The building's water pipes, dry for too long and rattled by exploding V-2 rockets,[6] were no longer watertight. I had heard all about these rockets from the concierge in my father's office building. She had told me of the fear of hearing a V-1 coming, but the V-2 was worse: it arrived unexpectedly. No alert could be sounded. No time to rush into a shelter. The thing was capable of destroying an entire city block. Her husband happened to be in the kitchen when a nearby building was hit. The blast only broke a few windows in her building, but her husband was at the opposite end of the corridor when he got up. The Germans had fired a large number of such rockets at Antwerp, which had become the major Allied facility for handling shipments of war supplies. One rocket had hit a movie house, killing hundreds of people. According to the concierge, Antwerp suffered more from the war after its liberation than before.

A plumber soon fixed the leak, and when our credenza and table arrived, retrieved from Delphine, they looked downright regal in this conference room. Substantial pieces, they had never come into their own in the smaller rooms of our house in the Zurenborgstraat.

But the beautiful ceiling of our new abode, having survived the war unscathed, remained permanently splotched.

In one half of the conference room, my father set up his office, using what office equipment he had not sold. "For the time being," he wrote his brother, "I must work without office and personnel," adding, between parentheses, "with the sole support of Alfred."

Indeed, he needed me. For him, Belgium had been just an assignment. He still corresponded with Lissauer in German. His secretaries always had to be fluent in German, French, Dutch, and English as well. Now the only person available to him who could satisfy these requirements was me.

Still, I intended to become a scientist and an inventor. Upon mentioning this to the Beumers, I heard that they knew a physics professor at the university in Brussels, Professor Balasse. I lost no time writing him, attaching sketches of several of my "inventions." One, I remember, was a concept for glare-free automobile headlights. I proposed to tint each headlight with one of a pair of complementary colors. In his reply, the professor did not comment on my drawings but urged me to attend college, not to study science on my own as I had done in the past.

But how could I afford the tuition at a Belgian university? My prewar enrollment at a trade school certainly did not qualify me for a scholarship. My father suggested that I emigrate to the United States, where I could study evenings while working full time. Thus I importuned Aunt Betty once more, wrote to relatives, and registered with the American consulate. In the meantime, I would be my father's secretary.

Sundays remained reserved for Goldine. My father was occasionally too busy to go, but I always went to see her. I might take her out for a walk and ice cream or even bring her to Antwerp for the day. Once I even kidnapped her. A letter, dated November 16, 1945, reported the event to my cousin Lotte, Uncle Anschel's daughter:

". . . Goldine is now seven years old, a bright and lively little girl. What a pleasure it was when, the day before yesterday, she came unexpectedly to us! As you know, she lives in the orphanage in Mariaburg. She became ill there (nothing serious), and was sent to a hospital here, where we could visit her every day. The day before yesterday, she had recovered, and was allowed to leave the hospital. As no one, however, arrived to pick her up, I took her home with me. That was not that simple, because it was not I who had signed her in. I presented myself, therefore, as someone sent from Mariaburg. (I have, after all, considerable practice telling outrageous lies!) The drowsy employee released her without suspecting a thing. How Goldine jumped and hopped once we were on the street! Delphine, the lady who had hidden her, happened to be at our house. The joy was great.

"That night, she slept in a full-sized bed. I loaned her my pillow, and put her to bed. I would never have believed that I'd make such a good nurse-maid.

"And yesterday, whenever the bell rang, our hearts fluttered, as someone was supposed to pick up Goldine. Nobody came, however. I taught Goldine to type on a typewriter, and she taught me how to properly dry dishes. Just imagine that a big boy like me didn't know how to do that! She also showed me how to click one's tongue, but I was unable to imitate that.

"That evening, two elderly ladies visited us. That turned out to be a merry evening. Goldine made the two ladies laugh, no, to shriek with laughter. It's been a long time since we laughed like this. . . ."

Life, people said, had returned to normal. How different, indeed, was it now compared with a year ago! Upon our arrival from Italy, everything had been in short supply. Trolley cars were the only local means of transportation. Streets looked deserted, and the main roads carried mostly military traffic. Nights were occasionally punctured by the repeated blasts of a brazen horn, hushed at first, presently louder and louder, reaching a maximum, and then decreasing, gradually, into silence. Such din registered the progress across the intersections of Antwerp's streets of some Allied military convoy, presumably carrying munitions.

Now all that seemed far away. An exhibit had opened on a public square downtown: its centerpieces, Hitler's armored limousine and a V-2 rocket. The war was becoming history.

One day a parade of brand new Ford automobiles, garishly placarded with a dealer's name, noisily honked their way through Antwerp's streets. Another time, a widely advertised contest promised prizes to those able to identify some fifty different brands. Everyone, it seemed, participated. The task was easy until one got to the last two or three brands, which no one had ever seen. Shortages, too, had become a thing of the past.

Theaters opened again, and I got to see my first opera. The elaborate scenery surprised me. I had thought of opera only as music. Next, when in the plush opulence of the municipal theater a show for children was staged, I took Goldine to see it. It was more than a play. Occasionally, the actors froze while a motherly lady came on stage, leaned over the edge of the proscenium and talked to the audience, making sure they understood what the actors were doing. After the prince's kiss revived the Sleeping Beauty, she came on stage and asked, "And now, what shall we do with the witch?"

"Kill her, kill her," cried the little tykes.

"Oh no, we can't do that," she said, and proceeded to explain why one should not kill even a witch.

Life had indeed returned to normal.

The supply of brass casings was ebbing. Battlefields had been gleaned clean. My father tried to locate other sources of metals to be recycled. He found some but not enough. After but a few months, his business was expiring.

One afternoon, with not much to do, my father surprised me by suggesting that we go see a movie. A movie? There was a local movie house nearby. What was playing? It didn't matter.

Thereafter, we went to the movies every Thursday afternoon. This was before TV made its appearance in Belgium. Of the movies we saw, I recall but one. It was my first Western. I remember it because there was a shoot-out. And with the first few shots, my legs began to tremble.

Normal?

About then, Associated offered my father a job. It was to sample ores, the job he had done for Lissauer as a young man. He began to travel again—to Trieste, to southern Italy, and to Turkey.

On one of his returns to Antwerp, my father remarried. Another step to a normal life. She was a widow who had lost husband and son during the war.

It is normal for a woman to scold a child, and for a cleaning lady to dust the house. But the woman was Sala, my father's new wife, and the child, Goldine, who was now living with us. Her relationship with Sala was not always smooth. In two years of institutional life, the tyke had learned to stand her ground. Sala did not know how to handle this. She would get angry with Goldine, raise her voice, and revert to Yiddish.

And the cleaning lady was Delphine. She had come to work for us again, one day each week. She had relinquished work elsewhere for the joy of being with Goldintje. It was not all joy, however. Once, as Sala scolded the little girl, I happened to catch a glimpse of Delphine, in a corner, furiously dusting one spot, tears rolling down her cheeks.

Can our lives ever return to normal?

A half century has passed since the end of the war. And still some people cannot come to terms with their memories.

My cousin Paula is one of these. That surprised me, for she had been out of German reach during the war. She was, as I have related, part of the massive 1938 deportation of Polish Jews from Germany. She lives in Israel now, and when I asked for her experiences of the war, she delayed her reply for several months. Her account, when it finally arrived, was incomplete. Her typing turned choppy before it reached the bottom of the first page. Words were missing, misspelled, or struck out. On the next page, she stopped her account. "The tale goes on," she wrote, "but I have decided to terminate this letter for the time being. I hope that [you] can use some of this for your book. From my scribbles you can see what anguish these memories cause me."

I did not trouble my cousin Paula further. I gathered what I could from others. There still was Aunt Betty, but my best source proved to be my cousin Josi, Aunt Minna's son. He was only seven in 1938 when he, as I have related, was deported to the German-Polish border along with his mother, his younger sister, and other relatives. We had known that in July 1939, when the Polish authorities allowed these deportees to enter Poland, his mother and Aunt Jettchen, with their children, had hastened to our relatives in Przeworsk.

More than half a century later, during a visit from Josi and his wife, I set up a tape recorder. Finally the questions my father had asked in the letter mentioned at the beginning of this chapter would be answered. In impromptu, unrecorded remarks afterwards, Josi kept adding details.

They had not been welcome in Przeworsk, Josi said. Their cousins, Gita Locker and Chana Eisner, had no space for them, not enough money, and other problems. They sent Aunt Jettchen with her children to her in-laws, the Beglückters, in another town. She was not welcome there either. Within a few weeks she was back.

This state of affairs didn't last long. In September 1939, the Germans invaded Poland. As the Polish defenses crumbled, my relatives fled on foot, residents and guests alike. Overtaken by the Germans, they returned to Przeworsk. Some weeks after the hostilities ended, the Germans forced all of them to leave town. They were told to go to the sector occupied by the Russians, who had invaded Poland from the east.

It took them a week or so to cover the forty miles to Niemirow. Crossing the San River, which separated the German and Russian forces, my relatives were surprised to see Russian soldiers who were Jews. These reassured them that the Soviet Union would take care of them. Indeed, after several months in Niemirow, the Russian authorities organized an election, which gave the refugees three options. They could return to German-controlled Poland, or become Russian citizens, or remain in Russia as foreigners.[7] Josi's mother, Aunt Minna, whose only wish was to join her husband in America, elected the last option, and the other relatives followed suit.

The Russians considered all those electing the last option to be undesirable elements and, in the spring of 1940, sent them to forced labor in the remoteness of Siberia. I read that they traveled by rail, packed as many as fifty or sixty to a freight car.[8] Food was scarce. At railroad stations they were offered *kipiatok,* which was simply hot water. The transports may, in fact, have been well provisioned, but the train crews or their Soviet guards would sell such food.[9] In all likelihood, my relatives by then were penniless. Their journey took about a month, during which time the lack of ventilation, primitive toilet conditions, and limited opportunity to wash oneself or one's clothes promoted the spread of lice and other parasites. From the train, they were taken by horse cart to their final destination, a camp somewhere south of Novosibirsk, in a forest covering the approaches to the Altai mountains. There were no fences. The immensity of the forest precluded escape.

The forest produced resin. Food rations depended on the amount of resin a worker brought back from the forest. My aunts were too weak and their children too young for that work. Paula was their only breadwinner. She was out all day. "It was so cold," her letter said, "that I was afraid my nose would freeze off."

Aunt Minna's competitive spirit had made her the fastest typist at Lissauer. In Cologne, she had gallantly rejected Aunt Betty's advice not to leave, accompanying instead her widowed sister Jettchen to Zbaszyn. But in the Siberian chill, that spirit failed her. She withered away. "Perhaps a third of the camp's inmates perished that winter," Josi said.

The German surprise attack and invasion of the Soviet Union in June 1941 went almost unnoticed in that remote camp. But as a result, in July a Polish-Soviet treaty was signed in London, followed by an amnesty encompassing all Polish exiles. Josi and the other relatives were released. "Word was," Josi said, "that they were to be replaced by German prisoners of war."

Free now, my relatives did not know what to do nor where to go. Housing was limited, food in short supply, and the Soviet state the only employer. To those that found work, the government paid wages so skimpy that workers at every level habitually stole from their places of employment.[10] The goods so obtained fueled a black market. There, I think, my relatives found a way to make a living. It was precarious, and they kept moving from place to place, drifting some six hundred miles in a southeasterly direction into Kazakhstan. Winter came, and Josi was surprised how warm it was. Then, in February or March 1942, the authorities resettled them in a kolkhoz—a collective farm—near Turkestan.

Even with a warm winter, life at kolkhoz Kaganovitch was no improvement over their first camp. The rations, distributed monthly, amounted to thirty grams of flour—hardly more than an ounce—per day. "It was not flour," said Josi, "but grain, which we ground down to flour, and from that flour we made soup because there was so little flour we couldn't make bread. So by diluting it in water, it was some food. But then the ration was curtailed even more.

"There was no work to be done. This was why the Russians gave us so little food. . . . The members of the kolkhoz wanted nothing to do with the refugees. Those people . . . were Asian people. They had to produce, whatever they produced, for the Russians. They hated the Russians, and they didn't want to have anything to do with us. . . . And we couldn't communicate with them. Their Russian was vague; they spoke their own language. Russian had been forced upon them."

Josi's sister, little Nelly, died first. "There were no doctors, no medicine," Josi commented.

"The Lockers [our Polish cousins] lived in a separate house. One morning we discovered that they were all gone. They had left on the sly. They must have realized they were in a death trap."

Nachman Rosenbaum, an uncle who had joined Josi's family before they left Poland, figured that the Lockers had gone to the city of Turkestan to try to make a living. He decided that the rest of the family must go there as well.

The city was thirty or forty kilometers [twenty to twenty-five miles] from the kolkhoz. Not everyone was able to undertake this walk. My cousin Paula left her mother, taking only her brother Shlomo along. Nachman Rosenbaum left his mother, Sarah-Esther. Chana Eisner, sister of Nachman, left her husband, Avromtsche, as well. And Josi, his father in America and his mother dead, was also left behind. "Nachman said he'd come back for us," Josi recalled.

"I don't know how long they were gone," Josi continued, "but I guess it was no more than a week later that Aunt Jettchen died. My grandmother [Sarah Esther] died.[11] And now I was left alone with this Avromtsche Eisner, who was sick. And we had those two bodies in our room. We could not even bury them; there was nobody to help us. So . . . we just laid there. I think we were waiting to die, too, Avromtsche and myself."

As Josi talked, I watched the tape recorder, making sure that it did its job. Happening to glance at Frances, my wife, I saw that she was in tears. Afterwards she said, "But Josi was only ten years old!"

I thought of my grandmother, fretting in St. Martin-Vésubie about the blood-red sky. I realized that by then her two daughters and Sarah Esther, her sister, had been dead for more than a year.

"One night, or in the morning, or whenever," Josi continued, "there was a knock at the door. Nachman had come back, alone, on a wagon with a horse, and when he saw what he saw, I guess he buried his mother and Aunt Jettchen. He put us on the wagon, Avromtsche and me, and drove off."

In the city, Nachman had located the Lockers. "He dumped me off with one of them, one of the girls. She said they'd take care of me. They took me to a local hospital. A Russian hospital. And I was accepted, I was sick. And I was in that hospital quite a while, because, when I got better, I got myself sick again. They gave me something to drink there, the kids. There were some other Jewish kids there, orphans, and they knew how to stay alive in the hospital and be sick. It was either a question of being sick in the hospital, or dead outside."

What news there was came as rumors. One rumor reached the hospital that Polish orphans were to be taken out of Russia, to

Palestine. "So," Josi continued his tale, "we decided, a group of these kids, to get healthy and get out of there. We had no time really, so we just jumped the wall of the hospital and escaped. At the orphanage, we had to prove that we were orphans. Polish orphans. The other kids had no problem, because they really were Polish orphans, but I had a problem. I found Uncle Nachman in the city someplace—I don't know how I found him—and he faked some papers that said that I was a Polish orphan.

"There were about thirty Jewish kids in that group, and about 250 non-Jewish kids going, not to Palestine, but out of Russia to Persia. Although we were Jews, we were Poles, and they had to take us. They mistreated us badly because we were Jews." Josi remembered that when, at mealtime, he was refused his tray of food and complained, the Polish supervisor went to fetch it and, using an expletive, said, "Here is your food!" and threw the tray to the floor.

The transport did not leave until a couple of months later. "The trains in Russia," Josi explained, "did not leave like here, where you know when they leave. If you got to the train station, you still had a day or two before the train would really leave. So I got off the train, or before I reached the train, and I went to where Nachman lived, and I found Paula and Shlomo. Paula was lying down, she had swollen feet, she couldn't move, and Shlomo was still OK, so I told him that he could go with me. . . . I guess he did not want to leave Paula, but Paula convinced him to go, and we went to Persia by train. In Teheran, we were taken out by social workers from the Jewish Agency, from the Hadassah organization, into a separate camp. Again, we were supposed to go to Palestine right away, but it took another three or four months."

The sudden arrival in Teheran of Jewish children from the Soviet Union had been unexpected. The British government, relenting on its immigration limitations, did grant eight hundred certificates to allow "Teheran children" into Palestine. But Iraq refused to let them through, and so did Turkey. It was against their principles to encourage Jewish immigration to Palestine.[12]

Thus when finally Josi's transport left Teheran, it went in the opposite direction: first to Karachi, then Bombay. "We went by ship," Josi said, "and from there we took another ship around the Arabian Sea, around Aden, up to the border of the Suez Canal. And this was in 1943, February or March 1943. And there the Jewish

Brigade that was in Egypt took us and put us on a train, and then we arrived in Palestine.

"When we came to Palestine, Shlomo and I were separated. He was a little sick, and I was sick, too. He was taken to Jerusalem to a hospital and I was taken to a recuperation place. I knew I had family in Palestine. I knew I had an uncle in Ben Yehuda Street, Tel Aviv. Maybe Shlomo knew more. While he was in the hospital in Jerusalem, there was a Dr. Wallach who knew Uncle Anschel. So when he called up and said, 'I have here a German kid, his name is Sali Beglückter,' which doesn't sound Polish, Uncle Anschel said, 'Beglückter? My sister married a Beglückter. Sali is Shlomo. It must be my sister's son.' This is how we were reunited."

In recoiling from her memories of the war, Cousin Paula was not alone. I noticed a similar reluctance among the congregants in the Eisenmann Shul in Antwerp. The synagogue had survived the war untouched, several of its former congregants had returned, and the cantor, Mr. Gans, officiated again. Services went on as before the war. The conversations seemed unchanged, more in the nature of social courtesies than exchanges of opinion. I did hear, but only in undertones, that this congregant and his family had been hidden by their servant, that another had returned from America to resume his business, and that yet another had lost his family. I recall no one summoning up the past.

How different this was from Italy where, when former partisans encountered each other, they would burst out with uproarious, back-slapping reminiscences. Yet they, like we Jews, had suffered many deaths.

I can understand my cousin Paula and all that silence. I know the cause. It is fear. The fear of sudden emotional upsets, such as the impact of my sisters' dresses as I lifted them from the hamper in my father's office. Such as the shoot-out I had watched in my first cowboy movie.

It is astonishing how long such torment can lie in abeyance before suddenly erupting. Many, many years after my arrival in the United States, I once happened to mention the fate of my mother and sisters to a young and impressionable woman, born long after all those events. Aghast, she could not suppress a scream.

Oh, that scream! How it upset me! In a flash I realized that none of the screams of the millions of Nazi victims had ever reached my ears. Until this moment when, in that single scream, I heard them all. Thus when, in 1993, the U.S. Holocaust Memorial Museum was inaugurated in nearby Washington, the fear of such an emotional upset kept me home.

Afterward, I read in the papers of the rain that fell that somber day, of the speeches that were made, of the sad silences in between, and of the distant shouts of "Lies!...lies!...lies!" that could then be heard. These came from demonstrators whose hatred, transcending rain and pain, had brought them to this ceremony to disturb it, to label it as a fraud, to convince the world that the Holocaust had never happened.

Some time later, in the library where I researched the background for this memoir, I chanced upon the book *Hitler's War,* by the British writer David Irving. Substantial, well written, and handsomely printed, I did not suspect that it might be anything other than honest historiography. However, the search that turned up this book retrieved also a slim volume by the German historian Eberhard Jäckel. This alerted me to historical inaccuracies in Irving's book.[13] Surprised, I checked Deborah Lipstadt's *Denying the Holocaust.*[14] There I read about Irving's contention that Britain made a tactical error in going to war against Germany in 1939, that he considers the Allies and the Nazis to have been equally at fault for the war and its atrocities, and that he concludes that gas chambers were but anti-German propaganda.

Since then, I have followed the lengthy trial in which Mr. Irving sued Ms. Lipstadt and her publisher for ruining his reputation and career. The verdict, when rendered, absolved Dr. Lipstadt and damned Mr. Irving. It was a relief to see truth prevail. It was a relief to see that libraries are still dependable. What would the world have come to had the Nazis prevailed?

I did go to the Holocaust Memorial Museum. It was a few months after its inauguration. A lecture had been scheduled about Jewish refugees in Italy. It included a screening of the movie, *The Righteous Enemy.*[15] This I wanted to see.

To avoid an emotional upset, I made a dry run several days ahead. I would see none of the exhibits. I would not even go inside the museum.

From the entrance on Fourteenth Street, I circled around the building to the entrance on Raoul Wallenberg Place. I had read laudatory reviews about the building's architecture, but, seeing it for myself, I was somewhat disappointed. Its understated opulence, its smooth, massive stones accented by austere touches of black iron, its entrances wide and its spaces ample had little relation to the squat, grimy barracks I had seen on a visit to Dachau. To me, the building did not evoke a concentration camp and seemed to have no relation to the memory of my mother and sisters. Neither they nor most of those who had perished had ever lived in anything like this. How strange, I thought, that a memorial should be so irrelevant to what it memorializes.

And yet the stones did something to me. Mingling with tourists, mostly young, in colorful summer clothes, I felt out of place. And when I walked—stopping to read every inscription—I could not dispel the sensation that I was advancing on tiptoes.

Unexpectedly, I faced the surprise that I so dreaded. Past the museum's Wallenberg entrance, a truck ramp abutted onto the street, painted in garish yellow and black. These were the colors of the Star of David–shaped badges that the Nazis had forced Jews to wear. And over the structure to which the ramp led, a bulbous top towered surmounted by a chimney. Bluish smoke rushed from it, faint yet unmistakable against the blue sky. From within the structure issued a subdued howl, sounding like a thousand choked screams. A crematorium? Impossible! After the first shock I realized that I was looking at an incinerator in which the adjacent Bureau of Engraving of the U.S. Mint burns shredded dollar bills. I also recalled that in German death camps, people were killed in gas chambers, not in crematoria. But for a brief eternity, my heart had stopped beating.

My father must have had similar upsets, but he never confided in me about his feelings. He was the father, and I was the son, and the distance between us remained unaltered. His remoteness may have been, I think, for my protection. It is just as well. I doubt that I would have been capable of listening to what that poor man, whose shoulders carried so much weight, must have gone through.

Like emotional upsets, regrets are traumatic. Regrets are different, however. They do not catch you unawares. Nor do they subside. Regrets remain forever.

How I wish that I had overcome my youthful pride in St. Martin-Vésubie and admitted to Cousin Moyne that the letter I was supposed to have mailed was still in my pocket! How the fate of the poor little Zilla still weighs on my conscience!

Another regret is not saying Kaddish for my mother.

Kaddish is recited by the mourner first at the funeral, then all through the following year, and then on the anniversaries of the death. It is an important prayer, requiring the presence of a quorum. In traditional Jewish circles, where it is recited only by males, a young boy and only son may be referred to—already during the lifetime of his parents—as a *Kaddishl,* the one who will recite the Kaddish when his parents pass away.[16]

My mother would have expected me to say Kaddish for her, and I would not have wanted to disappoint her. And yet . . .

The Kaddish is not a prayer for the mourned. Nor is it a lament. It makes no reference to the deceased. It is, my father once explained to me, the bereaved's proclamation of his submission to the will of God. Despite his grievous loss, the mourner steps forward in the synagogue, and says:

> Magnified and sanctified
> may His great Name be
> in the world that He created,
> as He wills,
> and may His kingdom come
> in your lives and in your days
> and in the lives of all the house of Israel,
> swiftly and soon, and say all amen!

The congregation responds:

> May his great name be blessed
> always and forever!

The mourner continues:

> Blessed
> and praised
> and glorified
> and raised
> and exalted

and honored
and uplifted
and lauded
be the Name of the Holy One
(He is blessed!)
above all blessings
and hymns, praises, and consolations
that are uttered in the world
and say all amen.

May a great peace from Heaven—
and life!—
be upon us and upon all Israel,
and say all amen!

May He who makes peace in His high places
make peace upon us and upon all Israel,
and say all amen![17]

I could never bring myself to step forward in a synagogue and deliver this. When religious services resumed at the Eisenmann Shul, no congregant, as far as I remember, said Kaddish for a deported relative. I suppose that doing so would have been an admission of lost hope. And I, before my hope vanished, had lost my faith.

Following our return to Antwerp, my father and I had resumed the practices of the Jewish religion. We ate kosher again, kept the Sabbath, and attended services when the Eisenmann Shul reopened. These observances easily took hold. They were the only parts of my former normal life to be restored to me. They helped fill the great void.

Not all survivors returned to their faith. Many had their beliefs shaken by the magnitude of the disaster that had befallen the Jewish people. My father and I, however, agreed with those who felt that we could no better honor the memory of our martyrs than by living as they had wished to live.

But my life did not turn out as my parents had intended it to be. I had grown, and what had been only a dream before now was a goal. I was determined to become an inventor. Why waste my life, so narrowly spared, doing anything but what I really desired?

My father, as I have said, did not dissuade me.

At a trade school, I took what part-time courses seemed appropriate—trigonometry and industrial draftsmanship. Beyond that, I read books about science, which had become easily available again.

Lewis Thomas, a popular author, wrote that twentieth-century science's most significant contribution is that it confronts the human intellect with the depth and scope of its ignorance.[18] There in Antwerp, immersed in those books, I began to have intimations of that confrontation. I began to understand how science works. I came to suspect that much of what had been inculcated in me before was no knowledge at all. As yet I was afraid to place much trust in my new notions. Their implications were too momentous. I was too uncertain.

The Zionist organization had reopened in Antwerp. Its nice quarters had been restored. Lectures were being held there, studies, organized discussions, chess games, outings, as well as amateur theatrical productions, and, in time, even an occasional ball. It was also a good place to meet girls.

Not many of the people I met there had lived in Antwerp before the war. Speaking Yiddish, we all managed to communicate. When it appeared—as happened twice—that the Soviet Union might occupy western Europe, there were enough Russians among them to teach the Russian language, interest in which vanished, however, the moment the danger passed. Not so the stories about life in Russia that they told. I remember one in particular. It was quite unlike the one I would hear much later from my cousin Josi.

The young man who told me this story had, like my cousin, been deported in 1940 from Poland to Siberia. He and his family had ended up in Kazakhstan and been put to work in a cannery processing peaches. His father, noticing that entire wagonloads of the fruit often arrived rotten and were dumped, told the overseer that this fruit was still suitable for making vodka and that he, being a chemical engineer, could do it. Impressed, the overseer contacted the local commissar, who agreed to let him try. When it seemed impossible to find the necessary equipment, the commissar proved resourceful. Would hoses from the fire department do? When the answer was the affirmative, the commissar did not hesitate to dismantle the refighting equipment. The vodka turned out superbly, and for the remainder of the war, my friend and his family lived like kings. Once a building caught fire and became a total loss when the hoses and pumps could not be flushed fast enough of their flammable alcohol. Unperturbed, the commissar remarked, "It was only a government building."

More than stories, I enjoyed discussions. Most were quite informal. They could spring up in corridors and even on outings. I remember an excursion when a couple of show-offs who were displeased by the turn of the arguments ended them by retreating to the platform of the trolley car on which we were riding and there, with arms folded and in a crouched position, exploding into the shouts and kicks of a Cossack dance.

Topics of discussions ranged widely, from the establishment of a Jewish state in Palestine to girls, if none were around. Religion was also a popular subject. Discussions on this topic often sprang up between just two individuals. There were those who denigrated faith and there were those who defended it. I was among the latter.

But during an argument with a friend who had a firm grip on science, I came to realize, deep inside, that he was right, and that my arguments were flawed. I was unable to admit this to him. While I cannot recall the arguments, I remember distinctly how vexed I was and how hopelessly I fumbled in attempting to defend my faith.

This, I realized, could not continue.

I confided to Goldine, then seven or eight years old, that perhaps God had not created the world, that God might be a myth. But this little girl, educated in a cloister and raised among Christians, was quick to confound me: "Who then," she countered, "created Shabbos?"

I held forth on my new notions on a long bicycle ride with a date. I must have bored or frightened her, for she promptly dropped me for another fellow.

One day, at a friend's home, his father cut me off when I mentioned faith, saying matter-of-factly that religion made no sense in the modern world. He was no young firebrand. He was a respectable man, with a nice family, in a Jewish-looking home. Once more, deep inside myself, I agreed with him, and once more, I was unable to admit this to him.

I knew then that I would have to confront my creator.

This happened, unpremeditatedly, on Yom Kippur—probably in 1947. On that day of fasting, services at the synagogue last all day. Around noon, however, I went home for a rest. There, on the credenza, stood a bowl of grapes. The thought hit me that, if really I was not a believer, what could hold me back from eating them? I picked one. On this, the holiest day of the year, I would perform deliberately an act of apostasy as well as a crucial scientific experiment. Alone before my maker, under the eyes of my mother looking down from heaven, I ate the grape. I did not choke to death. The heavens did not come crashing down. The earth did not open beneath me. I was almost astonished that nothing as much as stirred.

Thus I parted with the last remains of what had been my normal life. It caused me no pain, producing instead a great uplifting sense of relief.

Having confronted my creator, I now had to face the outside world. I hesitated. Religion deals harshly with its renegades. How contrary to science, which is open to challenges, where anything can be questioned, and where every refutation of a theory is a step forward![19]

For a while yet, I remained outwardly religious and inwardly upset to act like this. I averted my eyes when facing religious acquaintances. There were not many now. I have long asked myself whether, absent the upheavals of the war, I would have gone through with such a step.

Finally, I told my father about my change of mind. He was displeased, and very much so, but he would not disown his son.

How I regretted the pain I inflicted on my father. But what alternative did I have?

Five years after the end of the war I obtained my visa to the United States. Packing my belongings, I came unexpectedly across the gold embroidered, blue velvet satchel that contained my phylacteries and the tallis in which I would be buried. It was soft and prim and showed no wear. It gave me a shock to see it and, for some time, I contemplated what to do with it. On the eve of my departure for the New World, fretting about the awesome difficulties I was likely to encounter on my quest there, I decided that I could not allow my sensibilities to encumber me, and I left the satchel behind.

This too I have regretted ever since.

My father, with Sala and Goldine, eventually emigrated to the United States. There he met my wife and was gladdened to see two grandchildren. And in 1963, a year before he suffered a massive stroke, I was able to tell him of my first invention. He did not understand much about it, but from the commotion my invention created,[20] he sensed that it was important. It was a method to generate computer codes capable of dealing with the structures of the millions of chemical compounds that are known.[21] In time it displaced all earlier methods in use. Although I was too inexperienced to command royalties and made no other noteworthy inventions, it fulfilled my childhood dream. Thus I was spared one more regret. I am still amazed at the immense and enduring satisfaction this has given me.

16
The Past Revisited

I HAD NOT INTENDED TO EVER set foot in Germany again. But in 1966 I had to go there on business. Employed by a research facility of the U.S. government, I traveled with my superior, Dr. David P. Jacobus, and our division director, LTC Michael Daquisto, dressed in civvies.

Because the trip included a stay in Cologne, I took my family along. It might be my only opportunity to show them the place where I had grown up.

For my wife and children, it was their first trip abroad. But I too was curious. How did the Germans endure the shame of the Holocaust?

The many new buildings we saw indicated both the widespread destruction suffered by German cities and how well they had rebounded since the war. Their citizens appeared prosperous and busy. When Daquisto expressed some concern about the speed at which our taxi driver barreled along, she replied, "Time is money."

Talking with Germans proved weird. If I talked in their language, they did not suspect that I was a foreigner. After all, I spoke my mother tongue. My vocabulary, however, had remained that of a child and was dated. I did not know, for example, the correct term for a one-way street. When I attempted to explain what I had in mind, I noticed that people looked very strangely at me. On the other hand, if I spoke English, a keen German ear could easily recognize my German accent, which occasioned suspicious looks.

In Cologne, my grandparents' house still stood, and I also found the street where I had lived. I vaguely recognized them. And on the first weekend there, I took my wife and kids to the little town of Königswinter, which sits prettily next to the Rhine and the Drachenfels, the Rock of the Dragon, the site of a long-remembered vacation.

It was still light when we arrived at the small waterfront hotel, and from the window of our room we enjoyed the view of the Rhine with its incessant traffic of barges. As it grew darker, a crowd assembled on the river's edge in front of our hotel. The crowd grew thicker, noisier. Suddenly, through the open window, we heard repeated shouts of "*Sieg, Heil!*" I told my wife that this was a Nazi salute. Frances paled. She recalled that we had seen no other tourists on our way here and that the local people whom we encountered had stared at us with some persistence. Had it been because we were Americans? Could it be that they recognized us as Jews? "They are going to lynch us!" she said. I dismissed her concerns: this was not America. How surprised I was to have said that! But having erred in the past on the side of optimism, I placed a call to the American embassy, just across the river in the city of Bonn. A German guard answered, informing me that the embassy was closed. Calmly, without disturbing the children who were asleep by now, we barricaded the door with the room's furniture.

In the morning, I asked the proprietor about the commotion the evening before. "Oh, that was nothing," he jovially replied. "They just had a little too much beer."

We took the children up the Drachenfels, on the beribboned donkeys. They were still there.

Sunday, we took a steamer upriver on our way to Frankfurt, where a business meeting was scheduled for the next day. As the ship approached Remagen, I remembered that General Patton's troops had reached the Rhine there so quickly that the retreating Germans failed to blow up the bridge. When I asked a ship's officer the whereabouts of that bridge, he claimed total ignorance. Soon, however, the ship threaded its way past the piers that remained of that bridge. They were blackened still and unmistakable.

In the afternoon, the ship skirted the Lorelei, a steep, imposing hill that juts into the Rhine. According to legend, a maiden used to appear on its top and comb her golden hair in the evening sunshine while below many a fisherman, distracted by wild longings, would capsize with his boat in the treacherous current. Presently, the ship's PA system played the lovely song that recounts this legend. I had learned it at school. The music is set to a poem by Heinrich Heine, a Jew. As I have mentioned, the Nazis had attributed it to an "unknown" author. For me, the song was a reminder not of an old legend but of the war.

In Mainz, the cabbie taking us from the ship to the railroad station, hearing us speaking English and learning that we were Americans, informed us that 80 percent of his historic city had been destroyed by American bombers. "How," he asked indignantly, "could you have done that!"

From Frankfurt I went to Munich where the German executives we had come to see offered to show us some of the sights in town when we finished our business. I suggested the nearby concentration camp at Dachau. This was not what they had expected. There was a cold silence. Daquisto broke it, saying that he wanted to visit the camp as well. Dachau had been the very first of the Nazi concentration camps. None of our hosts, however, seemed to have heard of it. But as we left someone quietly approached us, telling us to go to the railroad station. There, sure enough, Dachau was shown as one of the suburban destinations.

In Dachau, the taxi driver knew where to take us. The place was immense and empty. Most of the barracks into which the inmates had been jammed had disappeared. Life still shunned this place. Among the rectangular traces of their foundations, I noticed not even a weed. Considerately, Daquisto left me alone. The only other visitors were a few nuns, guiding the quietest group of schoolchildren. Of the barracks that remained standing, two were open to the public. Inside were large photographs that depicted conditions in the camp. I hardly looked at them. I had seen such photos before. As I went from one barrack to the next, I noticed in the distance the only substantial constructions in the camp, two towers, recognizable as crematoria. Were there really two, or only one? My eyes, brimming with tears, were unable to tell.

As I write this some thirty years later, I read in a newspaper that "the generation born [in Germany] during or just after the war largely defined themselves against their parents and grandparents—not only against their acts but against the subsequent silence about those acts. . . . There are plenty of nasty exceptions in Germany, of course, but no society has more thoroughly and systematically repudiated its past and sought to remember its victims."[1]

With all my heart, I wish them well.

There are places that I would have liked to revisit. One of these is the mountain pass over which we crossed from France into Italy in

1943. That beautiful region has deservedly been designated as parks since then. The Italian side of the Cherry Pass is now the Parco Naturale Argentera, the largest in Italy. The French side is the Parc National du Mercantour.

I actually had made plans to go there a few years ago. Already in my seventies, I had seen my doctor who, after subjecting me to a stress test, pronounced me fit. I traveled to Italy with the novelist Mary Doria Russell, who was gathering material for a fictionalized account of our crossing of the Alps. My wife and children, now grown, came along as well. We had planned to retrace the crossing starting from St. Martin-Vésubie. We went to Valdieri, to Rittana, and up to Gorrè. But the Cherry Pass failed to shed its snow cover that summer. We had to forgo that visit.

Even if the snow had melted, it would have been difficult to retrace our path. I had noticed that current hiking maps do not show the stretch hewn into sheer rock nor what connects to it. Part of that trail may have been damaged during the war.

Back in the States, I eventually wrote to the park's director to seek confirmation. In reply I received not only a letter but also photos of the pass and of the rocky path that now leads to it from the bottom of the valley in a profusion of steep zigzags. Touchingly, the ranger who made this ascent, Patrick Ormea, included a handful of rocks and soil taken from atop the pass and a length of barbed wire that had been strung there during the war.

Thus, in a fashion, I did revisit the pass.

I have revisited Cuneo and Rittana on several occasions. My most recent visit was in 1998. It was a special occasion. A memorial was to be dedicated in Borgo San Dalmazzo. Situated near the railway station from which the refugees captured in 1943 had been sent to Auschwitz, it was, however, not intended to commemorate them. Another memorial had already been erected for that purpose. The new memorial, Enzo Cavaglion's idea, is different and rather unique. It is a thank-you note, engraved on a stele. This is its text, translated from the Italian:

> While racial hatred raged in Europe,
> Jewish refugees, uncertain of their fate,
> coming from distant countries—

Austria, Germany, Poland, Belgium—
found hospitality and safety in Borgo San Dalmazzo
and in these valleys.
Hidden in isolated cottages, protected by the population,
they awaited with trustful hope
for two long, interminable winters,
the return of liberty.
In homage to the memory of those who helped them,
the sons and descendants of these Jewish refugees
fraternally embrace the inhabitants of these noble valleys.[2]

The road to Gorrè, as already mentioned, is paved now, and the people in the region live incomparably better than before. At Tanara, Margherita, our former neighbor, talked about her grandchildren who, she said with pride, live on three different continents. She also showed me the house in which my father and I had spent one winter. I could not recognize it. Everything looked fresh, with flowers everywhere. Stables held no animals anymore. Without grazing cattle, the parklike setting of the chestnut trees, I noticed, has disappeared under a profuse vegetation. Virtually no one, I was told, harvests chestnuts anymore. The cave of San Mauro, of course, was still there, but even scrutinizing the cliff with binoculars, I could not make it out.

As we walked toward Gorrè, I was pleased to see that someone was rehabilitating Massimo's mill as a mountain retreat. In Gorrè Sottano, a modern house was going up. The drying shed where my father and I had lived was still standing and so was the stable in which Lieserl and her parents had lived. Only its outside balcony, made of wood, had rotted away, and dense vegetation made access to these buildings difficult. Still, I could point out to my children where the German soldiers stood and where Lieserl and I stood when she gave me that kiss.

A sudden downpour surprised us there, whereupon someone drove up to fetch us. It was Cesana Battista, who now resides at Tetto Ponte but who used to live at Battaglia. He was the boy whom Lieserl attempted to have released by the Germans. Now he had his grandson with him to do the driving.

Because of a travel mix-up, we could not attend the dedication of the stele. But Enzo did take us to the quarry where we saw its lettering being completed.

Later I read that a group of young people had come from St. Martin-Vésubie to attend the ceremony, retracing the crossing of the mountains by way of the Colle della Finestra, the other pass taken by some of the refugees.

Four participants of that crossing, William Blye, Harry Burger, Walter Marx, and Charles Roman, spoke at the dedication. As Marx talked, a woman suddenly screamed and ran up to the podium. He happened to mention her, and she had recognized him.

During the ceremony, standard bearers wearing sashes with the national colors held up the elaborately embroidered standards of their towns. In the forefront, I noticed from photos Enzo sent me, was that of Boves, the town the German SS had set afire and in which a number of victims were burnt alive.

The stele's unveiling had been integrated with another event, the march of the Fifth Peace Caravan, which assembled there. Sending it off, Don Aldo Benevelli said, "The thoughts inscribed on the posters carried along the route of the Peace Caravan reflect the audacity and the valor of the inhabitants of these valleys, who welcomed the famished fugitives in 1943–45. The touching gratitude of the surviving Jews points even today to the need for extraordinary actions to liberate those who, even on the threshold of the year 2000, are still slaves and victims. The challenge, this Sunday, is to retain our emotions, to educate ourselves to act justly before Him."

Three thousand persons then marched to Cuneo where eight thousand assembled on the Piazza Galimberti and four thousand attended a special concert at the Sports Palace. A theater screened *Schindler's List, Kapo,* and *La vita è bella,* the bittersweet, prize-winning film about a little boy who survives the concentration camp.

Marx had returned twice before to look for the lady whose scream had interrupted his speech. During the war, she had hidden him in her parents' hotel for a while. On those earlier visits, he had not found her. The hotel was no longer there, her parents were dead, and she, married, had another name. Now, however, he invited her to visit him in New York.[3] There he showed her the sights, and at the United Nations building she sat for a moment in the seat of the Italian representative at the General Assembly. A reporter happened to snap the picture, which the Italian newspaper *Oggi* published. "In the 45 years that Italy has been a member of the United Nations," the accompanying story declared, "about a dozen ambassadors replaced one another in that chair, but never did Italy have a more deserving representative sitting there than Nella Giraudo."[4]

From Cuneo, we traveled to Genoa, still changing trains in Savona. During the couple of hours that we waited there, I examined the train station where I had come so close to being apprehended. The station, however, had been renovated.

In Genoa, we met Professor Giovanni Varnier, who had graciously researched for me the fate of Cousin Moyne and his family. Separated from us in 1943 after our arrival in that town, they had been hidden in an institution in which families could live together. A month later, a cleric, Don Gian Maria Rotondi, had taken them, along with a few other refugees, to Switzerland. The last segment of this voyage was accomplished on Lake Maggiore, by boat, at night. As they reached the shore, Swiss border guards discovered them and turned them back. The boat took them to the Italian town of Voldomino, where they were hidden in the presbytery. But the Germans occupying this town heard of their misadventure and arrested them the next morning. In all likelihood, that was what had alerted the archdiocese of Genoa and prompted our precipitous return to the mountains.

On April 20, 1982, Don Francesco Repetto, who had managed these rescue efforts, was awarded the Medal of the Righteous among the Nations. In his acceptance speech, he chose to talk not of his successes but to dwell on those whom his efforts had failed to save. He mentioned, in particular, Cousin Moyne's little girl:

Cilli Rosenbaum. You guess from her name that she was a child, a six-year-old girl. For some time already she had been caught in the blizzard of persecution, had wandered with her parents through Europe. She came to Genoa one evening in November. She pressed herself against her father and her mother, and her eyes were deep with fear. But when she found herself in a warm room, with food and a little bed ready, caressed by the sisters, her daddy and mummy at ease, her little heart opened up in gestures and words of delightful affection. . . .

Years later, I mentioned Cilli to Don Rotondi. "I remember her still," he told me, "atop the truck onto which they had been crowded. She trembled and I wrapped her in my coat, to hide from her the weapon that the SS trooper aimed at us."[5]

They went to Auschwitz.[6] And here am I, still feeling guilty. Had I but admitted forgetting to post that letter. . . .

I have returned several times to Montagnac as well. In 1995, fifty years after the war's end, this old town, already so well endowed with stones from its once prosperous past, managed to acquire yet another one. There would be a memorial here as well.

To never have said Kaddish for my mother still weighed on my soul. It distressed me also that her loss, and that of my sisters, had caused me so little pain. The awareness came so imperceptibly. What I discovered during the three-month-long voyage from Gorrè to Antwerp had come indistinctly and in snatches, by surmise and by guess. As my mother's and sisters' names were not on any of the lists of survivors posted in Antwerp, it became evident that we would never see them again. There was, however, no proof of their demise, and in the absence of proof a wan hope lingered on. Even after my father remarried in 1947, I still considered it possible that one of my sisters might be living somewhere, undetected. For the span of nearly half a century that impossible hope refused to be extinguished. It died only when my trembling hand held Serge Klarsfeld's book that contained their names.[7]

As intangibly as that hope, my mother and sisters ceased to exist. Their deaths were witnessed by no living soul. They were buried in no grave, recorded on no stone, deprived even of their loved ones' tears.

The memorial in Montagnac would rectify that.

The town had acquired a gentrified appearance. Palm trees bordered the highway where it met the esplanade. Showy tropical plants ornamented many balconies and windows of its old houses. The collapsed buildings in the rue Badoc, next to the house that was our first abode there, had been rebuilt. The tinette that used to salute unkempt residents had been replaced by a modern sewage system. Blacktop now covered the cobblestones; gone were the rivulets of water that coursed down the middle of the streets. The town crier had passed away, and so had the local train, along with its station and railroad tracks.

People from the north, Mr. Grasset informed me, had bought up some of the old houses as vacation places near the Mediterranean. And viticulture had changed. Children no longer helped with the harvest. School openings were no longer delayed because of it. All work was mechanized now. And the cooperative wine cellars of Montagnac and vicinity are Europe's largest.

Mr. Grasset, although not a native of Montagnac—he married a local girl—is the person who, after I began writing my memoirs, verified for me innumerable details about Montagnac. In this town, numbering no more than four thousand souls, he represents a thriving historical society that holds annual meetings and publishes a journal as well as books, one of which encompasses its entire six-thousand-year history.[8]

I already knew that the Granals and even their children were no longer alive. Only two persons remained of those whom I had known. We visited Mrs. Lucienne Trebosc, who had hidden my father and me overnight in her house. At the time, she had seemed so calm and reassuring. Now homebound, unable even to come to the unveiling, she remembered mostly one thing: "Oh, the fear! the fear!" she kept exclaiming. The other person, Jean Vidal, had been a little boy who played in his grandmother's bric-a-brac shop. He remembered me buying the electrical resistances with which I repaired the refugees' hot plates.

Yet everyone knew who I was. "My name is Del Rey, my father was the baker," said one. His bakery was the one in which I had briefly worked after my arrival in Montagnac. Another remembered having played with David Bauminger, my cousin. One woman and then another came to tell me that they had been classmates of one of my sisters. Since my French was no longer what it used to be, Grasset hovered over me, admonishing those talking to me to speak slowly. What a contrast between this reception and the one I had experienced in Germany! Here, it was like coming home.

The cemetery bordered the route de Villeveyrac, a short distance from the Maurel house where we had lived. I had passed it innumerable times, coming and going from work. Now, accompanied by Grasset, I entered it for the first time. On the somber, cypress-bordered path that stretched ahead, many people preceded us. Grasset explained that the establishment of the cemetery, at the beginning of the nineteenth century, had been the first visible step in ending centuries of religious strife. Till then, Catholics had been buried in the churchyard and Protestants on whatever land might do. How fitting that the memory of victims of the Holocaust should be embraced by this hallowed place! And might it not portend the end of those many centuries of strife against the Jews?

A man was waiting for us on the path. He introduced himself as the representative of the Jewish community of the town of Béziers. It was Saturday, the Shabbat, he said apologetically, and therefore neither the rabbi nor the cantor could attend the ceremony. Further along I was introduced to the mayor, who fell in with us. Ahead I noticed a man carrying the French flag. We had a color guard. A contingent of veterans had joined us.

The cypresses ended, allowing the shimmering Mediterranean sun to illuminate a wall carrying the inscription, "Garden of Memories." To one side hung a black curtain. After a brief speech, and while the French flag bowed, the mayor pulled the curtain down. On a slab of shiny black marble sparkled in golden letters the names of my mother and sisters and their ages. Their ages, Grasset had informed me, would have a bigger impact than their birth dates. My youngest sister had been thirteen at the time, my oldest seventeen.

When it was my turn to speak, I said, "It still hurts too much to talk about that dark night." Instead, I mentioned some songs I had heard in my youth, in particular Brahms' lovely lullaby. I related that unforgettable occasion when my mother, discerning some jealousy as she sang it to my youngest sister, then a baby, sat down with me to sing that lullaby once more, just for me. "How much would I have liked to sing this lullaby to my children!" I said. "That was not possible . . . How can one sing German lullabies to American citizens? And my children are Jewish. One no longer sings German lullabies to them.

"But French wine," I said, "we still enjoy, despite what the Vichy government had done to my family. For many years after my arrival in the United States, I had seen no wine. But one day—I was married by then, and my children already went to school—I heard an advertisement on the radio. A merchant in downtown Washington, D.C., offered a 'special,' a French wine, for less than a dollar a bottle. Intrigued, I bought some, an ordinary but respectable table wine, and that evening, for the first time since leaving Montagnac, I had wine for dinner.

"And it seemed to me that, for the first time after so many years, I had eaten . . . a real repast. During the war, the enchantment of wine could pass off a mess of rutabagas or topinambours as a meal.

Now this enchantment took effect once more. Since then, we have had wine with most of our meals."

I noted that, had Montagnac left me with bitter memories, these would have soured for me the taste of wine. But I had no such memories. I remembered the people of Montagnac remaining decent and steadfast, when so many stumbled.

I related how the Granals counseled us about where we should work during the vendange, and how, when food became scarce, they regularly provided us with some of the produce from their garden. I mentioned Mr. Vidal, who delivered the bundles of brindilles that I had picked up, and the unknown proprietor of the trees that I felled alongside the Hérault, who never complained, and Jeanne Babau, the lady so poor that she wore a dress made from a flour bag, who let me borrow her donkey and cart to carry that wood but refused to accept my money in return.

I mentioned the dangers some of the people had risked for us. "What might have happened to our neighbors, the families Granal and Trebosc, had they been found hiding my father and me? . . . to the gendarmes, who alerted us of the imminent *rafle*? . . . to Brigadier Cregut, who told a captive Jewish girl to get out quickly, that the way was clear . . . to the firefighters who allowed my Aunt Charlotte, her children, and my German-speaking grandmother to live above the firehouse while the Germans occupied Montagnac?"

I mentioned the mayor, André Bringuier, with some sixty Jewish refugees under his jurisdiction who, though pressed by Vichy decrees, sent his chief of police to bring back Aunt Charlotte's brother from a work camp and who provided false identity cards to some of the refugees when this became necessary. I mentioned the prefect, Mr. Benedetti, who, when one of his councillors betrayed the mayor of Montagnac, summoned the latter to Montpellier, showed him the letter, and tore it up in front of him.[9]

In my audience, I was surprised to see eyes that were wet.

Here there were people who had known my mother and sisters, who remembered them, and who now cried for them.

"On the other side of the Atlantic," I concluded, "two people, my wife and I, lift their wine glasses every evening at dinner. This would not have happened but for the brave people of Montagnac. Thus, when we lift our glasses, it is always in your honor."

Afterwards, as people began to scatter, someone led my wife to my side and cameras clicked. That too ended, and we remained alone for a while, in silence, aware only of the glittering afternoon sun.

After my return to the United States, I received a letter from Mr. Pierre Embry, the president of the Montagnac committee of the Souvenir Français, which maintains the graves of those who died for the fatherland. In it, he assured me that every May (Liberation Day) and November (Armistice Day), when flowers are placed at those graves, flowers would be placed at my family's memorial as well. In perpetuity.

CHRONOLOGY

LETTERS

NOTES

Chronology

This chronology is selective. It focuses on events related in the memoir as well as events related to it. It includes, as reference, important events that have become milestones in history. *The Timetables of Jewish History* by Judah Gribetz (Simon and Schuster, 1993) and other reference works have been used liberally in compiling this chronology.

1922

                Germany: The value of the currency drops steadily.

1923

Aug. 7   Hamburg, Germany: Alfred Feldman is born.

Nov. 20   A new currency, the Rentenmark, is introduced, ending runaway inflation.

1925

Feb.   Hamburg: Alfred's sister Jenny is born.

1927

Mar.   Hamburg: Alfred's sister Hella is born.

1928

                Cologne, Germany: Alfred's father is transferred to the Lissauer company headquarters. The family lives in an apartment at Lütticherstrasse 13.

1929

                Cologne: Alfred's sister Edith is born.

                Cologne: Alfred enrolls in first grade.

1932

                Antwerp, Belgium: The family joins Alfred's father, who had been transferred to this port city. The family lives in an apartment on rue Montebello, no. 11. Alfred enters fourth grade at the German school across the street.

1933

Jan.	Germany: Hitler becomes chancellor of Germany, head of the German government.
	The Nazi SA organize a boycott of Jewish stores, standing at their entrances with placards that warn: "Germans! defend yourselves. Don't buy from Jews."
Mar.	Antwerp: It is the end of the school year and of Alfred's attendance at the German school in Antwerp.
	Germany: The SS establish the first concentration camp at Dachau.
Apr.	Germany dismisses Jews from government service and the universities, also forbids them to enter the professions.
May	USA: Newsweek magazine reports the arrest of 200 Jewish merchants in Nuremberg for "profiteering," the beating of American Jews in Berlin, and the closing of the Jewish Telegraphic Agency offices in Berlin.
May 10	Germany: The Nazis arrange the public burning in great bonfires of books by Jewish and non-Nazi authors.
Sept.	Antwerp: Alfred enters fifth grade at the "Yessode Hatorah" school.
Oct.	Czechoslovakia: Ethnic Germans create the Sudetendeutsche Heimatfront under the leadership of Konrad Henlein, a hitherto obscure bank clerk and gymnastics teacher. This organization disseminates frankly Nazi and violently anti-Semitic propaganda.
Oct. 14	Geneva, Switzerland: Germany leaves the League of Nations.
also in 1933	Germany: Alfred's uncle Jacob Bauminger leaves Hamburg and arrives in Antwerp.
	Germany: Alfred's maternal grandparents sell their bakery in Hamburg and retire to Antwerp.
	Palestine: Alfred's uncle Anschel Feldman emigrates to Tel Aviv where he establishes an eatery near a construction site. He leaves his wife in Cologne, in charge of their children and their dairy shop.

1934

    Germany: By the end of the year, more than 10 percent of the 500,000 Jews living in that country have emigrated.

    Palestine: Alfred's aunt Mala Feldman, with her children, rejoins her husband, Anschel, in Tel Aviv. Alfred's aunt Klara Ehrenfeld, takes over their dairy store in Cologne.

1935

Sept. Germany: The "Nuremberg Laws" are enacted, depriving German Jews of their citizenship and of virtually all rights. Specifically, these forbid marriages between Jews and persons of "German blood," forbid Jews to engage in sexual relations with Aryans, or to hire female non-Jewish workers.

Oct. Africa: Italian forces invade Abyssinia (Ethiopia).

Dec. Poland: A wave of anti-Jewish riots occurs in Polish universities. Special seats are assigned to Jewish students.

also in 1935 Germany: Hitler repudiates the treaty of Versailles, reinstitutes conscription, and begins to rearm.

1936

Mar. Poland: Three Jews are killed in a pogrom in Przytyk, and sixty are wounded.

Mar. Germany sends troops into the Rhineland in defiance of the Versailles treaty.

Apr. Palestine: Haj Amin Al-Husaini, mufti of Jerusalem, organizes a general strike to protest Jewish immigration. Armed volunteers from neighboring Arab countries join.

May Abyssinia (Ethiopia): Italian troops occupy Addis Ababa, the capital, and the country surrenders.

July 17 Spanish Morocco: An army mutiny erupts led by Gen. Francisco Franco. It spreads to Spain and, within forty-eight hours, involves the whole country in a civil war.

Oct. 21 Cologne: Alfred's uncle Oscar Beglückter is beaten up by Nazi thugs and dies.

1937

July Italy: Mussolini, persuaded that Germany will win

	the next war, has Italy join the German-Japanese anti-Comintern pact in Nov. and withdraws from the League of Nations in Dec. The next year Italy introduces racial laws against the Jews.
Aug.	Antwerp: Alfred turns fourteen and receives his first identity card.
Sept.	Antwerp: Alfred enrolls in a trade school for business.
Oct.	Free city of Dantzig, East Prussia, Germany: Local Nazis incite anti-Jewish riots.
Dec.	Rumania: King Carol II names Octavian Goga, an anti-Semitic Fascist, to head the government. Goga establishes a dictatorship and restricts and harasses Jews.
also in 1937	USA: Alfred's aunt Tilly Feldman, her mother, and daughter Ruth arrive in New York. Their affidavit being inadequate, Alfred's uncle Max remains in Germany.
	France: F. L. Destouches, a French author writing under the pen name Celine, argues that France is a country occupied by Jews and that a German invasion would be liberation.
	South Africa passes the Aliens Act that closes a loophole in the Quota Act of 1930 and halts the entry of Jews fleeing from Nazi Germany.

1938

Jan.	Rumania abrogates the minority rights of Jews.
Mar. 12	Austria is annexed by Germany (the "Anschluss"). It was invaded twenty-four hours before a plebiscite was to be held to decide this matter.
Apr.	USA: A public opinion poll reveals that about 60 percent of Americans believe that persecution of European Jews was either entirely or partly their own fault.
	Germany: Jews are required to inform authorities of their property worth over 5,000 marks.
May	Hungary adopts its first "Jewish Law." It restricts to 20 percent the number of Jews in the liberal professions, the commercial and industrial enterprises, and in the government.

May	USA: Alfred's uncle Shimon Rosenbaum arrives in New York. He leaves wife and children in Germany as his affidavit was found inadequate to cover them.
May	USA: Alfred's uncle Max Feldman rejoins wife and daughter in New York.
June	Germany: Jewish-owned businesses have to be registered and marked as such.
July	Germany: Munich's main synagogue is demolished on Adolph Hitler's express orders.
July	USA: The Roman Catholic priest James E. Coughlin, "the radio priest," charges that Jews are guilty of deicide and unscrupulous money lending, that they control international banking, are responsible for the success of the Russian Revolution, and for this nation's ills.
July	Antwerp: Ines Rosenbaum arrives to spend the summer with the family at the seashore.
Aug.	Germany: Jews are ordered to use only Jewish first names. Those with Aryan first names must substitute "Israel" or "Sarah" for them.
Sept. 30	Germany: Without consulting the Czechs, British prime minister Chamberlain and French premier Daladier sign the Munich accord, which gives the Sudetenland to Germany. Chamberlain returns to England describing the accord as heralding "peace in our time."
ca. Sept.	USA: Alfred's uncle Herman Knoll arrives in New York. His affidavit being inadequate to cover his family, he leaves wife and child in Germany.
Oct. 28	Germany: 15,000 Jews living in Germany who are Polish citizens are forcibly returned to the Polish border. Poland does not allow them to reenter the country, and they are trapped in a no-man's-land or held in the border town of Zbaszyn. Among them are Alfred's aunts Jettchen Beglückter and Minna Rosenbaum, their children (except Ines), and Alfred's uncle Adolf Ehrenfeld, as well as cousins Moyne Rosenbaum and his brother, Wolftsche.

Nov. 7	France: Herschel Grynszpan, a young Jewish exile in Paris whose parents had been deported to Poland by Nazi orders, assassinates Ernst vom Rath, a subordinate official at the German Embassy.
Nov. 9	Germany responds to Ernst vom Rath's assassination with a well-organized nationwide pogrom against Jews, the Kristallnacht. During several days and nights, synagogues in Germany and Austria are burnt down, ninety-one Jews are killed, thousands wounded, and 30,000 arrested and sent to concentration camps. The windows of Jewish stores are smashed and looted. Then the Jewish community is ordered to pay the incredible fine of four billion marks.
Dec.	Antwerp: Willi Rosenbaum (son of Moyne) arrives at the Feldmans' home.
1939	
ca. Jan.	Antwerp: Alfred's aunt, Klara Ehrenfeld's two oldest children, Dora and Bella, arrive at the Feldmans' home.
Feb.	Antwerp: Klara arrives at the Feldmans' home.
Feb.	Antwerp: Alfred's grandmother Chinka Feldman arrives at the Feldmans' home.
Feb.	Antwerp: Klara's two youngest children, Goldine, six months old, and her brother Mordechai, arrive at the family's home.
Mar.	India: Gandhi declares that Palestine belongs to the Arabs.
Mar.	Germany: Hitler summons the Czech president to Berlin and threatens to destroy Prague by air unless he surrenders the Czech territories to him. The president accedes.
Mar.	Spain: The Civil War ends with the Nationalists victorious.
Apr.	Italy occupies Albania.
May	London: British colonial secretary MacDonald issues a "White Paper" restricting Jewish immigration to Palestine and prohibiting the sale of land to Jews. He admits that "there was a little bit of

cynicism . . . in our policy on Palestine . . . We knew the Jews would be on our side in the war whatever happened . . . Therefore we probably made more concessions to the Arabs than we would otherwise have done. . . ."

May   Cuba: The SS St. Louis arrives in Cuba with Jewish passengers who, though they have visas, are denied entry.

May   Antwerp: Josef Rosenbaum (son of Moyne) arrives at the Feldmans' home.

June   Antwerp: The SS St. Louis, prevented from discharging her passengers in America, arrives in Antwerp, where some of the passengers are allowed to disembark.

July   German-Polish border: Alfred's relatives in Zbaszyn are allowed to enter Poland. They travel to Przeworsk, where they have relatives.

July 10   Belgium: After a twenty-four-hour walk, Alfred's aunt Betty Knoll and her son Moni (Simon) cross the border illegally from Germany and come to the family's house in Antwerp.

Sept. 1   Poland: The Germans invade.

Sept. 3   Great Britain and France declare war on Germany. Ireland, offshore: A German submarine sinks the British passenger liner Athenia, carrying 1,480 passengers and crew.

Sept. 17   North Atlantic: A German submarine sinks the British aircraft carrier Courageous.

Sept. 17   Poland: Soviet armies cross into Poland unopposed.

Sept. 30   Finland is invaded by Soviet forces.

ca. Oct.   Poland: Alfred's aunts Jettchen and Minna and their children walk from the German-occupied part of Poland to the Russian-occupied zone. They stay in Niemirow.

Oct. 14   Scapa Flow (Orkney Islands): A German submarine torpedoes the British battleship Royal Oak.

Dec. 8   Antwerp: Betty and her son Simon leave on the SS Veendam from Rotterdam, the Netherlands, for New York.

Dec. 13	Uruguay, offshore: The German battleship Admiral Graf Spee, raiding Allied merchantmen, is spotted by three British cruisers. When it is attacked, the ship seeks shelter in the neutral Montevideo harbor. It leaves four days later to scuttle itself.
Dec. 22	New York: After a circuitous fifteen-day crossing of the Atlantic, Betty and her son arrive in New York.

1940

Mar. 13	Finland capitulates to the USSR.
Spring	USSR: Alfred's Aunt Minna, Josi Rosenbaum and his sister Nelly, Aunt Jettchen, Paula, Shlomo, and other relatives are taken to a labor camp in the region of Novosibirsk, Siberia.
Apr. 9	Norway and Denmark are invaded by the German army.
May 8	Antwerp: Alfred's cousin Ines Rosenbaum embarks for New York.
May 10 (Fri.)	The German army invades the Netherlands, Belgium, and Luxembourg.
May 11 (Sat.)	At midday, after twenty-eight hours of battle, Eben Emael, a Belgian fortress on the German border, succumbs to an attack by a mere seventy-eight German soldiers who landed by gliders. The French First Army and the British expeditionary force arrive to support Belgium.
May 12 (Sun.)	Breaking out of the Ardennes, German armor crosses into France and reaches the banks of the Meuse River. The family leaves Antwerp in two separate groups. Alfred's father, grandmother, Jenny, and Alfred arrive in their car in Coxyde, a resort on the Belgian coast.
May 13 (Mon.)	France: German tanks cross the Meuse at several points at Sedan and at Monthermé. The Dutch queen Wilhelmina and her government flee to England. Alfred's mother and sisters join the family in Coxyde. Alfred's uncle Jacob and family find lodgings nearby.

May 14 (Tues.)	The Netherlands surrender.
May 15 (Wed.)	The Germans break out of their bridgehead in Sedan and turn westward to drive behind the backs of the Allied armies in Belgium to the Channel coast.
	Alfred's father briefly returns to Antwerp to pick up some cash.
May 16 (Thurs.)	The Germans are reported nearly fifty miles west of Sedan. In Belgium, the Allies abandon their fallback line on the Dyle River.
May 17 (Fri.)	German armored units coming from Sedan cross the Oise river. Although there is fighting at Rethel, thirty miles from Sedan in the direction of Paris, the crossing of the Oise river indicates that the Germans are heading toward the sea.
	Coxyde, Belgium: Alfred's father tells Jacob that it's time to leave. German troops enter Brussels.
May 18 (Sat.)	The Feldmans leave Coxyde, splitting up again, and cross the border into France.
	Antwerp falls to the Germans.
May 19 (Sun.)	Alfred, his father, Jenny, and Grandmother Feldman arrive in Bordeaux, France. There is no contact with Alfred's mother and her party.
May 20 (Mon.)	General Guderian's troops reach Abbeville, blocking all communication between the north and the rest of France. By night, they reach the North Sea.
May 26	Dunkirk, France: The British begin the evacuation of their expeditionary force from the beaches.
May 27	Belgium sues for an armistice.
May 28	The Belgian surrender takes effect.
June 3	France: The Dunkirk evacuation ends.
June 5	France: Germany launches its final offensive.
June 9	France: German armies cross the Seine.
June 10	Italy declares war on the Allies.
	France: The government is about leave Paris and move to Bordeaux. All foreign refugees there must leave. Alfred and the rest of his father's party are directed to a resort, Lacanau les Bains.

	Bordeaux, France: Before leaving town, mail is received from Alfred's mother's party. She writes from Montagnac, a small town in the Mediterranean region. Neither she nor any other refugees were allowed to leave their train in Bordeaux.
June 14	Paris: The Germans enter the city.
June 16	France sues for an armistice.
June 18	England: Charles de Gaulle starts his "Free French" (later "Fighting French") movement.
June 19	Lacanau les Bains, France: Ignoring their assigned residence, Alfred and the rest of his father's party return to Bordeaux, where his father obtains a Haitian visa. With this, he obtains Portuguese and Spanish transit visas. By telegram, he arranges to meet Alfred's mother.
	France: Germany delivers its terms for an armistice.
ca. June 21 (Fri.)	Alfred and his father's party arrive in Montagnac but find that Alfred's mother had left that day to meet them at the Spanish border. As public transportation is no longer available, Alfred's father remains in Montagnac, expecting that she will return.
June 22	France accepts the German terms in the forest of Compiègne, in the railroad car in which the 1918 German surrender had been signed.
June 25	France: The armistice takes effect. France is divided into two parts. One is occupied by the Germans, the other ruled by a French government in Vichy.
ca. July	Poland (Russian sector): Alfred's aunts Jettchen and Minna and their children are sent to Siberia.
July 7	France, unoccupied part: The Vichy government is formed. The Constitution of the Third Republic is revoked and Marshal Pétain is given the title of chief of the French state. The Senate and the Chamber of Deputies are adjourned indefinitely.
July 16	Germany: Hitler orders the German army to prepare for the invasion of England (operation Sea Lion), but the army is unprepared, having assumed

	that Great Britain would recognize "her militarily hopeless situation."
July 22	Vichy, France: The new government authorizes Minister of Justice Alibert to review grants of French citizenship. As a result, in the next three years over 7,000 French Jews lose their citizenship.
also in July	Montagnac, France: Alfred's mother and sisters rejoin Alfred and the rest of his father's party.
Aug. 8	England: The German air force begins steady assaults over England, starting the Battle of Britain.
Aug. 17	Somalia: The British, leaving by sea, abandon Somaliland, which is under attack by Italian troops from Abyssinia.
Aug. 27	France: The Vichy government abrogates the Marchandeau law that prohibits attacks on individuals in the press based on race or religion.
Sept. 13	North Africa: Italian troops cross the Cyrenaican frontier into Egypt.
Sept. 17	Egypt: The Italian forces reach Sidi Barrani.
Sept. 27	France: The Vichy government gives prefects the power to intern all male immigrants between the ages of eighteen and fifty-three judged to be "superfluous in the national economy."
Oct. 3	France: The Vichy government decrees its first Statut des Juifs, preempting German regulation of the issue. It authorizes prefects to intern, assign to supervised residence, or enroll in forced labor any foreign Jews in their departments as they see fit.
Oct. 23	Germany, despite intense French objections, sends 6,000 German Jews from western Germany to France.
Oct. 25	France: A new decree requires foreign Jews to obtain a permit (sauf-conduit) to travel outside their place of residence.
Oct. 28	Albania: Italian troops attack Greece from an occupied Albania.
Nov.	England: Despite a superiority of 3,000 to 800, the German air force suffers such heavy losses over England that it ends the "Battle of Britain." Said

Winston Churchill, "Never in the field of human conflict was so much owed by so many to so few."

Greece: On the Greek-Italian front, the initiative passes to the Greek forces.

Rumania joins the axis after the USSR, in June, occupies the Rumanian provinces of Bessarabia and Bukovina. German troops immediately infiltrate Rumania to secure the oil from the Ploesti oil fields.

Dec. 10   Egypt: The British launch a counteroffensive. They will retake Sidi Barrani, drive the Italian troops from Egypt advance into Cyrenaica, and take many prisoners.

Winter   Siberia: Alfred's Aunt Minna dies in the camp near Novosibirsk.

1941

France: The winter of 1940–41 is the coldest of the war.

Feb. 7   North Africa: The British cut off the Italian army, which surrenders, leaving Cyrenaica in British hands.

Feb. 8   Greece, under attack from Italy and anticipating a German attack from Bulgaria, asks for British help.

Mar. 1   Bulgaria joins the Axis and allows free passage to German troops. Within a week, seventeen divisions arrive from Rumania.

Mar. 7   Greece: The first British contingent arrives in Athens.

Mar. 24   North Africa: German troops brought in to rescue their Italian allies begin a second Axis offensive under Field Marshal Rommel, repulsing the British and occupying El Agheila in Cyrenaica.

Mar. 25   Yugoslavia: The government joins the Axis.

Mar. 27   Yugoslavia: The government is overthrown; the new government opposes the Axis.

Mar. 29   USA: "War by Refugee," a story in the widely read Saturday Evening Post, reports incorrectly that Nazi agents disguised as refugees have infiltrated the United States. It describes a Gestapo school that teaches spies to "speak Yiddish, read Hebrew, and pray." To make their disguise complete, spies are circumcised.

Apr. 3	North Africa: The British evacuate Benghazi, in Cyrenaica, and retreat to the Egyptian frontier. Tobruk, isolated, holds out and is supplied by sea.
Apr. 6	Yugoslavia is attacked by Axis troops. Abyssinia: After a year and a half of reverses, British troops, in the first morale-boosting success of the Allied armies, capture Addis Ababa, the capital.
Apr. 9	Greece: German troops enter from Yugoslavia.
Apr. 17	Yugoslavia falls to Germany.
Apr. 29	Greece: Under German attack, British and Greek forces evacuate the mainland, abandoning their equipment.
May 9	France: Paris police carry out mass arrests of foreign Jewish men.
May 20	Crete: German forces, landing with gliders and by sea, surprise the British and Greek forces that had withdrawn to this island.
May 29	Crete: The Germans complete the occupation of the island.
June 6	France: Alfred's father reports to the work camp in Agde.
June 18	France: Alfred's father is released from the work camp in Agde for medical reasons.
June 22	USSR: In a surprise attack and on a wide front, Germany invades the Soviet Union.
also in June	USA: Congress passes the Russell Act, which bars immigration to all persons with close relatives in Nazi-occupied Europe. USSR: German mobile killing squads begin mass murders in captured Soviet territories.
July 13	Marseilles, France: Alfred's father arrives to his appointment with the U.S. Consul to submit his immigration papers. The consul, already informed of the Russell Act, informs him of the "close relatives" restriction. It prevents his obtaining a visa as his sister Klara lives in Antwerp under German occupation.
July 30	London: Polish-Soviet treaty is signed.

Aug. 12	Moscow: As a result of the above treaty, the Soviet government grants amnesty to all Polish citizens. In time, Josi Rosenbaum and his sister Nelly, as well as Aunt Jettchen, Paula, Shlomo, and other relatives are released from their camp in Siberia.
Oct. 9	La Jonchère-St. Maurice (Haute Vienne), France: Alfred's sister Hella arrives at the children's home in the Château le Couret.
Nov. 18	North Africa: Second British counteroffensive begins.
also in Nov.	France: Salomon Rotenberg departs from France for Cuba.
	London: Thomas Mann, the German novelist, broadcasting over the BBC, mentions the "unspeakable" done to Jews and Poles.
Dec. 2	USSR: The Russian army under Zhukov surprises the Germans with a massive winter counteroffensive.
Dec. 7	Pearl Harbor: Arriving at dawn, Japanese airplanes bomb the naval base in a surprise attack.
Dec. 8	Hong Kong: Japanese airplanes bomb the city.
	Guam: The Japanese invade this key American base in the central Pacific as well as other islands.
	USA: The United States declares war on Japan.
Dec. 9	Malay peninsula: Japanese forces occupy Bangkok.
Dec. 10	Philippines: Japanese troops land in Luzon and quickly capture Manila, the capital.
	South China Sea: Japanese aircraft sink the British battleship Prince of Wales and the battle cruiser Repulse, conferring Japan naval superiority in the Indian and western Pacific oceans.
Dec. 11	Germany and Italy declare war on the United States.
Dec. 12	Paris: German police arrest French Jews.
Dec. 24	Hong Kong surrenders to a Japanese invading force.
Dec. 30	North Africa: Rommel withdraws to El Agheila in western Cyrenaica.
1942	
Jan. 20	Wannsee, Germany: A conference reviews the details of the "Final Solution" of the "Jewish problem," a program to kill all the Jews of Europe.

Jan. 22	North Africa: Rommel begins the third Axis offensive in North Africa.
also in Jan.	France: Alfred's uncle Jacob Bauminger departs France for Cuba.
Feb. 4	North Africa: Rommel retakes Benghazi.
Feb. 15	Singapore, the greatest naval base in the Far East, falls to the Japanese.
Feb. 26	Montagnac: Alfred obtains a receipt that he has registered as an Israelite who entered France after Jan. 1, 1936.
Mar. 27	Paris: The first transport for Auschwitz, Poland, leaves from France. SS captain Annecker, chief of the Gestapo's Jewish Office, personally accompanies it.
Apr. 18	Tokyo is bombed by sixteen planes from a U.S. carrier led by LTC James H. Doolittle.
also in Apr.	Kolkhoz "Kaganovitch," Siberia: Under unendurable conditions, Alfred's Aunt Jettchen and little Nelly die.
May 5	Coral Sea, Pacific Ocean: The first battle between aircraft carrier groups begins. It ends with a tactical victory for the Japanese but a strategic victory for the Allies, who prevented the capture of Port Moresby.
May 30–31	Germany: Cologne undergoes a saturation bombing raid. Within ninety minutes, 1,000 British bombers drop more than 2,000 tons of bombs. It is the first of many German cities to be thus ravaged.
May 31	Germany: Essen undergoes a saturation bombing raid by British bombers.
June 3	Pacific Ocean: The Battle of Midway is engaged, in which the Japanese lose four carriers while the United States loses only one. This battle is considered the turning point of the war in the Pacific, costing the Japanese their strategic initiative while allowing the United States to begin offensive operations.
June 6	Montagnac: Alfred receives an identity card and a permit to take a course in agriculture at a school in Agde established by the ORT, a Jewish organization. (By then Alfred had been in Agde several months already.)
June 11	Paris: SS captain Dannecker promises Eichmann, his direct superior in Berlin, 100,000 Jews from France.

	These would be delivered within the next eight months, and be aged from sixteen to forty. The age limits, which, because of practical difficulties, are raised to fifty-six are to disguise these earliest deportations as labor convoys.
June 14	Aleutian Islands: Japanese troops take Kiska, Attu, and Agattu. This will be the only part of North America invaded by the enemy during the war. Heavy losses at Midway prevent the Japanese from following up on this initial success.
June 25	Germany: Bremen undergoes a saturation bombing raid by British bombers.
June 28	Russia: Germany launches a major offensive in the south.
July 5	North Africa: The Germans reach El Alamein, 60 miles west of Alexandria. The British have lost 80,000 men.
July 6	Solomon Island, Pacific Ocean: Japanese troops land on Guadalcanal and begin the construction of an air base.
July 16	Paris: French police carry out the first roundup of Jewish families.
July 21	Gona, New Guinea: The Japanese land troops that advance toward Port Moresby, threatening navigation along the northern shores of Australia. After months of jungle combat, however, a mixed force of Australians and Americans vanquish the Japanese in New Guinea.
also in July	France: In camps in the occupied zone, children under fourteen are left to fend for themselves as parents are sent to Auschwitz.
Aug. 6	France: French police begin combing internment camps for foreign Jewish refugees to be delivered to the Germans for deportation.
Aug. 7	Pacific Ocean: U.S. Marines come ashore on Guadalcanal and adjacent islands and dislodge the Japanese.
Aug. 26	Hérault, France: During the night, police enter Jewish residences. Alfred's mother and sisters are taken. Round-ups elsewhere in the south of France continue through the twenty-eighth.
Aug. 28	Antwerp: Alfred's Aunt Klara and her three oldest children are arrested during the night.
Sept. 1	Belgium: Klara and children are sent to Auschwitz in convoy VII.

Sept. 11	France: Alfred's mother and sisters are sent from Drancy to Auschwitz in convoy 31.
Sept. 13	Auschwitz, Poland: Alfred's mother and sisters arrive at the camp.
Sept. 14	Auschwitz: On this day, presumably, Alfred's mother and sisters are killed.
also in Sept.	Hérault: Alfred travels to Le Puy en Velay with "Roche" (Kowarski) to join a "Groupement" of Young Workers.
	USSR: The advance of the German Sixth Army under General Paulus is checked in Stalingrad.
	Pacific Ocean: Throughout the fall, the Battle of Guadalcanal grinds on, ending in a hard-won American victory.
	London: Thomas Mann, on the BBC, signals the total extermination of European Jewry, mentions the gassing of thousands near Warsaw, and relates the tales of German locomotive conductors who had taken the trains to the death centers.
Oct. 23	El Alamein, Egypt: The British launch their third and final counteroffensive. It will have advanced 1,400 miles by Jan. 1943.
also in Oct.	New York: Despite being "highly" pregnant, Alfred's Aunt Betty travels to Washington, D.C., for a hearing on her appeal of the denial of a U.S. visa to Alfred's family. Betty's baby will be stillborn.
	The Jewish Telegraphic Agency releases press reports of German mass killings of Jews at death camps.
Nov. 8	Northwest Africa: American and British troops land on a massive scale on Africa's Atlantic and Mediterranean coasts.
Nov. 11	Northwest Africa: Morocco and Algeria surrender to the Allies.
	Southern France: Axis forces pour into the free zone of France to secure it. Germans and Italians occupy separate areas.
Nov. 20	Northeast Africa: The British capture Benghazi.
Nov. 23	USSR: The Russian counteroffensive encircles the Germans in Stalingrad. Another Russian force bars relief routes the Germans might use.

| Nov. 27 | Toulon, France: The French fleet is scuttled to keep it from falling into German hands. |

1943

Jan. 2 or 3	Palestine: Alfred's cousins Josi and Shlomo arrive in a roundabout way from the USSR.
Jan. 23	North Africa: The British Eighth Army takes Tripoli.
Feb. 2	Stalingrad, USSR: The German general Paulus, though just promoted by Hitler to field marshal, surrenders with his army.
Mar. 25	Nice, France: Alfred's father receives orders from the Italian occupation forces to report to the forced residence of St. Martin-Vésubie, France, on or by Mar. 28, 1943.
Apr. 7	North Africa: The British Eighth Army, coming from the east, makes contact with the U.S. II Corps, coming from the west.
May 10	North Africa: All organized Axis resistance ceases.
June 25	Nice: Alfred arrives in that city.
July 2	St. Martin-Vésubie, France: Alfred arrives in that resort.
July 5	USSR: A major German offensive launched at Kursk fails. The battle proves to be the largest tank engagement of the war. It ends with the retreat of the Germans who, thereafter, can no longer mount a serious offensive in Russia.
July 9	Sicily: Allied forces invade the island.
July 24	Rome: Mussolini's leadership is repudiated. He is arrested and the king appoints Marshal Pietro Badoglio to replace him.
July 25	Italy: The Fascist regime is abolished.
July 17	Sicily: The British enter Messina, completing the conquest of that island.
Sept. 3	Sicily: An Italian unconditional surrender is signed but kept secret.
	Sicily: Allied forces cross the Straits of Messina and land in Italy. They meet little resistance.
Sept. 8	Italy: Upon announcement of the Italian surrender, the Germans, with six divisions already in Italy, take control of the country. Italian troops disband.

Sept. 9	St. Martin-Vésubie: Germans troops arrive by evening. Rome is occupied by the Germans. Gulf of Salerno, Italy: Allied forces land and establish a bridgehead.
Sept. 10	Nice: The S.S. establishes itself and immediately rounds up the Jews. St. Martin-Vésubie: In the early afternoon, Alfred and his father join a scattered line of refugees going across mountain passes into Italy.
Sept. 12	Cuneo, Italy: The Germans occupy the city. Abbruzzi Mountains, Italy: In a daring exploit by air, the Germans free Mussolini.
Sept. 17	German commandos arrive at St. Martin-Vésubie.
Sept. 18	Valdieri, Cuneo Province: In this town, where most of the Jewish residents from St. Martin-Vésubie have gathered, two troopers of the SS "Leibstandarte Adolf Hitler" affix a proclamation ordering all "strangers" to surrender and threatening the life of anyone who helps them. Several hundred Jews are caught or surrender. The others scatter into the surrounding mountains.
Sept. 19	Boves, Cuneo Province: Having been challenged and fired upon by Italian partisans, SS burn the town and kill twenty-three civilians.
Sept. 21	Berthemont, Maritime Alps, France: German SS take the inmates of the Jewish nursing home for the aged and send them, including Grandmother Feldman, by train to the camp at Drancy.
Oct. 7	Drancy, France: Convoy 60, carrying Alfred's grandmother Chinka Feldman, departs for Auschwitz.
Oct. 12	Monte Cassino, Italy: After crossing the Volturno, the Allies are stopped before this abbey along the Gustav Line, which the Germans have been preparing since the Allies first landed in Italy. It will take them seven months to push through.
Oct. 25	Jewish refugees from St. Martin-Vésubie, now hiding in the Italian Alps, arrive at the archdiocese in Genoa, brought by Catholic clerics. Alfred, his father, and

	Moyne Rosenbaum and family arrive there probably on Oct. 29.
Dec. 3	Valdomino, Italy: Moyne Rosenbaum and family, having been taken to the Swiss border but been refused entry into Switzerland, are captured by the SS. The Archdiocese in Genoa, who directed this attempt, is compromised. All Jewish refugees on its premises, including Alfred and his father, must return immediately to the mountains.

1944

Jan. 4	Polish Russian frontier is crossed by advancing Russian forces.
May 18	Monte Cassino is finally conquered. The Allies advance again.
May 26	Cuneo Province, Italy: A flight of some 700 B-17/24s crosses the sky.
June 4	Rome is liberated.
June 6	Beaches of Normandy, France: The long-awaited Allied landing begins.
June 11	Beaches of Normandy: The Allies manage to join the different beachheads, achieving a solid front.
July 13	Cuneo Province: In the Stura Valley, partisans destroy the bridge over the Stura River, interrupting the road that connects Italy to France by the Maddalena Pass. They control the thirty miles of valley in between.
June 15	Italy: The Allies liberate Livorno and reach the River Arno.
June 26	France: The Allies have broken out of their beachhead and capture Cherbourg and its harbor.
July 20	Hitler's headquarters in East Prussia: Claus von Stauffenberg, a German officer, explodes a bomb near Hitler, but the dictator survives virtually unscathed.
July 31	Poland: The Red Army reaches the suburbs of Warsaw. It encourages the Polish underground to rise against the Germans, but then, under much-debated circumstances, stands by while the Germans suppress the Polish uprising.
Aug. 13	Italy: The Allies capture Florence.

Aug. 15	Beaches of southern France: The Allies land once again in France to support the troops advancing in the north of France.
Aug. 17	Franco-Italian border: The Germans go on the attack against the partisans in the Stura Valley and all along the Franco-Italian border.
Aug. 23	Rumania and Bulgaria: Both are occupied by the Red Army. Rumania sues for peace and changes sides in the war.
Aug. 24	Germany: The Official War Communiqué mentions the fighting along Franco-Italian border and claims that German forces have reconquered the Maddalena Pass.
Aug. 25	Paris: de Gaulle's army enters in triumph.
Sept. 1	France: The Allies capture Nice in the south, Dieppe in the north, and overrun Verdun.
Sept. 2	Italy: The Allies capture Pisa.
Sept. 4	Belgium: The Allies capture Antwerp.
Sept. 11	Germany: The U.S. First Army enters Germany near Trier.
Sept. 15	France: Allied forces that have landed in the south join with Patton's forces from Normandy, cutting off the German Nineteenth Army.
Oct. 2	Germany: The U.S. First Army breaches the Siegfried Line near Aachen.
Oct. 20	Yugoslavia: Russian forces liberate Belgrade.
Nov. 4	Hungary: Russian forces reach the suburbs of Budapest.
Dec. 16	Belgium: The Germans launch a counterattack in the Ardennes, near Bastogne.
1945	
Jan. 17	Poland: The Red Army, which had reached the suburbs of Warsaw six months earlier, goes on the offensive again and Warsaw falls.
Jan. 19	Germany: The Red Army crosses into Germany at the Silesian border.
Jan. 26	East Prussia, Germany: The Russians reach the Baltic, isolating all German forces east of Dantzig.
Jan. 30	Germany: Russian forces cross the Brandenburg frontier, barely a hundred miles from Berlin.

Jan. 31	Germany: Russian forces reach the Oder, forty miles from Berlin.
also in Jan.	The Soviet army liberates Auschwitz, but the report is delayed until May.
Mar. 3	Gorrè, Cuneo Province: Alfred faces a German execution squad but is released.
Mar. 7	Germany: The Allies capture Cologne.
Mar. 23	Germany: The Allies cross the Rhine at several points.
Apr. 9	Italy: The Allies begin an offensive into the Po Valley.
Apr. 11	U.S. troops enter the Nazi concentration camp of Buchenwald. The BBC temporizes in releasing the news, fearing it won't be believed.
Apr. 18	Czechoslovakia: U.S. troops enter the country.
Apr. 23	Berlin: Russian forces enter the suburbs.
Apr. 24	London: Big Ben lights up, ending the London blackout.
Apr. 25	Torgau on the Elbe, Germany: Russian and American forces meet.
	Cuneo Province: The bells ring throughout the mountains. The Germans are in retreat.
	Cuneo: A truck of the Brigate Nere stops at a prison, removes six Jewish partisans, and executes them.
Apr. 28	Dongo, near Lake Como, Italy: Partisans capture Mussolini and other Fascist officials on their way to escape into Switzerland. Mussolini and Clara Petacci are shot.
Apr. 30	Berlin: Hitler and Eva Braun commit suicide.
Apr. 31	Berlin: Goebbels kills his wife and six children, then commits suicide.
May 4	Brenner Pass, Italy: Elements of the U.S. Seventh Army, coming from the north through Austria, meet with a division of the U.S. Fifth Army, which had fought its way up the Italian boot.
May 8	V-E day is declared.
	At midnight, the German surrender takes effect.
May 28	Cuneo: A military truck takes Alfred, his father, and some other refugees back to France.
June 6	France: Alfred and his father arrive in Montagnac to meet Alfred's Aunt Charlotte.

Aug. 6	Japan: An American B-29 drops the first atomic bomb over Hiroshima.
Aug. 8	Japan: A second atomic bomb is dropped over Nagasaki.
Aug. 14	Japan: The emperor accepts the Allied terms of surrender.
also in Aug.	By the end of the month, Alfred and his father are back in Antwerp.
Sept. 10	Antwerp: Alfred's father writes to the director of the French police, inquiring about the fate of Alfred's deported mother, sisters, and grandmother. The police can provide only the date on which they left France.
Oct. 18	Berlin: An international military tribunal begins a tenmonth trial of major Nazi figures. Beginning on Nov. 20, it is held in Nuremberg.

1946

ca. Jan.	Palestine: Alfred's cousin Paula arrives from the USSR.

1948

France: Maurice Bardèche publishes a book in which he contends that at least a portion of the evidence regarding the German concentration camps has been falsified and that the deaths that occurred there were primarily the result of war-related privations. He further maintains that Nazi documents referring to the "final solution of the Jewish problem" are really referring to the proposed transfer of Jews to ghettos in the east. He will be followed by many others who deny the Holocaust.

Letters

Except as noted, the following wartime letters were saved by Aunt Betty. She received many more but was selective in what she kept. She did not keep copies of what she wrote. Of her letters, only one survived because it was returned undelivered. All family letters were written in German. The translation is by the author. Letters marked with an asterisk are stored at the American Jewish Historical Society, on the campus of Brandeis University at Waltham, Massachusetts.

Letter from Aunt Klara and Alfred's father in Antwerp to Aunt Betty and Uncle Herman in New York.

January 18, 1940

Dear Betty:

We are very surprised not to have heard from you thus far. Yet you have been already a month over there. Mother, in particular, cannot understand why she has received no news from you. If you write us, you must always use air mail. It takes much too long otherwise, and the content of your letter will be out of date. We assume that a letter from you is on its way, informing us about your arrival and how the voyage agreed with you and Moni. In the meantime, we have received the letter from Simon [Rosenbaum, Minna's husband], and you will have received our reply to him, from which you can see what we are attempting to do on Minna's behalf. With the exception of the telegram, we have however, not heard so far either from them, nor from the Red Cross. For Ines, we expect an appointment any day. Were you already at Adolf's cousin and what do you think about my voyage? Are you making efforts on behalf of Paula and Shlomo [Sali], whose turn has now arrived on the German quota. I hope that you have written us minutely about your impressions there. Here, thank

God, we all are well. Mother visits me frequently, in particular to enjoy Goldale [Goldine]. With every day she gets smarter; and has changed considerably in the time that you have been gone.

Heartfelt greetings and kisses, Klara

Dear Betty! (now I am taking dictation from Joa [Alfred's father, Joachim]). We worried much following your departure, and received the telegraphic notice of your arrival there after considerable anxiety. We had been able to determine already one day earlier that your ship had arrived. Mother however calmed down gradually only after the telegram's arrival. Time and again, she refused to believe that the ship was out of danger, and did not abandon her final doubts even after the telegram's arrival. She would gladly have liked to hear a word directly from you, and we certainly counted on the prompt arrival of an airmail letter from you. We are sorry to have to assume that you sent your account by ordinary mail, since we have received nothing from you in the past four weeks. We have received only last week Simon's airmail letter informing us that you were expected in a few days. Since the mail is so slow, and Mother so dotes on you and your boy, you will have to send, from time to time, a few lines by airmail, with which you will much gladden her. Here, nothing has changed since your departure. Although Mother complains about this and that, she generally feels good. She misses you a lot because with you she could best unburden herself. She keeps much company with my mother-in-law, who is now a frequent visitor here. One cannot go much outside because of the winter, and this time, it is a real winter. It is very cold and today high snow covers the street. Klara and her family freeze considerably in their apartment. About Ines I have everything in readiness. The papers were found completely in order, and I anticipate an appointment for her with the consulate any day. From Jettchen and Minna one hears nothing, as there is no postal connection to there [Soviet-occupied Poland]. I have long since turned to the Red Cross, and written to the Jewish relief society in Berlin as well. But as long as there is no postal service, one can't know what to do about Minna's departure. I asked the Red Cross and the relief society to enable Minna to reach the consulate in Stuttgart.—I do not know whether I can prevail from here to obtain ship's passage for Ines, and remember that Simon may have to

contact the HIAS about this. I hope that I may inform Simon soon
that Ines has her visa. Assuming that you have a different address
now, I am sending this letter to Simon's address, and remain, with
heartfelt greetings to all,

your Joa

Dear Simon [Rosenbaum]!

Your airmail letter reached us only a few days ago. I have long since
attempted everything imaginable. So far as anyone knows, no one has
received mail from there because postal connections have not yet been
established to there. As soon as I learn anything, I shall undertake
the necessary steps. For the time being, heartfelt greetings.

your Joa

*Letter dictated to Alfred by Alfred's Grandmother Feldman in Antwerp
and addressed to Uncle Herman and Aunt Betty in New York.*

Antwerp, March 24, 1940

Dear children,

You can not imagine my joy when they read your letter to me. I am
very pleased to hear that you are beginning to get accustomed to
life there. You should be satisfied. You wrote that, because of the
Shabbos, you have difficulties setting up a business. If it involves
the Shabbos, it is better to forego the business, the Eternal then will
not abandon you. Try to contact the family operating that camp,
so that you may spend the summer months there with your child,
if possible.

   I think that you should contact the family there, and get them
to sponsor Jettchen's children. Although you had so much trouble
with Moyne's papers, make the effort, even if you don't have time.
Describe the children's situation, inquire about what may be done
for them, go to the family owning the movie house, tell them they
wouldn't even see the children if they didn't want to, they should
only have pity, and sponsor them. If possible, one may take care of
Jettchen from here, as her quota comes up later. As you know me,
my eyes no longer drip with tears, but with blood; we have received
only two telegrams from the children. Minna has better prospects

than Jettchen. Joa has telegraphed a letter and ten dollars. That was already five weeks ago, and we still have no answer.

Then, dear Betty, you should undertake to break walls, and take Arale Neuwirth, and prevail upon Leibtsche on behalf of Moyne. It is a big thing. Then I pray you to write me where the father-in-law is. If he is not a refugee, attempt to bring him over, or send him something? I am very curious. I have already exerted myself enough to dictate this to you but will write you yet a few more lines. I am very curious, search out the family Körper, perhaps you can be of some assistance to them. Would you know where Simon's Feigale is? Write me also about her. Perhaps you can find someone with the name of Blaser, a brother of Hendel Schwebel, and children. Klara or Joa will write you about everything else, I have no patience anymore. I am closing this letter with heartfelt greetings and kisses to all. An extra 1,000 kisses for Moni; if he wants me to come right away, he must send me an air ship, and I will then bring him a present because he says the benedictions so nicely every morning. The air ship must be at least as large as his little trunk bed that is still here, so that I can bring along many presents.

[greetings and signature in Yiddish written with Hebrew characters]

Many greetings and kisses from Alfred.

P. S. Extra many greetings to my only brother, Jakob [Bezalel] Rotenberg. I wish him a kosher Passover and much joy.

Letter from Aunt Klara in Antwerp to her sister Betty in New York.

June 1940 [estimated date]

Dear Betty,

I can tell you only today that, after a journey of about 4 weeks, we have returned home, thank God, in good health. Joa, with family and mother, have not yet returned, though we expect them daily. We have heard of them from others who met them on the way. Joa did not travel with us because, at first, we had no intention to depart; but we then changed our mind. We left with Max [Moyne], Regine, and family, who are also, thank God, back and in good health. Ines really had some incredible luck. But we have not heard anything from her about her arrival, and hope that such news is on the way. Hopefully, she likes it as much there as here with Joa. Our journey was very stressful for the children and I am glad to be home again. Unfortunately, I cannot satisfy their desires, for example, to buy enough fruit, as my situation here is no better than before. It is evidently impossible to make ends meet with what I receive, especially since I am missing the subsidy from Joa. That which I had previously had evaporated during the journey, so that we are, as it were, broke. Did Joa write you on the way? I wish that they all were back again, as we feel very lonely here. Of the children, I can tell you that Goldale, thank God, makes good progress, repeating what everyone says, which is very funny, and is beginning also to turn catty. With respect to cockiness, Bella and the boy [Mordechai] have not at all improved, and Dörchen [Dora] is turning ever more serious. After the vacation, please God, Bella will go to school, and I shall then take Goldale to nursery school, assuming that she will be accepted. That would give me more time for housework, as I now also launder myself the entire wash at home. Adolf [Aunt Klara's husband] now helps me diligently with the household, as otherwise I would not know where to begin. How are you, and Herman and Moni, doing? I await a detailed letter from you soon, and I rejoice at the anticipation, as it makes one believe to be in conversation with you. How is Simon [Rosenbaum, Aunt Minna's husband and Ines's father] doing, and what writes Minna? It's been a long time since we have heard from Jettchen and Minna. What about Minna's voyage? How is your business doing? Please write Anselm [Feldman, their brother in Palestine] and Leo [Ehrenfeld, Aunt Klara's brother-in-law, in Palestine] immediately upon receipt of this letter, that we are, thank God, in good health, and inform Leo that we have received his last letter written after Easter. Is Moni eager to go to school, and does he already speak English well? Is Ines also going to school? Did Joa write you on the way? I hope to receive your reply soon, and I greet and kiss you many times, your

Klara

Dear Simon. Be happy and contented that you have at least Ines there. Hopefully, Minna and the children will soon arrive there as well. According to what I hear here, it should be possible to travel out of Russia. You should inquire about this. Perhaps she will have better luck this time, so that you will all be together again. Don't lose courage. What should we say!

Dear Ines. Please give us a detailed account of your impressions there.

Many greetings to all of you, including Herman and of course also Max, Tilly, Ruth, and the other relatives, as well as Ida, etc. Many cordial greetings from me.

Klara

Please forward the attached to:
  Hugo Weil
  Krispijnsche Weg
  Dordrecht, Holland

Letter from Alfred's father, Joachim, to Aunt Betty and Uncle Herman in New York. *

Montagnac, July 30, 1940

Dear Sister and Brother-in-law,

I see from a letter that arrived today from the brothers Rotenberg[1] that my telegram did arrive there. The Associated Metals did forward to you the telegram that I sent them. I am surprised, therefore, that I have not received an answer, either from you or from the company, either by telegram or by letter. I might have had a reply already a week ago, and by mail. According to the letter of the Rotenbergs, it would seem that I was either in Spain or in Portugal, which I don't understand, as I am still in France, in the unoccupied part. I hope that you haven't sent everything to Spain instead of to France.[2] We reside here in a small place pretty much cut off from the world. Money runs out, one sends telegrams and one writes, the last money is spent on that, but one receives no answer. Instead the news comes through other people that one is not here, but in Spain. It causes one to despair. I already wrote you in my last letter that airmail goes twice weekly. I notice again and again that if one writes at the correct time, the letter arrives promptly. Why then does it not work with me? I hope I won't lose my patience before I receive news from you. In the meantime, it appears that money cannot be transferred to us from the USA; I would like to hear from you in detail the how and why. Do you think we can live here without money? Doubtlessly, there are other ways for sending money here. Please talk with an experienced person, one that is not a dilettante. Also don't fall into the hands of a swindler. But above all, *write*. We here are completely free, as in nicest peacetime. There is no censorship, only foodstuffs are turning scanty. Mother, therefore, would like to move to you. What do you think of it? Please inquire whether there is a possibility that we all could come over there, as we dread a forced return to Belgium.[3] Be careful with the money, because it is the last that we can get our hands on. Pay careful attention to my address, so that your letters to me won't get lost. Put constant pressure on Neuwirth to write me directly because I must absolutely know what is happening on the business side.[4] How long can one thus float on air? May I expect something from the family? I must try to latch onto something somewhere. I hope that these lines opened your eyes somewhat, and made you recognize the situation in which we and all Israel are in. Could some close relative who is an American citizen[5] request Mother? Who could pay for the voyage? Please write your brother, who has become impatient, as soon as possible, and who, in the meantime, sends you his heartfelt greetings.

Joa

Please turn the page for my exact address
Mr. J. Feldman
chez Peyrottes, Boucherie
Montagnac (Hérault)
France

1. The letter was addressed to Alfred's aunt Charlotte Bauminger, sister of the Rotenberg brothers. She, her husband, and children had also been assigned a residence in Montagnac.

2. Alfred's father had obtained visas to Spain and to Portugal, but a mix-up had made it impossible to get out of France.

3. Before the Germans invaded Belgium on May 10, 1940, the Feldmans lived in Antwerp. They fled that city on May 12.

4. Adolf Neuwirth, a relative, was employed by the same company as Alfred's father, N. V. Oxyde, of Amsterdam, in the Netherlands. He had been able to make it to its New York subsidiary, Associated Metals and Minerals Corp.

5. Recently immigrated, Alfred's aunt and her husband were not yet American citizens and could not sponsor the immigration of relatives.

Letter from Aunt Klara, sent from the Feldman's house in Antwerp, to Aunt Betty in New York.

Klara Ehrenfeld,   Antwerp, October 22, 1940
Antwerpen
30, rue Zurenborg

Dear Betty!

Your letter from Brooklyn, which I have received, was about a month under way. I was very pleased, as this was the first news I received since our return here. I am now sending this letter through Levy via Cologne, as I hear that it may travel faster this way. I am pleased to learn from it that you are corresponding with Joa because we have received mail from him only once, and he does not seem to have received my letters. Since my return I have been living here at No. 30, and I am glad that I am home again with the children because they have endured much on the journey. Every day people return here, and I expect that Joa will return as well since it serves no purpose to remain on the way if he cannot continue. Also for our mother it is a great exertion to remain at large, without her comforts. Mrs. Rotenberg, with family, as well as Bertha Grünbaum and also Fanny Beck are all here again. Baruch Beck is in Portugal. From us here there is nothing in particular. The children go to school while the boy goes to nursery school, and during this time I carry out my household chores and relax my nerves. I can never finish and never manage to sew or mend a thing. Especially not now, during the holidays, which we have passed, thank God, rather well, and let us hope that this year our prayers will bring all that is good. How did you pass the holidays? Was Simon with you, and how does Ines feel there? She certainly has forgotten all of us already. What did the family have to say about Ines? What do you hear from Jettchen and Minna? Are there no prospects for Minna to come there? I was very sorry that you had again a miscarriage. You must spare yourself as much as possible. Does Ines help you in her spare time? We receive no mail at all from Jettchen and Minna. Now, above all, I want to wish you good luck with your business, and may it soon turn into a wholesale business with several employees. What foods do you sell there, many? Do you have also now such a comfortable apartment as in the Bronx, with central heating and running water? What actually does Simon, and why does he live in the Bronx? Does he earn better now? I have already followed your advice to contact L., and been turned down already long ago. I hear that Lissauer and Grieshaber are on their way to the USA or perhaps already there. Should Joa not already know about this, then please tell him this as he receives no mail at all from me. Perhaps you can tell me more about Joa, how come they were separated for about seven weeks, etc., since I have received mail from him only once, and short. Tell me also what Minna and Jettchen write you, as I receive nothing from them.

I completed this letter today, October 29, as I had little time during the holidays. I hope that all of you also passed the holidays well, and that your prayers will bring all that is good, and that henceforth we shall have only good notices to communicate to each other. To all of you our heartfelt greetings and kisses, also from the children and Adolf, your

Klara

Many greetings to Uncle Jakob and the children. Have you received mail, in the meantime, from Anselm and Leo?

Dear Ines. I was very pleased with your dear letter, since this was the first sign of life from you since I accompanied you to the ship. I still remember how you went all alone up the ship, then turned around to wave at us once more. You really were lucky. Hopefully, your mother will soon have the luck to come there with the children. Add a note to us on every letter, in particular about how you like it there. Many greetings and kisses.

Mrs. Koss, who now lives in my apartment at number 8, asks you to please tell her brother-in-law, Mr. Ast, that she and the child are well, thank God, and awaiting a letter from him. When you write me, write directly to this address, rather than through Germany, which is faster.

The address of Mr. Ast is: Mr. Ast, c/o Sobel, 902-51 Street, Brooklyn-New York.

Could he perhaps send her some money?

Letter from Alfred's father to Aunt Betty in New York. *

Montagnac, December 8, 1940

Dear Betty,

We just received your dear letter of the 12th with footnote dated the 19. We too have waited almost five weeks for a letter from you, since we received your last letter, dated 19 October, on 3 November. Therefore, you did not write between 19 October and 19 November. Alfred keeps a precise accounting, and if his accounting is correct, you allowed four weeks to elapse before writing us. Nevertheless, I cannot understand why you have to wait more than four weeks for a letter from us. We sent you various letters during October, which predated Alfred's accounting. In November, we included a letter for you, dated the 1st, in a letter sent to Jos.[1] On both the 4th and the 11th, we sent you letters directly and on the 21st we again included a letter for you in a letter sent to Jos. We hope that you have received these letters by now, and that you have found in them an enclosure to Associated,[2] and a draft on the bank to pay you $200. A week ago we finally received a small amount from Associated, namely $60, which we could exchange for only Fr2,650. We received this amount through a subsidiary of the Chase Bank, and as you see, the exchange rate is very bad. I surmise, however, that this amount originated not from Associated, but from Neuwirth, as Associated requested an authorization for $100. Please determine exactly whether this is indeed so. In the meantime, I heard from Schmeidler that he has not yet received his $100. This money has enabled us to keep our heads above water thus far, and I await your confirmation that the $100 have been repaid, either through Associated or through you. The exact address is . . .

I also expect to hear from you that you have paid the debt of $100 owed Bengio. I have already written you that I have asked Associated to pay you $100 monthly on my behalf, so that you can transfer this to me. Nothing is changed in our situation, but for the moment we are content, though we must do without quite a few things. It is now winter, and nights are usually quite cold. Our heating setup is very primitive, and we lack the supplies for it. We must seek our own wood, which doesn't yield much heat. Food is scarce. Paula [Alfred's mother] spends hours shopping each day, but most importantly, we eat our fill. The kids look healthy, and even gain weight, while we adults keep a negative balance-sheet. Paula has lost about 20 Kg, I have lost about 8 Kg. Mornings we face the problem of what to eat, yet evenings we go to bed satiated. The children, however, are voracious. Partly, this is caused by the healthy climate, but mainly, it is because the food is not nutritious. For many months, we have seen no butter, and we have to make do with 200 g of oil per head per month as our only source of fat. Fish are abundant here, but expensive, and we eat them almost daily. Being short of fat for frying, we usually boil them. Recently, we had butter on the table again but have lacked potatoes for the past several weeks. We now receive some meat and distribute 1 Kg over 3 to 4 meals. According to our most recent exchange rate, 1 Kg of meat of good quality, without bones, costs almost $1, and the fish are not much cheaper. With all that, [Alfred's father's and Aunt Betty's] mother is feeling well, and is surely capable of undertaking the voyage to the USA, should you be able to sponsor her. Consider whether this is possible. We can do very little about it. I was astonished to read in your letter that one can obtain a visa to Virginia. Since Virginia, to my knowledge, is a state of the union of the USA, this would be equivalent to a visa to the USA. Please inquire exactly under what circumstances such a visa is granted, and if you can, obtain an affidavit for us all. There is, of course, nothing we wish more than to immigrate into some civilized country. Our prospects for going elsewhere are virtually zero. Also we did hear that the mail has been reestablished with Belgium,[3] however, no direct mail has yet arrived. Letters reach us only by way of Switzerland. We are attempting to have some of our winter clothes, bedding, etc. sent here, but not much seems to be happening. You do not seem to have received mail from Klara[4] recently. She writes that all are well. Until now, Klara has not mentioned whether she is doing anything about her emigration. In my judgment, her quota's turn has come. I also do not understand why Max [Moyne] Rosenbaum can't do anything about that. So far, you have not sent us the requested addresses of Minna and Jettchen[5] (write clearly). Possibly we can write them directly from here. If, as you write, Simon [Aunt Minna's husband] is trying to obtain an affidavit for Minna, then emigration [to the United States] must be a possibility for her? Why did you mention nothing about Heumann; is he still in Cologne? Mother would like you to make inquiries about the Körper family, they are relatives on her side. As Paula wants to add something to this letter, I will close for today. I am enclosing once again the birth dates, from which you will notice that Mrs. Bauminger [Paula Feldman's mother] is also with us.[6] When you can send us money, consult with Jos Rotenberg, who has sent money to his brother. Because I have a hurt finger, I have dictated this letter to Alfred. I remain with best greetings and kisses

Your Joa

1. Jos Rotenberg, brother of Alfred's Aunt Charlotte. The latter, with husband and children, was also in Montagnac.

2. Associated Metals and Minerals Corp., New York, a subsidiary of N. V. Oxyde, in Amsterdam. Alfred's father was director of the Belgian subsidiary of the N. V. Oxyde.

3. The Feldmans lived in Antwerp, Belgium, when the Germans invaded that country on May 10, 1940.

4. Klara Ehrenfeld, one of Joachim's sisters, had been smuggled with family out of Germany to Antwerp before the German invasion of Belgium.

5. Two of Joachim's sisters, deported from Germany to the Polish border following the Kristallnacht in 1938. Jettchen, widowed, was deported with two children. Minna, whose husband and one daughter were already in the United States, was deported with two children.

6. This is the mentioned enclosure:

	born at:	date:
Joachim FELDMAN,	Zolynia (Poland)	October 5, 1891
Pauline FELDMAN born Bauminger	Krakow (Pol.)	February 12, 1898
Alfred Philip FELDMAN,	Hamburg (Germany)	August 7, 1923
Jenny FELDMAN	"	February 1, 1925
Rachel FELDMAN	"	March 24, 1927
Edith FELDMAN	Cologne (Germany)	March 19, 1929
Scheindel Chaja BAUMINGER born Deutscher	Krakow (Poland)	July 6, 1864
Chinka FELDMAN born Rotenberg	Zolynia (Poland)	July 17, 1860

14/12/1940

Dear Betty,

Although Paula wanted to add a few lines, she didn't have time. We learned today from Moritz Rotenberg, who expects to depart from Lisbon for the U.S. in about 8–14 days, that the U.S. quota for Poles[1] has been opened up, which means that we could promptly depart. We do not know, of course, how accurate this information is, but you can learn more over there. In particular, after Moritz has arrived, you can get him to arrange things also for us. In any event, always inform us in detail, because we are stuck in a small place and have little information. We have all registered with the American consulate in Marseilles. This consulate, however, is so overburdened that it will not reply. You see, therefore, how important it is that we are informed about everything from the outside. The faster we can get away from here, the faster we will be able to stand on our own feet. We have left money and valuables behind in Antwerp, but we do not know if and when we can regain control over these. Klara writes us to come back as soon as possible, as otherwise everything will be lost. But it is impossible to return to Belgium, in particular because we are a large family. Also, as Oxyde has liquidated, I would not know what to begin there. I must anticipate to . . . [The remainder of this letter is missing.]

1. Because Alfred's parents were born in Poland, their immigration into the United States was restricted by the Polish quota.

Letter from Alfred's father to Aunt Betty in New York.

Montagnac (Hérault), January 26, 1941

Dear Betty and dear Herman,

It has been a long time since we received mail from you. Your last letter was dated December 2. I write you today exceptionally by ordinary mail and, upon receipt of this letter, you should be in possession of my letters of January 16, January 1, and December 8. From my preceding letters, you will have seen that one must now seriously try to obtain affidavits for us. From that depends how soon we can get on from here. In addition to the "Affidavit of Support," one needs now also a so-called "Affidavit of Morality." You will learn all the details from the attached letter to Cousin Bernstein, to whom you will hopefully have transmitted also the enclosures to my letter of January 16. Additionally, I am enclosing a statement from [my New York] bank, so that it can be shown, in the Affidavit of Support, that I have about $2,000.—in my account there. You must now convince yourselves that Bernstein will really undertake everything quickly, otherwise you must look for someone else. As I have mentioned, all depends on obtaining most speedily a good affidavit. Perhaps Tilly can do something now in this matter. The recent news from Klara and Adolf is not good. Adolf had to leave Antwerp shortly before Christmas, and about 14 days later, Klara and the children had to follow him. They remained in Belgium, in St. Trond, about 100 Km from Antwerp. I do not know if it is an enforced residence, or a camp. Pappenheim [a relative of Alfred's mother, a refugee in Antwerp] wrote me that Klara, before leaving, had packaged the house's contents and put them in storage. I have received no further notice from Klara and do not know her address. In any case, you should contact Adolf's relatives there immediately. Perhaps it is possible to send them something. On my part, I shall try, of course, to do something through my friends in Antwerp. With regard to us, we worry a lot because no money reaches us. I hope that mail from you will soon arrive, and that you succeeded in transferring some money to us. I hope also that you have sent us, according to my last letter, a package of matzo, as well as matzo meal and fat. As I hear, packages do arrive here from the USA, and you should therefore endeavor to send us packages continuously. I am writing today, according to enclosure, to the firm, and believe that it will provide you the means to do this. Even if you should not hear from them right away, you must make a serious attempt, perhaps through a collection from the relatives, to send us something. You must ascertain, of course, that these shipments get through. Your relief organizations will inform you about this. The following items would be particularly desirable: semolina, Maizena, oat flakes, rice, legumes, flour, noodles, possibly sugar, kosher meat preserves, cocoa, soup cubes. If possible, package the individual articles inside.

Enclosed, a letter for Dr. Rothschild [an executive at Associated Metals and Minerals Corp]. The further annexes follow by airmail.

Letter from Aunt Klara to Alfred's father in Montagnac.

A. Ehrenfeld   Stevoort, February 1, 1941
                                                    Prov. Limburg (Belgium)

Dear Joa!

We left Antwerp about 14 days ago and live now with the children in the village of Stevoort. Since we did not have time to consult with you about what to do with the furniture and other things [in our house in Antwerp] we placed everything temporarily in storage. We have reached an agreement with the manager for 50% of the rent and have paid him so far three months rent and sent him the keys of the house. Your letter containing the keys did arrive timely in Antwerp. The safe deposit box has however not been opened. Paula could have settled this business had she come when Mrs. Hirsch was here. [A veiled hint that my father's safe deposit box at the bank was no longer accessible. Mrs. Hirsch was one of our fellow refugees in Montagnac who had risked the voyage to recover her family's valuables.] The trip would certainly have been worthwhile. In my opinion, it is preferable to defer the matter for the time being.

As for us, we have obtained here a scantily furnished two-room lodging. A part of our kitchenware as well as bedding has been forwarded to us here. We must accommodate ourselves as best we can and get used to life in the country. The children here are very wild, and we shall try to have them registered at school. We just received notice from the Pappenheims, who are still in Antwerp, that Jacob [Bauminger] is again with you. Is that true? [It was not.] Then he can truly be pleased. Now I would like to know how you all are doing, especially how dear Mother is faring, and the other Oma? Paula seems to be very busy keeping house, as Mrs. H. [Hirsch] told me, because she never adds a line. Dear Mother certainly worries about us, and about Jettchen and Minna. I have no news from any of the siblings; did you receive anything from them by way of Betty? Did you receive a suitcase with winter clothing? Does Oma think much about the children? Dörchen [Dora, Aunt Klara's oldest] has recently suggested that Oma needs to mend the pants, as the others are also torn. Well, hopefully we soon will all be joyfully reunited.

It is already rather late, the others are in bed already, and the room is turning cold as the stove went out. I therefore am closing for today with heartfelt greetings and kisses to all, also on behalf of Adolf and the children.

Your Klara

Letter from Alfred's father to Aunt Betty in New York.

Montagnac, February 20, 1941

Dear Betty,

Your airmail letter of January 28 arrived quickly this time. You will have noted meanwhile that I have been unfaithful to the airmail, after having observed that it did not function regularly for some time. Reconciled by the quick delivery of your last letter, I shall trust it with this letter. I am pleased to hear that I shall be sent money from various quarters; I have, however, not received anything to date. I am thankful to Maurice, respectively Jos [Aunt Charlotte's brothers in New York], for having delivered the package to Schmeid; I hope that they have asked for a written receipt. One must always request this for safety's sake. The sum that Maurice advises is very small. Given current circumstances, twice that would not be too much. Ask him, consequently, why that is so. Anyway, I am very thankful to them to send me at least this amount, as nothing could be worse [than a lack of money] in these times when, to remain healthy, one has to buy anything that is available. I am in constant correspondence with Minna Neuwirth, in friendly correspondence even. I am eager to see whether her brother will transfer her the amount that he owes me. I am happy that the company [Associated Metals and Minerals Corp., New York] will send me a further amount of $60. This proves to me, after all, that they won't leave me in the lurch. You will have received other letters from me to be forwarded to them in which I ask the company to deliver any further amounts to you and also to procure an affidavit for me. Already, I have repeatedly given you all our data, and you must have them ready at any time. You should also know that the Affidavit of Support must be accompanied by the sponsor's tax return for the past year, and by a so-called Political and Moral affidavit, in which the American citizen confirms knowing us well with respect to morals and politics. It is advisable that that citizen also has a reputable person provide him with a similar attestation. I have already mentioned this in my letters to Bernstein, which I sent you to forward to him. I repeat all of this for safety's sake so that the affidavit, when finally issued, is unobjectionable in any way. A little error, and a further inquiry can result in a delay of six months. The affidavit, also, should be sent out in at least two copies, so that, if one letter is lost, the second one is immediately available. In addition, the affidavit should be prepared by experienced and competent people, and one must be careful not to be taken in by a dabbler. Not everyone who asserts that he can prepare an affidavit is up on the latest restrictions. That which was perhaps unobjectionable the year before, today may no longer be acceptable. You can imagine the picking and choosing, when today one pays less attention to the quota than the affidavit. I am disappointed that Arthur Bernstein hasn't accomplished anything yet. I have assumed that, among his acquaintances at the stock exchange, he would have quickly located a suitable person with sufficient means to do us this strictly perfunctory favor. If you do not have the time, you should ask important acquaintances to remind him of this as often as possible. If he tries, he will certainly have someone ready in short order. He should be told that one may not waste any time. Tomorrow, conditions may turn, perhaps, much worse. I hardly expect that the firm will do anything in this regard. If, however, some important person could talk with them, I would be interested to see what their answer might be. For some time already, the firm has refused, because of overload, to provide affidavits. But as you know, Dr. Rothschild has found, among his acquaintances, providers of affidavits for various colleagues. With regard to our relatives, I do not think that Leo Rotenberg is capable of claiming us, as his affidavit was already insufficient for Max Rosenbaum [Cousin Moyne Rosenbaum]. I remember well his sister Chana [Hanna Eisner], but have heard too little from her to know whether she can claim us. You write that you wanted to talk with cousin Rintsche, and I am awaiting the result. If need be, the family must divide us, each claiming one or two of us. As to claiming our children, I have already sent you letters for several of our cousins and am waiting to see how they might react. Now, in the matter of food packages that, under current circumstances, are very important to us. We need no luxuries, such as tea or chocolate, but foods such as rice, semolina, oat flakes, flour, Tapioca, fat, and if available, kosher meat preserves. No sausages, no canned milk.

From Klara and Adolf I received recently better news. Adolf has been in town [Antwerp] for a short visit, to get some furniture and tableware. Pappenheim wrote me this; from Klara I have received no news since her departure. Talk with Uncle Jakob about mother wishing to go there, and that she would be glad to read a few lines from him, even if written by his children. Mother bears her years well and, with God's help, will be able to stand the voyage to America all right. But the uncle must see to it that she can undertake this voyage soon, before she is weakened too much by the general lack of food. I have written you already long ago whether you can send us matzo and hope to have your answer soon. I hope that the mail will be regular again and that we may be constantly in communication. We hope to hear soon that a good affidavit is on its way. You may even splurge on a telegram for this, to give me time for the necessary preparations here. Why do you mention nothing about Simon, and whether he earns well. Some time ago, I wrote Tilly a detailed letter by ordinary mail, so that she too might make inquiries about an affidavit, if need be. I will close for today and remain, with best greetings, your

Joa and Paula

Letter from Alfred's father to his cousins in New York. *

Montagnac (Hérault) France

February 1941 [estimated date]

Dear cousins Rifka, Feige, and Ida [daughters of Jakob Bezalel Rotenberg, who is mentioned in Alfred's grandmother's letter dated March 24, 1940],

My sister Betty has, no doubt, informed you sufficiently about our situation. There is some hope that we may go soon to the USA, and for some time Betty has been attempting to obtain affidavits for us. The task is not easy, but I hope that, with God's help, it will soon succeed. In the meantime, we have the opportunity to send our three youngest children to your country, taking advantage of a children's transport. Betty will arrange for their accommodation there. They will not become a burden to anyone. It is however required, that American citizens accept the children. I have consequently declared that my Rachel will be lodged by you, that is with [Ida] Lippel, 146, Ave. C. Her birth date is 24/3/1927. I hope that you will confirm, by return mail, that you will accept the child. If you can, I would even entreat you to undertake the necessary steps to speed the arrival of the children. I have declared that my cousin Feldman will take my oldest daughter, Jenny, born 1/2/1925. Please intervene with him, that he gives his consent like you do. Should cousin Feldman not agree, you will doubtlessly be able to arrange a substitute for him. The situation is so serious that nothing can be omitted that might cause a delay.

I hope that you all are well, and that we shall soon enjoy seeing each other again over there. I send my best greetings to all, and particularly to dear Uncle as well as to Aunt, which I do not know.

Your cousin
Joachim

It would please me greatly to receive a detailed letter from you. My Address is:

J. Feldman
Montagnac (Hérault)
France

Letter from Aunt Klara to Alfred's father in Montagnac. (Though dated February 10, this must have been in error, for mail dated February 24 and March 2 could not have been received by then. Alfred assumes the date to be March 10, 1941.)

Stevoort, February 10, 1941

Dear Joa!

We received both your letter and postcard of February 24, and we were very pleased with the specificity of both these missives. We were particularly pleased that our mother is doing well, and that the other Oma has recovered.

Now I shall answer all your questions. There are, in this village, already several refugees, but none of these are our acquaintances. We receive here unemployment compensation, which is much less than what we received in Antwerp. Subsistence for us is, of course, very difficult. We are pleased that you finally received the suitcase; we had been waiting for the acknowledgment of its receipt. If you had not always written that we should send you only the most important things for the winter, we would have sent you more. We have now asked Mrs. Engelmeyer to send you two suitcases of linen, and three bales of bedding. Hopefully you will receive these soon, as I imagine that these are urgently needed. I can well imagine that you are in want of everything, as we here are equally uncomfortable. Why does one hear nothing from Jettchen and Minna? They always did write to Betty. Did she not mention anything to you about this?

We receive mail regularly from my mother-in-law and, thank God, she is content. We do have the necklace as well as the other things that you forgot in the night table. We have put the furniture in storage with the company Pierre. As they have not yet gotten around to unload it, we do not yet have a receipt. The manager was here around Christmas, and we agreed verbally on a 50% discount. He wanted to send me the contract for this, but since, in the meantime, I departed, I have not received it. We could not know that you did not have his address. I have sent the manager three months rent and will yet settle the account with him for additional months. The stoves and the kitchen range, as well as the bathroom, are in storage. We have insured everything against fire. Mrs. Neuwirth and daughter did remain in Antwerp; she had obtained a [medical] certificate, and the daughter must care for her. Max [Moyne] Rosenbaum and Family now live in Brussels. We hear that he intends to visit you. Since our return, we meet him but rarely, as he always takes advantage of us. He borrowed from us Alfred's bicycle but has not returned it so far and does not think of returning it. Now I would like to know how you are doing. Mrs. Hirsch told us that you receive financial assistance. Can you manage with that, or do you supplement that from elsewhere, perhaps from where Betty is? We have, in general, gotten used to living here. The children go to school, and Dörchen and Bella are each the most studious in their classes. I find it difficult keeping house because of the inconveniences, and Adolf needs almost the entire day to purchase the necessities for the house. Dörchen helps me sometimes in the kitchen, and Goldi always dries the tableware. Goldi has established a strong friendship with the chickens here. They follow her into the kitchen and peck at her legs. The boy and Bella are almost always outside, in particular where there are swamps and mud, which redoubles my work. They know virtually all the children of the village. For lack of time, I go outdoors only on Shabbos. Also when I have to fetch water, which is down the road, I take a little walk. And to the toilet, which is not so simple.

In the meantime, we received your card of March 2. I wish you a kosher Passover, as well as possible, and have passed a nice Purim.

Letter from Aunt Klara to her sister Betty in New York.

A. Ehrenfeld, c/o Pappenheim   Stevoort, March 27, 1941
Antwerpen, Steenbockstr. 20

Dear Betty,

We can inform you that, for about three months, we have been living with the children in the village of Stevoort in Belgium. We have put Joa's furniture into storage and shipped our belongings here. Although we have never before lived in a village, we have become fairly used to village life. The children go to school here and seem to like it quite well. As we did in Antwerp, we receive financial assistance here and have to make ends meet with that. We are much surprised not to have received a letter from you in months, especially as we hear from acquaintances that they frequently receive mail from the USA. Do you have that little time for writing? Or what other reasons are there for not writing? Before going to Stevoort, we sent you a letter by way of Mr. Levy. Did you receive it? We would like to hear how you are doing, by way of health as well of business. Did you establish you business successfully, and is it progressing? Do you have sufficient income? How are Simon [Rosenbaum, the father of Ines] and Ines doing? We haven't heard from them either. Does he get mail from Minna and Jettchen? Does he have an income?

I can inform you now that we have received, from the American Consulate, the attached letter, according to which we can travel to the USA as soon as we have a complete and valid affidavit as well as ship's tickets. We would like to ask you whether you can possibly obtain the tickets for the passage, perhaps through a committee there, promising to repay these in installments after our arrival there. It is not advisable to turn to the sponsor [Israel Silberman] for the tickets, as he needs to renew our affidavit now and such a request might jeopardize the renewal of the affidavits. The tickets must be obtained there. Should it perhaps not be possible to meet the costs of the ship's tickets for all of us, then obtain them at least for Adolf and the boy, so that these can travel ahead. I, with the other children, could struggle through until my departure. We know that you do not have much time there for running around; nevertheless we entreat you urgently to use whatever means you have, so that we may finally reach a goal. Dear Betty, we hope that, upon receipt of this letter, you will undertake all the necessary steps and leave no stone unturned. I have given you Pappenheim's address, as, God willing, I shall return with the children to Antwerp in a few days. Adolf will remain temporarily here. It is possible that he, as well, will return to Antwerp. As soon as possible, please have Cousin J. Silbermann, Danbury Paint Supply Co., Inc., Danbury Conn., 284 Main Street, renew the affidavits of the persons for which you have a prospect to obtain their ship tickets. He will make the arrangements with the sponsor.

Do you have mail from Joa? How is Moni's progress in school, and how does Ines like it there? I close for today with affectionate greetings and kisses from me and the children, your

Klara

Do you have mail from Anselm, Mala, and Leo? Many greetings to Herman, Simon, Ines, and Moni.

Dear ones. Klara has already written you everything in detail and I hope that our wish, to see you there soon, will quickly be fulfilled. In the meantime I greet all of you cordially, as well as Simon and Ines, your

Adolf

Please give my cordial greetings to my cousin and my aunt.

Letter from Aunt Klara to Alfred's father in Montagnac.

A. Ehrenfeld, Antwerpen   Antwerp, May 1, 1941
Oostenstr. 36

Dear Joa,

For a few weeks already we are back in Antwerp, but only today do I finally have time to write you. Your latest cards and letters have been forwarded to me from Stevoort, and I was very happy to receive your mail. I had asked Pappenheim, in the meantime, to write you that we are all here together, about which, on the one hand, we are happy because life back there was very uncomfortable. On the other hand, however, it would have been much better for the children to spend the summer in the country. They all are run-down, especially Bella, who has developed glandular swelling. Also the food was much better there. As Pappenheim has already written you, we have here a two-room apartment with kitchen and managed to settle in it. How we shall raise the rent, we do not know. I have shown your card to Mrs. Engelmeyer concerning our financial assistance. She says that she has not yet heard anything from you about this. She has taken the card to H. and shown it there, but without success. I already contacted Dr. Lissauer about a subsidy, but he declined. Mrs. Engelmeyer thinks that you should write about this directly to H.

Now I shall reply to your letter. The address of Mrs. Engelmeyer is: Berchem, Uitbreidingstr. 558. I talked with her today, and she is surprised that you have received no mail from her. The things were sent already on March 13 by the Cook company and are presumably already in your possession. Mrs. Engelmeyer will make some inquiries. The furniture is stored in our name. Adolf has inspected it, and it seems to be well cared for. I am happy that you are receiving good mail from Betty but am surprised that she does not write to me. I have written her by airmail, still from Stevoort, asking her to obtain tickets for the passage, either for all of us, or otherwise only for Adolf and, perhaps, one child, so that finally we get a step further, but I hear nothing about this. If one can produce here the tickets and a valid affidavit, then the possibility of departure exists; but it seems impossible for Betty to obtain for all of us so many tickets. It would please me if also Minna were finally to make some progress. Can't you send me the address of Jettchen and Minna? It may perhaps be possible to write them from here. Adolf will inquire about the safe deposit box, whether it is still closed. I do not think it advisable to open it now. With Jacob and Charlotte [Bauminger] this is different. I have talked about this with Mrs. Rotenberg [Aunt Charlotte's mother. Regulations may have been different for Belgian citizens, such as Aunt Charlotte, and foreigners, such as Alfred's family].

I was pleased to see from your letter that you all had pleasant holidays, which we cannot say about us because we arrived here only shortly before the holidays and everything was very unsettled. I am pleased, also, that dear Mother is doing well. I would have liked to dash over to you to see how you manage. As in the past, I do not manage well, especially as I have so much to scramble about. The children can occupy one all day, so that one is dead tired by evening. They still quarrel a lot, though if it pleases Dörchen, she can play with them without there being a quarrel. I just hear that from where Betty is, one can send one-pound packages to here. Could you perhaps arrange for Betty to send us tea, flour, etc.? In the meantime, Adolf has inquired about the safe deposit box. It has been opened, and its contents are now sealed, but we may obtain the removal of needed documents upon written request. Please write me, therefore, what papers you need from it.

I anticipate your answer by return mail, and cordially greet and kiss many times, especially dear Mother, your

Klara

Many cordial greetings from Adolf and many kisses from the children.

Dear Mr. Jorysch.

As you see from this letter, I live again in Antwerp and no longer in Stevoort. My current address is Oostenstr. 36, Antwerp.

Best regards from your

K. Ehrenfeld

Letter from Alfred's father to Aunt Betty in New York.

Montagnac, May 19, 1941

Dear Betty,

In my letters to you, I have repeatedly enclosed additions to the letters that I sent to cousins Rosie and Ida, which you should have received in the meantime. From Portugal we have received altogether 9 packages in the meantime. Tea and coffee we would gladly have forgone if, instead, we could have obtained rice or flour. How is the payment of these packages taken care of, and how costly are they? I assume that Klara, in the meantime, will have received her packages as well. We finally have received a letter from Klara from Antwerp. We had been quite concerned, but she seems not to have much time for writing. Every 1–2 months a letter arrives from her. I wrote her to sell, if need be, some of the valuables, so that she will have some money. I am surprised that they are thinking, only now, about the possibility of their emigration, and that she wrote to you about money for the passage. Adolf, it seems to me, intended to turn to his cousin there when it came to that. I suppose that you have already contacted him. Mother is quite upset that no affidavit has arrived for her. What is the cause of this delay? Why doesn't our cousin Bernstein answer me? After all, I have written him several times. It is incomprehensible that no mail arrives anymore from Max and Tilly. They write, perhaps, only by ordinary mail, which perhaps gets lost. Did they receive my detailed letter? I hope that I have not hurt Tilly's feelings by asking her to do something for us, if need be, with regard to affidavits. I have retained until now the papers that Ida has sent me, hoping that they would soon be followed by the moral and political affidavit. Hopefully it will arrive soon, together with the affidavit for mother. In the meantime, I hope to slowly start the ball rolling at the consulate in Marseille. Unfortunately, nothing is happening concerning the transfer of money to us. Hopefully your next letters will bring something in this regard. Your Moni has doubtlessly recovered; let us hope that we will have the good fortune to personally admire his further progress there. Unfortunately, till then, there is more than one mountain to scale. Have you, in the meantime, talked with Neuwirth again? I still hope to break his long silence sooner or later. As you see from the enclosed letter from Klara, she wished to write to Jettchen and Minna. I shall send their address to her, in as far as I can get it copied here [the address was written in Cyrillic characters]. Write me how everyone is doing; even your husband might add a greeting, occasionally. We are OK so far. Two children have departed from here today [Frieda and Paula (alias Peshu) Weiss], i.e. their ship will leave Portugal only in approximately 3–4 weeks. I shall give you their address in my next letter, so that you can receive our personal greetings from these children. I close for today and remain with cordial greetings your

Joa

Klara and Adolf could possibly travel [to the United States] by way of Marseilles, which costs perhaps only $100 per person.

Letter from Alfred's father to Maurice Rotenberg in New York.

Montagnac, May 19, 1941

Dear Maurice,

Finally, it worked. After a long interruption, since Casablanca,[1] we have again received several packages from you, 9 altogether, and I will not omit to thank you kindly. I would like to know how much it all costs, and I hope that you will let me know. Your mother has recently written me that she, respectively your brothers, will repay me B.Fr.500.—that have been outstanding a very long time. Jack and Jos [brothers of Maurice Rotenberg, living then in New York] were then still in Antwerp. I hope that you are able to send me that money, and I expect indeed to receive the real value of that money at that time. I shall, no doubt, soon hear from you about this. I also hope to hear from you about how you have become accustomed there, and whether you earn an adequate income. Perhaps it shall be granted that we will meet there again soon. From Charlotte [Bauminger, Maurice Rotenberg's sister] and the children, I suppose that you hear enough. Unfortunately for Jacob [Aunt Charlotte's husband, still being held in the camp at St. Pons], the desired result has not yet been attained. I do not doubt that all of you there are doing everything in your power to help. I am afraid that our situation here, already quite desperate, may yet turn much worse. May the Almighty stand us by. Please give our best regards to your brothers and particularly to your sister-in-law, and accept our affectionate greetings, your

J. Feldman

1. Maurice Rotenberg managed to get from Bordeaux, where the Feldmans met him last, to Casablanca, before emigrating to the United States.

Letter from Alfred's mother to Aunt Betty in New York. *

Montagnac, June 10, 1941

Dear Betty,

As Joa has already written you, the affidavit for us is incomplete because the so-called 13 points, dealing with the political and moral certification, are missing. I am very sorry that the cousin who provided the affidavit did not consult with the HICEM [initials of a Jewish social service agency], despite Joa's repeated recommendation. In thus writing back and forth, much valuable time is lost, and two additional months are lost waiting for a notification from the American consulate. Most people, unfortunately, share this predicament that, by the time all papers have been assembled, the affidavit has expired, and must be renewed. Joa now has a notification from the American consulate in Marseilles for July 13; please spare no effort to get the missing papers here by the beginning of July. Who knows how long it may be before he can again obtain a notification. For us, all now depends on this notification. Since Friday, Joa is in a work camp [located in Agde, about 25 Km from Montagnac]. You can imagine what this means for a man of his age and his health. I, therefore, am staking all my hopes for him and Alfred on the American papers. Once these two are over there, we should be able to follow them. Had Alfred been 18 years old, he too would have had to go to the camp, and the respite is unfortunately very brief. Dear Mother is quite depressed and spiritless. And her affidavit is still not here. From Meno,[1] regretfully, I have received a totally negative letter, and I am utterly astonished at such incomprehension in the face of our situation. Meno writes that Joa should become self-supporting, should try to find something else, and forgets that Joa would have accepted any work had he been allowed to work. But we are not allowed to move from this village, and there is work here only for agricultural laborers, and one needs a work permit to boot. Our situation would have been quite different had the company not left us so completely in the lurch, and my husband could have remained with us. Since I don't see how I could obtain larger and more regular supplies of cash for the near future, the only option left to me is prompt emigration, and with that, dear Betty, you must help me. Remember that, when you stayed with us, I told you that we would always be there if someone needed help, but that, if we needed help, who would there be? This is, God forbid, no reproach to you, as I know that you exceed your strength in your efforts on our behalf. This is only to establish what bitter fate has befallen us. I believe that we will be permitted to withdraw funds from our account over there to pay the ship passage. The matter of most importance is thus that the missing papers reach us as soon as possible, that is, by the beginning of July. Otherwise there is nothing to report from here. From Klara [Ehrenfeld, Alfred's aunt] we have not yet heard again. Do you have any plans to begin something else during the quiet business period of summer? It seems that Charlotte's brothers[2] are quite satisfied over there. That would be a good profession for Alfred. For today, just many greetings for you all.

Paula

Many greetings and kisses

Have you already talked with the Weiss girls?[3] They departed today from Lisbon.

Alfred

Please give my greetings to my brothers, and ask them to obtain, as rapidly as possible, an affidavit, at least for Jacob [Bauminger, Charlotte's husband and Paula's brother]. Also the visas are urgently needed. Please communicate this to my brothers as soon as possible. Thank you.

With best regards and best wishes,

Salomon Rotenberg

1. Dr. Meno Lissauer, founder of the company of which Associated Metals and Minerals Corp. was a subsidiary, in New York. Joachim, engaged straight out of school, was one of the first employees when Lissauer originally set up business in Cologne, Germany.

2. Charlotte Bauminger, born Rotenberg. Her brothers are mentioned in the letter dated July 30, 1940.

3. Two of the children of a family of Jewish refugees living in Montagnac who managed to be sent to the United States.

Letter from Aunt Klara to Aunt Betty in New York.

Antwerp, June 18, 1941

Oostenstr. 36

Dear Betty, I received your letter with much pleasure, as it is the first letter to be received from you in a long time. At the same time I also received two letters from Joa, in which he gave me advice both about our voyage overseas and about the furniture. Times, however, have changed here in the meantime, and we are unable to follow his advice. Also it is no longer possible to turn, as you write we should, to the local committee for the tickets for passage. It no longer exists for this purpose. The tickets are valid only if they come from America. We are therefore unable to do anything with the affidavit, and we must, I think, have patience until the war is over. We did not receive the two packages that you sent us in December; they must have been returned to sender as, at the time, we were not in Antwerp. We would be very grateful, if you could send us new packages again. They help us very much, as the assistance we receive is still what it was at the time when you were here, but prices have risen considerably since then. People here receive such packages almost weekly. See thus to it that we receive something soon. If, as you wrote in your letter, you are not in a position to afford this, you could, perhaps, make a collection from our relatives. I am very sorry that you have so much trouble, nevertheless, you should be happy to be with your husband. I am pleased that Moni thinks about us. How is Ines doing? You did not mention her in your letter at all. What about Minna's voyage? By whom is Simon [Ines's father] employed? How are Max and family doing? Do you see him sometimes? Fanny Beck asks me to send you her regards. Since her return here, she is receiving financial support also. I am very pleased that Liba Heumann finally arrived there. Moyne and family live now in Brussels and intend to wait out the war there. He is doing better than we, as he does not have to depend on financial support. Not everybody is as capable as he. Please send the attached letter to my cousin, Isaak Silbermann. His address is: Danbury Paint Supply Co. Inc. 284 Main Street. As you see from it, we would like him to send us packages. How is your health? With us it is as usual. I still have much housekeeping to do and barely manage to keep up with the laundry. Were dear Mother here, she would have entire mountains of mending. The children are going to school, and even Goldi goes to nursery school until 4 P.M., so that I can rest at least my nerves during the day. I hope to hear from you again real soon, and close for today with cordial greetings to you, your husband, Moni, Ines, Simon, and the other relatives, your

Klara

Most cordial greetings also from me, specially to Moni. Your

Adolf

Letter from Alfred's father to Aunt Betty in New York.

Montagnac, March 30, 1942

Dear Betty,

I am writing you yet a few lines, as we just received notification from Ehrenfeld [Aunt Klara] that the company no longer pays the storage charges for my furniture. Unfortunately, I still do not know how much these charges amount to. In any event, if you talk with Meno [Lissauer, Joachim's employer], you can broach this subject. When my travel arrangements are complete, I shall have everything auctioned off anyway. Otherwise, for today, nothing special. The Ehrenfelds write that they are content. They hope that you can have packages sent to them from Portugal. The children grow up. Mrs. Ehrenfeld writes that the little Mordechai not only walks home alone from kindergarten, but also minds Goldi; both children come home by themselves, the boy does not want anyone to come for him. You have not mentioned whether you got back the $65 from Neuwirth. Also the Rotenbergs were to return you about $30. You need not make them a gift of anything. Write me everything accurately about cousin Klara.[1] Once again my warmest greetings, your

Joa

1. Aunt Klara was in fact his sister. In this letter, Joachim deliberately hid his relationship to her. In appealing the refusal of this U.S. visa due to the "close relatives" restriction, he must have denied that she was his sister. He warns Aunt Betty in a manner that would not attract a censor's attention.

Letter from Aunt Klara to Alfred's father in Montagnac.

May 1942 [estimated date: letter was written after Passover]
Dear Joa!

I was pleased to hear that you endured the winter well, in particular dear Mother. How is Paula's mother doing? How did you pass the holidays, and how did Hella [Alfred's sister] like being with you. Has she returned, or will she now remain with you? It would be a shame if she had to interrupt her education. What are Jenny and Alfred doing? One hears nothing from them. Edith is certainly still going to school? Is she a good student? I am pleased that Betty takes pains on your behalf. Hopefully she will achieve something good soon. The rest will fall into place on its own. Last week two packages of sardines arrived, which gave us much pleasure. I assume that these were also from Betty, who was to have sent them about half a year ago. They tasted well after such a long time. We passed the holidays well, thank God. The children, with the exception of Goldi, stayed up on both evenings [of the Seder], which takes a rather long time with us. The boy was much interested in everything. Only the traditional questions, those he could not ask. Hopefully he will make up for it the next year, in joy. My husband and children are, thank God, in good health, and we are making ends meet better than before. How are you doing? I would like it very much if Paula could write me. Did you hear anything from Jettchen and Minna?

Many heartfelt greetings from Adolf and children and your

Klara

Letter from Alfred's father to Aunt Betty in New York.

Montagnac, May 17, 1942

Dear ones,

I received your letter of March 18 with great pleasure, as we had been without news from your for a long time. Mother is always beside herself with joy when she receives news from her children, and let us hope, therefore, that you can write us soon something positive about Jettchen and Minna. We were quite amused by what you wrote about your boy. No harm is done by a fight in school, the main point is that he learns so well. We miss, long since, a letter from Ines. From the children's letters one learns many a thing that a grown-up never thinks of writing. I see from your letter that you meet oftentimes also with Tilly and Max [Feldman, Joachim's brother]. Admonish them to write at less long intervals, to give pleasure to Mother and also to us. Ruth may certainly write in English; we shall translate everything for Mother. It surprised me greatly to read in your letter that you have had the first affidavit for us since the beginning of December. Inasmuch as you still didn't have the second affidavit by mid-March, I can hardly believe that Nathan, after three months, will change his mind. Was there no other way out? In the meantime, it would appear that one cannot depart from here altogether. I have not yet been able to ascertain this positively. After receipt of Arthur's telegram in February, I had undertaken here various steps, and incurred several expenses, to prepare for the departure. In spite of everything, the illusion was worth it; of the disappointment we won't talk. Paula did not doubt for a moment that it couldn't happen and thus maintains that she was not at all disappointed. With your letter to Meno [Lissauer, Joachim's employer], you have, dear Betty, waited two months too long. Should Meno notice that one leaves him in peace so long, he believes that one can struggle through without him. In the introduction, you should also have referred to me, and I hope that, henceforth, you will make it clear to him at every opportunity that your situation, in the meantime, has worsened. I was very pleased to see from your letter that Neuwirth responded so positively, though I have not received anything thus far. At any rate, I shall search for the two addresses and ask you to send them to me as soon as possible in the event that you can obtain them from Neuwirth. Did you already meet Neuwirth's sister there? My brother-in-law Jacob [Bauminger, recently arrived in Cuba] can perhaps help you with . . . [The remainder of this letter is missing.]

Letter from Alfred's sister Jenny to Aunt Betty in New York.

Montagnac, August 19, 1942

Dear Aunt Betty,

We were terribly pleased to have received, on Saturday, two letters from you and one letter from Ines. I was very surprised that my letter from December did arrive, I thought that it had been lost long ago. I hope now to receive soon a reply from the cousins. The news here is not particularly delightful, instead of freezing, we are now perspiring, and how! You cannot imagine this. As Papa has written you, I was at a Beth-Jacob school in Marseille, supposedly for 6 months, to be trained as a teacher, but I had to return after 14 days because of difficulties with red tape, but I hope to return soon to Marseille. Things there are very interesting, and we learn a fantastic amount, and I liked it very much. I almost forgot to write you that Aunt Charlotte has given birth, Friday, to a little girl, mazel tov, her name is Paulette. Both are doing well. Dear Simon, do not think that, because I am not writing you, I do not think of you. I would have liked to see you once, to see how much you have grown. Hopefully, that will be very soon.

Many greetings and kisses from
Jenny

Many greetings and kisses

Hella

Heartfelt greetings and kisses from

Alfred

Letter from Alfred's father to Aunt Betty in New York.

Montagnac, August 21, 1942

Dear Betty,

This time you shall have the pleasure to receive a few lines from my daughters. As they are not accustomed to write in German, their letters did not come out too well. Last week we received from you, once more, three letters together and, for the moment, there is no shortage of news from you. And yet we miss the main news, that our visa has been approved. I have requested the HICEM to intervene somehow, to obtain a decision about the visa as quickly as possible, as our situation here has become uncertain once more, and we do not know what the next day may bring. As you see from the back side, a week ago today, thus on August 14, Charlotte gave birth to a daughter; she is in a maternity hospital in Montpellier, and mother and daughter are doing very well. I have sent a telegram to Jacob [Bauminger, the baby's father] and he has already telegraphed his congratulations together with greetings from Holles. As soon as Charlotte is back home, we shall telegraph Jacob once more that everything is OK. Here, all our children, with the exception of Edith, are back home. I always wanted to give you the address of Edith; it is: Edith Feldman, Château le Couret, par La Jonchère-St. Maurice (Haute Vienne) France.

We have not yet received the greetings from Holles.

Cordial greetings from all, your

Joa

Should we no longer be here, which we do not hope, then you can always write to Charlotte. But for safety's sake, keep Edith's address.[1]

1. This note was probably added after the *rafle,* which took place in the early hours of August 26, 1942.

Letter from Alfred's father to his cousin Adolf Neuwirth in New York written for Aunt Betty's signature. *

August 23, 1942

Dear Adolf,[1]

I don't know whether I should laugh or be annoyed at the impudence of your letter of 18/8. Let us finally establish factually that, since June 1940, you have let your sister Martha educate you in how best to avoid paying your debts.

You could have made things easier by asking your sister Minna here what the exchange rate was at the time the good-natured Joachim Feldman, on the flight, handed you his hard-to-spare money. How come the expert businessman, Adolf Neuwirth [spelled "Neuwirt" in the original], looked for ways to repay a loan by circuitous routes such as a cable transfer to Paris, through friends in France, and through Cuba, while my brother [Joachim Feldman] had given me power of attorney to accept this sum.

I would now like to enlighten you, dear Adolf, that the exchange rate at the time was not 80/90, but 40/45.—I thank you for your readiness to help Joachim. I inform you that I have neither time nor desire for a dispute with you about the rest of the sum, and that this shall be the last letter in this distressing money matter. I shall seek advice as to whether you are entitled to arbitrarily select a convenient rate of exchange, and shall seek this from Dr. L. [Dr. Meno Lissauer], with whom I have a meeting upon his return from his vacation that, his secretary wrote me, would be in a few days. I am sending Joachim a copy of this letter, to allow him to convince himself of the truth of the proverb that ingratitude is the world's reward. I can, however, not indulge the luxury of waiting for Joa's reply, as I am intensely busy procuring money for the passage, and need every amount.

Best greetings, Betty

1. Aunt Betty only signed and transmitted this letter. It was written by Joachim Feldman in Montagnac (Hérault) in France.

The following letter is the only surviving letter written by Aunt Betty. Accompanied by the note from Tilly and Max, it was addressed to Mrs. Paula Feldman, Montagnac (Hérault) France. It survived because it could not be delivered. On the envelope, Aunt Betty had declared "written in

German." The envelope had been opened and resealed, the seal carrying the caption "Opened by Examiner 764." A stamp on the envelope read "Service suspended. Return to sender." Service was suspended because on December 11, 1941, while this letter was still in transit, Germany declared war on the United States.

Betty Knoll   Brooklyn, September 23, 1942
2032 Bath Ave.

Dear ones,

Yesterday I received your letter of August 14, with a copy for the bank. However the letter of August 13, of which you notified me, still has not arrived. In contrast, I received from Simon Pappenheim a letter from London that was only 18 days under way. Then, by way of the letter to Simon, I received, after a long time, again mail from you. On Saturday I received a letter from the local HIAS informing me that they had received a cable from their affiliate in Marseille [France] that asked whether affidavits had been filed for you. Naturally I went immediately to the HIAS, even though it was the eve of Yom Kippur, asking them to cable back that I had filed the affidavits already by the middle of May with the State Department, and for the entire family, 8 persons altogether. May it please the Almighty that visas be soon granted and that you may depart as soon as possible. Cousin Arthur promised me to intervene through a friend. I have reminded him of that several times, both verbally and in writing. He came by on Sunday, and mentioned to Herman that he had written his friend in this matter, but only this Saturday. At the time I was in New York at the HIAS. Hopefully, the time will soon come that I do not have to waste good words on my dear cousin. I had an audience with Meno [Lissauer] last week. He categorically refused any financial assistance. My friend is good, but fearful. I directed him to the Quakers. He seized the opportunity immediately. Consequently, one can expect soon to hear from the Quakers over there. He did not know that the food packages no longer arrive. I have sounded out Martha Anfänger [Lissauer's secretary] about the possibility of obtaining a subsidy for the passage. She thinks this will not be denied. In general, she thinks that if only you manage to arrive here, you will receive every help. For the time being, I did not want to mention anything about the passage, as I hope the HIAS will be satisfied with what is in your account. Neuwirth did send me another 20 dollars. I have received altogether $50 from him so far. I am not satisfied with that and am insisting on receiving the remaining 17 dollars. We carry on a charming exchange of letters. I write him in the most polite, guileless tone, unveiling thereby his true character, so that he turns green and yellow. His replies testify to that. I keep the entire correspondence with him. Hopefully, you will come soon to see it.

Now I would like to tell you a little about us. Our business has not at all improved; it has, on the contrary, rather deteriorated. Our rental agreement expired in August, and Herman finally decided to look for something else. Indeed, for the past eight weeks, he has been learning to cut diamonds, several hours per day. His workplace is in Manhattan, and travel and work takes nearly half a day. He leaves the house about 3 o'clock and returns home only around 11 P.M. For me, that means even more work than before. In September, the schools opened. Simon arrives home only after 4 o'clock. The child must remain in the store until I have prepared his food. Evenings he must bathe by himself and go to bed. The boy has become quite self sufficient. All mothers are amazed to see him riding the bus to school by himself. Simon longs already for the time when we give up the store and move to a private lodging. I long for it no less, because, save for minor interruptions, I am so tied to the store. Afterward, I still have the housekeeping, for which I use the late evening hours, as I cannot close before 9:30 P.M. I am always tired. I now understand dear Mother, who liked to lay down for a nap around noon. I get up at 6 A.M. already tired. Moreover, Simon has bespoken a little sister. We expect the baby, with luck, early next year. Since last week I already feel its quickening. I have not yet found time to consult a physician. Everything is so distant, to everywhere one must ride, which always takes several hours. Herman has to pay for his apprenticeship. Fourteen days later, Simon (Rosenbaum) has begun to learn diamond cutting as well. He does it on evenings too, after work. I hope that both will complete their apprenticeships soon and begin to earn something. Simon works at Frommer's like a coolie for low wages. Though it caused me much more work, I did invite Simon and Ines for the Sukkoth days. Also the sleeping arrangements were difficult. But I cannot leave those two alone for the holidays. Ines had school until 3 P.M. on the eve, and Simon worked Thursday until 11 P.M. When were they to shop and to cook! At my place, they found the table set.

Tilly visited me again last week. Jos Rotenberg did receive mail from Mala [Uncle Anschel's wife, and Rotenberg's aunt]. Two photos of Anselm and his children were included. I recognized Anselm, but the children have much changed. The letter must have come by [illegible]. May you have prayed for a good and happy year. May you have a good Quittel. This is fervently wished by your Betty, Herman, and our Simon.

Dear Joa:

We always await your letters with great suspense and wish fervently that you might be here already. On your behalf, everything possible is being done. Betty leaves no stone unturned and shuns no means or effort. Tilly dispatches letters to the authorities by return mail, for she says always that "every minute counts." The new year is now coming about, and we wish that it may be a good one, and bring us the fulfillment of our wishes, and that we shall be reunited in health and good fortune. This we wish you, as well as dear Mother, and Paula, as well as the dear children, Mrs. Bauminger, and all who are with you, a prosperous year, in which you may attain all that you long for.

Tilly and Max

Letter from Samuel Knoll in New York to his sister-in-law, Alfred's Aunt Betty.

Samuel Knoll   October 1942 [estimated date]
215 E. 164 St.
Bronx, New York

Dear Betty

From the enclosed timetable you will see that a train leaves Pennsylvania Station, 7th Avenue and 33rd Street, at 12:30 midnight and arrives in Washington at 5:15 in the morning. It takes one hour from your house to the subway station because you will have a fairly long walk from the subway to the train station, so don't leave the house any later than 11 o'clock, preferably sooner. It is dark now outside the station, which is therefore difficult to find when one is not familiar with the area. Thus, allow enough time.

I wish you success in this voyage.

Sam

DEPARTMENT OF STATE
WASHINGTON

In reply refer to
VD 811.111 Feldman, Joachim

November 27, 1942

Mrs. Branel Knoll,
2032 Bath Avenue,
Brooklyn, New York.

Madam:

As the persons in whom you are interested reside in territory where no American consular visa services are available, no steps may be taken at this time with a view to providing them with visas for admission into the United States.

In the event that they should proceed to some territory where they will be able to apply at an American consular office for visas, you may write to the Department for advice as to the procedure to be followed in presenting their cases. The cases should not be taken up with the Department, however, until definite information can be furnished to show that the persons in question have actually arrived in the territory where they will apply for visas.

No assurance may be given that an alien will receive a visa at an American consular office until he appears in person and is found upon examination to qualify in all respects under our immigration laws.[1]

Very truly yours,
H. K. Travers
Chief, Visa Division

1. Doubt cast by this sentence on the granting of a U.S. immigration visa will deter any country from granting the transit visa needed to reach a U.S. consulate.

Notes

1. How We Arrived in Germany, and How We Left

1. "Germany, Years of Crisis (1920–23)." *Encyclopedia Britannica,* 10:337, 1970.

2. "Jewish Holidays, Pesach." *Encyclopedia Britannica,* 12:1042, 1970.

3. Psalms, 79:6–7.

4. Psalms, 69:24.

5. Lamentations, 3:66.

6. Rabbi Charles A. Spirn, personal communication.

7. Stanislaw Koziarski, *Siec Kolejowa Polski W Latach 1842–1918* (Opole, Poland: Panstwowy Instytut Naukowy, Instytut Slaski, 1993), 190.

8. Hillel Halkin, in his introduction to Sholem Aleichem's *Railroad Stories* (New York: Schocken, 1987), xxxiii.

9. My father's report card showed "Hausierer" as his father's profession.

10. Simon Dubnow, *Weltgeschichte des jüdischen Volkes,* 10 vols. (Berlin: Jüdischer Verlag, 1925).

11. Saul Friedländer, *Nazi Germany and the Jews,* vol. 1, *The Years of Persecution, 1933–1939* (New York: HarperCollins, 1997), 167.

12. Henry L. Feingold, *The Politics of Rescue: The Roosevelt Administration and the Holocaust, 1938–1945,* rev. ed. (Washington, D.C.: U.S. Holocaust Memorial Museum, 1980), 16.

13. Judah Gribetz, *The Timetables of Jewish History* (New York: Simon and Schuster, 1993), 417.

14. Feingold, *Politics of Rescue,* 350.

15. *New York Times,* Oct. 29, 1938, p. 1.

16. *New York Times,* Nov. 2, 1938, p. 13.

17. Not her real name, which Aunt Betty has forgotten.

18. Friedländer, *Nazi Germany ,* 277.

19. Hans-Dieter Arntz, *Judenverfolgung und Fluchthilfe im deutsch-belgischen Grenzgebiet* (Euskirchen, Germany: Kümpel, Volksblatt-Druckerei + Verlag, 1990).

20. *New York Times,* Feb. 16, 1939, p. 11.

2. The Halfway House

1. Mark Zborowski and Elizabeth Herzog, *Life Is with People: The Culture of the Shtetl* (New York: Schocken Books, 1995), 92, 96.

2. Composer André Modeste Grétry was born in Liège in 1741.

3. Inventor Zénobe Gramme was born near Liège in 1826.

4. Simon Dubnow, *Weltgeschichte des jüdischen Volkes,* 1: xiii.

5. Zborowski and Herzog, *Life Is with People,* 116.

6. Otto Willi Gail, *Mit Raketenkraft ins Weltenall: vom Feuerwagen zum Raumschiff* (Stuttgart: K. Thienemann, 1928).

7. Proverbs, 31:10–31.

8. Psalms, 128:3.

9. Exodus, 35:3.

10. Clyde Sanger, *Malcolm MacDonald: Bringing an End to Empire* (Montreal: McGill-Queen's University Press, 1995), 175.

11. Sanger, *Malcolm MacDonald,* 170.

12. Arthur D. Morse, *While Six Million Died: A Chronicle of American Apathy* (Woodstock, N.Y.: Overlook Press, 1983), chap. 15.

3. Practice Makes Perfect

1. James E. Mrazek, *The Fall of Eben Emael: Prelude to Dunkerque* (Washington, D.C.: Luce, 1970).

2. William L. Shirer, *Berlin Diary: The Journal of a Foreign Correspondent 1934–1941* (Boston: Little, Brown and Co., 1940, 1941), 417.

3. Alistair Horne, *To Lose a Battle: France 1940* (Boston: Little, Brown, 1969), 230.

4. Jenny's Belgian ID card, which has survived, was stamped there on May 19.

5. Jenny's ID card has the stamp of Lacanau-Océan, entered on June 6.

6. Eva Fogelman, *Conscience and Courage: Rescuers of Jews During the Holocaust* (New York: Anchor Books, 1994), 200–202. See also Jose-Alain Fralon, *A Good Man in Evil Times: Aristides de Sousa Mendes* (London: Viking, 2000).

7. My father obtained the Haitian, Portuguese, and Spanish visas also for his mother. Her passport has survived.

4. A Crazy Summer

1. I have donated the originals of the letters mentioned here to the American Jewish Historical Society, Waltham, Mass. The appendix holds a translation of these letters.

2. "Shir Ha-emek," in *Sefer shirim u-manginot,* ed. Moshe Gorali and David Samburski (Jerusalem: Kiryat Sefer, 1946–51), 2: 37.

5. Time Turns Back

1. Michel Cepède, "Agriculture et Ravitaillement," in *La France sous l'occupation* (Paris: Presses Universitaires de France, 1959).

2. René Blockouse, *Gazogène ou gaz comprimé?* (Liège, Belgium: Vaillant Carmanns, 1940).

3. Michael Robert Marrus and Robert O. Paxton, *Vichy France and the Jews* (Stanford, Calif.: Stanford University Press, 1995), 3.

4. Marrus and Paxton, *Vichy France and the Jews,* 69.

5. Susan Zuccotti, *The Holocaust, the French, and the Jews* (New York: Basic Books, 1993), chap. 3.

6. Gérard Bouladou, *L'Hérault dans la résistance, 1940–1944* (Nîmes: C. Lacour, 1992), 33.

7. *Midi Libre,* Aug. 27, 1944, p. 6.

8. *Paris-Soir,* Feb. 12, 1941.

9. Bouladou, *L'Hérault,* 32.

10. Bouladou, *L'Hérault,* 44.

11. Now in the Special Collections Department of the Judaica Department at the Brandeis University Library, Waltham, Mass. The leaflets the rabbi left with us are glued against the inside of the Haggada's cover.

12. Feingold, *Politics of Rescue,* 155.

13. Carol Iancu, *Les juifs à Montpellier et dans la Languedoc à travers l'histoire du moyen age à nos jours* (Montpellier, France: Centre de recherches et d'études juives et hébraïques, Université Paul Valéry, 1988), 348.

14. Feingold, *Politics of Rescue,* chap. 6

15. Feingold, *Politics of Rescue,* 131.

16. Feingold, *Politics of Rescue,* 157.

17. Feingold, *Politics of Rescue,* 160.

18. Feingold, *Politics of Rescue,* 126.

19. Alexander Rotenberg, *Emissaries, A Memoir of the Riviera, Haute-Savoie, Switzerland and World War II* (Secaucus, N.J.: Citadel Press, 1987), 71–74.

20. On March 11, 2002, in Montagnac, a delegate from the State of Israel, in a ceremony with speeches, church bells ringing, and a banquet, bestowed Medals of the Just among Nations to our wartime neighbors, the Granals, and to the mayor, Andre Bringuier. As they were no longer alive, the medals were handed to their relatives. But earlier that day I had quietly gone to the cemetery and placed flowers on the graves of the Granals and the mayor. My most expensive bouquet, however, went to the grave of Jeanne Babau, the woman who, although her dress was a flour sack, refused to let me pay for using her donkey and cart.

21. Marrus and Paxton, *Vichy France and the Jews,* 187. See also Henri Amouroux, *La grande histoire des français sous l'occupation,* vol. 5, *Les passions et les haines* (Paris: Laffont, 1981), part 2, "Des hommes et des femmes comme les autres." 149–344.

22. André Nos, *Montagnac, 6,000 ans d'histoire* (Montagnac, France: Les Amis de Montagnac, 1991), 102–10.

23. Nos, *Montagnac,* 101.

24. Nos, *Montagnac,* 132.

25. Nos, *Montagnac,* 155.

26. Nos, *Montagnac,* 143.

27. Nos, *Montagnac,* 147.

28. Nos, *Montagnac,* 283.

6. The Warmth of a Mother's Love

1. Iancu, *Les juifs à Montpellier,* 351.
2. The Canal du Midi.
3. Bouladou, *L'Hérault,* 48.
4. In 2001, Mr. and Mrs. Granal were awarded posthumously the Israeli Medal of the Righteous among the Nations.
5. This camp was located near Perpignan, in the unoccupied zone of France.
6. The arrest of my sister Edith is reported in the third supplement of S. Klarsfeld, *Le Mémorial des Enfants Juifs Déportés de France* (Les Fils et Filles des Déportés Juifs de France, 32 rue La Boétie, 75008 Paris, France). 31–32.
7. She had three younger siblings who were not taken since they were born in Belgium. Her parents were allowed to stay with them. But Rachel had been born in Poland.
8. Bouladou, *L'Hérault,* 46.
9. Serge Klarsfeld, *Memorial to the Jews Deported from France, 1942–1944: Documentation of the Deportation of the Victims of the Final Solution in France.* (New York: B. Klarsfeld Foundation, 1983), 260–68.
10. Zuccotti, *The Holocaust, the French, and the Jews,* 112.
11. Klarsfeld, *Memorial to the Jews,* 261.

7. My Life as Somebody Else

1. Groupement de Jeunes Travailleurs.
2. Translation: "Youth!"
3. W. D. Halls, *The Youth of Vichy France* (New York: Oxford University Press, 1981), 269.
4. The day was Nov. 11, the anniversary of the World War I armistice.
5. René-Pierre Audras, *Le Velay: Le Puy, cité ancienne au cœur de la France* (Paris: Pygmalion/G. Watelet, 1981), 65.
6. Bouladou, *L'Hérault,* 51.
7. These exhibits, since renovated, are in the Alexandre Clair Collection at the Musée Crozatier. Even after an interval of some fifty years, I could recognize the remembered machines in a catalog kindly sent me by the museum. Thus, I retrieved the names of their inventors.
8. Zuccotti, *The Holocaust, the French, and the Jews,* 228.
9. In 2001, Mr. Bringuier was awarded posthumously the Israeli Medal of the Righteous among the Nations.

8. A Biblical Migration

1. Alberto Cavaglion, *Nella Notte Straniera,* 3d ed. (Cuneo, Italy: L'Arciere, 1991), 32 n. 10.
2. Jonathan Steinberg, *All or Nothing: The Axis and the Holocaust 1941–1943* (London: Routledge, 1990), 126. See also Daniel Carpi, *Between Mussolini and Hitler: The Jews and the Italian Authorities in France and Tunisia* (Hanover, N.H.: University Press of New England, 1994).

3. Cavaglion, *Nella Notte Straniera,* 34. See also Renée Poznanski, *Être juif en France durant la seconde guerre mondiale* (Paris: Hachette, 1994), 561–71.

4. The documentary movie *The Righteous Enemy,* written and directed by Joseph Rochlitz and made from film clips of these events, also uses the word "biblical." It is available from the National Center for Jewish Film, Brandeis University, Waltham, Mass.

5. Cavaglion, *Nella Notte Straniera,* appendix 1.

6. American Jewish Joint Distribution Committee, organized at the beginning of World War I for the relief of Jewish war sufferers.

7. Anny Latour, *The Jewish Resistance in France (1940–1944)* (New York: Schocken, 1981), 150–51.

8. Feingold, *Politics of Rescue,* 175. See also Walter Laqueur, *The Terrible Secret: Suppression of the Truth about Hitler's Final Solution* (Boston: Little, Brown, 1981; repr., New York: Penguin, 1982).

9. Aunt Klara and her three oldest children were deported in convoy VII, which left on Sept. 1, 1942, for Auschwitz. (Serge Klarsfeld and Maxime Steinberg, *Memorial de la déportation des juifs de Belgique* [New York: Beate Klarsfeld Foundation, 1982]).

10. Susan Zuccotti, *Under His Very Windows: The Vatican and the Holocaust in Italy* (New Haven: Yale University Press, 2000), 143–47.

11. Cavaglion, *Nella Notte Straniera,* 55–57.

12. Cavaglion, *Nella Notte Straniera,* 54. A stele, erected in St. Martin-Vésubie in 1995 to commemorate this exodus, also calls it a "biblical migration."

13. Bronka Halpern, *Keren or ba-hashekhah* (Jerusalem: Rubin Mass, 1967), 41.

14. Danielle Baudot-Laksine, "Le mouvement Franc-Tireur Vésubie," *Pays Vésubien,* no. 6, 2005, pp. 19–46.

15.Reginald John Farrer, *Among the Hills* (London: Headley, 1911; repr. London: Waterstone, 1985), chaps. 5 and 6.

16. Cavaglion, *Nella Notte Straniera,* 66.

17. Cavaglion, *Nella Notte Straniera,* 73.

9. *Vogelfrei*

1. James J. Weingartner, *Hitler's Guard: The Story of the Leibstandarte SS Adolf Hitler, 1933–1945* (Carbondale: Southern Illinois University Press, 1974).

2. Carlo Gentile, "Tedeschi in Italia: Presenza militare nell'Italia nordoccidentale." *Notiziario dell'Istituto Storico della Resistenza in Cuneo e Provincia* 40 (1991): 17.

3. Gerhard Schreiber, *Deutsche Kriegsverbrechen in Italien: Täter, Opfer, Strafverfolgung* (Munich: Beck, 1996), 129–35.

4. Appears on maps as the "Bedale."

10. A Failed Rescue

1. Mario Giovana, "Il 'distretto' Paralup," in *Valle Stura in Guerra 1940–1943 1943–1945,* ed. Michele Calandri, Mario Cordero, and Stefano Martini (Cuneo,

Italy: Comunità Montana Valle Stura, Centro di Documentazione), 35. Available from the Istituto Storico della Resistenza in Cuneo e Provincia, Corso Nizza 17, Cuneo, Italy.

2. Zuccotti, *The Italians and the Holocaust: Persecution, Rescue, and Survival* (New York: Basic Books, 1987), 93.

3. Professor Giovanni B. Varnier suggested that it may have been the Palazzo Vittorino de Feltre, on Via Maragliano.

4. Carlo Brizzolari, *Gli Ebrei nella storia di Genova* (Genoa: Sabatelli, 1971), 306.

5. Cavaglion, *Nella Notte Straniera*, 98, 109 n. 13.

11. The Cave of San Mauro

1. Shelley Stock Volpi, "I rapporti della Militärkommandantur tedesca 1020: Cuneo settembre 1943–ottobre 1944," in "Il presente e la storia," *Notiziario dell'Istituto Storico della Resistenza di Cuneo e provincia* 42 (Dec. 1992): 186.

12. The Privilege to Be Shot as a Partisan

1. Appears on maps as "Tagliarè." The peak rises to 5,425 ft.

2. Bronka Halpern, *Keren or ba-hashekhah.*

3. Michele Calandri, Mario Cordero, and Stefano Martini, eds., *Valle Stura in Guerra 1940–1943 1943–1945* (Cuneo, Italy: Comunità Montana Valle Stura, Centro di Documentazione), 137, item 1.

4. Benjamin Graf von Rumford, *An essay on chimney fire-places: with proposals for improving them, to save fuel, to render dwelling-houses more comfortable and salubrious, and effectually to prevent chimneys from smoking* (Dublin: R. E. Mercier and Co., 1796).

5. In Piedmontese dialect, commonly spoken in those parts.

6. Dr. Sergio Arneodo, Museo Etnografico, S. Lucia di Monterosso Grana, Cuneo, Italy, personal communication.

7. The loom belonged to and was operated by the brothers Pietro and Bastianin Cesana. It is located now in the above-mentioned Museo Etnografico.

8. Kit C. Carter and Robert Mueller, *U.S. Army Air Forces in World War II, Combat Chronology, 1941–1945/World War II* (Washington, D.C.: Center for Air Force History, 1991), 352.

9. Geoffrey Perret, *Winged Victory: The Army Air Forces in World War II* (New York: Random House, 1993), 338.

10. Dante Livio Bianco, *Guerra Partigiana* (Turin, Italy: Einaudi, 1973), 74–75.

13. The Oldest Instinct

1. Catherine Andreyev, *Vlasov and the Russian Liberation Movement: Soviet Reality and Émigré Theories* (Cambridge: Cambridge University Press, 1987), 57. Livio Bianco, in *Guerra Partigiana,* mentions on page 123 that about twenty such soldiers had joined the partisan brigade "P. Braccini" entrenched in Val Grana, a valley next to ours. The band I encountered may have been part of this brigade.

2. Michele Calandri and Mario Cordero, "La Valle Stura dalla guerra fascista alla Liberazione," in *Valle Stura in Guerra 1940–1943 1943–1945,* 20.

3. Calandri and Cordero, "La Valle Stura," 21.

4. Calandri and Cordero, "La Valle Stura," 19–20.

5. Calandri and Cordero, "La Valle Stura," 23–24.

6. Calandri and Cordero, "La Valle Stura," 25–31.

7. Sept. 15, 1944.

8. Exodus 7:5.

9. Livio Bianco, *Guerra Partigiana,* 91.

10. This leaflet is presently in the collection of the U.S. Holocaust Memorial Museum in Washington, D.C. (see figure 16).

11. Giorgio Bocca, in *Partigiani della Montagna: Vita delle Divisioni 'Giustizia e Liberta' del Cuneese,* 2d ed. (Borgo San Dalmazzo, Italy: Bertello, 1945), 28, claims that these cadavers, which the Fascists exhumed, had been mutilated by frost.

14. A Voyage of Discovery

1. Cavaglion, *Nella Notte Straniera,* 106.

2. Deborah E. Lipstadt, *Denying the Holocaust: The Growing Assault on Truth and Memory* (New York: Free Press, 1993), 245.

3. Laqueur, *Terrible Secret,* 1.

4. See chap. 7.

5. Her remains were reburied in the Jewish cemetery in Montpellier, France.

6. A headline in the *New York Times* of Apr. 18, 1945, mentions "Death Factory" but applied it to Buchenwald, which was not an extermination camp.

15. Aftershocks

1. Bob Warnier, *Spoorloos bij een Spoorwegman . . .* in "Brugge & September '44, Deel I. Rond de Bevrijding (Brugge, Belgium: Uitgaven West-Vlaamse Gidsenkring), pp. 162–183.

2. Sidney Finkel, *The Four Seasons of My Life* (Baltimore: published by the author, 1995), 98–99.

3. Justyna Pawlak, "With Remorse, Poland Recalls a Pogrom," *Forward,* June 28, 1996, p. 5.

4. Yad Vashem, Dept. for the Righteous, Dossier No. 1949. Hector and Delphine Janssens and Marie Janssens, Belgium.

5. Associated Metals and Minerals Corp.

6. In the 1991 Persian Gulf War, these became known as Scud missiles.

7. See Dov Levin, "The Fateful Decision: the Flight of the Jews into the Soviet Interior in the Summer of 1941," *Yad Vashem Studies* 20 (1990). See also Jan T. Gross, *Revolution from Abroad: The Soviet Conquest of Poland's Western Ukraine and Western Belorussia* (Princeton: Princeton University Press, 1988).

8. Yosef Litvak, "The Plight of Refugees from the German-Occupied Territories," chap. 4 of *The Soviet Takeover of the Polish Eastern Provinces, 1939–41,* ed. Keith Sword (New York: St. Martin's Press, 1991). See also Gross, *Revolution from Abroad,* 20.

9. Litvak, "The Plight of Refugees," 20.

10. Litvak, "The Plight of Refugees," 62.

11. Josi's parents were cousins. Nachman was both his uncle and his mother's cousin. Sarah-Esther and my grandmother were sisters and both his grandmothers.

12. Joan Dash, *Summoned to Jerusalem* (New York: Harper and Row, 1979), 300–301. A number of other authors also have described the plight of these refugees, known as "Teheran children."

13. Eberhard Jäckel, *David Irving's Hitler: A Faulty History Dissected, Two Essays* (Port Angeles, Wash.: Ben-Simon Publications, 1993).

14. Lipstadt, *Denying the Holocaust*, 161.

15. Rochlitz, *The Righteous Enemy.*

16. Alfred J. Kolatch, *The Jewish Mourner's Book of Why* (Middle Village [Brooklyn], N.Y.: Jonathan David Publishers, 1993), 130.

17. Leon Wieseltier, *Kaddish* (New York: Alfred A. Knopf, 1998), xiii.

18. Lewis Thomas, "The Hazards of Science," in *The Medusa and the Snail: More Notes of a Biology Watcher* (New York: Viking Press, 1979), 73.

19. Sir Karl Raimund Popper, *Conjectures and Refutations: The Growth of Scientific Knowledge* (London: Routledge, 1989), vii, 57.

20. "Federal Role Grows in Handling Technical Data." *Chemical and Engineering News* (Sept. 30, 1963): 21–22.

21. I described the invention in the *Journal of Chemical Documentation* 3 (1963): 187–89, under the title: "The Automatic Encoding of Chemical Structures." The following patents were issued for it:

Alfred Feldman, "Two Dimensional Structure Encoding Typewriter." U.S. Patent 3,358,804 (Dec. 19, 1967).

Alfred Feldman, "Two Dimensional Structure Encoding Typewriter." U.S. Patent 3,476,311 (Nov. 4, 1969).

16. The Past Revisited

1. Stephen Greenblatt, "Ghosts of Berlin," *New York Times,* Apr. 28, 1999, p. A27.

2. Author's translation from the Italian.

3. Corey Kilgannon, "From a Wartime Escape to a Stateside Reunion," *New York Times,* May 7, 2000, metro section, p. 54.

4. John Cappelli, "Un grande gesto 'normale,'" *Oggi,* May 21, 2000, p. 6B.

5. Francesco Repetto, "La consegna della Medaglia dei Giusti fra le Nazioni," *Liguria* 49, 3 (1982): 28.

6. Liliana Picciotto Fargion, *Il Libro della Memoria* (Milan: Gruppo Ugo Mursia, 1991).

7. See chap. 6, n. 9.

8. Nos, *Montagnac.*

9. Personal communication from Lucien Bringuier, the mayor's son.

ALFRED FELDMAN was born in Hamburg, Germany, in 1923. He was a chemist and computer systems consultant.